EQUAL STATUS ACTS 2000–2011

EQUAL STATUS ACTS 2000–2011

Discrimination in the Provision of Goods and Services

Judy Walsh

*Published in association with
the Irish Council for Civil Liberties*

BLACKHALL
Publishing

Published by Blackhall Publishing
Lonsdale House
Avoca Avenue
Blackrock
Co. Dublin
Ireland

e-mail: info@blackhallpublishing.com
www.blackhallpublishing.com

© Irish Council for Civil Liberties, 2012

Paperback ISBN: 978-1-84218-190-4
ePub ISBN: 978-1-84218-254-3
Kindle ISBN: 978-1-84218-255-0

A catalogue record for this book is available from the British Library.

Printed in Ireland by SPRINT-print Ltd.

For George, Katherine and Louise

About the Author

Judy Walsh teaches courses on discrimination law and human rights at the School of Social Justice, University College Dublin, where she is also Director of the Equality Studies Research Centre. Judy collaborates with several organisations working on social justice issues in Ireland.

The Irish Council for Civil Liberties

The Irish Council for Civil Liberties (ICCL) is Ireland's independent human rights watchdog, which monitors, educates and campaigns in order to secure full enjoyment of human rights for everyone. Founded in 1976 by Mary Robinson, Kadar Asmal and others, the ICCL has played a leading role in some of Ireland's most successful human rights campaigns, including for the establishment of an independent Garda Ombudsman Commission, the right to divorce, securing more effective protection of children's rights, decriminalising homosexuality and the introduction of enhanced equality legislation. The ICCL has tirelessly worked to ensure the full implementation in Ireland of international human rights standards and has campaigned for constitutional reform on a range of issues since its foundation. The ICCL is a non-party-political, non-governmental organisation that receives no state funding.

Preface

Discrimination law applies to everyday activities like accessing transport and social welfare, dealing with landlords and attending school. However, the Equal Status Acts use complex language and a large volume of cases has shaped what the law means in practice. In writing this book I tried to strike a balance between accuracy and accessibility. Using legal 'jargon' and concepts was unavoidable but I hope this book will be useful to people seeking information about their rights and responsibilities.

Part 1 of the book deals with the substance of the law. It explains the types of discrimination prohibited by the Equal Status Acts and sets out the contexts in which these prohibitions apply. Chapter 2 is of central importance to the book as a whole because it addresses the scope of the law. It deals with both the discriminatory grounds that people must base a complaint on and the types of services that are covered by the law. It also outlines the numerous exceptions and exemptions that save certain actions and omissions from being considered discriminatory. People who want to understand how any particular discrimination prohibition operates (e.g. reasonable accommodation) should, therefore, refer back to Chapter 2.

Part 2 addresses the implementation of the law. It explains how the Equal Status Acts are triggered both by individuals who take cases and by the Equality Authority. The Equality Authority is a specialised body that promotes compliance with the law and also plays an important role in enforcement through mechanisms like litigation. It is expected that from late 2012 the new Irish Human Rights and Equality Commission will carry out the Authority's functions (see further Chapters 10 and 11).

The law is up to date as of 2 April 2012. I have endeavoured to include information about appeals to the Circuit Court but because transcripts of such cases are not generally available that information is necessarily incomplete. Since the final draft of this book was written there have been a couple of significant developments I address here. First, it appears that the new employment rights and industrial relations body to be formally established in 2012/2013 will hear equal status complaints. The Workplace Relations Commission will replace the Equality Tribunal and several other bodies (see further Chapter 11). The Minister for Jobs, Enterprise and Innovation told the Joint Oireachtas Committee on Jobs, Enterprise and Innovation on 11 July 2012 that equal status cases will transfer from the Tribunal to the new forum. Appeals will continue to be dealt with by the Circuit Court. Second, an important case concerning the entitlement of surrogate mothers to maternity or adoptive leave has been referred to the Court of Justice of the European Union. The Equality Tribunal effectively found that the issue fell outside the scope of the Equal Status Acts (*A Complainant v Department of Social Protection*, DEC-S2011-053). It remains to be seen whether the Oireachtas will take action to protect the interests of such families before the Court of Justice rules on the matter.

Several people contributed to the process of writing this book. Noeline Blackwell, Cathal Kelly and Tanya Ward generously read an early draft. Síle Larkin provided crucial guidance and access to materials, as did Siobhán Cummiskey. I am extremely grateful for their invaluable suggestions and support. Thanks also to the staff of various Circuit Court offices for enabling access to information about appeals.

My colleagues and the students at the UCD School of Social Justice are a constant source of inspiration. I am indebted to them for everything they have taught me. Sincere thanks to the former and current staff of the ICCL, in particular Lorraine Curran, Mark Kelly, Stephen O'Hare and Tanya Ward, who were directly involved with the production of the book at various stages. I am also very grateful to all at Blackhall Publishing, especially Eileen O'Brien and Elizabeth Brennan for their exceptional professionalism and kindness.

Finally, thank you to my family and friends for their love and support. A special note of thanks to Adele, Ann, Clair, George, Katherine, Louise, Maggie, Marie, Maureen, Michael, Olga, Theresa and Val.

Contents

Contents

Contents

Contents

Table of Cases

Table of Cases

Table of Cases

Table of Cases

Labour Court

Table of Cases

Table of Cases

SUPREME COURT

Table of Cases

COURT OF JUSTICE OF THE EUROPEAN UNION

Table of Cases

EUROPEAN COURT OF HUMAN RIGHTS

OTHER JURISDICTIONS

United Kingdom

Table of Cases

Table of Cases

Table of Legislative Instruments

Table of Legislative Instruments

COUNCIL OF EUROPE
(in chronological order)

INTERNATIONAL
(in chronological order)

List of Abbreviations

ART	Assisted reproductive technology
CEDAW	United Nations Convention on the Elimination of all Forms of Discrimination Against Women
CERD	United Nations Committee on the Elimination of Racial Discrimination
CJEU	Court of Justice of the European Union
DART	Dublin Area Rapid Transit
EC	European Community
ECHR	European Convention on Human Rights
ECtHR	European Court of Human Rights
EEA	Employment Equality Acts 1998–2011
ESA	Equal Status Acts 2000–2011
EU	European Union
HSE	Health Service Executive
IBEC	Irish Business and Employers Confederation
ICERD	International Convention on the Elimination of all Forms of Racial Discrimination
ICTU	Irish Congress of Trade Unions
NGO	Non-governmental organisation
UNCRPD	United Nations Convention on the Rights of Persons with Disabilities
UDHR	Universal Declaration of Human Rights
UK	United Kingdom
US	United States of America

Glossary of Terms

Amicus curiae	An *amicus curiae* ('friend of the court') is essentially an impartial bystander whose expertise is called upon to assist courts in their deliberations.
Comparator	An actual or hypothetical person used to assess the treatment complained of in a discrimination case.
Complainant	A person who pursues a legal action in the form of a complaint.
Direct discrimination	Less favourable treatment of a person related to a prohibited ground of discrimination.
Directive	A type of European Union law that requires member states to achieve particular results but leaves some discretion as to how those results are to be achieved.
Disability	A socially constructed disadvantage experienced by people with physical, mental or intellectual impairments or conditions.
In camera	A legal hearing to which the public is not admitted.
Institutional discrimination	Institutional discrimination consists of policies, practices and patterns of behaviour that are embedded in the systems and structures of an organisation, which have the effect of disadvantaging some categories of people relative to others. These policies, etc. appear to be neutral but have an exclusionary impact.
Judicial review	A legal remedy available in situations where a public body or tribunal has acted in excess of legal authority or contrary to its duty.
Locus standi	The capacity of an individual or other litigant to commence legal action.
Prima facie	Evidence which on its face is sufficient to prove a given case.

Race	The terms 'race' and 'racial' are used widely in anti-discrimination law to identify groups that are subjected to racism. It is a legal term that does not imply acceptance of theories which attempt to divide human beings into different 'races' on the basis of biological criteria.
Respondent	A person or other party against whom a legal action is taken.
Statutory instrument	An order, regulation, rule, scheme or by-law made in the exercise of a statutory power. Statutory instruments are most often issued by ministers.
Transgender	'Transgender' is used in this book to refer to individuals whose gender identity and/or gender expression differs from conventional expectations based on the physical sex assigned to them at birth (McIlroy, 2009).
Transsexual	The term 'transsexual' is used to signify people who do not identify in the sex assigned to them at birth. In case law it tends to refer to people who have undergone, are undergoing or intend to undergo medical gender re-assignment procedures.
Vicarious liability	The allocation of legal responsibility to employers and other parties for the wrongdoing of employees or other persons under their control.

I

PROTECTION FROM DISCRIMINATION

1

Overview

1.1 Introduction

For just over a decade the Equal Status Acts 2000–2011 (ESA) have prohibited certain types of discrimination by both public and private sector providers of goods and services. This book illustrates how that law operates in practice. It explains the types of actions or omissions that amount to discrimination, examines relevant case law and looks at how the Acts are enforced. Before exploring those areas in some detail, this opening chapter situates the legislation in a broader context. First it considers the relationship between 'inequality' and 'discrimination', two concepts that are often erroneously thought of as meaning the same thing. This brief account is designed to illustrate the limits of discrimination in addressing deep-rooted injustices that stem from unequal social relations in contexts like the economy or the family. The chapter then addresses the origins of the ESA and its relationship with other sources of discrimination law.

1.2 Inequality and Discrimination

At a general level, equality is a relationship, of some kind or other, between two or more individuals or groups of people, regarding some aspect of those people's lives. If equality was a simple idea, it would be obvious what this relationship is, who it is about and what aspect of their lives it concerns. Theorists have grappled with these questions for centuries and have arrived at various conceptions of equality, which Baker, Lynch, Cantillon and Walsh (2009) have loosely categorised as basic, liberal or radical.

Basic equality imports the widely accepted idea that at some very basic level all human beings have equal worth and importance, and are therefore equally worthy of concern and respect. The concept of discrimination evolves from that premise and from liberal political theory, which insists that individuals should be judged on their personal attributes. Distinctions drawn on the basis of social status, group affiliation or identity and irrelevant physical characteristics are generally regarded as arbitrary and unjust (Fredman, 2002, pp 66–67). As we will discover, discrimination law aims to outlaw harmful distinctions, while preserving those that are considered legitimate.

Liberal models of equality supplement basic equality with a concern for distributive justice. The fact that social goods are not spread evenly amongst populations but tend to cluster is seen as problematic. However, according to Baker et al. (2009, p 25) the assumption remains that there will always be major inequalities between people in their status, resources, work and power. Within liberal models, the role of the idea of equality is to provide a fair basis for managing inequalities, by strengthening the minimum to which everyone is entitled and by using equality of opportunity to regulate the competition for advantage. The equal opportunity principle has two major interpretations. Formal equality of opportunity classically gives rise to the idea that all persons should be treated in the same manner. This is sometimes termed a 'sameness' approach to equality and is embodied in legal prohibitions against direct discrimination (see Chapter 3). A stronger version, substantive equality of opportunity, insists that people should not be advantaged or hampered by their social background and that their prospects in life should depend entirely on their own efforts and abilities. In turn, such an approach can give rise to laws and policies which mandate that in certain contexts (typically the public sphere and the market) people should be treated differently so that they arrive at an equal starting point in the competition for advantage (sometimes labelled a 'difference' approach to equality). The ESA provides for substantive equality of opportunity through provisions such as those on reasonable accommodation for disabled people (Chapter 6) and by providing for exceptions to the underlying ideal of sameness which cater for the particular needs and interests of some social groups (Chapter 2). However, as we will see, the law's potential in this regard is undercut by a number of broad exemptions. The ESA also permits limited forms of positive action (Chapter 8).

'Equality of condition' is a radical model. It rests on the insight that inequality is rooted in changing and changeable social structures, particularly in structures of domination and oppression (Baker et al., 2009; Crowley, 2006). These structures create, and continually reproduce, the inequalities that liberal conceptions of equality see as inevitable. This emphasis on social structures affects the way equality of condition should be understood and embedded within the legal system. For example, in contrast to the tendency of liberal models to focus on the rights and advantages of individuals, equality of condition also pays attention to the rights and advantages of groups. Equality of condition is concerned with how people are related, particularly through power relations, as well as with how things are distributed. Moreover, equality

4

of condition regards the private dimension of people's lives, such as their care needs and care work, as a central political concern.

As this brief summary illustrates, the idea of equality embraces a wide spectrum of beliefs and resultant strategies. Basic and liberal equality principles underpin human rights guarantees and anti-discrimination laws. The idea of basic equality clearly informs international human rights standards. Article 1 of the Universal Declaration of Human Rights (UDHR), for example, proclaims 'All human beings are born free and equal in dignity and rights.'[1] Shaped over several decades of activism and international negotiation, the human rights agenda promoted by bodies such as the United Nations and the Council of Europe is primarily concerned with setting minimum standards and promoting key principles of non-discrimination. A variety of international covenants spell out basic entitlements that should be secured for every person as a matter of right, with each instrument stipulating that these rights should be upheld in a non-discriminatory manner. The unequal position of various social groups is underscored by the development of thematic conventions that address the particular concerns of children, disabled people, ethnic minorities, women and so on. These conventions call on states to institute a range of policies, programmes and laws aimed at securing substantive equality of opportunity (Vandenhole, 2005).

On the national plane, constitutional bills of rights generally, explicitly at least, deal with so-called 'first generation' civil and political rights, including the rights to freedom of expression, privacy and liberty. Welfare states tend to supplement these protections with legislation and policies aimed at securing a floor of basic socio-economic entitlements and achieving equality of opportunity in certain settings. In the case of Ireland, the principle of non-discrimination, although not addressed in explicit human rights terms, features throughout the core anti-poverty instruments, particularly through the targeting of groups such as Travellers, older people and disabled people. Specific groups are not dealt with separately in the *National Action Plan for Social Inclusion 2007–2016*, but rather are addressed within the various lifecycle and communities chapters (Government of Ireland, 2007). Several other national strategy documents address the position of particular groups experiencing inequality, including the *National Children's Strategy* (2000–2010), the *National Women's Strategy* (2007–2016), the *National Disability Strategy* and the *National Action Plan against Racism* (2005–2008). As the National Economic and Social Forum (2008, p 158) notes, however, 'significant challenges remain to secure their implementation'. It observes that such policies have been criticised for failing to include the achievement of specific outcomes (National Economic and Social Forum, 2008, p 158).

---

[1] The UDHR was adopted by the General Assembly of the United Nations in 1948.

The principles associated with liberal equality of opportunity inform significant Irish and European Union (EU) laws. Primary examples of Irish laws are the Employment Equality Acts 1998–2011 (EEA) and the subject of this book, the Equal Status Acts 2000–2011 (ESA). The EEA applies to the context of employment, which includes self-employment, access to employment, vocational training and work experience, while the ESA governs the provision of goods and services.

1.3 Overview of the Equal Status Acts

The Acts outlaw certain discriminatory practices in the field of public service provision and also limit the rights of private property owners who transact with the public (or a section of the public). The prohibitions on discrimination are directed at a range of entities and persons who provide goods, services, accommodation and education, such as landlords, shopkeepers, financial institutions, universities, schools, government departments and statutory agencies.

In relation to private sector service providers, the ESA essentially modifies the usual right to choose whether and how to 'do business' with any given person. Such regulation is considered legitimate because service providers derive incomes and profits through their business activities. Along with other legal obligations like complying with health and safety laws and filing tax returns, discrimination law imposes duties on those who benefit from transactions with members of the public. The ESA does not apply unless goods and services are offered to the public at large or a section of the public. For example, a woman driving a private car who only stops for female hitchhikers is carrying out a purely private activity and it is not unlawful for her to discriminate against men. By contrast a taxi driver is licensed to provide a service to the general public and so cannot lawfully decide to select customers based on their gender or any other discriminatory ground.

Two specialised statutory bodies, the Equality Authority and the Equality Tribunal, currently play a major role in the implementation of the legislation. Chapter 11 looks at their functions and powers. Briefly, the Equality Tribunal is currently the main forum for hearing and determining complaints about breaches of the law. Under a process to be commenced in autumn 2012 the Tribunal will be wound down. Its functions, along with those of a number of employment rights bodies, will be carried out by a new institution called the Workplace Relations Commission (Department of Jobs, Enterprise and Innovation, 2012). At the time of writing it is not clear whether the new body will hear ESA cases; the implications of these changes are discussed in Part II.

The Equality Authority provides various stakeholders, including members of the general public, with information on relevant rights and responsibilities. It offers legal advice and assistance to some people pursuing discrimination complaints. The Authority also engages in promotional activities and exercises some enforcement powers. In 2012 the Equality Authority will merge with the Irish Human Rights Commission to form a new Human Rights and Equality Commission.[2] It remains to be seen how the new body will operate across its revised mandate (Chapter 11).

Referring a complaint to the Equality Tribunal is the main way of activating the ESA (Chapter 12). The Tribunal will investigate the complaint and successful claims will usually attract an award of compensation. Other remedies may include directions to a service provider to change its practices and policies. Complaints may be resolved through mediation, in which case the Tribunal will assist the parties to arrive at a confidential and binding agreement. Generally speaking, only individuals who have been personally affected by the actions of a service provider can make complaints (Chapter 12.3.2). A person who refers a complaint is known as a 'complainant'. The goods or service provider against whom a complaint is made is referred to as a 'respondent'.[3]

It is important to appreciate that the legislation does not give people a right to obtain a particular item or service, e.g. healthcare, childcare, education or housing. Rather it seeks to ensure that where goods and services are already provided the conditions under which they are supplied are cleansed of bias against members of particular social groups (direct discrimination) and that unjustifiable conditions that disadvantage those people are eliminated (indirect discrimination).[4] As with the Employment Equality Acts 1998–2011, harassment, sexual harassment and victimisation are also prohibited, positive action is enabled and reasonable accommodation must be provided on the disability ground. Basically, the prohibitions on harassment and sexual harassment are aimed at ensuring that goods and services can be accessed in an environment that respects people's dignity. The legal remedies for victimisation are

---

[2]　See further: <http://www.inis.gov.ie/en/JELR/Pages/PR11000174>. The Irish Human Rights Commission was established in July 2001 as a consequence of undertakings set out in the Good Friday Agreement. The Commission's powers and functions derive from the Human Rights Commission Acts 2000 and 2001: <http://www.ihrc.ie/>.

[3]　The terms 'complainant' and 'respondent' are defined in section 20 of the ESA.

[4]　People seeking a right to a particular social good must instead look to other legislation that confers such rights or to the Constitution. While civil and political rights such as the right to liberty, to vote and to freedom of expression are relatively well secured, socio-economic rights including the rights to health and shelter are rooted far less firmly within the legal system (Irish Human Rights Commission, 2006; O'Connell, 2008; Whyte, 2002). The Health Act 1970 creates an entitlement to certain health services and places a duty on the Health Service Executive (HSE) to provide those services. The right to education is addressed under Article 42 of the Constitution and in a series of laws (O'Mahony, 2006, 2009).

designed to prevent people from being negatively treated for invoking the legislation or enabling others to do so. Reasonable accommodation involves making changes to rules, standards, policies or physical environments to ensure that they don't have an exclusionary effect on disabled people.

Subject to important exemptions (see Chapter 2.4–2.6), all goods and services that are available to the public, or a section of the public, are covered by the ESA. In order to be protected by the legislation it must be established that the treatment complained of is related to at least one of the nine specified grounds: age, disability, gender, family status, membership of the Traveller community, civil status (the marital status ground until 1 January 2011), race, religion and sexual orientation. Chapter 2.3 considers how these grounds are defined.

The vast majority of cases to date concern allegations of direct discrimination. In the early years of the law's operation a considerable proportion of those concerned refusals to provide various services to Travellers. According to Joyce (2003, p 16), the ESA has 'been relatively successful in addressing the socially ingrained practice of maintaining "Traveller Free premises" carried out by some providers of goods and services, in particular licensed premises'.

In relation to all types of discrimination claims, from 2005 to 2010 the disability ground witnessed the highest volume of referrals to the Equality Tribunal (Equality Tribunal, 2006, pp 13–14, 2007a, p 12, 2008, p 16, 2009a, pp 16–17, 2010a, p 11, 2011a, p 9). The Traveller community, race and age grounds comprise the next largest categories for five of those years (2005–2009 inclusive), with gender overtaking age in 2010. There are consistently very few complaints on the family status, gender, marital status, religion and sexual orientation grounds. For instance, in 2009 the family status and marital status grounds saw only one referral each (Equality Tribunal, 2011a, p 9). That year there was no sexual orientation case and just five and four in the gender and religion categories respectively. The following year, 2010, followed a similar pattern with no referrals on the marital status and religion grounds, five in the gender category, and two family status and sexual orientation ground referrals (Equality Tribunal, 2011a, p 9). One hundred and twenty-nine people referred complaints to the Tribunal in 2010 (Equality Tribunal, 2011a, p 9).

1.4 Origins of the Equal Status Acts

The initial law in this area, the Equal Status Act 2000, was widely regarded as innovative because it extended the principle of non-discrimination beyond the workplace. One of the stated aims of the Act was securing compliance with Ireland's international law obligations, particularly those under the UN Conventions on Women's Rights (CEDAW) and Racism (ICERD) (Bolger and Kimber, 2000, Chapter 13).[5] In enacting the law, the Oireachtas also followed the example set by the parliaments of several countries. For instance, in the United States 'public accommodation' laws were first introduced in the form of the Civil Rights Act 1964, Section II of which prohibits discrimination based on race in places that serve the public.

Just as the civil rights and other social movements were key drivers of legal change in the United States, Irish non-governmental organisations (NGOs) were instrumental in placing discrimination on the political agenda (Crowley, 2006, pp xiii–xvii). The so-called 'Rainbow Coalition' of the mid-1990s (comprising Fine Gael, the Labour Party and Democratic Left) established the Department of Equality and Law Reform. That Department carried out a comprehensive review of equality issues which resulted in the Employment Equality Bill 1996 and the Equal Status Bill 1997. However, on referral to the Supreme Court both bills were found to be unconstitutional on a number of grounds.[6] For the purposes of this book the most significant finding concerned the reasonable accommodation requirement in the Employment Equality Bill. Essentially, the provision obliged employers to accommodate the needs of people with disabilities by providing treatment or facilities unless the costs of doing so would cause an employer 'undue hardship'. According to the Court, that measure would infringe the constitutional property rights of employers. Notably, the parallel provision in the Equal Status Bill was not addressed in the judgment on its constitutionality and it is arguable that different considerations should apply to service providers. In any event, the incoming Fianna Fáil and Progressive Democrats coalition revised both bills in light of the Supreme Court judgments, and the reasonable accommodation requirement was diluted, as we will see in Chapter 6.

After a lengthy gestation period, the Equal Status Act 2000 came into force on 25 October 2000 and has since been amended a number of times. Some revisions were mandated by European Community (EC) law developments, as discussed below, while others flowed from internal sources. Following pressure exerted by vintners' organisations, the Intoxicating Liquor Act 2003 brought about a number of changes that are discussed in the body of this book (Crowley, 2006, pp 101–106). One of the most important was the transfer of jurisdiction from the Equality Tribunal to the District Court for cases of discrimination against licensed premises. As a consequence, the number of claims in that area has dropped considerably (Chapter 12.2).

---

[5] See 505 *Dáil Debates* Col 336 (Second Stage); 162 *Seanad Debates* Cols 550–552 (Second Stage).

[6] *Article 26 of the Constitution and the Employment Equality Bill 1996, Re* [1997] 2 IR 321 and *Article 26 of the Constitution and the Equal Status Bill 1997, Re* [1997] 2 IR 387.

Significant elements of the 2000 Act were amended by the Equality Act 2004 to bring the law into line with a number of EC directives, in particular the Racial Equality Directive, which prohibits discrimination on the basis of race or ethnicity in the field of goods and services. Another EC directive in the area, this time dealing with the gender ground, was adopted in 2004 and the ESA was again amended. European Union law is examined further in the next section. Finally, changes to discrimination law procedures were effected under the Civil Law (Miscellaneous Provisions) Act 2011 (see Part II). Collectively, the Equal Status Act 2000 and the various laws that have amended it are referred to as the Equal Status Acts 2000–2011.

1.5 The Impact of European Union Law

Article 13 of the Treaty of Amsterdam, now article 19 of the Treaty on the Functioning of the European Union (TFEU), granted the EC competence to combat discrimination based on sex, racial or ethnic origin, religion or belief, disability, age and sexual orientation. To date the provision has been used to generate three directives, two of which overlap with areas covered by the ESA: the Racial Equality Directive and the Gender Goods and Services Directive.

In June 2000 the Council of Ministers adopted Directive 2000/43, which is generally referred to as the 'Racial Equality Directive' or the 'Race Directive'. And in November of that year Directive 2000/78, known as the 'Framework Directive', was adopted. It covers discrimination on the grounds of religion or belief, disability, age and sexual orientation in the field of employment and occupation. While the Racial Equality Directive encompasses 'social protection, including social security and healthcare; social advantages; education; and access to and supply of goods and services which are available to the public, including housing' (article 3), the Framework Directive is much more limited in scope. It applies to discrimination within employment, vocational training and membership of organisations of workers or employers. Social security, the supply of goods and services, and so on are excluded. It does not, therefore, apply to the fields governed by the ESA. The Framework Directive is implemented in Irish law through the Employment Equality Acts 1998–2011.

A directive on gender discrimination in the field of goods and services followed in 2004 (the Gender Goods and Services Directive 2004/113). It applies to goods and services that are 'available to the public' such as housing, banking and insurance, whether provided by the public or private sector (article 3(1)). Its exact scope is uncertain in the absence of case law from the Court of Justice of the European Union (CJEU). But it is clear that education, advertising and media content are not covered (article 3(3)). The terms 'goods' and 'services' are defined with reference to EU economic law and so seem to be confined to goods or services provided for payment.[7] However, Ringelheim (2010, p 12) points out that this includes services which are not paid for by the recipient; it is enough that there is payment from some party. Healthcare provided in the context of a social security scheme may therefore be covered where fees are paid out of state funds to a service provider.[8] In any event, the Gender Goods and Services Directive is narrower in scope than the Racial Equality Directive. Member states were required to transpose the Gender Goods and Services Directive into national legislation by December 2007. Changes to Irish law were introduced in the Civil Law (Miscellaneous Provisions) Act 2008.

The latest EU initiative dates from July 2008, when the European Commission produced a draft directive that will extend EU law on discrimination in goods and services to the grounds of age, disability, religion and belief, and sexual orientation.[9] As of July 2012 negotiations on the text are ongoing before the Council of the European Union.[10] Some member states have questioned the Union's powers to legislate in the way proposed in the areas of housing, education and health services (Bell, 2009, pp 11–12; Bell, 2010a). Competence to address discrimination is limited to the fields that fall within the powers conferred on the Union by the various treaties.[11] Yet to date these fields have not been defined with any precision. It remains to be seen what form the final law will take. As it stands, the Draft Goods and Services Directive prohibits direct and indirect discrimination, as well as harassment, and it requires reasonable accommodation to be provided to disabled persons. Provisions of the draft law will be referred to throughout this book where relevant.

When the Lisbon Treaty entered into force in 2009 it altered the status of the Charter of Fundamental Rights, making it a legally binding document with the same status as the EU treaties. As a result, the institutions of the

---

[7] See recital 11, Directive 2004/113. Recitals are set out in the preamble to EU directives. They introduce the main provisions of a directive and explain the reasons for its adoption. Recitals do not have legal force but courts may take the recitals into consideration to ascertain the intentions of the Council and Parliament when drafting certain provisions.

[8] Gender discrimination concerning some aspects of social protection is covered by other directives: Directive 79/7EEC (statutory social security) and the Recast Directive 2006/54 (occupational social security). The extent to which non-employment-related benefits are covered either under these measures or by the Gender Goods and Services Directive is not clear (Craig and de Búrca, 2007, pp 932–949).

[9] 'Proposal for a Council Directive on implementing the principle of equal treatment between persons irrespective of religion or belief, disability, age or sexual orientation', COM/2008/0426.

[10] See <http://ec.europa.eu/prelex/detail_dossier_real.cfm?CL=en&DosId=197196>.

[11] Upon the entry into force of the Lisbon Treaty article 13(1) of the Treaty of Amsterdam was replaced by article 19 of the TFEU.

EU are bound to comply with it. EU member states must also comply with the Charter, but only when implementing EU law.[12] National courts need to apply the Charter to cases involving the application of EU law (including equality directives). In domestic cases, therefore, individuals may now lodge complaints to the effect that the ESA, in so far as it implements EU law, violates the Charter.[13] A further significant development occurred in December 2010 when the European Union ratified the UN Convention on the Rights of Persons with Disabilities (UNCRPD). The UNCRPD is likely to become a reference point for interpreting EU law concerning discrimination on the disability ground (Clifford, 2011).

As discussed further in Chapter 1.6, EU law in this area is highly significant since all domestic law must conform to it. It would appear that the ESA meets the requirements of the Gender Goods and Services Directive (aside from the area of insurance and possibly registered clubs), but that it does not fully implement the Racial Equality Directive. For example, there appears to be inadequate provision for remedies in cases of race ground discrimination under the ESA and its scope may also be too narrow.[14] Significantly, the applicable EU laws set minimum requirements and each of the applicable directives contains a principle of non-regression. This means that measures implementing changes required by EU law should not reduce the level of protection already afforded against discrimination in national law. These matters are revisited throughout the book, while general issues concerning the interpretation of the Acts are dealt with in the next section.

1.6 Interpretation

The words and phrases used in the ESA must be interpreted, that is, their meaning in any given case must be established. This task falls to the bodies

---

[12] Article 51 of the Charter; see, for example, *Association Belge des Consommateurs Test-Achats ASBL v Belgium*, Case C-236/09, [2011] 2 CMLR 38, discussed in Chapter 2.6.4.4.
[13] Article 21 of the Charter contains a prohibition on discrimination on various grounds. It provides: '1. Any discrimination based on any ground such as sex, race, colour, ethnic or social origin, genetic features, language, religion or belief, political or any other opinion, membership of a national minority, property, birth, disability, age or sexual orientation shall be prohibited. 2. Within the scope of application of the Treaties and without prejudice to any of their specific provisions, any discrimination on grounds of nationality shall be prohibited.' The Lisbon Treaty accords the same legal value to the Charter as to the Treaties (article 6 of the Treaty on European Union).
[14] In 2007 the European Commission began enforcement proceedings against Ireland. It issued a Reasoned Opinion, which is the second stage of infringement proceedings against member states that it considers are in default. Those proceedings were closed in 2011: <http://ec.europa.eu/eu_law/eulaw/decisions/dec_20110406.htm#ie>.

that hear complaints in the first instance, namely the Equality Tribunal and the District Court, and ultimately to the ordinary courts on appeal.[15]

When interpreting legislation, the fundamental objective of any court or tribunal is to give effect to the intention of the Oireachtas (Donlan and Kennedy, 2006; Law Reform Commission, 2000). That intention should be derived from the wording of the legislation. If the meaning of a statutory provision is ambiguous or an absurd result would follow from a literal reading, a court or tribunal may apply other rules of interpretation, including the purposive approach.[16] The purposive approach involves looking behind the words used to establish the overall objective of the legislation in question. The long title to an Act is important in identifying its purpose.[17] The title of the ESA describes it as:

> An act to promote equality and prohibit types of discrimination, harassment and related behaviour in connection with the provision of services, property and other opportunities to which the public generally or a section of the public has access ....

It is clear from that title and indeed from the provisions of the ESA that it is a remedial law, designed to tackle the problems generated by discrimination in Irish society.

The Equality Tribunal and the Circuit Court have adopted a purposive approach to the interpretation of equality legislation when they have

---

[15] Decisions made by lower courts and tribunals are supervised by the High Court through the mechanism of judicial review. The High Court is largely concerned with how the decision was made and whether fair procedures were followed, rather than with substituting its own findings on the merits of the case for those of that lower court or tribunal. In line with well-established administrative law principles, a court will generally defer to the specialist expertise of bodies like the Equality Tribunal in interpreting discrimination law. According to Hamilton J, '... the courts should be slow to interfere with the decisions of expert administrative tribunals. Where conclusions are based on an identifiable error of law or an unsustainable finding of fact by a tribunal such conclusions must be corrected' (*Henry Denny & Sons (Ireland) Ltd v Minister for Social Welfare* [1998] 1 IR 34, at pp 37–38). In *Eagle Star Life Assurance Company of Ireland Ltd v Director of the Equality Tribunal & Another* [2009] ELR 295 the High Court held that primary responsibility for interpreting the provisions of the ESA rests with the Equality Tribunal.

[16] See section 5 of the Interpretation Act 2005 and the Supreme Court judgments in *Howard v Commissioners of Public Works in Ireland* [1994] 1 IR 101; [1993] ILRM 665 and *Crilly v T. & J. Farrington Ltd* [2001] 3 IR 251; [2002] 1 ILRM 181. For an example of the Tribunal's engagement with these rules see *Gloria – Ireland's Gay and Lesbian Choir v Cork International Choral Festival Ltd*, DEC-S2008-078, paras 5.3–5.5.

[17] See the judgment of Murray CJ in *Bupa Ireland Limited & Anor v Health Insurance Authority & Ors* [2009] 1 ILRM 81. See also *Dunbar v ASTI*, DEC-E2009-054, paras 6.24–6.26.

encountered ambiguous words or phrases.[18] In so doing, those bodies have relied on Supreme Court findings that remedial laws should be construed as widely and as liberally as possible.[19] For example, in an equal status appeal before the Circuit Court Hunt J stated:

> I adopt the starting point for the construction of this statute, which is a statute intended to confer rights on the citizen, that I should adopt the construction and proceed on the basis of an interpreta-tion which is consistent with the broadest possible application of statutory rights to the citizens, or indeed to give effect to a European directive if necessary.[20]

The Equality Authority v Portmarnock Golf Club[21] is the main case to date in which the Superior Courts have examined provisions of the ESA. At issue was the right of women to join a golf club that only accepts men as members. The Courts involved at every level did not consider that there was a need to adopt a purposive approach to interpreting the sections concerning registered clubs. This was because the meaning of the words in question was regarded as unambiguous. However, various judges reached different conclusions as to what those words meant (Chapter 9.3). Denham J commented on the interpre-tive approach that should be adopted in relation to the ESA:

> [I]f there were any ambiguity, which I do not find, the Act of 2000 should be interpreted purposively. The Act of 2000 should be inter-preted in accordance with the intent of the legislature. The Act of 2000 was a remedial social statute. Its purpose was to promote equality and prohibit certain forms of discrimination.[22]

---

[18] See, for example, *McClean v The Revenue Commissioners*, DEC-S2004-016, para 6.7 and *Persaud v The Shelbourne Hotel*, DEC-E2004-075, paras 5.3–5.5. In *Corcoran and Others v The One Foot Inn, Burnfoot, Co. Donegal*, DEC-S2007-004, the remedial purpose of the ESA was taken into account in considering the level of formality that participants in Tribunal proceedings should expect. On complying with the technical aspects of referring a complaint see *Comerford v Trailfinders Ireland Ltd*, DEC-S2011-013 and *Fitzgerald v McCaul*, DEC-S2011-026.

[19] See *Bank of Ireland v Purcell* [1989] IR 327 and the judgment of McGuinness J in the case of *Western Health Board v M* [2002] 2 IR 493.

[20] *Dublin City Council v Deans* (Circuit Court Dublin, Hunt J, unreported, 15 April 2008), at p 28.

[21] [2005] IEHC 235 (High Court); *Equality Authority v Portmarnock Golf Club & Ors.* [2010] 1 ILRM 237 (Supreme Court).

[22] *Equality Authority v Portmarnock Golf Club & Ors* [2010] 1 ILRM 237, at p 301.

The ESA must be interpreted in a way that conforms to superior sources of law. Applicable EU law takes precedence over all the national laws of member states. For that reason, Irish courts and tribunals are obliged to interpret national legislation implementing an EU directive, as far as possible, in light of the wording and purpose of that directive.[23]

The ESA, in part, implements the Racial Equality Directive and the Gender Goods and Services Directive. When courts and the Equality Tribunal are interpreting those elements of the ESA they are obliged to have regard to the purpose of the two Directives. At this stage, however, there is very little CJEU case law to clarify what those Directives require. It is by no means certain that the Court will apply discrimination law principles in a uniform manner across the grounds and fields covered by the various directives (O'Cinneide, 2010). We cannot assume, therefore, that concepts developed primarily in the context of gender-related employment discrimination will apply in the same manner to the grounds of gender and race in the goods and services area.

The Irish Constitution, *Bunreacht na hÉireann*, is the fundamental legal document of the Irish state. All other national laws, including the ESA, must comply with it.[24] The ESA was therefore drafted with the Constitution in mind. However, it is difficult to predict the effects of laws in the abstract; those effects become clearer when they are applied in actual cases. The constitutional fundamental rights guarantees may prove significant in cases that involve tensions between the right to equal treatment and other human rights, or indeed where there are perceived clashes between non-discrimination on different grounds. A person could, for example, maintain that the provisions on harassment interfere with the right to freedom of expression or the right

---

[23] *Murphy & Ors v Telecom Eireann No. 2* [1989] ILRM 53 and *Nathan v Bailey Gibson* [1998] 2 IR 162. Relevant CJEU cases include *Von Colson and Kamann v Land Nordrhein-Westfalen* [1984] ECR 1891; *IMPACT v Minister for Agriculture and Food & Others*, Case C-268/06, [2008] ELR 181; *Marleasing SA v La Comercial Internacional de Alimentacion SA* [1991] ECR 1-4135 (applied in *Kelly v University College Dublin* [2008] IEHC 464); *Pfeiffer v Deutsches Rotes Kreuz Kreizerband Waldshut EV* [2005] IRLR 137; and *Mangold v Helm*, Case C-144/04, [2004] ECR 1-9981. The High Court has found that the Equality Tribunal cannot re-order national law to bring it into line with an EU provision: *Minister for Justice, Equality and Law Reform v Director of the Equality Tribunal* [2010] 2 IR 455; [2009] ELR 116. This decision is under appeal to the Supreme Court. For a critical assessment of the High Court's judgment see Fahey (2009).

[24] All legislation enjoys a presumption of constitutionality. In other words, the courts assume that an Act of the Oireachtas complies with the terms of the Constitution. A number of consequences flow from this presumption, including the double construction rule of interpretation. That rule dictates that where two meanings of a legislative provision are open, the meaning that complies with the Constitution should be adopted by a court. See further Doyle (2008, Chapters 16–17).

not to be discriminated against on the religion ground where the conduct in question flows from a religious belief (McColgan, 2009; McGlennan, 2010).

To date, just one direct constitutional challenge has been mounted to an ESA provision. In *The Equality Authority v Portmarnock Golf Club*[25] the High Court dismissed an argument that the provisions on discriminating clubs violated the right to freedom of association. On appeal the Supreme Court found, however, that the constitutional question was not relevant and so should not have been dealt with by the High Court. As a result the courts have yet to fully assess a supposed conflict between the Constitution and the ESA.[26]

Several constitutional provisions may prove relevant in future cases. Many reinforce the right to equal treatment and freedom from discrimination secured in the goods and services context by the ESA. The guarantee of equality before the law under Article 40.1 is of most immediate relevance. It prohibits arbitrary and invidious differences in treatment based on characteristics such as gender, 'race' or ethnicity, religion, language or political opinion.[27] Differential treatment may serve a legitimate legislative purpose and in that event there will be no discrimination.[28] Since the courts tend to accept that government classifications serve a legitimate purpose the equality guarantee has not been a useful tool for minority groups (Constitution Review Group, 1996).[29] It did not avail David Norris, for instance, in his challenge to the criminalisation of consensual sex between men.[30] Relevant constitutional provisions and case law are referred to throughout the book.

It should also be noted that the ESA interacts with other Acts of the Oireachtas. As we will see from the Tribunal decisions discussed in this book, when

---

[25] [2005] IEHC 235 (High Court); *Equality Authority v Portmarnock Golf Club & Ors* [2010] 1 ILRM 237 (Supreme Court).

[26] The Equal Status Bill 1997 was declared repugnant to the Constitution on the basis that it contained two provisions that were identical in all material terms to sections in the Employment Equality Bill 1996, which had previously been struck down. But the Supreme Court did not examine the remainder of the Bill and so no part of the 2000 Act was examined in light of the Constitution: *Article 26 of the Constitution and the Equal Status Bill 1997, Re* [1997] 2 IR 387.

[27] In *Article 26 of the Constitution and the Employment Equality Bill 1996, Re* [1997] 2 IR 321, Hamilton CJ said 'The forms of discrimination which are, presumptively at least, proscribed by Article 40.1 are not particularised: manifestly, they would extend to classifications based on sex, race, language, [and] religious or political opinions' (at p 347).

[28] See, for example, *de Búrca v Attorney General* [1976] IR 38; *(D.P.P.) v Quilligan and O'Reilly (No. 3)* [1993] 2 IR 305; *Article 26 and the Illegal Immigrants (Trafficking) Bill 1999, Re* [2000] 2 IR 360; *Murphy v Attorney General* [1982] IR 241; and *Article 26 and Part V of the Planning and Development Bill 1999, Re* [2000] 2 IR 321.

[29] It is not clear whether, or at least to what extent, Article 40.1 applies to the actions of private individuals (Banda, 2009).

[30] *Norris v Attorney General* [1984] ILRM 167.

deciding on the meaning of particular provisions the equality officers who investigate cases frequently rely on Tribunal decisions under the EEA. The two laws are inextricably linked, sharing common definitions and grounds of discrimination, for example.[31] According to the Supreme Court:

> It is a well established principle to be applied in the consideration of an Act that, where a word or expression in an earlier Act has received a clear judicial interpretation, there is a presumption that the subsequent Act which incorporates the same word or expression in a similar context should be construed so that the word or expression is interpreted according to the meaning that has previously been ascribed to it, unless a contrary intention appears.[32]

When an ordinary court considers a provision of the ESA it must interpret that provision in light of the state's obligations under the European Convention on Human Rights (ECHR).[33] That interpretive duty does not extend to the Equality Tribunal and it cannot assess whether a public body has breached the European Convention on Human Rights Act 2003 in addition to the ESA.[34] The European Court of Human Rights has produced a vast body of law, some of which is directly relevant to the question of discrimination in accessing goods and services. Relevant cases are dealt with throughout the book.

The Equality Tribunal only has jurisdiction to consider compliance with the ESA and other defined discrimination laws (Chapter 11.2). An equality officer cannot, therefore, establish whether a respondent has breached another law that may be relevant to a complaint. As we will see from the cases discussed in this book, other laws may nonetheless be relevant in deciding whether discrimination has occurred.

Finally, it is worth noting that the Equality Tribunal and courts often draw on United Kingdom (UK) cases. Those cases do not enjoy the force of law but are sometimes considered to be of persuasive value, especially where similar wording and concepts are in issue.[35]

1.7 The Structure of the Acts

The Equal Status Acts 2000–2011 are divided into five parts: (I) Preliminary, (II) Discrimination and Related Activities, (III) Enforcement, (IV) Equality

---

[31] The Supreme Court acknowledged the inextricable links between the two laws in *Article 26 of the Constitution and the Equal Status Bill 1997, Re* [1997] 2 IR 387.

[32] *Cronin v Youghal Carpets (Yarns) Ltd* [1985] IR 312, per Griffin J at p 321.

[33] Section 2, ECHR Act 2003.

[34] See, for example, *A Patient v Health Service Provider and a Hospital*, DEC-S2010-053.

[35] See, for example, *O'Brien v Iarnród Éireann*, DEC-S2003-029, at para 7.5.

Authority and (V) General. For our purposes the first three are the most important.

Briefly, Part I of the ESA (sections 1–4) sets out the definitions used in the legislation – most significantly of the discrimination grounds (section 2), of services and goods (section 2), of direct and indirect discrimination (section 3) and of reasonable accommodation (section 4).

Part II of the ESA (sections 5–19) goes on to specify how the discrimination principle is to be applied in various contexts, defines harassment and sexual harassment (section 11), and contains a series of general exemptions. Section 5 deals with the general arena of goods and services provision, section 6 applies to the sale of property and provision of rental accommodation, while section 7 concerns education. Registered clubs are the subject of sections 8–10 and advertising is dealt with in section 12.

Enforcement is provided for under Part III of the ESA and its provisions are discussed in Chapters 10 to 12 of this book.

2

Scope

2.1 Introduction

As noted in Chapter 1, the ESA does not apply universally but only targets certain activities of public and private bodies. The term 'material scope' refers to those areas that fall under the remit of the ESA. The reach of the Equal Status Acts appears to be very wide. It covers the use and provision of a wide range of services (e.g. banking, insurance and entertainment), the purchase and sale of goods, advertising, the disposal of property and the provision of accommodation and education. However, certain key activities of public bodies are not subject to the ESA: most policing and immigration practices, aspects of the operation of prisons and of the implementation of tax, social welfare and planning codes fall outside its remit. Two provisions are especially relevant in setting the material scope of the Acts: the definition of 'service' in section 2 and section 14(1)(*a*). Section 14(1)(*a*) excludes the taking of any action required by or under 'any enactment' from the ambit of the Acts, which means that the legislation cannot be used to challenge other *laws* that may be discriminatory. These major exemptions are considered further in Chapters 2.4 and 2.5.

The scope of the ESA is also confined to discriminatory treatment that is related to nine specified grounds. These grounds are in turn linked to personal identities or statuses. A person who advances a discrimination complaint must place it under at least one of the protected categories and so the nine grounds restrict the personal scope of the ESA (Chapter 2.3). As discussed in Chapter 2.6, particular exceptions apply to safeguard treatment on some of those discriminatory grounds that would otherwise breach the ESA.

2.2 Other Avenues for Challenging Discrimination

Where a particular issue falls outside the scope of the ESA an individual may challenge alleged discrimination by a public body using other sources of law within the ordinary courts system. However this route is considerably more expensive, requires professional legal expertise and will generally take a longer period of time to be heard.[36] Any such challenge would usually take the form of a judicial review[37] application or constitutional litigation before the High Court and be based on the equality guarantee of the Constitution. The European Convention on Human Rights Act 2003 (ECHR Act) can also be used to advance discrimination claims that fall outside the scope of the ESA (De Londras and Kelly, 2010; Kilkelly, 2009; O'Connell, Cummiskey, Meeneghan and O'Connell, 2006). Under that Act 'organs of the state' are required to carry out their duties and functions in a manner that is compatible with the provisions of the ECHR.[38] Failure to do so will expose the public body in question to an award of damages. Additionally, Irish courts are obliged in interpreting and applying any statutory provisions or rule of law to do so 'in a manner compatible with the State's obligations under the Convention provisions'.[39]

Discrimination encountered in the course of accessing many public services can also be raised in complaints to bodies such as the Ombudsman or the Ombudsman for Children. Detailed consideration of these alternative avenues is beyond the scope of this book but they are referred to where relevant and a brief account of their operation is set out in Chapter 10.5.

2.3 Personal Scope: The Discriminatory Grounds

2.3.1 Introduction

The ESA does not prohibit all forms of discrimination but only those connected to a fixed set of grounds or bases: age, disability, civil status, gender, family status, membership of the Traveller community, race, religion and sexual orientation.[40] When making a complaint under the ESA the first thing a person must establish is that he/she is covered by at least one of those nine grounds. Technically, 'victimisation' constitutes a further ground under the Acts but,

---

[36] Part II of this book discusses the benefits of the Equality Tribunal system.

[37] Judicial review is a legal action used where a public body or tribunal has acted in excess of legal authority or contrary to its duty. Questions about the constitutional validity of legislation are usually raised in plenary proceedings but may arise in judicial review applications (Collins and O'Reilly, 2004, p 158).

[38] Section 3, ECHR Act 2003.

[39] Section 2, ECHR Act 2003.

[40] Protection on other grounds, such as socio-economic status and political opinion, is provided for in other jurisdictions (Kilcommins, McClean, McDonagh, Mullally and Whelan, 2004; MacKay and Piper, 2009). The selection of discrimination law grounds, and how those grounds are defined in the first instance as well as through interpretation, is the subject of much commentary (see, for example, McCrudden, 2004; Fredman, 2010).

following the practice of the Equality Authority (2010a), it is considered a distinct form of discrimination in this book (Chapter 3.5).

Section 3(2) provides:

> As between any two persons, the discriminatory grounds (and the descriptions of those grounds for the purposes of this Act) are:
>
> (*a*) that one is male and the other is female (the 'gender ground'),
>
> (*b*) that they are of different civil status (the 'civil status ground'),
>
> (*c*) that one has family status and the other does not or that one has a different family status from the other (the 'family status ground'),
>
> (*d*) that they are of different sexual orientation (the 'sexual orientation ground'),
>
> (*e*) that one has a different religious belief from the other, or that one has a religious belief and the other has not (the 'religion ground'),
>
> (*f*) subject to *subsection (3)*, that they are of different ages (the 'age ground'),
>
> (*g*) that one is a person with a disability and the other either is not or is a person with a different disability (the 'disability ground'),
>
> (*h*) that they are of different race, colour, nationality or ethnic or national origins (the 'ground of race'),
>
> (*i*) that one is a member of the Traveller community and the other is not (the 'Traveller community ground')[41]

As discussed in subsequent chapters, the grounds operate differently depending on the form of discrimination at issue. Generally speaking, the grounds are used to compare the position of the complainant with that of other persons.

The personal statuses or identities that underpin six of the nine grounds are defined in section 2, with 'age', 'gender' and 'race, colour, nationality or ethnic or national origins' being the exceptions. The next section looks at how the grounds are defined, while case law dealing with each of the grounds is considered in the remainder of Part I.

2.3.2 Age

Protection is only provided against age discrimination for people aged over 18. 'Age' is not defined under the ESA. The discriminatory ground refers to

---

[41] The victimisation ground (section 3(2)(*j*)) is dealt with in Chapter 3.5.

people being of 'different ages', but, beyond that, the Acts offer no guidance on the nature of age-based discrimination.

2.3.3 Civil Status

The Civil Partnership and Certain Rights and Obligations of Cohabitants Act 2010 amended the ESA by replacing the definition of 'marital status' with that of 'civil status'. Civil status 'means being single, married, separated, divorced, widowed, in a civil partnership within the meaning of the Civil Partnership and Certain Rights and Obligations of Cohabitants Act 2010 or being a former civil partner in a civil partnership that has ended by death or been dissolved'.[42] The Act came into force on 1 January 2011. In effect, the new definition extends protection to civil partners and to people whose civil partnership has been dissolved or has been ended by the death of their partner. Along with that of family status this ground covers a range of family forms and relationships but many more, such as those involving siblings and other relatives, are not specifically addressed by the ESA.[43]

2.3.4 Disability

'Disability' has a broad meaning for the purposes of the Acts:

> 'disability' means—
>
> (*a*) the total or partial absence of a person's bodily or mental functions, including the absence of a part of a person's body,
>
> (*b*) the presence in the body of organisms causing, or likely to cause, chronic disease or illness,
>
> (*c*) the malfunction, malformation or disfigurement of a part of a person's body,
>
> (*d*) a condition or malfunction which results in a person learning differently from a person without the condition or malfunction, or

---

[42] Section 103(2)(*a*) of the Civil Partnership and Certain Rights and Obligations of Cohabitants Act 2010. The definition of 'near relative' under section 2 is also amended to include civil partners. But that change seems unnecessary since the term 'near relative' only appeared in subsections of the 2000 Act (section 6(2)(*b*) and (*d*)), which were repealed by section 49 of the Equality Act 2004.

[43] The status of relatives such as siblings for discrimination law purposes is not very secure under the ECHR either: *Burden v United Kingdom* (2008) 47 EHRR 38. On broadening the ground to include a range of care relationships see Ontario Human Rights Commission (2007).

(*e*) a condition, illness or disease which affects a person's thought processes, perception of reality, emotions or judgement or which results in disturbed behaviour[44]

Case law has established that the definition includes, for instance, depression,[45] epilepsy,[46] claustrophobia and agoraphobia,[47] alcoholism,[48] facial scarring,[49] Attention Deficit Hyperactivity Disorder (ADHD),[50] HIV infection,[51] diabetes[52] and dyslexia.[53] Literacy difficulties that stem from poor educational opportunities as opposed to a 'cerebral impairment' do not amount to a disability for the purposes of the Acts.[54]

The Irish provision goes further than EU law because it covers transient conditions arising from perhaps an illness or an accident.[55] So, for the purposes of the parallel definition under the EEA, whiplash injury is considered a 'malfunction' of the body under paragraph (*c*), while serious neck injuries sustained in a car accident also comprised a disability in an ESA case.[56] Additionally, unlike many provisions applicable in other countries, the Irish definition does not require a certain severity of 'impairment' or of 'functional limitation' (Schiek, Waddington and Bell, 2007, Chapter 1.3.9). In some employment discrimination

---

[44] Section 2.

[45] *Mr X v A Town Council*, DEC-S2008-042. See the detailed consideration of depressive illnesses as a 'disability' for the purposes of the EEA in *A Government Department v A Worker* (ADE/07/23; EDA/094, 25 March 2009) and the discussion of that and similar cases by Whelan (2009, pp 428–430).

[46] *Forde v The Body Clinic*, DEC-S2007-085.

[47] *Ms D (a tenant) v A Local Authority*, DEC-S2007-057.

[48] *A Complainant v Café Kylemore*, DEC-S2003-024. In the employment arena see the Labour Court decision in *An Employee v A Government Department* [2006] ELR 225.

[49] *Carey v McDonalds Restaurant*, DEC-S2005-044.

[50] *Two Complainants (a mother and her son) v A Primary School*, DEC-S2006-028.

[51] *Goulding v O'Doherty*, DEC-S2009-073.

[52] *Mr A v A Life Assurance Company*, DEC-S2011-008; *Connery v Coiste an Asgard*, DEC-S2006-034.

[53] *Two Named Complainants v Minister for Education and Science*, DEC-S2006-077.

[54] *Two Complainants (a mother and her son) v A Primary School*, DEC-S2006-028, para 4.3.

[55] According to the CJEU, sickness in itself is not enough to qualify as a 'disability' for the purposes of the Framework Directive. 'Disability' is a long-term limitation which results from physical, mental or psychological impairments and hinders participation in professional life (para 43): *Chacón Navas v Eurest Colectividades SA*, Case C-13/05, [2006] ECR 1-6467. See further Waddington (2007). It is important to note that the EU equality directives set out minimum requirements. Member states may therefore provide for a higher level of protection against discrimination in national legislation.

[56] See respectively, *Customer Perception Ltd v Leydon* [2004] ELR 101 (Labour Court) and *Banjoko v Mellon t/a Dolmen Nursery & Montessori School*, DEC-S2009-020.

cases, however, the Tribunal and Labour Court have found that disability ground protection will not apply where the symptoms or effects associated with a condition or impairment are present to an insignificant degree.[57]

As with the other grounds, in cases of direct discrimination (i.e. less favourable treatment) the disability may no longer exist, or indeed it may have never existed but have been wrongly attributed to a person.[58] What this means is that someone need not 'have' one of the conditions or impairments outlined in section 2 in order to avail of the Acts. It is enough that they are treated less favourably because a service provider (incorrectly) assumes that they have a disability. People will also be protected where they are discriminated against because of a condition or impairment they had in the past, which should be especially important for individuals with a history of mental health problems.

For Degener (2004, p 10) the Irish definition endorses the social model of disability: 'it does not portray disabled persons as helpless or needy, because it makes no assumptions about the effects of a given impairment or malfunction.' In addressing the inequalities encountered by disabled people, the social model of disability focuses on socially constructed barriers instead of considering an impairment or condition as a problem that ought to be fixed (Barnes and Mercer, 2005).

2.3.5 Family Status

People in specific relationships of dependency are covered by the 'family status' definition. It is also aimed at pregnancy-related discrimination:

'family status' means being pregnant or having responsibility—

(*a*) as a parent or as a person *in loco parentis* in relation to a person who has not attained the age of 18 years, or

(*b*) as a parent or the resident primary carer in relation to a person of or over that age with a disability which is of such a nature as to give rise to the need for care or support on a continuing, regular or frequent basis,

and, for the purposes of *paragraph (b)*, a primary carer is a resident primary carer in relation to a person with a disability if the primary carer resides with the person with the disability.

---

[57] *Colgan v Boots Ireland Ltd*, DEC-E2010-008; *O'Rourke v JJ Red Holdings Ltd t/a Dublin City Hotel*, DEC-E2010-045; *A Government Department v A Worker* (ADE/07/23; EDA/094, 25 March 2009).

[58] *Ms X v Electronic Component Co.*, DEC-E2006-042 and *A Health Service Employee v Health Service Executive*, DEC-E2006-013.

The terms 'parent' and 'person *in loco parentis*' appear to be broad enough to cover legally recognised parents and their partners (married or otherwise), along with other adults who play a parental role in a child's life. It should protect, for example, foster family relationships and parents in gay or lesbian relationships. Parents of minors are afforded more extensive protection than that accorded to those caring for disabled people since there is no requirement that they be resident or primary. There is no guidance as to the meaning of the term 'primary carer', but presumably it refers to the person who provides the majority of care. The residence requirement could have the effect of excluding the primary carers of persons who spend some time in care institutions (Power, 2003).[59]

2.3.6 Gender

'Gender' is not defined under the ESA but the gender ground refers to one person being a man and the other being a woman. The sex discrimination provisions of EU law extend to the protection of transsexual persons, that is, a person who intends to, is undergoing or has undergone gender reassignment.[60] Although the ESA is broader in terms of its material scope than EU law at present, it is to be expected that a single definition of gender to include transsexual people will apply to all areas subject to the ESA. A number of cases involving transsexual people have been settled with the assistance of the Equality Authority, and the first Tribunal decision concerning a transsexual person was issued in March 2011.[61] This employment case is discussed in Chapter 3.3.4. The extent to which transgender people more broadly are protected from discrimination is not clear at present (Chapter 3.3.4).

Under the Gender Goods and Services Directive less favourable treatment of women for reasons of pregnancy and maternity (including IVF treatment)[62] is a form of direct discrimination based on sex (article 4(1)(*a*)). The gender ground under the ESA must be read in light of that Directive

---

[59] In its submission on the Equal Status Bill 1999, the Irish Council for Civil Liberties recommended that the residency requirement be deleted. See the debate before the Select Committee on Justice, Equality, Defence and Women's Rights on 3 November 1999 and 512 *Dáil Debates*, Cols 1595–1597 (Report Stage).

[60] See *P v S and Cornwall County Council*, Case C-13/94, [1996] ECR 1-2143; *KB v National Health Service Pensions Agency and Another*, Case C-117/01, [2004] ECR 1-541; *Richards v Secretary of State for Work and Pensions*, Case C-423/04, [2006] ECR 1-3585. See also recital 3 of the Recast Directive.

[61] *Hannon v First Direct Logistics Limited*, DEC-E2011-066.

[62] See *Mayr v Bäckerei und Konditorei Gerhard Flöckner OHG*, Case C-506/06, [2008] ECR 1-1017. The case concerned the Equal Treatment Directive 76/207, but the principle established should also apply to Directive 2004/113.

and so it overlaps to an extent with 'family status', which explicitly covers pregnancy.

2.3.7 Race

The race ground embraces 'race, colour, nationality or ethnic or national origins'. None of these terms is defined. According to the High Court the term 'ethnic origins' under the ESA will usually refer to an immutable characteristic over which an individual has no control.[63] Hogan J adopted the definition of 'ethnic group' used in a House of Lords judgment. In that case Lord Fraser found that such a group must regard itself and be regarded by others as a distinct community by virtue of certain characteristics. He set out the following essential characteristics which help to distinguish the group from the surrounding community:

> (1) a long shared history, of which the group is conscious as distinguishing it from other groups, and the memory of which it keeps alive; (2) a cultural tradition of its own, including family and social customs and manners, often but not necessarily associated with religious observance. In addition to those two essential characteristics the following characteristics are, in my opinion, relevant; (3) either a common geographical origin, or descent from a small number of common ancestors; (4) a common language, not necessarily peculiar to the group; (5) a common literature peculiar to the group; (6) a common religion different from that of neighbouring groups or from the general community surrounding it; (7) being a minority or being an oppressed or a dominant group within a larger community, for example a conquered people (say, the inhabitants of England shortly after the Norman conquest) and their conquerors might both be ethnic groups.[64]

Applying this formula the High Court concluded that for the purposes of the ESA farmers are an occupational group, not an ethnic group. The complainant could not, therefore, base a discrimination complaint on his status as a member of the farming community.

In a 2007 decision, *O'Brien and Others v Florry Batts*,[65] the complainants were refused service in a pub in Kenmare, Co. Kerry on the basis that they were not from the locality. Their discrimination claim also failed because

---

[63] *Fitzgerald v Minister for Community, Equality and Gaeltacht Affairs* [2011] IEHC 180, at para 10.

[64] *Mandla v Dowell-Lee* [1983] AC 548, at p 562.

[65] DEC-S2007-063. See also *Kelly v Greville Arms Hotel, Granard*, DEC-S2006-009.

they could not establish that it came within any of the nine grounds provided for under the ESA. According to the equality officer, because 'the majority of those who are locals in Kerry are of the same race, colour, nationality and ethnic origin as the complainants, any less favourable treatment of the complainants is not based on their race'.[66]

The inclusion of both 'nationality' and 'national origins' suggests that these terms refer to distinct statuses. In *Sabherwal v ICTS (UK) Ltd*[67] the equality officer equated 'nationality' with 'citizenship'. Australian[68] and UK[69] case law regards 'national origin' as a status that is fixed at the time of birth whereas nationality has been characterised as a 'transient status' that may change over the course of a person's life. The distinction between these various components of the race ground is significant since certain exceptions provided for under the legislation apply only to one element of the ground. As discussed further below, the broadest exceptions concern 'nationality' (see Chapter 2.6.2.4).

Any one person may fall under several elements of the race ground. For example, a Kenyan individual may be defined by colour, nationality or ethnic or national origins.

In a 2010 decision the Tribunal found that the race ground does not cover Travellers.[70] The equality officer did not elaborate on the reasons for his finding. Subsequent decisions appear to leave the matter open in referring to the complainants' failure to adduce relevant evidence.[71]

A related matter that remains to be resolved is whether Travellers are covered by the terms of the Racial Equality Directive, which addresses discrimination on the grounds of 'racial or ethnic origin'. The term 'racial or ethnic origin' is not defined in the Directive and has yet to be interpreted

---

[66] See also the EEA case of *Curran v The Department of Education and Science*, DEC-E2009-075.

[67] DEC-S2008-037.

[68] See, for example, *AB v New South Wales* (2005) 194 FLR 156 and *Macabenta v Minister of State for Immigration and Multicultural Affairs* (1998) 154 ALR 591.

[69] See, for example, *Ealing London Borough Council v Race Relations Board* [1972] AC 342.

[70] *Mrs X (on behalf of her son, Mr Y) v A Post-Primary School*, DEC-S2010-009, at para 4.17.

[71] *Mrs K (on behalf of her son) v A Primary School*, DEC-2011-003, at para 4.15; *Cash v Murphy Property and Finance Ltd*, DEC-S2011-031, at para 4.9; and *Burke v Kerry County Council*, DEC-S2011-043, at para 5.11. It may be that equality officers are in effect applying the legal maxim *expressio unius est exclusio alterius* (the expression of one thing is to the exclusion of another). In other words, since membership of the Travelling community is recognised as a specific ground of discrimination, the Oireachtas did not intend that the wider 'race' ground would also apply to Travellers or non-Travellers. For a discussion of that rule of interpretation in the context of the ESA see *Joyce v Madden* [2004] 1 ILRM 277.

by the CJEU (Farkas and European Network of Legal Experts in the Non-Discrimination Field, 2007, pp 16–23; Howard, 2008). However, the weight of precedent under both the European Convention on Human Rights (ECHR)[72] and from the UK courts[73] suggests that Travellers are an ethnic group for the purposes of human rights and discrimination law (Equality Authority, 2006a; Irish Human Rights Commission, 2004a, 2007; McVeigh, 2007; Sandland, 2008). Since the ECHR forms part of the body of human rights standards protected under EU law (De Schutter, 2005a), the CJEU can be expected to take a similar approach.[74] This question is of major importance since the material scope of the Racial Equality Directive is much broader than that of the ESA. Most significantly, the Racial Equality Directive can be used to challenge laws that may be discriminatory.

A further question that remains to be determined is whether groups such as Sikhs and Jews are ethnic groups, as is the case under UK anti-discrimination law, and so covered by the race ground as well the religion ground.[75] As discussed further in Chapter 3.3.6, this may have implications for certain exceptions provided for under the ESA.

2.3.8 Religion

Section 3(2)(*e*) defines the religion ground as: 'that one has a different religious belief from the other, or that one has a religious belief and the other has not'. According to section 2, 'religious belief' includes 'religious background

---

[72] In *Timishev v Russia* (2007) 44 EHRR 37 (at para 55) the European Court of Human Rights stated that ethnic groups may be defined with reference to objective criteria such as 'common nationality, tribal affiliation, religious faith, shared language, or cultural and traditional origins and backgrounds'. Travellers also fulfil the ethnic minority criteria under the International Convention on the Elimination of All Forms of Racial Discrimination (ICERD) and for that reason the United Nations Committee on the Elimination of Racial Discrimination has continually recommended that the Irish Government recognise Travellers as an ethnic group (United Nations Committee on the Elimination of Racial Discrimination, 2011, para 12).

[73] *Commission for Racial Equality v Dutton* [1989] 1 All ER 306 (Romany Gypsies) and Irish Travellers in *O'Leary and Kiely v Punch Retail* (unreported, London County Court, 29 August 2000); cited by Turner (2003, p 408).

[74] Following the entry into force of the Lisbon Treaty, on 1 December 2009, the EU Charter of Fundamental Rights has become legally binding on the EU's institutions and on member states when they act within the scope of EU law. It entrenches all the rights found in the European Convention on Human Rights as well as other rights and principles resulting from the common constitutional traditions of the EU member states, the case law of the CJEU and other international instruments. Under article 53 of the Charter the level of protection provided by the Charter must be at least as high as that under the Convention.

[75] *Mandla v Dowell-Lee* [1983] AC 548; *R (Watkins Singh) v Governing Body of Aberdare Girls' High School* [2008] ELR 561; *R (E) v Governing Body of JFS & Anor* [2010] 2 AC 728.

or outlook'. The Labour Court has found that the words 'background' and 'outlook' used in the identical provision under the EEA refer to an opinion or conviction which a person may hold or to a point of view or an attitude to life: *Irish Prison Service v Morris*.[76] The complainant, a Catholic priest, was working as a chaplain in a prison and sought to compare his work conditions with laypersons employed in the Prison Service. The Court pointed out that the difference in treatment was grounded in the office or position held by the complainant and not on the religion which he professes or practices. According to the Court the definition does not encompass a person's status or position within a particular religion.

To date the religion ground has been invoked by individuals with no religious belief as well as people from some of the dominant religious traditions recognised in Ireland, including Islam and denominations of Christianity such as Catholicism and Protestantism. It is to be expected that 'religious belief' will apply to other major religions such as the Baha'i faith, Buddhism, Hinduism, Jainism, Judaism, Rastafarianism, Sikhism and Zoroastrianism. It is not clear from *Morris* or from relevant Equality Tribunal decisions whether the ground covers secular beliefs or philosophies. For example, in *Sheeran v The Office of Public Works*[77] the equality officer expressed some doubt as to whether humanism could be counted as a religious belief. It appears from the wording of the provision that the belief in question must be a religious one and so the current definition will probably be inadequate to meet the requirements of the proposed EU directive, which will prohibit discrimination on the grounds of religion *or* belief. Significantly, religious belief is also the subject of a substantive right under the ECHR (article 9). Case law on article 9 is referred to in the chapters on direct discrimination and indirect discrimination.

2.3.9 Sexual Orientation

'Sexual orientation' means heterosexual, homosexual or bisexual orientation. Gay men and lesbian women have referred a number of cases. To date there are no findings of discrimination against a heterosexual. It appears that just one bisexual individual has lodged a complaint on this ground.[78]

2.3.10 Traveller Community

In debates surrounding the draft equality law, Travellers' rights NGOs and other bodies such as the National Economic and Social Forum (1996) sought

---

[76] ADE/06/10; EDA/074, 28 February 2007. This case was under appeal from the Tribunal finding in *Mr M v A State Authority*, DEC-E2006-015.

[77] DEC-S2004-015.

[78] *A Complainant v A Fast Food Franchise*, DEC-S2008-036.

legislative recognition of Travellers as a distinct ethnic group.[79] The defini-tion of the ground arose in *McCarthy v Davitt's Nite Club*.[80] It was argued that several of the complainants lived in England and did not have a nomadic lifestyle as required by section 2(1), which provides:

> 'Traveller community' means the community of people who are commonly called Travellers and who are identified (both by them-selves and others) as people with a shared history, culture and traditions including, historically, a nomadic way of life on the island of Ireland.

The equality officer did not accept that argument:

> The definition of Traveller under the Act does not require the complainants to have a nomadic way of life so long as historically they or their ancestors had a nomadic way of life and that they are identified as Travellers by both themselves and others. I am satisfied that the complainants satisfy these criteria and that they are members of the Traveller community as defined by the Act (para 6.4).

2.3.11 Multiple Grounds

Complainants frequently take cases on multiple grounds, but there are few find-ings of cumulative discrimination (aside from those establishing victimisation in addition to discrimination on another ground). The case law also reveals that there is a close relationship between several of the bases, such as that between race and religion, and between family status and gender. For example, a landlord who will not rent a house to a single mother may discriminate on the gender, family status and civil status grounds. As discussed further in Chapter 4, the close relationship between various grounds is particularly significant in the area of indirect discrimination. For example, discrimination against carers (family status ground) may also amount to indirect discrimination on the gender ground.[81]

2.4 Material Scope

2.4.1 Introduction

The ESA only addresses certain activities of public and private bodies. This section looks at various factors that set the material scope of the legislation

---

[79] See 512 *Dáil Debates* Cols 1606–1608.
[80] DEC-S2005-005/011. See also *Connors v Crowe*, DEC-S2001-003; *O'Brien v Killarney Ryan Hotel*, DEC-S2001-008; *Maughan v Dolly Heffernan's Pub*, DEC-S2002-010/011; and *Ward v Paddy Keane Auctioneers*, DEC-S2008-119.
[81] From the available statistics it appears that the majority of carers are female (Central Statistics Office, 2007a, pp 19–21).

including the definition of services as well as numerous exceptions, which remove some activities from the reach of the ESA. First it examines the general contexts the Acts apply to, then it explains what types of goods and services are covered by the ESA. This section concludes by considering the public sector in some detail.

2.4.2 Contexts

Here we look in broad terms at the areas of activity covered by the ESA. As Table 1 illustrates, section 5 applies to the general arena of goods and services provision, while other fields are dealt with separately under sections 6–10.

Table 1: The Material Scope of the Equal Status Acts

Provision of ESA	General Area	Sectors Covered
Section 5	Disposal of goods and provision of services	Banking, insurance, entertainment and leisure (e.g. hotels, restaurants, shops), transport (e.g. public transport, car hire, taxis, air travel), healthcare (e.g. medical practitioners, hospitals), social welfare (Licensed premises are generally dealt with under the Intoxicating Liquor Act 2003)
Section 6	Disposal of premises and provision of accommodation	Rented accommodation and premises, public housing and accommodation (e.g. halting sites, accommodation provided by voluntary housing associations), sales of houses and other premises
Section 7	Education	Pre-school, primary, secondary and tertiary educational establishments *Vocational training is subject instead to the EEA*
Sections 8–10	Registered clubs	Treatment of members and access to membership of clubs that hold a certificate of registration

Section 5(1) states:

> A person shall not discriminate in disposing of goods to the public generally or a section of the public or in providing a service, whether the disposal or provision is for consideration or otherwise and whether the service provided can be availed of only by a section of the public.

The rest of that section essentially provides for various exceptions (see Chapter 2.6). The term 'discriminate' includes direct and indirect discrimination as well as the duty to reasonably accommodate disabled persons (harassment and sexual harassment are dealt with separately under section 11).[82] Matters dealt with in the Tribunal decisions under section 5 include banking, insurance, car hire, air travel, hotel, restaurant and leisure facilities, and stays in hospitals. The phrase 'for consideration or otherwise' means that coverage extends beyond contexts where goods and services are purchased. Section 5 has been applied to statutory bodies that provide healthcare, transport and grants of various types.

Transactions concerning premises and the provision of accommodation are governed by section 6 (hotel and other overnight accommodation is usually dealt with under section 5).[83] Section 6(1) provides:

> A person shall not discriminate in—
>
> (*a*) disposing of any estate or interest in premises,
>
> (*b*) terminating any tenancy or other interest in premises, or
>
> (*c*) providing accommodation or any services or amenities related to accommodation or ceasing to provide accommodation or any such services or amenities.

The remainder of section 6 clarifies the obligations incurred and lists numerous exceptions.

The phrase 'discriminate' includes direct and indirect discrimination as well as the duty to reasonably accommodate disabled persons.[84] It operates so that, for example, landlords and estate agents cannot base refusals to rent premises or decisions to terminate lettings on the nine grounds.[85] Supposedly neutral

---

[82] Section 2(1).

[83] See *Martin v Esplanade Hotel*, DEC-S2010-034, para 5.2.

[84] Section 2(1). Application of the reasonable accommodation duty to this field is reinforced under sections 4(6)(*c*) and 4(6)(*d*).

[85] See, for example, *De Burca and Fernandez v Homelocators*, DEC-S2004-030/031

conditions or other measures applied by service providers could also have the effect of disadvantaging people covered by those grounds and so fall foul of the indirect discrimination prohibition (Chapter 4). The most frequently litigated aspect of section 6 appears to be subsection 6, which permits housing authorities and voluntary housing bodies to take into account family size, family status, civil status, disability, age or membership of the Traveller community when providing housing. These and other exceptions concerning accommodation and property are discussed in Chapter 2.6. Harassment and sexual harassment liability in this context is dealt with separately under section 11.

Section 7 applies the prohibitions on direct and indirect discrimination along with the reasonable accommodation provision to 'educational establishments'.[86] Again, harassment and sexual harassment liability are dealt with under section 11. The 'educational establishments' covered are:

> ... a pre-school service within the meaning of *Part VII of the Child Care Act, 1991*, a primary or post-primary school, an institution providing adult, continuing or further education, or a university or any other third-level or higher-level institution, whether or not supported by public funds.[87]

Private schools, colleges and similar institutions are clearly included. A pre-school service 'means any pre-school, play group, day nursery, crèche, day-care or other similar service which caters for pre-school children, including those grant-aided by health boards.'[88]

---

and *Cassidy and Wesemann v Doherty*, DEC-S2003-040/041 (both on the family status ground); *McCann v Dún Laoghaire–Rathdown County Council*, DEC-S2008-004 and *Ward v Paddy Keane Auctioneers*, DEC-S2008-119 (the Traveller community ground); and *Cementwala v Colbert, Winters Property Management & Crescent Green Ltd*, DEC-S2005-184/186 and *McGreal v Clúid Housing*, DEC-S2011-004 (disability ground). Note that on occasion cases involving rental accommodation have been dealt with under section 5(1): *Cantwell v Giles & Co., Tralee*, DEC-S2007-010; and *McDonagh v Duff*, DEC-S2005-012. In *McDonagh v O'Keeffe, Ocean View Park*, DEC-S2005-161/164 a complaint concerning the provision of holiday accommodation at a caravan park was determined under section 6(1)(*c*).

[86] Application of the reasonable accommodation duty to this field is copper-fastened by section 4(6)(*e*).

[87] Section 7(1). Individual teachers are also under a duty not to discriminate in contravention of the professional codes of conduct for the profession. See further the website of the Teaching Council: <http://www.teachingcouncil.ie/>.

[88] Section 49, Child Care Act 1991; according to section 52 of that Act a pre-school service does not include: '(*a*) the care of one or more pre-school children undertaken by a relative of the child or children or the spouse of such relative, (*b*) a person taking care of

Under section 7(2) educational establishments cannot discriminate on each of the nine grounds in relation to:

(*a*) the admission or the terms or conditions of admission of a person as a student to the establishment,

(*b*) the access of a student to any course, facility or benefit provided by the establishment,

(*c*) any other term or condition of participation in the establishment by a student, or

(*d*) the expulsion of a student from the establishment or any other sanction against the student.

Paragraph (*c*) embraces school codes of conduct, assessment procedures and teaching methods. To date several Tribunal decisions have dealt with the accommodation of disabled students (Chapter 6.7) and broader questions of access across all levels of the education system,[89] while uniform policies and suspensions have featured in cases concerning schools.[90] A range of exceptions allow, for example, third level institutions to reserve places for mature students and set different fee scales for EU nationals and persons from other countries. Perhaps the most controversial one concerns the admission criteria of denominational schools. This is discussed in Chapter 2.6.2.3. As we will see, discrimination in the context of secondary and primary level education is complex because of a number of overlapping laws that govern students' rights (see Chapter 6.7).

Section 7 only refers to students or prospective students. But other people, such as parents of pupils, can refer cases against schools or other educational establishments under section 5 (provided they are accessing a service, good or facility).[91] The Department of Education and Skills is not an 'educational

---

one or more pre-school children of the same family and no other such children (other than that person's own such children) in that person's home, (*c*) a person taking care of not more than 3 pre-school children of different families (other than that person's own such children) in that person's home.'

[89] See, for example, *Mr X and Ms Y (on behalf of their daughter Z) v A Boys National School*, DEC-S2009-017 (gender ground); *Mrs A (on behalf of her son, B) v A Childcare Facility*, DEC-S2009-041 (disability ground); *Faulkner v St Ita's & St Joseph's School, Tralee*, DEC-S2006-037 (Traveller community ground); and *Lyamina v The Department of Education and Science*, DEC-S2009-016 (race ground).

[90] *Knott v Dunmore Community School*, DEC-S2009-008; *A Male Student v A Secondary School*, DEC-S2009-010; *Carr v Gaelscoil Mhainistir na Corann*, DEC-S2009-023; *A Complainant v A Secondary School*, DEC-S2009-074 (all on the gender ground).

[91] See, for example, *A Separated Father v A Community School*, DEC-S2010-049: access

establishment' but may be regarded as providing goods and services under section 5 (Chapter 2.4.4).[92]

Discrimination in the context of vocational training falls under the Employment Equality Acts 1998–2011.[93] Section 12 of the EEA imposes similar obligations on educational or training bodies to section 7 of the ESA. But the duty to provide reasonable accommodation to disabled people is more onerous under the EEA, a point that is re-visited in Chapter 6.7. Vocational training is defined as:

> … any system of instruction which enables a person being instructed to acquire, maintain, bring up to date or perfect the knowledge or technical capacity required for the carrying on of an occupational activity and which may be considered as exclusively concerned with training for such an activity.[94]

Social employment schemes come under the definition, for example.[95] A Masters in Social Science degree programme that comprised 50 per cent academic and 50 per cent practical work was not vocational training according to the Equality Tribunal 'as it was not exclusively concerned with perfecting

---

to students' records was a service provided to parents having regard to both the ESA and the Education Act 1998.

[92] For example, *Two Named Complainants v Minister for Education and Science*, DEC-S2006-077 and *Lyamina v The Department of Education and Science*, DEC-S2009-016.

[93] The definition of 'service' under section 2 excludes 'a service or facility' to which the EEA applies.

[94] Section 12(2) EEA. For consideration of the definition see *Eng v St. James's Hospital*, DEC-E2001-041; *Kelly v University College Dublin* [2008] IEHC 464; and *Ngongban v Dublin Institute of Technology*, DEC-E2011-144. The definition of vocational training developed by the CJEU in the context of free movement of persons law is broader than the EEA definition. In *Blaizot v University of Liège*, Case 24/86, [1989] 1 CMLR 69 the Court held that a university course would comprise vocational training unless its purpose was to improve general knowledge without any element of preparation for a future occupation (see also *Commission v Austria*, Case C-147/03, [2005] ECR 1-5969). Should a similar definition be adopted under the EU equality directives, the EEA definition may have to be revised. This would in turn have consequences for the application of the ESA to third level educational establishments. In practice a gap between EU requirements and Irish law is most likely to arise in the context of reasonable accommodation since less onerous duties are imposed under the ESA (Chapter 6.7).

[95] FÁS, Ireland's National Training and Employment Authority, currently operates such schemes. A new agency, SOLAS, is to replace FÁS: <http://www.citizensinformation.ie/en/education/vocational_education_and_training/fas_training_programmes_and_supports/fas_training_courses.html> [accessed 2 April 2012]. Relevant case law includes, *Mr W v A FÁS Social Employment Scheme*, DEC-E2008-069 and *Byrne v FÁS*, DEC-E2002-045.

the knowledge or technical capacity to carry out an occupational activity'.[96] The complaint was therefore one that came within the ambit of the ESA. A graduate course in Pharmaceutical Quality Assurance and Biotechnology prepared students for a range of careers across the pharmaceutical, chemistry and biochemistry industries and so was not restricted to equipping a person with the knowledge or capacity for a specific profession or occupation. As a result, it too did not constitute vocational training within the meaning of section 12 of the EEA.[97] In a 2009 decision the Tribunal found that a Higher Diploma in Public Health Nursing was a course that was covered by the ESA.[98] On other hand, the provision of medical training to doctors is considered vocational and so falls to be examined under the EEA.[99]

Issues concerning membership and the treatment of members of registered clubs are treated exceptionally under the ESA (sections 8–10) and are the subject of Chapter 9. Significantly, the ESA does not deal distinctly with other forms of associations or clubs, that is, ones that are not registered. Clubs are, however, mentioned in the definition of 'services' in section 2 (see Chapter 2.4.3). Whether such an organisation is subject to the legislation will depend, therefore, on whether it is providing goods or services to the public or a section of the public. Examples of clubs or associations that would be covered include those that anyone can join after payment of a membership fee such as a film club or health and fitness club. Clearly in that case the club is providing a service to a section of the public. Associations that provide services to members after a selection process governed by the association's rules, because they demonstrate, for example, affiliation to certain political ideals, also fall within the reach of the ESA.[100] UK case law has drawn a distinction between clubs based on how membership is acquired. In a case under the Race Relations Act 1968 the House of Lords decided that the words 'the public or a section of the public' must be interpreted in

---

[96] *Kelly v University College Dublin*, DEC-S2006-076. The decision in this case is the subject of ongoing proceedings before the High Court; a question of law was referred to the CJEU: *Kelly v National University of Ireland*, Case C-104/10, (2010/C 134/29). In one of the judgments associated with those proceedings McKechnie J expressed some doubt as to whether the course could not be considered vocational training for the purposes of EU law: *Kelly v University College Dublin* [2008] IEHC 464, at para 27.

[97] *Ngongban v Dublin Institute of Technology*, DEC-E2011-144.

[98] *A Complainant v An Educational Institution*, DEC-S2009-076.

[99] *Mr X v A Third Level Educational Establishment*, DEC-E2008-062. Cases concerning training provided to people with disabilities by the same college have been lodged under both the EEA and the ESA: *A Complainant v National Training and Development Institute*, DEC-E2002-037; *Hendrick v National Learning Network t/a Roslyn Park College*, DEC-S2009-013.

[100] See *Egan v Young Fine Gael*, DEC-S2011-001, discussed in Chapter 2.4.3.

contrast to 'private'.[101] It found that when the rules of a club provided for nomination and personal selection, and when there was nothing to indicate that those rules were mere formalities, a club was to be considered as private and as not providing goods or services to a section of the public. To date there is no Irish case law distinguishing clubs or associations according to membership criteria.

All of the provisions concerning educational establishments, clubs, providers of accommodation and other services use the definitions of 'goods' and 'services' set out under section 2. We now turn to explore the meaning of those terms.

2.4.3 Definitions of Goods and Services

The definition of 'goods' is straightforward. It refers to 'any articles of movable property' (i.e. property apart from land) and has not been contentious in the case law to date. By contrast the meaning of 'service' has been tested in a number of important decisions.

According to section 2:

> '[S]ervice' means a service or facility of any nature which is available to the public generally or a section of the public and, without prejudice to the generality of the foregoing, includes —
>
> (*a*) access to and the use of any place,
>
> (*b*) facilities for —
>
> > (i) banking, insurance, grants, loans, credit or financing,
> >
> > (ii) entertainment, recreation or refreshment,
> >
> > (iii) cultural activities, or
> >
> > (iv) transport or travel,
>
> (*c*) a service or facility provided by a club (whether or not it is a club holding a certificate of registration under the Registration of Clubs Acts, 1904 to 1999) which is available to the public generally or a section of the public, whether on payment or without payment, and
>
> (*d*) a professional or trade service,

---

[101] *Charter v Race Relations Board* [1973] AC 868. See also *Dockers Labour Club and Institute Ltd v Race Relations Board* [1976] AC 285. UK law on private associations and clubs has since been amended a number of times, most recently by Part 7 of the Equality Act 2010.

but does not include pension rights (within the meaning of the Employment Equality Act, 1998) or a service or facility in relation to which that Act applies.

The list of services is not meant to be comprehensive but simply indicates the Acts' potential areas of application. Aside from the reasonable accommodation duty (Chapter 6), the prohibitions on discrimination in the Acts are directed at 'persons'. Section 2 defines 'person' as including an organisation, public body or other entity. Public bodies are, therefore, subject to the ESA when they are providing a good or a service to the public or a section of the public (Chapter 2.4.4).[102]

Goods or services that are not supplied on a commercial basis are included (i.e. money need not be exchanged).[103] The Acts apply, therefore to competitions, subsidies and other types of benefit. It is clear from the decisions considered below that government grants and schemes of various sorts fall within the remit of the ESA.

The Tribunal examined the meaning of the term 'facility' in *Two Complainants v Department of Education and Science*.[104] The equality officer noted that the same word was also used and not defined in UK equality legislation. He quoted the definition of 'facility' set out in a UK textbook on discrimination law:

> [A] facility is usually a manner, method or opportunity for the easy or easier performance of anything. It might enable a member of the public to have easier access to a service; a cash machine facilitates the withdrawal of money from a bank. It may present a method of obtaining goods; a collection point in a department store facilitates the purchase of heavy or bulky commodities. The term should cover most instances where a person is not actually providing goods or a service himself, but is providing a means to obtain access to those goods or that service (para 7.2).

On that basis he concluded that maintenance grants for third level students were a 'facility' for the purposes of the ESA.

---

[102] In *Donovan v Garda Donnellan*, DEC-S2001-011, the equality officer stated: 'While State services are not specifically mentioned as being covered they are not specifically excluded either and I believe it is clear that certain services provided by the State are available to the public and are covered by the Act, e.g. social welfare services, health services, etc.' See also the discussion at 512 *Dáil Debates* Cols 1601–1606 and *Lyamina v The Department of Education and Science*, DEC-S2009-016.

[103] Section 5(1) states that the discrimination prohibition applies 'whether the disposal or provision is for consideration or otherwise …'.

[104] DEC-S2003-042/043.

The words 'grant' and 'facility' cover benefits provided under various social welfare schemes. For instance, in a 2009 case the equality officer reasoned as follows:

> I am of the view that the financial assistance given under the Disabil-ity Allowance benefit can be described as a grant in the ordinary meaning of that word which is available to a section of the public. I am also of the view that the Free Travel Scheme constitutes a facility that is made available to a section of the public by the respondent which enables the recipients to access public transportation services free of charge. I therefore find that both the payment of Disability Allowance and the Free Travel Scheme constitute a service within the meaning of section 2 of the Equal Status Acts.[105]

McCall v Area Development Management Ltd[106] raised several points about the ambit of the legislation. The case concerned the Taxi Hardship Payments Scheme introduced to ease the effects of the liberalisation of the taxi industry. The respondent maintained that the Government's power to allocate public funds was not liable to action under the ESA: because this was a power derived from the Constitution, courts and tribunals should not interfere with its exercise. Furthermore, it was argued, the Government is not included in the category of respondents set out in section 2, which provides that 'person' includes 'an organisation, public body or other entity'. Relying on a Supreme Court judgment, the equality officer concluded that any such exemption from the Act would have to be expressly provided for.[107] The payment scheme was a 'facility' and so was subject to the obligation not to discriminate. However, the Tribunal's findings in relation to the Taxi Hardship Payments Scheme were overturned by the Circuit Court in an appeal from the decision in *Hoey v Area Development Management Ltd*.[108] A copy of that Circuit Court

---

[105] *Mrs X (on behalf of her daughter, Ms Y) v The Minister for Social and Family Affairs*, DEC-S2009-039, para 5.1. See also *Walczak v Minister for Social Protection*, DEC-S2012-011, which addressed delays in processing applications for jobseeker's benefit and the jobseeker's allowance.

[106] DEC-S2007-058. Applied in *Hegarty v Area Development Management Ltd*, DEC-S2009-004.

[107] In *Howard v Commissioners of Public Works in Ireland* [1994] 1 IR 101, at p 161, Denham J stated: '[The] concept of equality, allied to the doctrine of the separation of powers, and to the absence of any specific provision in the Constitution to give to the executive a special position in relation to the legislature, convinces me that the executive has no such special position. Thus, in legislating in accordance with the Constitution, the Oireachtas legislates for all, and that includes the executive.'

[108] DEC-S2008-010.

judgment is not available but the following account of it was included in a 2012 Tribunal decision:

> Learned Judge Reynolds issued her judgment in the Circuit Court on the appeal on 14 April 2011. The judge found that the Tribunal erred in allowing Mr. Hoey's complaint against the respondent to proceed. Her reasoning was that the respondent was merely administering the scheme in accordance with the criteria established by the Executive. The judge found that for the respondent to have done otherwise would have been *ultra vires* its powers and unlawful. Furthermore, she was of the view that the Tribunal had no jurisdiction to entertain Mr. Hoey's complaint as by doing so the Tribunal was purporting to review a decision of Government, thus acting *ultra vires* of its powers conferred by the Equal Status Acts (para 3.4).[109]

Although the exact reasons for the judgment are unavailable it appears that the Court concurred with the arguments of the respondent in *McCall*. Certain *ex gratia* (i.e. voluntary) schemes established by the Government may not amount to services or facilities for the purposes of the ESA.[110] However such schemes would appear to fall within the ambit of the Racial Equality Directive (Chapter 2.4.5). The implications of the Circuit Court judgment will no doubt be examined in future case law.

A website operated by a voluntary organisation was found to amount to a service in *Dalton v Aspire*.[111] The equality officer had regard to the definition in section 2 and stated: 'By applying clear, everyday language to this definition it is clear that a website is a service within the meaning set out by the legislature' (para 5.3). It has yet to be determined whether the media more generally, in publishing newspapers and broadcasting television programmes and so on, is providing 'services' to the public. Based on the reasoning used in *Dalton*, it may well be. Advertising is subject to separate regulation under section 12.

---

[109] *Brennan and Others v Area Development Management Limited – Taxi Hardship Payments Scheme now POBAL*, DEC-S2012-010. As a consequence, a number of other complaints concerning the Scheme were dismissed as misconceived under section 22 of the ESA (see further Chapter 12.5.5).

[110] It may be that the Circuit Court applied *Bode (A Minor) v Minister for Justice, Equality & Law Reform & Ors* [2007] IESC 62. In that case the Supreme Court held that the Minister was not obliged to have regard to the ECHR and constitutional rights of applicants under a scheme which allowed certain foreign nationals to apply for permission to remain in the state. The scheme was *ex gratia* in nature and '[s]uch an arrangement is distinct from circumstances where legal rights of individuals may fall to be considered and determined' (para 22).

[111] DEC-S2009-062.

An allocation of bonus shares by a cooperative society to its members is a service for the purposes of the ESA, as is an option for holders of public service vehicle licenses to buy shares in a business.[112] It is important to note that in these and several other cases the service or facility is not available to the public at large but only to a limited group of people who nonetheless amount to 'a section of the public'. *Egan v Young Fine Gael*,[113] for example, involved access to membership of a political party. The equality officer had regard to the broad definition of 'service' under the Acts and found 'that the youth wing of a political party can be defined as a service to a certain section of the public and therefore it constitutes a service within the meaning of section 2 of the Equal Status Acts' (para 4.2). Likewise a choir[114] and a shooting club[115] were providing services as defined under the ESA and so subject to its terms. As discussed in the next section, people who are involuntarily detained in prisons or other institutions may also be 'a section of the public'.

2.4.4 Distinction between Public Functions and Services

The nature of state activities has been discussed extensively in ESA decisions and in similar case law in other countries. Government departments and a host of public bodies engage in activities that affect all of our lives on a daily basis. The main question for discrimination law purposes is when those bodies can be regarded as providing goods and services.

Donovan v Garda Donnellan[116] was the first ESA decision to consider the meaning of 'service' in that context. At issue was whether the investigation and prosecution of crime by the Gardaí is a service that is 'available to the public' within the meaning of section 2(1). In that case four horses had strayed onto a road but only one of the owners, a Traveller, was prosecuted. The other horse owners were apparently members of the settled community and the complainant argued that he had been subjected to discrimination on the Traveller community ground by the investigating Garda.

The equality officer quoted a statement made by the Minister for Justice, Equality and Law Reform in the course of the Dáil debates on the Bill:

> Not all actions of the State *vis-à-vis* members of the public can be regarded as services. There is a difference between controlling duties exercised by the State and services provided by the State. I am

---

[112] See respectively, *Fitzgerald v Dairygold Co-Operative Society Ltd*, DEC-S2009-083 and *Oladoyin and Others v Abby/Eco Taxis*, DEC-S2011-009.
[113] DEC-S2011-001.
[114] *A Complainant v A Choir*, DEC-S2012-004, para 4.1.
[115] *Brooks v BRC Shooting Club*, DEC-S2010-042, para 5.3.
[116] DEC-S2001-011. Applied in *A Complainant v An Garda Síochána*, DEC-S2005-037.

advised that immigration and citizenship matters, for example, are not services within the meaning of the Equal Status Bill but rather an expression of the State's duty as a sovereign power to control who it admits to the State. Controlling duties in the areas of policing, defence, and prisons would likewise not be regarded as services.

The service aspect of policing, immigration, defence and prisons will, however, come within the scope of the Bill. For example, while a decision to grant a visa would not be covered by the Equal Status Bill, the interaction between officials and the visa applicant and collateral services and facilities, such as access to buildings and information, would come within the scope of the legislation.

In the policing area, for example, while riot control or apprehending a criminal gang could not be regarded as services, information and assistance provided by [Gardaí], including responding to reported crimes, would be regarded as services within the scope of the equal status legislation.[117]

According to the equality officer in *Donnellan* it is:

[C]lear and plain from the wording of section 2(1) that the investigation and prosecution of crime are not services which are available to the public, or a section of it, within the meaning of service defined therein. It is my belief that these are State functions which are carried out by Gardaí (and the Director of Public Prosecutions) on behalf of and for the benefit of the public and society as a whole. They are clearly not services which the public have access to in the way that other services clearly are, such as access to facilities for banking, leisure or travel (para 5.2).

As a result the complaint fell outside the scope of the ESA. Similar decisions were reached in other cases involving the investigation of crimes by the Gardaí.[118] The Equality Tribunal has also established, however, that the customer service aspects of the force's duties, such as providing information to and liaising with victims of crimes, are subject to the legislation.[119] As for immigration matters, the Director of the Equality Tribunal made the following

---

[117] 512 *Dáil Eireann Debates* Col 1604 (Equal Status Bill 1999: Report Stage. 15 December 1999).

[118] See *Woodhead and Sparkes v Swinford Garda Station*, DEC-S2008-064 and *A Complainant v An Garda Síochána*, DEC-S2005-037. Such matters could be referred instead to the Garda Síochána Ombudsman Commission.

[119] See *Buckley v An Garda Síochána*, DEC-S2008-006 and *A Named Individual v A*

comments in a case concerning the treatment of a Turkish man by an immigration officer when he was renewing his permission to remain in the state:

> My preliminary view is accordingly that, on the one hand, certain decisions made by the State on applications concerning immigration and the entry of non-nationals may well also be the exercise by the State of controlling functions which are not covered by the Equal Status Acts. On the other hand, by analogy, it appears that the treatment by the State or its officers (including [Gardaí]) of a person wishing to make an application in an immigration matter may involve provision of a service to the public and thus may come within the Equal Status Acts (para 5.7).[120]

Because the complainant did not appear at the hearing no actual findings were made on the issue and so the Director's comments are only indicative of the approach that might be adopted by the Tribunal. It appears that the approach will be similar to that in the policing context so that for example, while a decision to grant a visa would not be covered, the interaction between officials and the visa applicant and services and facilities such as access to buildings and information would come within the scope of the legislation.

In support of its conclusions on public functions the Tribunal has often relied on the persuasive value of UK case law. Equivalent UK provisions have been subject to fairly extensive interpretation (McColgan, 2005, pp 255–285; Monaghan, 2007, pp 505–508). In a number of cases UK courts concluded that 'services' were confined to acts of a similar kind to acts that might be carried out by a private person.[121] Therefore, functions that are of a public law nature (i.e. enforcement, regulatory and control functions) have fallen outside the scope of that country's non-discrimination legislation.[122] The ramifications for policing were explored by the UK Court of Appeal in *Farah v Commissioner of Police for the Metropolis*:[123] certain activities including giving assistance

---

Named Detective Garda Immigration Office, An Garda Síochána, Limerick, DEC-S2004-187, paras 5.7–5.8.

[120] *A Named Individual v A Named Detective Garda Immigration Office, An Garda Síochána, Limerick*, DEC-S2004-187.

[121] *R v Entry Clearance Officer (Bombay) ex parte Amin* [1983] 2 AC 818. See also *R v Immigration Appeal Tribunal ex parte Kassam* [1980] 1 WLR 1037.

[122] The Race Relations (Amendment) Act 2000 remedied this gap by extending protection against race discrimination to all actions of public authorities with some exemptions (section 19B). It also created a new duty on public authorities to take action to eliminate racism (section 17). UK equality law was upgraded substantially under the Equality Act 2010 (Chapter 10.3).

[123] [1998] QB 65.

and protection to a victim of crime could constitute a service but investiga-tive functions would not. The plaintiff in *Farah* was assaulted and called the emergency services but instead of investigating the crime the police officers in question arrested and detained her. Her claim was that she did not obtain the protection others would have been afforded on racial grounds. The Court of Appeal held that in such circumstances a claim of unlawful discrimination under the Race Relations Act 1976 was maintainable against the police.

An earlier case concerning the Inland Revenue drew a similar distinc-tion between the function of collecting taxes and other services that body provides.[124] The former was a duty owed to Parliament, not something that benefited the taxpayer. However, when giving people information and advice, making repayments of tax and granting tax relief the Inland Revenue was providing services to a section of the public and so was covered by discrimi-nation legislation.[125]

UK cases have also addressed situations in which public functions and services are provided 'simultaneously' to a complainant. For example, in a judgment concerning the scope of the Disability Discrimination Act 1995 the Court of Appeal held that fulfilling the public duty of immigration law enforcement and providing services could occur at the same time. A disa-bled man lodged a discrimination complaint about services provided to him in an immigration detention facility. The services in question included access to toilet and bathroom facilities, the provision of suitable bedding and the provision of medical services. On appeal the Home Office accepted that those services were subject to the Act and the claimant conceded that the recep-tion procedures and acts of searching him did not.[126] Likewise in *Conwell v Newham London Borough Council*[127] the UK Employment Appeals Tribunal

---

[124] *Savjani v Inland Revenue Commissioners* [1981] QB 458.

[125] Australian tribunals and courts tend to interpret 'services' more broadly than their Irish and UK counterparts. For example, in *Russell v Commissioner of Police, New South Wales Police Service* [2001] NSWADT 32; [2001] NSWSC 745, a tribunal and the New South Wales Supreme Court on appeal found that the police were providing a 'service' under the state's Anti-Discrimination Act 1977 when effecting an arrest and detaining a person in custody. 'Services' were characterised as 'a public duty to provide to the late Mr Russell police services by way of the protection of his person from injury or death, and the protection of his property from damage': [2001] NSWSC 745, at para 44.

[126] *Gichura v Home Office and Another* [2008] ICR 1287; applied in *R (Gill) v Secretary of State for Justice* [2010] MHLR 135. See also *Veysey v Canada (Correctional Service)* (1990) 1 FC 321: although that case was not about the meaning of services as such, it is an example of discriminatory treatment of incarcerated people. A prison inmate and his male partner were denied participation in a family visit programme. The Federal Court of Canada quashed that decision on the basis that it violated the equality guarantee of the Canadian Charter.

[127] [2000] ICR 42. See also *Applin v Race Relations Board* [1975] AC 259.

found that where a local authority is acting pursuant to statutory duties and is making decisions which require the exercise of discretion and judgment in the performance of those duties its actions do not fall outside the scope of the UK Race Relations Act 1976.[128] It concluded that when looking after children in care a local authority is a 'person' concerned with the provision of goods, facilities or services to the public or a section of the public and so must comply with anti-discrimination law.

Another case established that prisoners are a section of the public and that inmates' access to prison work is a service, which could be challenged as discriminatory on racial grounds. A black inmate was repeatedly refused work in the prison kitchens while a white prisoner who had been found guilty of poisoning was given such work, as was a white man who was serving a sentence for murder.[129] By contrast, the accommodation and transportation of prisoners were not considered services in a case heard by the Australian Federal Court.[130] However, Rees, Lindsay and Rice (2008, p 414) note that the narrow view of services adopted is at odds with other case law and that it was doubted on appeal. According to the appellate Court 'although the meaning of "service" is not simple to resolve, and the matter was not argued in depth, we see some strength in the view that the provision of transport and accommodation, even in a prison, may amount to a service or facility.'[131]

In a 2010 decision the Tribunal applied similar reasoning to that adopted by the UK courts. It found that a person detained in a mental health institution could avail of the ESA to contest the nature of the facilities provided there (*A Patient v Health Service Provider and A Hospital*[132] (discussed in Chapter 3.3.4)). The respondent argued that because the accommodation provided was as a consequence of involuntary detention under the Criminal Law (Insanity) Act 2006 it could not be considered a service. The equality officer disagreed. She found that the very purpose of the hospital was to provide medical treatment and healthcare to a section of the public. It was irrelevant whether such services were availed of involuntarily.

The Tribunal examined the relationship between public functions and services in *Fogarty v Employment Appeals Tribunal*.[133] At issue was the accommodation afforded an individual who communicated through sign language in the course of an employment rights case lodged with the respondent (the EAT). The equality officer examined the statutory functions of the

---

[128] Applying *Farah v Commissioner of Police for the Metropolis* [1998] QB 65.
[129] *Alexander v Home Office* [1988] 1 WLR 968.
[130] *Rainsford v Victoria* [2007] FCA 1059.
[131] *Rainsford v State of Victoria* [2008] FCAFC 31, at para 9.
[132] DEC-S2010-053.
[133] DEC-S2009-087.

EAT as well as a number of relevant precedents. She concluded that some of the body's functions are also 'services' for the purposes of the ESA. According to the equality officer:

> These functions, which can be distinguished from the decision making functions, are the reception and processing of complaints and the organising and hearing of complaints. I note that the respondent is obliged to receive the claim and then they are obliged to hear the parties and any evidence relevant to the appeal. I am of the view that this part of the functions, i.e. the administrative matters in relation to receiving the claim or appeal and the organising and hearing of the claim or appeal, is a service or a facility under the ES Acts. The respondent has a statutory function to provide a mechanism to enable a person, who believes that they have been unfairly dismissed, to seek redress or to appeal a recommendation of the [Rights] Commissioner. For this reason, I find that these functions are a service or facility for a person who finds themselves in such a position (para 4.7).

A decision of the High Court of Australia was considered to be of persuasive value.[134] Several of the judgments in that case referred to the need to interpret the definition of services broadly in light of the remedial purposes of anti-discrimination law. The Tribunal's decision in *Fogarty* was appealed to the Circuit Court and the appeal was due to be heard in March 2012. No details as to the outcome of that appeal were available at the time of writing.

Fogarty was applied in *O'Neill v Garda Síochána Ombudsman Commission*.[135] Here too, the equality officer distinguished between the various activities of the statutory body. The Commission had turned down an application to extend the time limit for lodging a complaint and Mr O'Neill sought to challenge that decision as discriminatory. Its decision-making function was not a service and so the Tribunal found it could not be reviewed under the ESA.[136]

Questions as to the boundaries between 'functions' and 'services' have also been explored in Australian case law. Where governmental activity provides benefits to an individual it tends to be considered as a service, but a great deal

---

[134] *IW v City of Perth* (1997) 146 ALR 696.

[135] DEC-S2010-037.

[136] See also *Stokes v Christian Brothers' High School, Clonmel and Department of Education and Skills*, DEC-S2010-056: a Department of Education and Skills committee tasked with hearing appeals from school enrolment decisions under the Education Act is not providing a service under section 5 of the ESA.

too rests on the facts of the case (Rees et al., 2008, pp 401–414). As is the position under UK law, in some situations the performance of statutory duties may also amount to a service provided to a particular individual. Alteration of a person's gender on the register of births is a service, for instance.[137] In *Director General, Department of Community Services v MM*[138] the Supreme Court of New South Wales held that an agency which offered people the opportunity to become foster parents was providing a service within the meaning of the state's Anti-Discrimination Act 1977. The applicant was therefore entitled to bring proceedings claiming that he had been discriminated against on the ground of disability in respect of becoming a foster carer. In 2010 the Equality Tribunal heard a complaint about the assessment of a couple's suitability to adopt by the Intercountry Adoption Services. The published decision indicates that the respondent did not dispute that it was providing a service for the purposes of the ESA.[139]

Both the Equality Tribunal and the High Court of Australia have examined planning permission applications. In *IW v City of Perth*[140] a local government body refused planning approval for a drop-in centre for people with HIV. A majority of the judges hearing the case decided that a decision to grant or withhold planning permission was not a service (Rees et al., 2008, p 405). However, the Court was divided as to what aspects of the planning approval process were subject to discrimination law. A majority found that the act of considering the application and providing access to the local government planning approval process were services, while the quasi-judicial function the authority exercised when deciding whether to grant planning approval was not. No such distinctions were drawn in an Equality Tribunal decision concerning an application for planning permission and so it would seem that it considers such processes to be services under the ESA: *O'Donoghue v North Tipperary County Council*.[141] There were two distinct elements to the complaint. One was on the Traveller community ground and concerned the alleged influence brought to bear on the process by local settled residents. The

---

[137] *AB v Registrar of Births, Deaths and Marriages* (2006) FCA 1071.

[138] (2003) NSWSC 1241.

[139] *A Couple v The Intercountry Adoption Services*, DEC-S2010-002. On appeal to the Circuit Court the Tribunal's decision was set aside by consent and so it has no real weight as a precedent. The ECHR Act 2003 could also be relied upon in this type of case. In *EB v France* (2008) 47 EHRR 21 the Court clarified that government actions concerning prospective adoptive parents fall within the ambit of article 8 and so can be assessed for compliance with the Convention's discrimination prohibition (compare *Fretté v France* (2002) 38 EHRR 438).

[140] (1997) 146 ALR 696.

[141] DEC-S2008-097. This decision is in line with several of the minority judgments in the *Perth* case.

other was referred on the disability ground and related to an alleged failure to consider the needs of the complainant's disabled son in the actual decision. *O'Donoghue* seems to be at odds with the distinction drawn in *Fogarty* between the actual decisions made by a body and the processes and services surrounding that decision-making function.

Government departments frequently set general policy objectives which are implemented in turn by service providers on the ground. Amongst other matters *Lyamina v The Department of Education and Science*[142] considered whether the Department of Education was a service provider for the purposes of the ESA. A complaint was referred by a young woman against the Department, alleging that while she was a student living in a Gaeltacht area it failed to provide for her education through the medium of English. The respondent maintained that while the Minister for Education carries out certain legally prescribed functions those functions relate only to providing for education rather than providing education itself. The equality officer undertook a detailed review of various sections of the Education Act 1998, as well as the Department's mission statement, statement of strategy and customer service charter. He concluded that the Minister and the Department have a pivotal role to play in planning and coordinating the provision of education in recognised schools and centres for education. He noted that the Act states that it shall be a function of the Minister to monitor and assess the quality, economy, efficiency and effectiveness of the education system provided in the state by recognised schools and centres for education. Given its roles and functions the Department was subject to the ESA. However, the particular decision at the centre of the complaint fell within the exclusive competence of the school's board of management. In conjunction with another school it had decided to discontinue the practice of offering classes through the medium of English. As a consequence the Department was not the appropriate respondent and the complaint failed for that reason.

Lyamina was applied in two subsequent cases which challenged a policy decision taken by the Department of Education in relation to the education of disabled students.[143] It is clear then that Department policies are subject to the ESA when they concern the provision of a good or service to a section of the public.

The implications of this and other decisions concerning schools are that complaints about admissions, as well as those concerning a child's day-to-day

---

[142] DEC-S2009-016.

[143] *Mrs Cr (on behalf of her daughter Miss Cr) v The Minister for Education and Science*, DEC-S2009-051 and *Mrs Kn (on behalf of her son Mr Kn) and Others v The Minister for Education and Science*, DEC-S2009-050. See also *Two Named Complainants v Minister for Education and Science*, DEC-S2006-077: in that case the service provided by the Department was the certification of educational accomplishment by examination.

education, should generally be taken against the school's board of management.[144] Boards are accorded responsibility for the running and management of schools under section 15 of the Education Act 1998 (where relevant on behalf of the patron). It should be noted, however, that the boards of Vocational Educational Committee (VEC) schools do not have a separate legal identity, and so the correct respondent in such cases is the relevant Vocational Educational Committee.

2.4.5 Compliance with International and EU Law

This section briefly assesses whether the material scope of the ESA complies with EU law and with Ireland's international human rights obligations.

When examining Ireland's combined initial and second reports under the International Convention on the Elimination of all Forms of Racial Discrimination (ICERD), the relevant United Nations committee recommended that the state 'consider expanding the scope of the Equal Status Act so as to cover the whole range of government functions and activities, including controlling duties' (United Nations Committee on the Elimination of Racial Discrimination, 2005, para 19). Another international human rights body, the European Commission against Racism and Intolerance,[145] made a similar recommendation in its *Third Report on Ireland* (2007).

The ESA implements the two EU Directives that apply to the field of goods, services, education and accommodation (Chapter 1.5). In the absence of case law on the issue from the CJEU the material scope of the Racial Equality Directive is unclear. Article 3(1) provides:

> Within the limits of the powers conferred upon the Community, this Directive shall apply to all persons, as regards both the public and private sectors, including public bodies, in relation to:
>
> [...]
>
> (e) social protection, including social security and healthcare;
>
> (f) social advantages;

---

[144] See also *Stokes v Christian Brothers' High School, Clonmel and Department of Education and Skills*, DEC-S2010-056. On the respective roles and responsibilities of schools and the Department of Education see further the Supreme Court decision in *O'Keeffe v Hickey* [2008] IESC 72.

[145] Established by the Council of Europe in 1997, the ECRI is an independent human rights monitoring body specialising in racism. It comprises independent members who are appointed on the basis of their expertise in dealing with racism, xenophobia, anti-Semitism and intolerance: <http://www.coe.int/t/e/human%5Frights/ecri/>.

(*g*) education;

(*h*) access to and supply of goods and services which are available to the public, including housing.

The text does not distinguish between services and functions and it remains to be seen whether Irish law complies with the Directive. Several commentators maintain that the Directive can and should be read so as to include the activities of public bodies such as the police (Brown, 2001; Farkas, 2006). The concept of 'social advantage' has been interpreted quite broadly under EU law (Craig and de Búrca, 2007, pp 774–782). According to Ellis (2003, p 642) it is meant to 'cover benefits of an economic or cultural nature granted either by public authorities or private organisations', including such things as 'concessionary travel on public transport, reduced prices for cultural or other events and subsidized meals in schools for children from low income families'. It clearly then encompasses benefits granted on a discretionary basis.[146] Bamforth, Malik and O'Cinneide (2008, p 154) explain that social protection:

> … includes all those matters which protect individuals in their life in society. Social security and health care are given as examples, but social protection includes all forms of protection of the individual that the state confers on society. There are literally hundreds of ECJ cases in which this concept has been considered, and it would be wrong to read it down to protection which is equivalent to social security and health care.

The phrase 'within the limits of the powers conferred by the Community' in article 3(1) means the Directive only applies to matters over which the EU has competence. So its reach into areas like education, healthcare and housing is uncertain. As case law emerges from the CJEU the extent to which the ESA corresponds with EU law requirements should be clarified.

2.5 Exemption for Actions Required by Law

From the point of view of prospective complainants, the blanket exemption for any action that is required by or under 'any enactment' is very problematic.[147] It means the ESA cannot be used to challenge other laws that are discriminatory

---

[146] See, for example, *Netherlands v Reed*, Case 59/85, [1986] ECR 1283, at para 25; applied in *Secretary of State for Defence v Elias* [2006] 1 WLR 3213 to a compensation scheme for former prisoners of war.

[147] Section 14(1)(*a*)(i). The Equality Authority notes that the exemption limits the contribution it can make in relation to discrimination by public bodies and has consistently called for its

and so it limits the scope of the anti-discrimination provisions significantly. For example, in recent years changes were made to the jobseeker's allowance to allow lower rates of payment for people aged under 25. Those changes are set out in legislation and, therefore, are covered by the exemption.[148] The exemption also means that successful equal status challenges can be reversed by simply amending the ESA[149] or by bringing in another law.

The word 'enactment' is not defined in the ESA. It certainly covers Acts of the Oireachtas and statutory instruments.[150] Department circulars and other administrative rules are not law (Hogan and Morgan, 2010, p 63), and have not been considered enactments for the purposes of the ESA.[151]

The exemption has been applied to actions taken by respondents in compliance with numerous laws, including those relating to health and safety,[152] freedom of information,[153] and the prevention of criminal offences.[154] In *A Complainant v Department of Social and Family Affairs*[155] the equality officer

---

amendment (e.g. Equality Authority, 2003, p 9, 2004, p 35, 2008a, pp 60–61). Section 14(1) (*a*) also covers actions required by court orders and under other laws. It provides: 'Nothing in this Act shall be construed as prohibiting—

    (*a*) the taking of any action that is required by or under—

        (i) any enactment or order of a court,

        (ii) any act done or measure adopted by the European Union, by the European Communities or institutions thereof or by bodies competent under the Treaties establishing the European Communities, or

        (iii) any convention or other instrument imposing an international obligation on the State'.

[148] See section 6, Social Welfare and Pensions Act 2009 and section 6, Social Welfare and Pensions (No. 2) Act 2009.

[149] See discussion of section 7(5)(*b*) ESA in Chapter 2.6.2.4.

[150] Secondary legislation is covered by the term 'enactment' in section 14(1)(*a*)(i). Following the entry into force of the Equal Status Act 2000 section 2(1) of the Interpretation Act 2005 defined 'enactment' to mean 'an Act or statutory instrument or any portion of an Act or statutory instrument'. The Interpretation Act was applied in *Dowd v Minister for Finance*, DEC-S2011-061 to find that tax regulations were enactments and so immune from challenge under the ESA. See also *Dowd v Gilvarry & HSE West*, DEC-S2011-060.

[151] See, for example, *Health Service Executive v Quigley* (Circuit Court Dublin, Linnane J, unreported, 26 April 2010).

[152] See, for example, *Gahan v Valour Investments t/a Shell Mulhuddart*, DEC-S2009-021 and *Murphy v Spawell Centre*, DEC-S2004-036.

[153] *Chawla v Irish Wheelchair Association*, DEC-S2009-024: files held by the respondent in relation to the complainant's mother could not be released to him as the respondent was prohibiting from doing so under section 28 of the Freedom of Information Acts.

[154] Information submitted by a bank which was required to comply with money-laundering laws (*A Nigerian National v A Financial Institution*, DEC-S2005-114) and EU security regulations (*Hassan v Western Union Financial Services*, DEC-S2006-004).

[155] DEC-S2008-013. See also *King v The Voluntary Health Insurance Board*,

found that the ESA could not be used to challenge the method of calculating Pay Related Social Insurance (PRSI) contributions for the purposes of the old age contributory pension. The scheme in question is governed by statute.[156] It has also been applied to defeat an age discrimination complaint concerning access to licensed premises. The equality officer accepted that denying entry to a pub was legitimate since the complainant produced a student ID card and under the provisions of the Intoxicating Liquor Act 2000 the respondent was entitled to only accept a Garda age card as valid proof of age.[157]

An airline company successfully invoked the exception in *Kane v Eirjet Ltd*.[158] A man with Down syndrome was asked to vacate a seat located in an emergency exit row. The equality officer had regard to the terms of the respondent's *Passenger Information Manual* and also took note of Irish and EU safety regulations, which require that airlines have procedures in place to ensure that passengers are seated where they may best assist and not hinder evacuation from the aircraft. The regulations provide that certain categories of passenger, such as children, persons who are 'substantially blind or substantially deaf' and those who have 'an obvious physical or mental handicap' should not be allowed to occupy such seats. Having regard to the nature of the complainant's disability and in light of the obligations that were imposed upon airline operators, the equality officer found that the actions of the respondent complied with the safety obligations and so did not amount to discrimination on the disability ground. A complaint of harassment was, however, upheld (see Chapter 5.4).

Litigation concerning a gay couple demonstrates how passing another law can effectively undo case outcomes. A man who sought and was refused a travel pass under the non-statutory Free Travel Scheme for his cohabiting male partner successfully settled an action taken against the Department of Social and Family Affairs in 2003 (Equality Authority, 2004, pp 105–106). The Department accepted that the decision amounted to unlawful discrimination on the sexual orientation ground in contravention of the Equal Status Act 2000. Statutory social welfare schemes were immune to challenge, because of the exemption for any measures required by law, but as an administrative scheme the Free Travel Scheme was covered by the ESA.

Following the case the Oireachtas amended the principal social welfare statute so that the pre-existing definition of 'spouse' or 'qualified adult', which encompassed only married and opposite-sex cohabiting couples, would also

---

DEC-S2008-116.

[156] Section 108 of the Social Welfare Consolidation Act 2005 (as amended by section 8 of the Social Welfare Law Reform and Pensions Act 2006).

[157] *Thornton v Turner's Cross Tavern*, DEC-S2004-142.

[158] DEC-S2008-026.

apply to some administrative social welfare schemes.[159] The amendment was designed to ensure that for the purposes of those schemes same-sex couples would essentially be treated as single persons *as a matter of law*. The move ran contrary to international human rights law and in particular to ECHR case law on sexual orientation discrimination (Walsh and Ryan, 2006, pp 105–106). That change has now been reversed. In 2011 the social welfare code was amended in line with the changes brought about under the Civil Partnership Act 2010.[160] Civil partners will now be treated in an equivalent manner to married spouses for social welfare purposes, and the definition of 'couple' and 'cohabitant' will include both same-sex and opposite-sex couples.[161]

Returning to the ESA, where some element of discretion exists in relation to the grant of a benefit, other good or service the statutory exemption is inapplicable since it relates only to discriminatory treatment *required* by law.[162] During the Seanad debates on the Equal Status Bill 1999 the Minister for Justice, Equality and Law Reform stated: 'I stress that this exemption applies only to actions which are mandatory under the relevant statute and not to the discretionary actions of statutory bodies or public officials.'[163] Such an argument was advanced in a 2006 settlement of a social welfare case (Equality Authority, 2007a, p 30). The Department of Social and Family Affairs sought to rely on section 14 in refusing an adult dependant allowance to a gay man who had left paid employment to care for his partner. Following intervention by the Equality Authority the allowance was paid on an *ex gratia* (i.e. voluntary) basis. The Authority pointed out that section 2(2) of the Social Welfare (Consolidation) Act 2005 allows the Minister to specify persons to be adult dependents. It argued that the Minister's failure to exercise that discretion to

---

[159] Section 19 of the Social Welfare (Miscellaneous Provisions) Act 2004.

[160] Social Welfare and Pensions Act 2010. The sections dealing with civil partners were commenced by the Social Welfare and Pensions Act 2010 (sections 15 to 26) (Commencement) Order 2010 (SI 673/2010). The Order provides that these amendments came into effect on 1 January 2011.

[161] Section 172 of the Civil Partnership and Certain Rights and Obligations of Cohabitants Act 2010.

[162] In *Sabherwal v ICTS (UK) Ltd*, DEC-S2008-037, the equality officer (at para 5.8) noted: 'While section 14(1) of the Acts may allow for certain measures and activities under national legislation, European legislation and/or legally binding international obligation on Ireland, it certainly does not mean that those measures and/or activities should be provided in a less favourable manner on the grounds of race or any of the other equality grounds unless the legislations and/or conventions specifically require them to do so. Section 14 of the Acts cannot be extended to legislation enacted in the United States.' See further the recommendations in *Murphy v Spawell Centre* (DEC-S2004-036) and *Roche v Alabaster Associates Ltd t/a Madigans* (DEC-S2002-086).

[163] 162 *Seanad Debates* Col 586 (Second Stage).

specify the claimant and his partner as a couple amounted to discrimination under the ESA (Equality Authority, 2007a, p 30).

Likewise, the Tribunal will not permit respondents to avail of the exemption where no law *requires* different treatment. In a case concerning refusal to admit a woman and her infant child to a cinema the respondent tried to rely on section 12 of the Safety, Health and Welfare at Work Act 2005.[164] Section 12 provides that: 'Every employer shall manage and conduct his or her undertaking in such a way as to ensure, so far as is reasonably practicable, that in the course of the work being carried on, individuals at the place of work (not being his or her employees) are not exposed to risks to their safety, health or welfare.' The equality officer did not accept that this provision made it necessary to impose a blanket ban on the admittance of children under the age of two years, when accompanied by a parent or adult, to an afternoon screening of a children's film.

EU law is again relevant to discrimination on the basis of gender and racial or ethnic origins. The Racial Equality Directive does not envisage any blanket exemption for discriminatory measures required by law. Nor is such an exemption provided for under the Gender Goods and Services Directive. Arguably, the ESA should be amended to take account of this divergence, at least in relation to the gender, race and Traveller community grounds.

A challenge to legislation that made trespass on land a criminal offence was due to be heard by the High Court in 2008.[165] Submissions by the Equality Authority (2009a, pp 22–23) and the Irish Human Rights Commission (2007) raised compliance with the Racial Equality Directive and the ECHR respectively.[166] When applying domestic law and in particular legislative provisions specifically adopted for the purposes of implementing the requirements of a directive, national courts of EU member states are bound to interpret it, as far as possible, in the light of the wording and purpose of the directive concerned in order to achieve the result sought by the directive (Chapter 1.6).[167] The

---

[164] *Flanagan Talbot v Casino Cinemas Limited t/a Killarney Cineplex Cinema*, DEC-S2008-053, at paras 4.8–4.12. See also *Collins v Drogheda Lodge Pub, Finglas*, DEC-S2002-097/100, at para 7.17 and *Ms A (on behalf of her sister Ms B) v Aer Lingus*, DEC-S2009-038, at para 5.13.

[165] *Lawrence and Others v Ballina Town Council and Others* (High Court, Murphy J, unreported, 31 July 2008). The legislation in question is section 24 of the Housing (Miscellaneous Provisions) Act 2002, which amended the Criminal Justice (Public Order) Act 1994. See further Law School, Trinity College Dublin (2002).

[166] Both the Irish Human Rights Commission and the Equality Authority acted as *amicus curiae* in *Lawrence*. An *amicus curiae* ('friend of the court') is essentially an impartial bystander whose expertise is called upon to assist courts in their deliberations. For an account of the Commission's role in the case see: <http://www.ihrc.ie/enquiriesandlegal/amicuscuriae/criminaltrespass.html> [accessed 13 July 2012].

[167] See *Marleasing SA v La Comercial Internacional de Alimentacion SA* [1991] 1 ECR

breadth of the exemption in the ESA may well, therefore, have been tested in light of the Racial Equality Directive had the litigation proceeded. However, those elements of the case concerning the criminal trespass law were settled prior to hearing and so the Court did not rule on the matter (Equality Authority, 2009a, pp 22–23; Irish Human Rights Commission, 2009, p 37). Apparently Murphy J's judgment accepted that the trespass legislation could be indirectly discriminatory but suggested that the objective justification defence might apply (*Irish Times*, 2008a). Indirect discrimination tackles neutral provisions that disadvantage persons protected by discriminatory grounds (Chapter 4). For now, then, the compatibility of the section 14 exemption with EU law remains in question.

The exemption is likely to arise when the Oireachtas legislates in the area of assisted human reproduction (AHR) (Commission on Assisted Human Reproduction, 2005; *Irish Times*, 2008b; S. Ryan, 2008). Currently such services are subject to the ESA and so service providers should not discriminate on the basis of civil status, family status, sexual orientation and so on. Less favourable treatment on any of the discriminatory grounds would have to be justified with reference to one of the exceptions expressly provided for under the ESA, such as the one concerning clinical judgment (Chapter 2.6). Regulatory legislation may take the area outside the reach of the equal status law because of section 14(1)(*a*). However, again owing to the supremacy of EU law, national legislation would have to comply with both the Racial Equality Directive and the Gender Goods and Services Directive.[168] In practice, discrimination on the grounds of age, civil status, disability or sexual orientation are likely to prove most relevant (Commission on Assisted Human Reproduction, 2005, pp 135–137; Rehnstrom, 2005; Women's Health Council, 2009, p 35).[169] EU discrimination law in the services context does not yet extend to any of those grounds. As it stands, the Draft Goods and Services Directive expressly excludes matters concerning reproductive rights from its scope.[170] It would therefore appear that were legislation to sanction discrimination against, for instance, lesbian women or unmarried persons in access to AHR their rights

---

4135; *Pfeiffer v Deutsches Rotes Kreuz Kreizerband Waldshut EV* [2005] IRLR 137; and *Mangold v Helm*, Case C-144/04, [2004] ECR 1-9981.

[168] The exemption in the Gender Goods and Services Directive for services 'which are offered outside the area of private and family life' appears to refer to the sphere of interpersonal relationships as opposed to services contracted for on the market: article 3(1).

[169] In *McBain v Victoria* (2000) 99 FCR 116 the Federal Court of Australia noted that a provision of the Infertility Treatment Act 1995 (a statute of the State of Victoria) required a provider of infertility treatment to discriminate on the ground of marital status. That section and a number of other provisions were found to be inconsistent with the Sex Discrimination Act 1984.

[170] Council Document 8889/10, 28 April 2010, article 3(2)(*a*).

would ultimately fall to be tested under the terms of the ECHR Act 2003 and the Constitution. Preferences for married heterosexual families enjoy robust constitutional protection (Hogan and Whyte, 2003, Chapter 7.6). According to the Commission on Assisted Human Reproduction (2005, p 137), the issue:

> ... is whether *the State can oblige clinics to provide a service to non-marital families*, either as a result of the existing provisions of the Equal Status Acts 2000–2004 or as part of any possible future legislation regulating AHR. In order to establish the unconstitution-ality of a legislative requirement that AHR services be provided to non-marital families, one would have to argue that such a provision amounted to the promotion of alternative social units to the marital family and that such promotion amounted to a failure by the State to guard with special care the institution of marriage, contrary to Art.41.3.1 [emphasis in original].

The age and disability grounds are addressed below in light of the clinical judgment exception (Chapter 2.6.4.5).

2.6 Specific Exceptions

2.6.1 Introduction

The ESA sets out numerous general exceptions and several that apply to discrete grounds. Both courts and the Equality Tribunal consider that excep-tions should be applied narrowly because the purpose of the legislation is to provide remedies for acts of discrimination.[171]

2.6.2 Ground-Specific Exceptions

2.6.2.1 Gender

On the gender ground differences in treatment of persons are permissible:

> In relation to services of an aesthetic, cosmetic or similar nature which require physical contact between the service provider and the recipient;[172]

---

[171] See Chapter 1.6 on the purposive approach to interpretation of the ESA. This approach has been applied in several cases: *Dublin City Council v Deans* (Circuit Court Dublin, Hunt J, unreported, 15 April 2008), at p 28; *A Post-Leaving Certificate Student v An Educational Institution*, DEC-S2009-043, at para 5.10; *McClean v The Revenue Commissioners*, DEC-S2004-016, at para 6.7. On employment equality legislation see *Harrington v East Coast Area Health Board*, DEC-E2002-001.

[172] Section 5(2)(*c*).

Where embarrassment or infringement of privacy can reasonably be
expected to result from the presence of a person of another gender.[173]

A shop specialising in bridal wear sought to avail of the latter exemption in
McMahon v Bridal Heaven Ltd.[174] The equality officer did not accept that
the blanket 'no men' policy was permissible given that the privacy of female
customers could be secured by availing of dressing rooms and by the option
of making a private appointment. In reaching this conclusion she stressed
that any departure from the overarching principle of equal treatment must 'be
construed in the narrowest possible sense' (para 5.3). On the other hand, a
man who was asked to leave another bridal shop when female customers were
trying on dresses did not succeed in his complaint of gender discrimination.
The respondent did not operate a general exclusion policy and could legitimately avail of the section 5(2)(*g*) exemption on the facts.[175]

The exception also featured in *Curran v Total Fitness*[176] but only as a
background to a proven case of victimisation (Chapter 3.5). A gym reserved
an area for the exclusive use of women and when Mr Curran inquired as to
whether men would be allowed into the space his membership of the club was
terminated. The equality officer did not consider whether the reservation of a
women-only area was justified because a complaint on the gender ground was
withdrawn prior to the hearing.

There is no case law to date on 'services of an aesthetic, cosmetic or similar
nature' but across Europe several challenges have been successfully mounted
to, for example, differential pricing by hairdressers along gender lines (Burri
and McColgan, 2008). It is not clear whether the exception provided for under
the ESA would cover that type of practice. The provision simply refers to
'differences in treatment' in relation to services. But it seems that prices would
be included since gender discrimination was found in a case of free access for
women while men had to pay a fee to gain entry to a nightclub.[177]

The exception concerning embarrassment and privacy is reiterated in the
specific context of accommodation provision, permitting single-gender rooms
in hostels, for instance.[178]

---

[173] Section 5(2)(*g*).

[174] DEC-S2008-015.

[175] *Blaney v The Bridal Studio*, DEC-S2008-032.

[176] DEC-S2004-164.

[177] *O'Connor v The Icon Nightclub*, DEC-S2004-001 (discussed in Chapter 8.2).

[178] Section 6(2)(*e*) provides that the discrimination prohibition does not apply in respect
of 'the provision of accommodation to persons of one gender where embarrassment or
infringement of privacy can reasonably be expected to result from the presence of a person
of another gender.'

Many voluntary bodies provide services either primarily or exclusively to men or to women. For instance, NGOs working on issues of domestic and sexual violence may offer advice and other services such as accommodation to persons of one gender only. Some of these services may not be justified by reference to embarrassment or privacy considerations. But exceptions provided for elsewhere under the ESA could be availed of. In relation to accommodation in the form of a shelter or refuge, for example, it is acceptable to reserve such premises or accommodation for use by a particular category of persons (see Chapter 2.6.3). Other services like advice, counselling and so on could be included under the exception for services that are either suitable only for the needs of certain persons or that promote the interests of persons within a particular category (Chapter 2.6.4.3).

Section 7, which deals with educational establishments, sanctions the existence of single-gender primary and secondary schools[179] and provides that where an institution is established for the purpose of providing training to ministers of religion and admits students of only one gender it may validly refuse to admit a person who is not of that gender.[180]

As for EU law, the Gender Goods and Services Directive does not prohibit differences in treatment if the provision of goods and services exclusively or primarily to members of one sex is justified by a legitimate aim and the means chosen to achieve that aim are appropriate and necessary (article 4(5)). In other words, there is no closed list of exceptions in cases of direct discrimination. The preamble to the Directive gives some examples of sex-segregated service provision that may be justified:

> Differences in treatment may be accepted only if they are justified by a legitimate aim. A legitimate aim may, for example, be the protection of victims of sex-related violence (in cases such as the establishment of single-sex shelters), reasons of privacy and decency (in cases such as the provision of accommodation by a person in a part of that person's home), the promotion of gender equality or of the interests of men or women (for example single-sex voluntary bodies), the freedom of association (in cases of membership of single-sex private clubs), and the organisation of sporting activities (for example single-sex sports events). Any limitation should nevertheless be appropriate and necessary in accordance with the criteria derived from case law of the Court of Justice of the European Communities (recital 16).

---

[179] Section 7(3)(*a*). See *Mr X and Ms Y (on behalf of their daughter Z) v A Boys National School*, DEC-S2009-017.
[180] Section 7(3)(*b*).

Many of the exceptions spelled out under the ESA cover similar situations to those listed here, but in the absence of EU case law it remains to be seen whether the Irish legislation is fully in line with the Directive. The position with single-gender registered clubs is addressed in Chapter 9.

2.6.2.2 Age

Under the age ground, section 3 of the Acts sets out a major exemption in stating that:

> (3)(*a*) Treating a person who has not attained the age of 18 years less favourably or more favourably than another, whatever that person's age, shall not be regarded as discrimination on the age ground.

This section essentially means that minors cannot base direct discrimination claims on the age ground.[181] A limited exception applies to the provision of car insurance under section 3(3)(*b*). While this may be valid since it covers various situations in which licensed activities and certain goods such as alcohol and tobacco are confined to those aged over eighteen on health and safety grounds, the exception is unduly broad in that it also exempts discrimination *as between* children of different ages. For instance a health authority could decide that speech therapy will only be afforded to children aged under 6, introducing an arbitrary cut-off point for access to a vital service. Such a decision cannot be challenged using the ESA because of section 3(3)(*a*). The appropriate avenue in such a case would be to challenge the policy decision by making a complaint to the Ombudsman for Children (Chapter 10.5).[182] Section 3(3)(*a*) only refers to 'less' or 'more' 'favourable treatment' and so arguably is confined to direct discrimination complaints even though the exception is contained within the section that defines both direct and indirect discrimination. It certainly should not prevent a child taking a harassment claim on the age ground under section 11. Of course children may refer complaints on any of the other eight grounds.

Further age-related exceptions include:

- An age requirement for eligibility as an adoptive or foster parent, where the requirement is reasonable having regard to the needs of the child or children concerned;[183]

---

[181] *Scanlon and Ryan v The Russell Court Hotel*, DEC-S2001-013, para 6.2.

[182] Complaints about the administration of services should be referred directly to the HSE. See Health Service Executive (2009b).

[183] Section 5(2)(*j*). Currently there is no *statutory* upper age limit for adoptive parents, however in practice many adoption agencies apply such criteria (Department of Health and Children, 2005, pp 38–42).

- The allocation of third level educational places to 'mature students';[184]

- A minimum age threshold (other than the legal minimum of 18) in relation to selling alcoholic drinks, e.g. an over 21 only policy, provided that a notice to that effect is displayed in a prominent place and the policy is implemented in good faith.[185]

2.6.2.3 Religion

On the religion ground differences in treatment are permitted where goods or services are provided for a religious purpose.[186] The difference in treatment must be on the religion ground and so a religious body could not use it to justify discrimination on other grounds such as sexual orientation, gender, civil status or family status. There is no case law on this exception yet. Presumably it will operate in a narrow range of circumstances to permit, for example, a church to confine access to a ceremony to members of its faith.

A number of exceptions apply to the education sector. Section 7 prohibits discrimination on each of the nine grounds in relation to admission of, access to or expulsion of a student from an educational institution or in relation to the terms or conditions of participation in that institution by a student. However, as is the case with the gender ground, educational establishments that were set up to train ministers can refuse to admit persons that do not hold that religious belief.[187] An exemption is also provided in relation to discrimination on grounds of religion for denominational schools. Under section 7(3)(*c*):

> Where the establishment is a school providing primary or post-primary education to students and the objective of the school is to provide education in an environment which promotes certain religious values, it admits persons of a particular religious denomination in preference to others or it refuses to admit as a student a person who is not of that denomination and, in the case of a refusal, it is proved that the refusal is essential to maintain the ethos of the school.

---

[184] Section 7(3)(*e*). Mature students are students who are 23 years of age or over in the year they enter, or re-enter, third level education (section 2 of the Local Authorities (Higher Education Grants) Act 1992).

[185] Section 15(4).

[186] Section 5(2)(*e*). On the constitutional position see *Quinn's Supermarket Ltd v Attorney General* [1972] IR 1, in which the Supreme Court considered a challenge to the provisions of a Ministerial Order which exempted the proprietors of kosher shops from a ban on evening opening in order to facilitate the purchasing of meat on the Sabbath. The exemption was justified as it safeguarded the free profession and practice of religion guaranteed under Article 44 of the Constitution.

[187] Section 7(3)(*b*).

The section allows schools to prefer members of a certain religion at the access stage. If adopted, that preference must be publicised since under the Education Act 1998 the board of management of each school must devise an admissions policy, which must be made available to parents (Glendenning, 2008a).[188] In relation to refusal of access, discrimination is only permissible where it is *essential* to act in that manner in order to maintain the ethos of the school. According to Bolger (2004, p 55) a school that refuses access on that basis must meet a high standard of proof. However, in practice it is likely that refusal of access and preferences will arise in the same situation and it remains to be seen how they will be read together. So for example, where a Catholic school has fewer places than applicants the exception suggests that it can first allocate those places to Catholics, but in so doing other children are in effect denied admission for not being Catholic. The interrelationship between these dual elements of the provision was the subject of extensive media commentary in August and September of 2007, when a large number of children from ethnic minorities could not secure primary school places in Balbriggan, Co. Dublin.[189]

The exception has yet to be considered in case law. The definition of 'ethos' should prove crucial and is one that will ultimately be set by courts (Bolger, 2004; Glendenning, 2008b, pp 343–347). In a Supreme Court case about state funding of denominational education Barrington J examined a particular constitutional provision and found it meant that 'if a school was in receipt of public funds any child, no matter what his religion, would be entitled to attend it.'[190] It may be then that the exception will be interpreted strictly. Indeed, Eardly (2005, pp 163–164) suggests that section 7(3)(c) may be unconstitutional. Other commentators adopt a more cautious position, arguing that in light of the competing constitutional principles involved some leeway may be afforded to denominational schools on the question of admissions (Hogan and Whyte, 2003, paras 7.8.103–7.8.105; Whyte, 2010).[191] The exception is discussed further in Chapter 3.3.7.

---

[188] Section 15(2)(*d*).

[189] See, for example, *Irish Times* (2007a, 2007b and 2007c).

[190] *Campaign to Separate Church and State v The Minister for Education* [1998] 3 IR 321, at p 356. The constitutional provision in question, Article 44.2.4°, provides: 'Legislation providing State aid for schools shall not discriminate between schools under the management of different religious denominations, nor be such as to affect prejudicially the right of any child to attend a school receiving public money without attending religious instruction at that school.' See also the High Court judgment in that case: *Campaign to Separate Church and State v The Minister for Education* [1998] 3 IR 321.

[191] See the UK Supreme Court decision in *R (E) v Governing Body of JFS & Anor* [2010] 2 AC 728. A majority of the Court found that a Jewish school's admission policy based on matrilineal descent amounted to direct discrimination on the grounds of race. Lady Hale

2.6.2.4 Race

The nationality component of the race ground also forms the basis of a number of exemptions. In terms of its personal scope EU law is more restrictive than the ESA. Article 3(2) of the Racial Equality Directive provides:

> This Directive does not cover differences of treatment based on nationality and is without prejudice to provisions and conditions relating to the entry into and residence of third-country nationals and stateless persons on the territory of Member States, and to any treatment which arises from the legal status of the third-country nationals and stateless persons concerned.

Since the Irish Government is not obliged by EU law to prohibit discrimination as between EU nationals and nationals of other countries it has a free rein when it comes to the breadth of nationality-based exceptions contained in the ESA.[192] It has made use of this freedom to narrow the scope of protection on the ground considerably in recent years.

In 2004 the Equal Status Act was amended, overturning an Equality Tribunal finding that confining eligibility for educational grants to EU nationals would amount to unlawful discrimination (Free Legal Advice Centres, 2004).[193] Under the 2000 Act it was already permissible to set higher fees and apply different entry requirements for non-EU nationals (aside from refugees). The 2004 amendment extended this discrimination to student grants. Section 7(5)(*b*) now reads:

> The Minister for Education does not discriminate where he or she (i) requires grants of third level institutions to be restricted to persons who are nationals of a member state of the European Union or (ii) requires such nationals and other persons to be treated differently in relation to the making of grants.

In its submission on the draft legislation the Irish Human Rights Commission (2004b, pp 8–9) objected to the change arguing that it would be likely to have a 'serious detrimental effect' on access to education, which in turn would impact

---

accepted there might be valid reasons for providing such an exemption from the provisions of the Race Relations Act 1976, but that it ought to be explicitly provided for by Parliament (paras [69]–[70]).

[192] Such differences in treatment could, however, be challenged in constitutional litigation or by way of judicial review, employing the constitutional equality guarantee and by way of judicial review or plenary summons relying on provisions of the ECHR Act 2003.

[193] *Two Complainants v Department of Education and Science*, DEC-S2003-042/043.

on employment prospects and wider economic, social and cultural rights. The new exemption was applied in *Yushchenko v Department of Education and Science*.[194] A Russian national, who was granted leave to remain in the country on the basis that he had an Irish child, challenged a third level education grant scheme. The equality officer found that the Department was entitled to deny the complainant access to a student support grant on the basis of his immigration status. The decision was upheld on appeal to the Circuit Court.

The Human Rights Commission (2004a) also took issue with a second amendment of section 14(1) of the Equal Status Act 2000, introduced by section 52 of the Equality Act 2004. Section 14(1)(*aa*) provides that nothing in the Acts shall be interpreted as prohibiting:

> [O]n the basis of nationality –
>
> (i) any action taken by a public authority in relation to a non-national—
>
>> (I) who, when the action was taken, was either outside the State or, for the purposes of the Immigration Act 2004, unlawfully present in it, or
>>
>> (II) in accordance with any provision or condition made by or under any enactment and arising from his or her entry to or residence in the State,
>
> or
>
> (ii) any action taken by the Minister in relation to a non-national where the action arises from an action referred to in subparagraph (i) ...

While the exact parameters of this section have yet to be tested in case law it appears to grant some discretion to public authorities[195] to discriminate against

---

[194] DEC-S2009-034.

[195] Under section 14(2) public authority is defined as '(*a*) a Minister of the Government, (*b*) an immigration officer appointed or deemed to have been appointed under section 3 of the Immigration Act 2004, (*c*) the Commissioners of Public Works in Ireland, (*d*) a local authority within the meaning of the Local Government Act 2001, (*e*) the Eastern Regional Health Authority, (*f*) an area health board within the meaning of the Health (Eastern Regional Health Authority) Act 1999, (*g*) a health board, (*h*) a harbour authority within the meaning of the Harbours Act 1946, (*i*) a board or other body (not being a company) established by or under statute, (*j*) a company in which all the shares are held by, or on behalf of, or by directors appointed by, a Minister of the Government, or (*k*) a company in which all the shares are held by a board or other body referred to in paragraph (*i*), or by a company referred to in paragraph (*j*).'

migrants and asylum seekers, but only on the basis of nationality.[196] During the Oireachtas debates on the Equality Bill 2004 the Minister of State explained that the provision was designed to clarify that 'any decision taken in the context of asylum and immigration applications is not open to challenge under the Equal Status Act 2000.' He made specific reference to 'direct provision', the system that provides separate housing, food and social welfare entitlements to people who have applied for asylum (Free Legal Advice Centres, 2009).[197] Indeed, it appears that the primary objective behind the section was to safeguard that non-statutory system because decisions in immigration matters and on applications for refugee status are not services within the meaning of the Acts (Chapter 2.4.4).[198] It seems, therefore, that the main effect of this amendment is to prevent an ESA challenge to the existence of that system, which clearly treats people differently based on their nationality.[199]

The ESA should still apply, however, to the day-to-day operation of direct provision and the associated system of 'dispersal' to designated accommodation centres.[200] Significantly, the exemption is limited to nationality-based discrimination and so discrimination on other grounds (including the other elements of the race ground, i.e. 'race', 'colour' and 'ethnic or national origins') is not permissible. A complainant would have to show that the treatment complained of happened in the context of accessing a good or service.

---

[196] See the exemption for nationality-based discrimination as between EU citizens and nationals of third countries under article 3(2) and recital 13 of the Racial Equality Directive.

[197] 175 *Seanad Debates* Cols 835–836 (Equal Status Bill 2004: Committee Stage, 18 February 2004). Section 14(1)(*aa*)(i)(I), which refers to any action taken by a public authority in relation to a non-national 'who, when the action was taken, was ... outside the State ...', may have been designed to avoid the situation that arose in *R (European Roma Rights Centre) v Immigration Officer at Prague Airport* [2005] 2 AC 1. In that case the House of Lords found that the entry clearance procedure operated by British immigration officers at Prague Airport unlawfully discriminated against Roma contrary to the Race Relations Act 1976. However, that type of activity would almost certainly be regarded as a state function and not as a service for the purposes of the ESA.

[198] *A Named Individual v A Named Detective Garda Immigration Office, An Garda Síochána, Limerick*, DEC-S2004-187. The decision did not refer to the changes effected under the Equality Act 2004, presumably because the new provisions were not in force at the time of the incidents complained of.

[199] It is open to individuals affected by such discrimination to rely on other sources of law, including the ECHR Act 2003. The Convention's non-discrimination prohibition (article 14) explicitly refers to 'national or social origin' as a ground on which adverse treatment may be challenged. See, for example, *Gaygusuz v Austria* (1996) 23 EHRR 364.

[200] Asylum seekers are initially accommodated in a 'reception centre' before being transferred, or 'dispersed', to designated direct provision accommodation. See generally Free Legal Advice Centres (2009). Private companies run most direct provision accommodation and so the relevant service provider is arguably not the Minister or a public body.

That should not be an obstacle for most aspects of the system, because service provision and the exercise of government functions can occur at the same time (Chapter 2.4.4). The real difficulty will perhaps lie with establishing a case of direct discrimination, which relies on a complainant comparing treatment with someone *in similar circumstances*. These matters are revisited in Chapter 3.3.6.

2.6.2.5 Disability

Finally, an exception is provided for in the education context on the disability ground. Section 7(4)(*b*) provides that the discrimination prohibition directed at educational establishments does not apply 'to the extent that compliance with any of its provisions in relation to a student with a disability would, by virtue of the disability, make impossible, or have a seriously detrimental effect on, the provision by an educational establishment of its services to other students.' During the Dáil debates the Minister stated:

> The exclusion of a person by a school on foot of this provision must meet a very strict test, namely, that the person's disability must make impossible or have a seriously detrimental effect on the school's provision of its services to other students .... It is not intended to cover cases where it would inconvenience the school to have a pupil with a disability nor are the perceptions or attitudes of other pupils or their parents relevant. The criteria are extremely strict and the exemption can be invoked only in limited circumstances.[201]

The exception has been considered in a number of Equality Tribunal decisions, most of which concern the application of disciplinary procedures.[202] These are discussed further in Chapter 6.6.3, which deals with the duty to reasonably accommodate students whose behaviour is considered problematic.

Section 7(4)(*b*) was applied at the admissions stage in *Mrs A (on behalf of her son, B) v A Childcare Facility*,[203] which addressed the terms on which the complainant's child (B) was to be admitted to a crèche. She was informed that a place would not be available unless the boy was accompanied by a full-time personal assistant, a requirement which the respondent maintained was necessary due a combination of factors. The respondent referred to its

---

[201] 513 *Dáil Debates* Col 959 (Equal Status Bill 1999: Report Stage (Resumed)).
[202] *A Post-Leaving Certificate Student v An Educational Institution*, DEC-S2009-043; *Mrs A (on behalf of her son B) v A Boys National School*, DEC-S2009-031; *Clare (A Minor) v Minister for Education and Science and Others* [2004] IEHC 350.
[203] DEC-S2009-041.

obligations concerning child–staff ratios under the Child Care Act 1991 and the Child Care (Pre-School Services) Regulations 2006 and to the fact that due to a disability B was unable to physically move on his own without assistance. Having reviewed the submissions of both parties the equality officer concluded that the educational establishment had not directly discriminated against the complainant on the disability ground:

> I am satisfied that it is reasonable to conclude that if the respondent had admitted the complainant's son without the assistance of a personal assistant on a full-time basis that this would have placed excessive pressure on the staffing resources available to it at that juncture with the result that it would not have been in a position to provide the required level of care and the standard of service that it was obliged to provide to the other children that were already under its care. Having regard to the provisions of Section 7(4)(*b*) of the Equal Status Acts, I find that the respondent did not subject the complainant's son to discrimination in the present case in terms of its requirement that he be assisted on a full-time basis by a personal assistant in order to be granted a place in its crèche. I therefore cannot accept the complainant's contention that the respondent was operating in a discriminatory manner in terms of its policy regarding the admission of children with Special Needs to its crèche. Based on the evidence presented, I am satisfied that the respondent was operating an inclusive policy for all children irrespective of whether the child was disabled or not and this is evidenced by the fact that it was already providing care for a number of children with Special Needs when the complainant sought to enrol her son in the crèche (para 4.5).

2.6.3 Multiple Ground Exceptions

Several other exceptions are permitted under a range of grounds. In relation to the grounds of gender, age, disability, national origin or nationality, discrimination is permitted in a sporting context provided the differences in treatment are reasonable and relevant to the facility or the event.[204] In relation to the gender ground, Bolger and Kimber (2009, pp 446–448) argue that the exception is

---

[204] Section 5(2)(*f*). This exception is replicated in the education context but confined to fewer grounds: section 7(4)(*a*) permits educational establishment to treat students differently on grounds of gender, age or disability in relation to the provision of sporting facilities, or organisation of sporting events, to the extent that the differences are reasonably necessary having regard to the nature of the facilities or events. The exception was raised in *MacMahon v Department of Physical Education and Sport, University College Cork,*

broad and unsophisticated. They call for a more nuanced approach, which factors in differences in physical strength between men and women and allows younger boys and girls to play and compete with each other.

Drama and other entertainment are also mentioned in the ESA. Discrimination reasonably required for reasons of authenticity, aesthetics, tradition or custom on the grounds of gender, age, disability or race is possible.[205] This exception would allow the selection of females, for example, to play roles generally allocated to women or girls.[206]

Clubs which have the principal purpose of catering for the needs of persons who are members of the Traveller community or people of a particular gender, sexual orientation, religious belief (or persons of no religious belief), family status, civil status, age, disability, or nationality or ethnic or national origin can restrict membership to people from those groups (see Chapter 9). The 'race' and 'colour' aspects of the race ground are not exempt.

Providers of goods, services and accommodation may impose or maintain a 'reasonable preferential fee, charge or rate' for persons with their children, married couples, persons in a specific age group or persons with a disability.[207] Clubs may also offer such concessions to members, but the exception does not extend to educational establishments. As discussed further in Chapter 8.2, this exception sanctions reduced payments for goods and services by persons covered by the age and disability grounds, as well as certain aspects of the family status and civil status grounds. It was applied in *Dalton v Limerick City Council*.[208] The Council charged householders a set fee for weekly collection of refuse contained in a standard size bin provided by the Council. People aged over 65 (provided they lived alone, or with only one other person who was also aged over 65) could avail of a preferential rate if they used a smaller size bin. Mr Dalton wanted to use the smaller bin and maintained that he should be entitled to the preferential rate even though he was aged under 65. He argued that the Council's failure to extend the rate to him amounted to discrimination on the age ground. The equality officer was satisfied that the exception under section 16(1)(*a*) applied to this practice and so the Council was acting in accordance with the ESA.

There have been no cases to date on the matter but 'rate' could be taken to include the amount payable under various social welfare schemes.

DEC-S2009-014. But since the complainant did not establish a *prima facie* case of discrimination the equality officer did not need to consider whether the exemption applied.

[205] Section 5(2)(*i*).

[206] See comments of the Minister for Justice to that effect before the Select Committee on Justice, Equality, Defence and Women's Rights, 3 November 1999 (Equal Status Bill 1999, Committee Stage).

[207] Section 16(1).

[208] DEC-S2004-042.

Section 6(5) provides for an exception that straddles several grounds. It applies where premises or accommodation is reserved for a particular category of persons for a religious purpose or as a refuge, nursing home, retirement home, home for persons with a disability, hostel for the homeless, or for a similar purpose. Refusal to dispose of the premises or provide accommodation to people outside that category will not constitute discrimination.

In the same general context section 6(6) sets out an important exception regarding public housing, which has been central to a number of cases (O'Neill, 2010). It provides:

Nothing in subsection (1) shall be construed as prohibiting –

(*a*) a housing authority, pursuant to its functions under the Housing Acts, 1966 to 1998, or

(*b*) a body approved under section 6 of the Housing (Miscellaneous Provisions) Act, 1992,

from providing, in relation to housing accommodation, *different treatment* to persons based on family size, family status, civil status, disability, age or membership of the Traveller community [emphasis added].

The equality officer in a 2009 case pointed out that the provision only relates to the management of housing lists and 'is not a defence to matters concerning eviction or disciplinary proceedings concerning accommodation'.[209]

The Housing Acts address a range of matters, including the provision of social housing. Under those Acts a housing authority, which is basically the same as a local authority,[210] is required to make a scheme setting out the order of priority to be given to applicants for housing.[211] It may stipulate that certain categories of people should be prioritised, such as applicants living in over-crowded conditions or in dwellings that are considered unfit or dangerous.

Section 6(6)(*b*) refers to cooperative housing societies and voluntary housing associations or trusts that have received approved status under section 6 of the Housing (Miscellaneous Provisions) Act 1992.[212]

During the Seanad debates on the Equal Status Bill 1997 the Minister explained that the exemptions were designed to afford housing bodies a

---

[209] *Husband and Wife v A Voluntary Housing Association*, DEC-S2009-071, para 5.3.
[210] See the definition of 'housing authority' in section 23 of the Housing (Miscellaneous Provisions) Act 1992 and the Housing (Transfer of Functions) Order 2011 (SI 85/2011).
[211] Section 60, Housing Act 1966.
[212] For further details see the website of the representative body for the housing association sector, the Irish Council for Social Housing: <http://www.icsh.ie/>.

degree of flexibility 'in allocating dwellings in order to ensure that purpose built and designated dwellings – for example, elderly persons' dwellings and accommodation for travellers, etc. – continue to be used for their original purpose.' Flexibility was also required to 'ensure an appropriate social mix' in that, for example 'local authorities and voluntary bodies may have to ensure a particular type of family does not predominate in one estate.'[213]

The complainant in *Jones v Dún Laoghaire–Rathdown County Council*[214] had been on the Council's housing list for six years when he referred a discrimination complaint. He had not been offered any accommodation, and since his position on the list had not improved significantly he had little prospect of securing housing in the near future. Mr Jones argued that the Council should afford him and others in his position reasonable accommodation[215] and that it was discriminating by failing to operate a distinct housing list to meet the needs of disabled people similar to that in place for older people. Since section 6(6) permits 'different treatment' the equality officer concluded that the respondent had not discriminated against the complainant in providing special housing facilities for older people.

The nature of the exception also arose in a 2007 High Court case concerning housing authorities' duties towards Travellers.[216] At the outset of the hearing South Dublin County Council accepted that the subsection did not afford a blanket exemption and could not be used to justify less favourable treatment. In other words, the Council conceded that the reference to 'different treatment' in subsection (6) is meant to sanction benign schemes that meet the particular needs of those with larger families, disabled people and so on. For the Equality Authority (2007b, p 26) this was 'a very significant and important concession'. In its experience housing authorities had sought to rely on section 6(6) to make discriminatory provision of accommodation immune from challenge under the ESA.

Reinforcing this approach in an appeal to the Circuit Court under the Acts Hunt J stated:

> I cannot construe subsection 6 of that section as exempting a housing authority in its entirety from all application of the equality legislation. It appears to me simply to provide that a housing authority is entitled to base its priorities and its housing plan on different

---

[213] 150 *Seanad Debates* Cols 1487–1488 (Second Stage).
[214] DEC-S2004-081.
[215] Reasonable accommodation is dealt with in Chapter 6.
[216] *Doherty & Anor v South Dublin County Council & Ors* [2007] 2 IR 696.

treatment to persons based on family size, family status and the other considerations set out in the subsection.[217]

In a series of recent decisions the Equality Tribunal has determined that section 6(6) does not allow a housing authority to discriminate against the categories of persons referred to, but rather means that it can prioritise in favour of those categories of people.[218] However O'Neill (2010) argues that the lack of transparency in how housing lists operate means that perceived cases of less favourable treatment are virtually impossible to prove.

2.6.4 General Exceptions

2.6.4.1 Overview

Across all grounds there are exceptions for different treatment that concerns private activity, insurance and other risk assessment, clinical diagnoses and capacity, and measures designed to promote special treatment of particular categories of people.

2.6.4.2 Private Activity

The ESA only applies where goods or services are provided to the public or a section of the public. It is not, therefore, directed at purely private activities. So that, for instance, while a taxi driver should not discriminate against prospective passengers, a person driving a private car is free not to offer a lift to someone because of their gender, sexual orientation and so on. A number of specific exceptions reinforce that general approach.

Under section 5(2)(*k*) an exception applies to the disposal of goods by will or gift. This exception is relatively straightforward and means that an aggrieved person cannot challenge the terms of a will using the ESA, or claim that a gift was given in a discriminatory manner. The term 'gift' is not defined but presumably is an entirely private offering that can be distinguished from grants, prizes, awards and so on, which are given to persons who meet

---

[217] *Dublin City Council v Deans* (Circuit Court Dublin, Hunt J, unreported, 15 April 2008), at p 29.

[218] *A Complainant v A Local Authority*, DEC-S2007-049; *Mr X v A Town Council*, DEC-S2008-042; *Boland v Killarney Town Council*, DEC-S2008-069; *McCann v Dún Laoghaire–Rathdown County Council*, DEC-S2008-004; *O'Donnell v Roscommon County Council*, DEC-S2008-113; *Cleary v Dublin City Council*, DEC-S2009-028; *Cleary v Waterford County Council*, DEC-S2009-085 (equality officer's decision upheld on appeal to the Circuit Court); *Cleary v Waterford City Council*, DEC-S2010-003.

eligibility criteria or other conditions of a scheme that is directed at the public or a section of the public.

Rental of a room or part of a private home is also treated exceptionally. Section 6(1) prohibits discrimination in disposing of any estate or interest in premises, providing accommodation or any services or amenities related to accommodation or ceasing to provide accommodation or any such services or amenities. Section 6(3) makes it clear that the prohibition includes 'the termination of any tenancy or other interest in those premises or ceasing to provide such accommodation services or amenities'. However, section 6(2)(*d*) goes on to specify a number of exceptions; one of these situations is where the property being disposed of is a part (other than a separate and self-contained part) of the home of the person engaging in the discrimination.

2.6.4.3 Special Treatment

Section 5(2)(*h*) allows differences in treatment in relation to services that are provided for the principal purpose of promoting the special interests of people in a particular category. Any difference in treatment of people in that category must be reasonably necessary to promote their special interests and be undertaken in a bona fide manner. Bona fide means 'in good faith'.

Egan v Young Fine Gael[219] involved an age discrimination complaint in relation to membership of the youth branch of a political party. Young Fine Gael's constitution confines membership to persons under the age of 31. Mr Egan's application was turned down as he exceeded that age limit by some 20 years. The respondent argued that the age limit was a bona fide measure saved by section 5(2)(*h*). The Tribunal agreed that it was entitled to rely on the exemption: 'I accept the information put forward by the respondent, in that Young Fine Gael was established as a forum for young people to engage together for political discourse, to speak freely, that it is an embryonic association for persons within their own peer group to not be shy about speaking their minds and that the parent party can be stifling for younger people' (para 4.8).

By contrast, in *Keane v World Travel Centre*[220] a company that offered reduced fares on flights only to Filipino nationals could not justify its policy under section 5(2)(*h*). World Travel Centre maintained that it was engaging in 'positive discrimination'. The Equality Officer disagreed and found that it did not meet any of 'the strict and comprehensive criteria required by Section 5(2)(h)' (para 5.5). The sole purpose of the special offer was to gain a commercial advantage over competitors and not to advance the special interests of the Filipino community.

---

[219] DEC-S2011-001.
[220] DEC-S2011-035.

In *Shanahan v One Pico Restaurant*,[221] the equality officer noted that the meaning of the subsection was ambiguous and commented: 'On the basis that the treatment must flow from the promotion of the special interests of persons in the category, it is my opinion that this sub-section of the Equal Status Act, 2000 will normally, if not always, relate to the justification of more favourable treatment of a particular category of persons' (para 7.2).

That approach was also adopted in a 2006 Tribunal decision on the exemption and annotation system applied to dyslexic students' Leaving Certificates.[222] The Tribunal found that the annotation was discriminatory; the reasonable accommodation afforded students through a grammar waiver in some subjects was not preferential treatment or positive action but simply a non-discrimination measure. Neither the waiver nor the annotation could be regarded as promoting the special interests of the students. However, on appeal the Circuit Court found that the system was designed to promote those interests as envisaged under section 5(2)(*h*).[223] The matter subsequently came before the High Court, which found that the Circuit Court had applied the law correctly in arriving at its decision but did not specifically address the meaning of section 5(2)(*h*). This judgment is examined in detail below (Chapter 6.7). More recently, Denham J has commented as follows on the section:

> This refers to the special needs of groups, to disadvantaged groups, where the discrimination is reasonably necessary. For example, where the State provides language classes for foreign nationals, nationals are excluded.[224]

In sum then it appears that the exception will usually serve to protect positive action measures from challenge as discriminatory. However, the possibility remains open that adverse or unwanted treatment from a complainant's perspective may also be saved.

Section 5(2)(*l*) contains another broad and vague exception in relation to goods or services that can 'reasonably be regarded' as 'suitable only to the needs of certain persons'. This provision has not been explored to any great extent in case law to date. It featured in *Travers and Maunsell v Ball Alley House*[225] and *Shanahan v One Pico Restaurant*,[226] which addressed the admission of parents with children to a pub and a restaurant respectively. In

---

[221] DEC-S2003-056.

[222] *Two Named Complainants v Minister for Education and Science*, DEC-S2006-077.

[223] *The Minister for Education and Science v Hollingsworth*, Circuit Court Dublin, Hunt J, unreported, 19 October 2007.

[224] *Equality Authority v Portmarnock Golf Club & Ors* [2010] 1 ILRM 237, at p 290.

[225] DEC-S2003-109/110.

[226] DEC-S2003-056.

Shanahan the equality officer reasoned that the provision of fine dining was not only suitable for corporate clients but for all persons who wished to access high quality food.

The complainants in the *Travers* case had been asked to leave a pub at 7 p.m. because they had a nine-month-old baby with them. According to the respondent the service it provided was only suitable to the needs of adults. It pointed out that no prepared food was available in the pub and that there were no facilities such as a garden or games room for children to play in. However, the equality officer did not accept that argument. The fact there were no special facilities for children did not mean that some of the services provided were not suited to children. Children had been allowed on the premises prior to a 'watershed' of 6 p.m. These factors demonstrated that the pub did not cater exclusively for the needs of adults, and so the respondent could not claim an exemption under section 5(2)(*l*). However, the equality officer noted that as the evening progressed, the emphasis might shift more towards the provision of alcohol to adults, and suggested that there might be a strong case for introducing an evening watershed to deal with the risks associated with unsupervised children on the premises. The equality officer also commented that a licensed premises which provided 'adult' entertainment would in his view be highly likely to fall within section 5(2)(*l*) (para 7.7).

It should be noted that the Intoxicating Liquor Act 2003 introduced amendments to the ESA so that licensees have discretion as to whether to admit children accompanied by parents at defined times.[227] In other words, pub owners are now free to exclude children from their premises without risking a discrimination complaint. Complaints about discrimination occurring at the point of entry to or on licensed premises are heard by the District Court since 2004 (Chapter 12.2.2).

2.6.4.4 Risk Assessment

A broad exemption applies to services that involve risk assessment, typically insurance policies but also loans (Hynes, 2010). The discrimination prohibition does not apply to differences of treatment of people in relation

---

[227] Section 25 of the 2003 Act amended section 15 of the Equal Status Act 2000 by adding subsections (3) to (5). Section 14 of the 2003 Act prohibits persons under 18 from entering licensed premises. However, under subsection (2), a licensee can permit a child aged under 15 to be in the bar *before 9 p.m.* if accompanied by a parent or guardian. Subsection (4) gives licensees discretion to allow a child accompanied by a parent or guardian or a person aged fifteen to seventeen to be in the bar after 9.00 p.m. on the occasion of a private function at which a substantial meal is served to persons attending the function, e.g. a wedding reception. For a discussion of the exact dates on which the new provisions came into force see *Grogan v Crocketts on the Quay, Ballina*, DEC-S2009-001.

to 'annuities, pensions and insurance policies or any other matters related to the assessment of risk', where that treatment is based on reliable actuarial or statistical data or other relevant or commercial underwriting factors.[228] The gender ground is treated exceptionally, as discussed further below.

In order to avail of the exemption a respondent must show that a difference in treatment is (1) effected by reference to actuarial or statistical data which was obtained from a source on which it was reasonable to rely and it is reasonable having regard to the data or other relevant factors *or* (2) is effected by reference to other relevant underwriting or commercial factors and it is reasonable having regard to the data or other relevant factors.

The breadth of the exemption has been criticised as effectively removing the field of insurance from the reach of discrimination law. Bolger and Kimber (2000, pp 444–446) argue for greater intervention in the market in the interests of the common good.

In practice the exemption is most relevant to life, travel, motor and income protection insurance products. Private health insurance, which helps cover costs incurred as a private patient, is governed by additional laws, which also in effect prohibit discrimination.[229] Insurers must accept all applicants for private health insurance cover, irrespective of their gender, health status or age. A community rating system also applies to such products, which means that everyone pays the same premium for a given health insurance plan (subject to a limited number of exceptions that allow, for instance, less expensive premiums for dependant children). It is unlawful to use genetic data in relation to insurance policies or mortgages under section 42(2) of the Disability Act 2005.[230]

Differential treatment based on many of the discriminatory grounds is widespread in the financial services and insurance sectors. For example, insurance companies use the medical history of a patient in assessing premiums for life, income protection and medical policies, which implicates the disability ground. Age-based differences are common across various policies and lending practices (Oxera, 2009). Differences in treatment could include refusal of coverage or a loan, the loading of premiums, or distinct transaction

---

[228] Section 5(2)(*d*).

[229] See the Health Insurance Acts 1994–2009, which provide for community rating in relation to premiums, open enrolment (i.e. equal access) and lifetime cover (renewal of polices). During the Dáil debates on the Equal Status Bill 1999 an amendment was sought to secure the community rating system. The Minister for Justice did not accept that such as amendment was necessary: Select Committee on Justice, Equality, Defence and Women's Rights, 3 November 1999 (Committee Stage). For further information see the website of the Health Insurance Authority, which is the body charged with regulating the private health insurance market: <http://www.hia.ie/>.

[230] For a discussion of European debates on this issue see Liukko (2010).

processes (such as requesting additional information or medical tests) from some prospective customers.

From the decisions to date it appears that blanket refusals to offer coverage to people covered by the discriminatory grounds will not be saved by the exemption. But it will apply where an insurer can demonstrate that an assessment of the individual's application was made, based on appropriate data as required by the ESA.

In *O'Donoghue v Hibernian General Insurance*[231] the equality officer decided that different motor insurance quotes for 31-year-olds and 41-year-olds were not unlawful. The model used to assess the relative risks and weight insurance policies accordingly was found to be a reliable one. The respondent's evidence was based on an assessment, by three actuaries, of the company's claims records and statistics. The complainant's evidence was inadequate to counter that expert testimony. It is regrettable that proportionality cannot be factored into such cases. In other words, while it may be legitimate to load premiums, some assessment of the extent of the penalty imposed for being of a given age, etc. would enhance the protection afforded by the ESA.

In a 2009 case the respondent insurance company was entitled to refuse life insurance cover to an applicant with a history of self-harm.[232] The Tribunal was satisfied that the processes in question were reasonable based on the information available about the complainant's health status. As a result there was no discrimination on the disability ground. In reaching that conclusion the equality officer found:

- The insurer is not operating a blanket policy of excluding people who have had mental health difficulties including self-harm and/or suicidal tendencies.

- The respondent has a considered approach in determining whether any individual is given cover and this approach is applied in a transparent and concise manner.

- In this case the respondent is relying on data that it has reason to rely on and the data used is of relevance when assessing risk (para 5.4).

On the other hand, in *Ross v Royal & Sun Alliance Insurance plc*[233] the Tribunal found that a company's 'across the board' policy of refusing motor insurance to persons aged over 70 was unlawful:

---

[231] DEC-S2004-201.
[232] *A Complainant v A Life Insurance Provider*, DEC-S2009-033. See also *Mr A v A Life Assurance Company*, DEC-S2011-008.
[233] DEC-S2003-116. See also *Burke v Lynskey Ryan Insurance Limited, Galway,*

[I]t is clear that reliable actuarial and statistical data is essential to the insurance industry in conducting risk assessment and I note that the data provided by the respondents, despite its flaws, does indicate that higher claim costs are more likely to arise from accidents involving elderly drivers than those involving middle-aged drivers. On this basis, I consider that there is a case to be made for a company quoting proportionately higher premiums to older drivers, based on the results of their actuarial reviews. What cannot be accepted is the complete refusal of a quotation based solely on a person's age (para 7.11).

The statistics used were found to be incomplete and inaccurate in parts and the commercial or underwriting factors unreasonably selective. Hynes (2010) notes that two cases involving people aged under 25 were settled following the decision in *Ross*.

We now turn to risk assessment exceptions applicable to the gender ground. In *King v The Voluntary Health Insurance Board*[234] the complainant argued that the respondent insurance company subjected him to gender discrimination because he was obliged to pay for maternity-related benefits as part of his health insurance premium. Since he could never avail of such benefits he wanted those aspects of cover removed from his policy but the respondent informed him that maternity-related benefits were a composite part of the overall insurance plan. The equality officer held that the treatment complained of was required by a legislative enactment and therefore fell under the exemption provided for in section 14(1)(*a*) of the ESA (Chapter 2.5). The VHI is legally obliged to include maternity benefits in every health insurance contract it offers and is not permitted to charge a lower premium to persons based on their gender.[235]

Following this decision the ESA was amended to take account of the Gender Goods and Services Directive.[236] Sex discrimination in insurance is now separated out from the other grounds so that, for example, the Central Bank and Financial Services Authority are obliged to compile, publish and maintain data on gender as an actuarial factor in the assessment of risk.[237] Section 5(4) was inserted to cover the precise situation at issue in *King*. As of 21 December 2009 it prohibits differences in the treatment of persons in rela-

---

DEC-S2006-071.

[234] DEC-S2008-116.

[235] Health Insurance Acts 1994–2009 and the Health Insurance Act 1994 (Minimum Benefit) Regulations 1996 (SI 83/1996).

[236] See section 5(2)(*da*) and sections 5(3)–5(5), which were inserted by section 76 of the Civil Law (Miscellaneous Provisions) Act 2008.

[237] Section 5(5).

tion to premiums and benefits payable under insurance policies based, whether in whole or in part, on costs incurred by insurers in relation to pregnancy and maternity.

Article 5 of the Directive provides that the use of sex as a factor in calculating premiums and other benefits in respect of insurance should not result in differences in premiums or benefits to an individual. However, article 5(2) contains an exemption to this prohibition which permits proportional differences in premiums or benefits where the sex of an individual is a determining factor in the assessment of risk (based on relevant and accurate actuarial and statistical data). The exemption was contentious, with discrimination law experts such as Bell (2007, p 303) commenting that it 'is difficult to find any principled basis for why EC legislation treats sex stereotyping in insurance as permissible whilst ethnic stereotyping is unlawful'. In any event, article 5(2) will cease to apply from 21 December 2012 following a judgment of the CJEU. A consumer group along with two individuals challenged the exemption (as implemented in Belgian law) on the basis that it conflicts with the overarching principle of equal treatment of men and women under EU law. On 1 March 2011 the CJEU agreed and found that different insurance premiums for men and women amounted to sex discrimination. It held that article 5(2) is not compatible with two provisions of the Charter of Fundamental Rights – articles 21 and 23 – which provide respectively that any discrimination based on sex is prohibited and that equality between men and women must be ensured in all areas.[238] It was also clear from the wording of the Gender Goods and Services Directive that men and women were considered to be in a comparable situation as regards insurance services. Men and women should, therefore, be treated the same in this context. The Court acknowledged that at the time the Directive was adopted the use of actuarial factors related to sex was widespread in the insurance sector. While it was acceptable for EU law to provide for a transitional arrangement there was a risk that the exemption would continue to apply indefinitely. The Court decided that article 5(2) should cease to apply from 21 December 2012. The ESA must be amended before that date.

It should also be noted that the Racial Equality Directive does not contain any equivalent exemption to section 5(2)(*d*) and so at a minimum the race and Traveller community grounds ought to be removed from its scope. In a report published in 2006 the National Consultative Committee on Racism and Interculturalism (2006) gathered anecdotal evidence of discriminatory practices directed at people who were nationals of African countries or had spent a significant amount of time on that continent.

---

[238] *Association Belge des Consommateurs Test-Achats ASBL v Belgium*, Case C-236/09, [2011] 2 CMLR 38.

To sum up, the current statutory exemption needs to be amended to take account of EU law. Any such reforms could be used as an opportunity to clarify other problems with the section, some of which have arisen in Tribunal decisions. For example, the meaning of 'other relevant underwriting or commercial factors' in section 5(2)(*d*) is vague and arguably allows insurance companies too much scope to evade application of the ESA. Complainants are placed in a very difficult position with respect to evidence where companies do not disclose the reasons for refusal or apply confidential risk assessment criteria. A statutory code of practice could be useful in this regard.

2.6.4.5 Clinical Judgments and Capacity

Under section 16(2)(*a*) it is not discriminatory to treat a person differently 'solely in the exercise of a clinical judgment in connection with the diagnosis of illness or his or her medical treatment'. The term 'clinical judgment' is not defined but a similar exception applies to the statutory complaints system with respect to health services set up under Part 9 of the Health Act 2004.[239] Section 2 of that Act defines 'clinical judgment' as 'a decision made or opinion formed in connection with the diagnosis, care or treatment of a patient'. From relevant decisions of the Tribunal to date it seems that similar matters are immune from challenge under the ESA.

The exception has been applied to decisions made by medical practitioners about the appropriate form and timing of treatment in several cases. *Mr X v Health Service Executive*[240] involved a complaint of disability discrimination under section 4, which requires the provision of special treatment or facilities unless this would impose more than a nominal cost on the service provider (Chapter 6). Mr X alleged that the HSE failed to provide special treatment or facilities in the form of the services of a psychologist as part of his treatment for schizophrenia. The equality officer was satisfied that no discrimination claim could be sustained in relation to part of the period in question as the medical team did not consider such services necessary: that is, the clinical judgment exception applied (see further Chapter 6.5). The exception was also successfully availed of in *Hallinan v O'Donnell*,[241] which concerned the treatment afforded a quadriplegic man while in hospital. Mr Hallinan argued that a delay in providing physiotherapy treatment and X-rays amounted to direct discrimination on the disability ground. In his evidence to the Tribunal the respondent explained that in his assessment physiotherapy would have exacerbated another condition the complainant was suffering from and that all

---

[239] Section 48, Health Act 2004.
[240] DEC-S2008-112.
[241] DEC-S2006-069.

patients experienced delays in receiving X-ray reports. According to the equality officer 'treating a person differently while exercising clinical judgment in connection with that person's diagnosis or treatment cannot amount to discrimination.'[242] The complaint did not, therefore, succeed. Likewise a doctor's decision to discharge a man from hospital following an assessment of his medical condition could not amount to discrimination in a 2010 case.[243] A similar finding was issued in *A Patient v Health Service Provider and a Hospital*,[244] where a number of the facilities provided to a person who was detained in a mental health facility were found to fall within the exception (Chapter 3.3.4).

According to the Equality Authority (2005a, p 10) the exception should apply on a 'case by case basis and cannot be used to justify a general practice, policy or approach'. It would seem, therefore that denying medical services to a group of people protected by the discriminatory grounds is not permissible. The Commission on Assisted Human Reproduction (2005, p 137) suggests that the exception could apply to decisions not to afford fertility treatment because the client is considered too old.[245] In light of the Authority's reasoning each case should be considered on its merits. The boundaries between clinical judgments and criteria informed by socially constructed evaluations of people's eligibility for services might not be straightforward in relation to judgments based on age and disability.

The exception does not apply to the general services and facilities available to people when accessing healthcare. In a 2009 decision the equality officer upheld a complaint of disability discrimination that involved access to appropriate toilet and bathing facilities during a hospital stay. Since the treatment in question did not concern diagnosis or medical assessment more broadly the exemption was inapplicable.[246] Similarly in *Goulding v O'Doherty*[247] a chiropodist's refusal to treat a person with HIV amounted to discrimination. The respondent's decision was not based on knowledge of HIV infection or

---

[242] See also *Traynor v Health Service Executive Dublin North East*, DEC-S2009-072, in which a delay in providing methadone treatment was based on genuine medical reasons and so was covered by the clinical judgment exception.

[243] *Ms A (on behalf of her brother, Mr B) v A General Hospital*, DEC-S2010-044, para 4.8.

[244] DEC-S2010-053.

[245] In a UK case a 37-year-old woman sought judicial review of a decision to refuse assisted reproductive treatment services to her on the grounds that she was over the 35-year age limit. The High Court found that the age limit was neither irrational nor unreasonable because clinical findings indicated treatment was less effective above the age and the local health authority was entitled to impose such criteria in a context of limited funding: *R v Sheffield Health Authority, ex parte Seale* (1994) 25 BMLR 1.

[246] *A Patient v Mater Misericordiae University Hospital*, DEC-S2009-057.

[247] DEC-S2009-073.

clinical developments in the area, since he did not have such expertise. While an expert report stated that there were more suitable facilities available to the complainant the equality officer found that this did not negate the duty to comply with the ESA; other facilities may have been preferable but they were not necessary.

Finally, section 16(2)(*b*) provides that treating a person differently shall not constitute discrimination where the person is incapable of giving informed consent or of entering into an enforceable contract, and for that reason the treatment of the person is reasonable in the particular case. Capacity and consent issues typically arise with respect to certain disabled persons (Whelan, 2009, Chapter 13). According to the Law Reform Commission (2005, p 124) it is likely that 'incapacity will be judged as a question of fact rather than on the basis of the subjective judgment of the supplier.' The Commission (2005, p 125) refers to a UK disability discrimination case in which 'an agent of a gas company refused to accept the signature of a woman on a contract for the supply of gas and electricity without the countersignature of a neighbour. The woman had a neurological condition that caused her to shake but was of full mental capacity. The company's policy that all contracts with older people and disabled people were to be countersigned was found to be discriminatory and unlawful under Part III of the UK's Disability Discrimination Act 1995.' The Commission's suggestion that a similar view would be taken by the Equality Tribunal is borne out by a 2012 decision. In *Complainant A and Complainant B (through their next friend and father) v Caledonian Life*[248] an insurance company refused to enter into life assurance contracts with two men who had been diagnosed with autism spectrum disorder. The Tribunal found that the respondent's actions fell within the section 16(2)(*b*) exception. Its decision was based on medical evidence which indicated that the men's conditions were severe. Moreover, the complainants' father, who referred the case on behalf of his sons, estimated that their developmental ages were between 9 and 12 years of age. He explained that both men were 'non-verbal and cannot write' (para 5.5). The equality officer noted that the father's expertise as to his children's capacities had been communicated to the respondent in writing. In light of this information and given the intricacies of the contract in question it was reasonable for the respondent to conclude that both complainants could not give informed consent.

Legislation reforming the general law on capacity is due to be published in 2012.[249]

---

[248] DEC-S2012-007.
[249] See   <http://www.taoiseach.gov.ie/eng/Taoiseach_and_Government/Government_ Legislation_Programme/SECTION_A1.html> [accessed 13 July 2012].

2.7 Conclusion

The precise scope of the ESA is uncertain, as the meaning of key terms like 'service' continues to evolve through interpretation. Indeed, several provisions have yet to be tested. Some exceptions appear to be out of step with EU law requirements and so we can expect further developments when relevant case law emerges from the CJEU.

Since it covers a wider range of activities than the 'services' addressed by the ESA, the ECHR Act 2003 may prove important in relation to alleged discrimination by public authorities. As we have seen, the ESA does not cover some key governmental functions. There is no such limitation under the ECHR Act; it would appear that all functions of an organ of the state are subject to it. For instance, an Garda Síochána is an 'organ of the State' for the purposes of the 2003 Act. Investigation, arrest, detention, stops and searches on the grounds of sexual orientation, membership of the Traveller community or other grounds could violate article 14 in conjunction with article 5 (deprivation of liberty) or article 8 (respect for private and family life). Significantly, an Irish law that does not comply with relevant Convention provisions can be declared incompatible with the ECHR.[250] As we have seen, discriminatory treatment required by law cannot be challenged under the ESA. The 2003 Act may be especially useful then for groups who encounter discrimination that is entrenched in law. Indeed, current developments to afford transgender people legal recognition are a direct consequence of ECHR litigation pursued by Dr Lydia Foy with the support of the Free Legal Advice Centres (Gender Recognition Advisory Group, 2011; Transgender Equality Network Ireland, 2010).[251]

The remainder of this part of the book revisits the exceptions discussed in this chapter as we learn how they have been applied in cases.

---

[250] Under section 5 of the ECHR Act 2003 the High Court or Supreme Court may declare that a statutory provision or rule of law is incompatible with the Convention provisions, 'where no other legal remedy is adequate and available.' A court may only issue such a declaration where it is not possible to interpret the law in question compatibly with the Convention provisions. A plaintiff may be awarded compensation but a declaration does not affect the validity of the law in question. The appropriate response to a declaration of incompatibility is ultimately a matter for the Oireachtas.

[251] *Foy v An t-Ard Chláraitheoir & Ors* [2007] IEHC 470. See Farrell (2008).

3

Direct Discrimination

3.1 Overview

3.1.1 Introduction

Section 3 of the ESA prohibits less favourable treatment of a person on any (or several) of the nine grounds. It tackles detriments experienced by people 'because of' age, civil status, disability, family status, gender, race, religion, sexual orientation or membership of the Travelling community. The prohibition of less favourable treatment is known as 'direct discrimination', although that phrase is not used in the legislation.

The basic idea behind direct discrimination prohibitions is that individuals should be treated according to their actual characteristics rather than on the basis of prejudicial or stereotypical assumptions. It should operate as a means of eliminating illegitimate considerations from service providers' processes and practices. As we will see below, less favourable treatment is sometimes overt but it can also be unconscious or unintentional.

Under the ESA direct discrimination cannot be justified.[252] But, as the case law considered in Chapter 3.3 demonstrates, a respondent may seek to avail of an exception provided for under the legislation (Chapter 2.4–2.6). In other words, once it has been established that less favourable treatment on a prohibited ground has occurred the only way of avoiding liability is to demonstrate that the treatment is covered by an explicit exception.

The relevant part of section 3 provides:

(1) For the purposes of this Act, discrimination shall be taken to occur—

(*a*) where a person is treated less favourably than another person is, has been or would be treated in a comparable situation on any of

---

[252] See, for example, *Ghetau v New Ross Coarse Angling Ltd*, DEC-S2011-059, para 4.3.

the grounds specified in *subsection (2)* (in this Act referred to as the 'discriminatory grounds') which—

(i) exists,

(ii) existed but no longer exists,

(iii) may exist in the future, or

(iv) is imputed to the person concerned,

(*b*) where a person who is associated with another person—

(i) is treated, by virtue of that association, less favourably than a person who is not so associated is, has been or would be treated in a comparable situation, and

(ii) similar treatment of that other person on any of the discriminatory grounds would, by virtue of *paragraph (a)*, constitute discrimination

The prohibition incorporates situations where a discriminatory ground existed but no longer exists, may exist in the future or is imputed to the person concerned. People are protected, therefore, where membership of a category is temporary or episodic (as is the case with some forms of condition or impairment under the disability ground, for example). Significantly, a person experiencing less favourable treatment 'on any of the grounds' does not have to possess the relevant characteristic or status themselves. The ESA includes situations where a person has been wrongly perceived as 'belonging' to the group in question (section 3(1)(*a*)(iv)). In addition, people are protected against discrimination because of their association with someone who is protected by a discriminatory ground (discrimination by association under section 3(1)(*b*)). These elements of direct discrimination are considered further in the next two sections.

3.1.2 Discrimination by Association

Discrimination by association occurs where someone associated with a person who is covered by a specified ground is treated less favourably because of that association (Honeyball, 2007).[253] As the cases discussed below demonstrate, it usually happens when two or more people encounter discriminatory treatment

---

[253] Section 3(1)(*b*). A complainant must have been subjected to less favourable treatment themselves; they cannot use discrimination by association to object to the treatment of another person: *O'Rourke v JJ Red Holdings Ltd t/a as Dublin City Hotel*, DEC-E2010-045.

when accessing a service *together*, and the 'reason for' that treatment is the protected characteristic of just one of them.

There is no requirement, however, for the person the complainant is associated with to be present or indeed to have ever accessed a service provided by the respondent. All that is required by the wording of section 3(1)(*b*)(ii) is that similar treatment of that other person on any of the discriminatory grounds would constitute discrimination. For example, a woman views a property that she is interested in renting. In the course of a conversation with the owner, who is showing her around the house, she mentions that her boyfriend is Syrian. The owner refuses to rent the house to her because he thinks visits by 'a foreigner' would upset the neighbours. She has been discriminated against by virtue of her association with a person who is covered by the race ground. Similar treatment of her boyfriend would constitute discrimination. Her boyfriend is not accessing a service (accommodation under section 6) and has never even met the service provider (landlord).

It is not clear from the wording of section 3(1)(*b*) whether the association has to be with actual people the complainant knows on a personal basis. There may have to be such a connection because the provision refers to 'a person who is associated with another person'. On the other hand, the ESA should be interpreted purposively (Chapter 1.6) and there is persuasive UK case law in favour of a broad reading of direct discrimination in such situations (Pilgerstorfer and Forshaw, 2008).[254] Arguably then discrimination by association could also occur if a service user is treated less favourably because of their involvement in a cause or campaign, say, about the rights of transsexual people.

All of the ESA decisions to date have concerned associations between people who know each other on a personal basis. *Cassidy and Wesemann v Doherty*[255] dealt with a heterosexual couple's treatment in private rented accommodation. According to the equality officer the man in question was covered by both the gender and family status grounds:

> Mr Cassidy claims that he was treated less favourably by the respondent because of his gender. Since Mr Cassidy adduced no evidence to show, nor did he suggest, that Mr Doherty treats women more favourably, Mr Cassidy's claim on the gender ground appears to be on the basis of his association with Ms Wesemann. Mr Cassidy attained family status on the birth of his baby. Prior to that date he had family status by association with his partner Ms Wesemann

---

[254] See *Showboat Entertainment Centre Ltd v Owens* [1984] 1 WLR 384 and *Weathersfield Ltd v Sargent* [1999] IRLR 94 (discussed in Chapter 7.4).
[255] DEC-S2003-040/041.

while she was pregnant. On that basis both the gender and family status grounds apply to Mr Cassidy.

A group of people were refused access to a pub in *Six Complainants v A Public House, Dublin*.[256] One of the claimants (Mr McM) had a condition that affected his facial expressions and occasionally caused him to stagger. The equality officer concluded that the doorman's decision was based on the first complainant's demeanour, since 'these attributes are identical to those which would give the appearance of drunkenness to any person charged with making a snap decision in the matter' (para 7.3). Having found that the denial of access to Mr McM constituted discrimination on the disability ground, she found that the exclusion of the remaining five members of the group accompanying him amounted to discrimination by association.[257]

There are several cases of discrimination by association on the Traveller community ground. For example in *Battles v The Killarney Heights Hotel*[258] the equality officer found that the complainant, a Traveller, and her husband, a settled person, had been discriminated against when refused service in a hotel. Mr Battles' claim was that of discrimination by association under section 3(1)(*b*).[259]

In all of the foregoing cases the complainant and the person he/she was associated with were accessing services together. The case of *O'Brien v Dunnes Stores, Tralee*[260] was different in that respect. A man was refused access to a store some weeks after his brother had been asked to leave while he was shopping there. The brother had notified the respondent in writing that he intended to lodge an equal status complaint. When the complainant tried to enter the shop he was denied access by a security guard who told him that it was because his brother 'was taking a case to the court'. By suggesting that he was going to refer a complaint the man's brother was covered by the victimisation ground. The victimisation ground protects people from adverse treatment for using or indicating an intention to use the ESA (see Chapter 3.5). In being denied access a few weeks later the complainant was therefore

---

[256] DEC-S2004-009/014.

[257] The decision was overturned on appeal but the principle established on discrimination by association was not affected. For a discussion of the Circuit Court appeal see Equality Authority, 2006b, pp 50–51.

[258] DEC-S2004-143/144.

[259] See also *Sweeney v The Ship Inn, Sligo*, DEC-S2002-032; *Dooley and Boyne v The Grand Hotel*, DEC-S2002-015/016; *Feighery v MacMathuna's Pub*, DEC-S2003-051; *Kiernan v The Newbury Hotel*, DEC-S2006-080; *McDonagh v O'Keeffe, Ocean View Park*, DEC-S2005-161/164 (all of which were successful claims of discrimination by association on the Traveller community ground).

[260] DEC-S2007-038.

treated less favourably by virtue of his association with someone covered by a discriminatory ground.

Significantly, the CJEU has held that the Framework Directive must be interpreted to protect people subjected to direct discrimination or harassment on the grounds of their association with a disabled person (on harassment see further Chapter 5.2). *Coleman v Attridge Law*[261] established that the principle of equal treatment enshrined in the Directive applies not to a particular category of person but by reference to the grounds mentioned in article 1 (at para 38). The Court held that the wording of article 13, which constituted the legal basis of the Directive, supports such an interpretation. Consequently it would appear that the Court's analysis applies with equal force to the other directives that stem from that Treaty provision, including the Racial Equality Directive and the Gender Goods and Services Directive (Pilgerstorfer and Forshaw, 2008; Waddington, 2009). In light of the *Coleman* decision the Draft Goods and Services Directive includes an express prohibition against direct discrimination or harassment by association.[262] The decision reinforces the approach adopted by the Oireachtas in explicitly providing for protection against direct discrimination by association on all nine grounds.

3.1.3 Discrimination by Imputation

Discrimination by imputation has not featured much in equal status case law.[263] In some other countries it is referred to as 'perceived discrimination' or 'discrimination by assumption'. This feature of discrimination law reflects the fact that people are often subjected to negative treatment because membership of a group is inaccurately attributed to them. For example, a man who is refused service in a shop because the teller assumes he is Muslim could refer a complaint of less favourable treatment on the religion ground, even though in fact he is an atheist. Outlawing such behaviour, even where the claimant does not in fact belong to the protected group, is designed to further the overall goals of discrimination law: it focuses on discriminatory treatment rather than the attributes of the complainant.[264]

---

[261] Case C-303/06, [2008] EC 1-5603; [2008] ICR 1128.

[262] Council Document 6092/10, 11 February 2010, article 2(1)(*f*).

[263] For examples of established discrimination by imputation in the employment field see *Ms X v Electronic Component Co.*, DEC-E2006-042; *Mr A v A Public Sector Organisation*, DEC-E2006-056; *A Health Service Employee v Health Service Executive*, DEC-E2006-013.

[264] In *Timishev v Russia* (2007) 44 EHRR 37 (at para 58) the European Court of Human Rights established that discrimination on account of one's actual *or perceived* ethnicity is a form of racial discrimination.

O'Brien v Killarney Ryan Hotel[265] involved a complaint of discrimination on the Traveller community ground. The ground covered Mr O'Brien because even though he did not self-identify as a Traveller and had a settled way of life his parents were Travellers and so membership of that group could be imputed to him. In *Cullen v Castle Inn*[266] the complainant claimed that he was discriminated against either (i) on the basis that membership of the Traveller community was imputed to him by the respondent or (ii) because the respondent believed that he was not Irish (discrimination on the grounds of race by imputation). The equality officer did not accept 'on the balance of probabilities, that the fact that he was poorly dressed gave rise to the imputation on the respondent's part that he was a member of the Traveller community or that the fact that he was heavily tanned gave rise to discrimination, by the respondent, on the race ground by imputation' (para 6.2). Case law under the EEA has established that people who are treated less favourably because of their body mass are subjected to disability discrimination by imputation (Morgan, 2009).[267]

3.2 Proof and Evidence

3.2.1 Establishing a Prima Facie Case

Section 38A deals with the burden of proof in discrimination complaints:[268]

(1) Where in any proceedings facts are established by or on behalf of a person from which it may be presumed that prohibited conduct has occurred in relation to him or her, it is for the respondent to prove the contrary.

(2) This section is without prejudice to any other enactment or rule of law in relation to the burden of proof in any proceedings which may be more favourable to the person.

Basically, the provision puts an onus on the complainant to provide evidence from which it may be presumed that prohibited conduct has occurred. This is referred to as establishing a *prima facie* case. Equality officers in ESA cases

---

[265] DES-S2001-008.

[266] DEC-S2002-028.

[267] *A Health Service Employee v Health Service Executive*, DEC-E2006-013. On the relationship between body mass and disability discrimination see further Aphramor (2009).

[268] The provision was introduced in the Equality Act 2004 to take account of the requirements of article 8 of the Race Directive. See also article 9 and recital 22 of the Gender Goods and Services Directive.

consistently use the following Labour Court statement in explaining what a complainant must do:

> [A] claimant must prove, on the balance of probabilities, the primary facts on which they rely in seeking to raise a presumption of unlawful discrimination. It is only if those primary facts are established to the satisfaction of the Court, and they are regarded by the Court as being of sufficient significance to raise a presumption of discrimination, that the onus shifts to the respondent to prove that there was no infringement of the principle of equal treatment.[269]

A *prima facie* case of direct discrimination establishes three things:

1. The complainant is covered by the relevant discriminatory ground(s).

2. There was specific treatment by the respondent.

3. The treatment of the complainant was less favourable than the treatment that was or would have been afforded to another person (the comparator) in similar circumstances.

The standard or level of proof required is on the balance of probabilities, i.e. it must be more likely than not that the proposition is true.

As we will see below, if and when those elements are established the burden of proof shifts, meaning that the difference in treatment is assumed to be discriminatory on the relevant ground. The burden or onus is then on the respondent to rebut or disprove the inference of discrimination.[270]

Criterion 2 rests to a large extent on the evidence presented on behalf of both parties at the hearing. Frequently there will be a dispute as to what actually took place, e.g. what was said by the respondent in refusing access to a particular service.[271] In such cases the equality officer will assess the credibil-

---

[269] *Mitchell v Southern Health Board* [2001] ELR 201.

[270] This approach to the burden of proof was adopted prior to its explicit inclusion under the Equality Act 2004. In *O'Brien v Scruffys Bar, Killarney Towers Hotel*, DEC-S2002-012, having reviewed relevant case law the equality officer noted that the practice of shifting the burden of proof once a *prima facie* case has been established was 'an indigenous development in Irish discrimination law, which was in advance of Community law. There is no reason why it should be limited to employment discrimination or to the gender ground' (at para 7.1). See also *Axinte v Q-Bar Dublin*, DEC-S2004-188, citing *Mitchell v Southern Health Board* [2001] ELR 201, and *Ross v Royal & Sun Alliance Insurance plc*, DEC-S2003-116, at paras 7.1–7.4.

[271] See, for example, the very different versions of events presented by the complainants and respondents in *A Complainant v A Fast Food Franchise*, DEC-S2008-036; *Kelly v*

ity of the complainant and the respondent as well as that of any witnesses. The officer will also take into account other evidence that supports either party's version of events, such as CCTV footage, incident logbooks or reports made to third parties.[272] Frequently, there will be no overt evidence of discriminatory treatment, so that all of the surrounding circumstances need to be examined. As the House of Lords has pointed out, 'because people rarely advertise their prejudices and may not even be aware of them, discrimination has normally to be proved by inference rather than direct evidence.'[273]

Criteria 1 and 3 are interrelated in that a claimant must establish that they fall within (at least) one of the nine grounds and then compare the treatment complained of with that accorded a comparator in similar circumstances. The comparator will depend on the ground(s) in issue. Section 3(2) sets out the discriminatory grounds, specifying the categories of people against whom comparisons in treatment may be drawn:

(2) As between any two persons, the discriminatory grounds (and the descriptions of those grounds for the purposes of this Act) are:

(*a*) that one is male and the other is female (the 'gender ground'),

(*b*) that they are of different civil status (the 'civil status ground'),

(*c*) that one has family status and the other does not or that one has a different family status from the other (the 'family status ground'),

(*d*) that they are of different sexual orientation (the 'sexual orientation ground'),

(*e*) that one has a different religious belief from the other, or that one has a religious belief and the other has not (the 'religion ground'),

---

Dunhill Enterprises Ltd, DEC-S2007-007; *Ms A (on behalf of her brother, Mr B) v A General Hospital*, DEC-S2010-044; *Connors v Mothercare Ireland Ltd*, DEC-S2011-027; *Carthy v Brennan*, DEC-S2011-045; *Fizel v Health Service Executive*, DEC-S2012-001.

[272] On CCTV footage see *Sweeney v Equinox Nightclub*, DEC-S2002-031; *Connors and Wall v The Firhouse Inn*, DEC-S2007-001; *O'Brien v Mustang Sally's Pub*, DEC-S2008-052; *A Complainant v A Fast Food Franchise*, DEC-S2008-036; and *A Complainant v A Supermarket*, DEC-S2010-013. Audio recordings made secretly by complainants (i.e. without the respondent's knowledge or consent) have been admitted as evidence in some Tribunal cases: *Laurentiu v The Central Hotel*, DEC-E2010-147 and *McDonagh v McHale*, DEC-S2011-025. For a discussion of the privacy and data protection issues raised by such evidence see Compton and Dillon (2010).

[273] *R (European Roma Rights Centre) v Immigration Officer at Prague Airport* [2005] 2 AC 1. See also the comments of Hedigan J in *Iarnród Éireann v Mannion* [2010] IEHC 326, at para 11.

(*f*) subject to *subsection (3)*, that they are of different ages (the 'age ground'),

(*g*) that one is a person with a disability and the other either is not or is a person with a different disability (the 'disability ground'),

(*h*) that they are of different race, colour, nationality or ethnic or national origins (the 'ground of race'),

(*i*) that one is a member of the Traveller community and the other is not (the 'Traveller community ground')[274]

Many cases fail because although the complainants establish that they are covered by a protected ground and provide evidence of poor treatment, they do not show that that treatment was not or would not have been experienced by a comparator.[275] This vital aspect of a discrimination law claim is addressed further in the next section. Complainants can seek further information about the circumstances surrounding a possible incident of discrimination in the notification form that must be sent to a service provider within two months of that incident (Chapter 12.3.4).

3.2.2 Comparator

Direct discrimination is not aimed at all adverse treatment of people by service providers. It is only aimed at treatment that occurs on a discriminatory ground. In order to establish whether the treatment in question was related to that ground, the law requires a comparison to be made with a person who was in a similar situation but does not share the complainant's characteristic or status. The basic idea is that the reason for the treatment in question can be isolated because the difference between the two persons is the protected ground. The person used for the purposes of comparison is known as a 'comparator'.

Classically persons alleging discrimination had to point to an actual person in a comparable situation (an actual comparator) by reference to whom they received less favourable treatment. However, the Employment Equality Act 1998 sanctioned the use of a hypothetical comparator instead, i.e. a person could claim that they were treated less favourably than for example a man/

---

[274] The victimisation ground (section 3(2)(*j*)) is dealt with in Chapter 3.5.

[275] See, for example, *Walczak v Community Welfare Services, HSE West*, DEC-S2011-056 and *Jedruch v Adelaide and Meath Hospital*, DEC-S2011-058. In such cases equality officers routinely apply a Labour Court decision which emphasises that unfavourable treatment, in the absence of evidence of less favourable treatment, is insufficient to establish a *prima facie* case of discrimination under the EEA: *Valpeters v Melbury Developments Ltd* [2010] ELR 64.

settled person *would have been treated* in similar circumstances. That position was replicated in the 2000 Equal Status Act.

In the absence of an actual comparator departures from, or compliance with, standard practice are often used to evaluate the treatment afforded the complainant(s).[276] A hypothetical comparison may be especially useful in situations where all of the possible actual comparators are of the same group as the complainant (in situations where goods or services are accessed on a segregated basis). For example, where all recipients of a service are single it may be possible to argue that the treatment of the complainant was less favourable than that which would have been afforded to married people. A complainant in such a case is asserting that a general discriminatory practice operates in relation to single people (i.e. on the civil status ground). This means of using hypothetical comparators was endorsed in *McGreal v Clúid Housing*.[277] Mr McGreal was a tenant in housing provided exclusively to older people but was able to compare the treatment he received from the respondent with that which would have been afforded to a younger person. Several examples of Tribunal findings involving hypothetical comparators are dealt with below.

Since the Tribunal is an investigative forum, equality officers often construct a hypothetical comparator in order to assess whether there has been less favourable treatment. In doing so they have approved UK practice, which places tribunals and courts under a *duty* to consider introducing a hypothetical comparator where there is no suitable actual comparator.[278]

In many cases the choice of comparator is relatively straightforward. For example, a Traveller may have been refused admission to a nightclub while a group of settled people gained entry. The claim here is on the Traveller community ground, the complainant is a Traveller and the comparators are settled persons. However the appropriate comparator may not be that obvious in more complex discrimination claims. Courts have struggled with

---

[276] See, for example, *Conroy v Carney's Public House*, DEC-S2001-002; *Coffey, Quilligan and McCarthy v The Blasket Public House*, DEC-S2001-010; *McDonagh v Tesco Ireland Limited Waterford*, DEC-S2001-016; and *Stanev v Pearse College*, DEC-S2007-008. In *Eupat Ltd v Businkas* (ADE/09/28; EDA103, 13 April 2010) the Labour Court endorsed the approach adopted by the Equality Tribunal as regards the use of hypothetical comparators. The Tribunal had found that a hypothetical comparator could be used in appropriate situations such as where it is shown that the existing actual comparators were unsuitable for one reason or another. However, the existence of actual comparators could not be overlooked where there was no reason to disregard them: *Businkas v Eupat Ltd*, DEC-E2009-039.

[277] DEC-S2011-004.

[278] See, for example, *O'Brien v Iarnród Éireann*, DEC-S2003-029 (at para 7.5) citing *Balamoody v United Kingdom Central Council for Nursing, Midwifery and Health Visiting* [2002] IRLR 288 and *Shamoon v Chief Constable of the Royal Ulster Constabulary* [2003] 2 All ER 26.

identifying the appropriate comparator in cases involving transsexual people, for example (Wintemute, 1997). In a UK case, *Croft v The Royal Mail*,[279] a transsexual woman was refused permission to use the women's bathrooms at work. She was required instead to use the unisex disabled people's facilities. In effect, her claim failed because the Court found that she was not entitled to be treated as a woman from the very outset of the gender re-assignment process. The CJEU accepts that the classic comparison between a man and a woman is not appropriate in such cases. Instead, the correct comparator is a woman or man of the same gender as the complainant whose identity is not the result of gender reassignment (Chapter 3.3.4).[280] Age ground cases also raise particular difficulties (Chapter 3.3.1), as do complaints on multiple grounds (Chapter 3.3.10).

As can be seen from the decisions discussed in Chapter 3.3, cases often fail because the complainant cannot show that they were treated less favourably than someone else was or would have been *in a comparable situation*. In other words, the equality officer decides that in similar circumstances, the same treatment was or would have been encountered by a person not sharing the complainant's characteristic or status. For example, a complaint about a delay in reconnecting phone services at a halting site did not succeed because the Tribunal accepted that the respondent's inaction was due to industrial relations and planning considerations.[281] Similar difficulties would probably have occurred if the same situation had arisen in a non-Traveller estate (para 7.7).

3.2.3 Less Favourable Treatment

What constitutes 'less favourable treatment' will depend on the facts of the case. Many of the decisions address situations where a facility, benefit or service has been withheld from a complainant, or where they have been denied access to a place where services and goods are obtained. Different payment rates for a service have breached section 3(1).[282] Remarks made in the context of obtaining or seeking access to goods or services may amount

---

[279] [2003] IRLR 592.

[280] *Richards v Secretary of State for Work and Pensions*, Case C-423/04, [2006] ECR 1-3585.

[281] *McCann, Collins and 31 Others v Eircom Ltd*, DEC-S2003-076/108.

[282] See, for example, *O'Connor v The Icon Night Club*, DEC-S2004-001 and *Keane v World Travel Centre*, DEC-S2011-035. Different payment rates may be saved by section 16(1), which permits providers of goods, services and accommodation to impose or maintain a 'reasonable preferential fee, charge or rate' for persons with their children, married couples, persons in a specific age group or persons with a disability. See further Chapter 2.6.3 and Chapter 8.2.

to 'less favourable treatment'.[283] Depending on the nature of the remarks, a case of harassment or sexual harassment could also be made out (Chapter 5.4.4). Less favourable treatment can arise where a service provider deviates from standard practice and applies relatively harsh procedures to a person covered by a ground of discrimination.[284] A delay in service provision could also ground a claim of direct discrimination.[285]

A *difference* in treatment is not necessarily less favourable treatment, as illustrated by the case law considered below on dress codes in schools (Chapter 3.3.4).[286] In other words, the complainant must have experienced some form of detriment.

The UK courts consider that the denial of a choice between options that are apparently of the same value can amount to less favourable treatment. For example, in *R v Birmingham City Council ex parte Equal Opportunities Commission*[287] the Council provided fewer selective school places to girls as a whole and as a result they had to achieve higher marks than boys in an assessment in order to secure a spot. A boy who obtained equivalent results to a girl would have the option of attending a selective school, whereas she would not. The House of Lords held that this amounted to direct discrimination in spite of evidence that the education standards of selective and comprehensive schools were comparable: girls were treated less favourably because they were denied a choice that was valued by them or their parents (McColgan, 2005, p 249).

Significantly, 'less favourable treatment' does not just arise where people in comparable situations have not been treated in the same manner, it may also comprise failure to afford different treatment to persons who are differently

---

[283] See, for example *Forrestal v Hearns Hotel Clonmel*, DEC-S2001-018 and *Crawford v The Bootlegger Bar*, DEC-S2003-146/147, paras 6.8–6.9.

[284] See, for example, the 2011 decisions in *McGreal v Clúid Housing*, DEC-S2011-004 and *Mrs K (on behalf of her son) v A Primary School*, DEC-S2011-003.

[285] See section 2(3)(*b*), which provides that in 'any proceedings a respondent is presumed, unless the contrary is shown, to fail to do something when ... the period expires during which the respondent might reasonably have been expected to do it'. That subsection is discussed in *A Traveller v A Local Authority*, DEC-S2010-052. *Walczak v Minister for Social Protection*, DEC-S2012-011 addressed delays in processing applications for social welfare payments. However, the complainant was unable to demonstrate that the delays amounted to less favourable treatment. The Tribunal accepted evidence put forward by the respondent to the effect that similar treatment was experienced by all service users because of staff shortages and a substantial increase in demand for its services.

[286] See also the comments of Hunt J in *Minister for Education and Science v Hollingsworth* (Circuit Court Dublin, Hunt J, unreported, 19 October 2007), at p 85; *Walsh v Health Service Executive*, DEC-S2008-014, at para 5.2; *A Patient v Health Service Provider and a Hospital*, DEC-S2010-053, at para 6.3.4; *Fizel v Health Service Executive*, DEC-S2012-001, at para 5.5; *A Complainant v Dublin City Council*, DEC-S2012-006, at para 5.5.

[287] [1989] 1 AC 1156. See also *Gill v El Vino Co Ltd* [1983] QB 425.

situated (Reynolds, 2008).[288] One of the main decisions on this aspect of direct discrimination is that of the Labour Court in *Campbell Catering v Rasaq*.[289] A Nigerian woman was dismissed for allegedly stealing fruit. The Court concluded that she was not afforded fair procedures, and was treated less favourably than someone of different ethnicity would have been treated. It referred to decisions of the CJEU to the effect that discrimination can arise where the same rules are applied to different situations.[290] In the case of disciplinary proceedings employers should take account of the particular circumstances of foreign nationals: 'special measures may be necessary' and 'applying the same procedural standards to a non-national worker as would be applied to an Irish national ... could in itself amount to discrimination.' Arguably such decisions oblige employers to accommodate the particular needs of individuals covered by the discriminatory grounds.[291] However the precise parameters of this duty, and its application in the services context, await further case law. Clearly the obligations incurred cannot be so extensive as to fall foul of the Supreme Court judgment in *Re Article 26 of the Constitution and the Employment Equality Bill 1996*.[292] A nominal cost ceiling would, therefore, seem to implicitly apply here and so a service provider's obligations will depend on its resources and capacity (see Chapter 6.5).

---

[288] See, for example, *Maughan v The Glimmer Man Limited*, DEC-S2001-020, discussed in Chapter 3.3.2 below. Similar principles apply under the ECHR. In *Thlimmenos v Greece* (2001) 31 EHRR 15 the applicant was denied membership of the Greek Institute of Chartered Accountants because of a rule that prohibited the appointment of persons who had been convicted of criminal offences. He had a conviction for refusing to wear a military uniform, which was in turn related to his religious beliefs as a Jehovah's Witness. Essentially he argued that he had been subject to discrimination in the exercise of freedom of religion guaranteed by article 9. According to the Court: 'The right not to be discriminated against in the enjoyment of the rights guaranteed under the Convention is also violated when States without an objective and reasonable justification fail to treat differently persons whose situations are significantly different' (para 44). See also *Price v United Kingdom* (2002) 34 EHRR 53: in addressing the conditions under which a disabled woman was incarcerated, Greve J noted that 'the applicant is different from other people to the extent that treating her like others is not only discrimination but brings about a violation of Article 3' (para 113). Article 3 prohibits torture and inhuman and degrading treatment.

[289] [2004] ELR 15.

[290] *Finanzamt Köln-Altstadt v Roland Schumacker*, Case C-279/93, [1995] ECR 1-225. See also *Gillespie v Northern Health and Social Services Board*, Case C-342/93, [1996] ECR 1-475; and *Spain v Council of Ministers*, Case C-203/86, [1988] ECR 4563, at para 25.

[291] See also the employment cases of *Fifty-Eight Named Plaintiffs v Goode Concrete Limited*, DEC-E2008-020; *Panuta v Watters Garden Sheds Ltd & Watters Garden World Ltd*, DEC-E2008-059; *Golovan v Porturlin Shellfish*, DEC-E2008-032; and *Zhang v Towner Trading (t/a Spar Drimnagh)*, DEC-E2008-001.

[292] [1997] 2 IR 321.

3.2.4 Onus of Proof

Once the complainant establishes that there is evidence of less favourable treatment and that they are covered by one of the discriminatory grounds, the onus should shift to the respondent to rebut the *prima facie* case.[293] The complainant does not need to prove that there is a link between the treatment and the membership of the ground; instead the respondent has to prove that there is not.[294]

The Equality Tribunal and the Irish courts have adopted the approach to proof first set out by the UK House of Lords in a race discrimination case.[295] According to the House, where there is less favourable treatment and a difference in race there is *prima facie* evidence of discrimination and it is for the respondent to provide a non-discriminatory explanation. The Labour Court has explained the rationale in the following terms:

> This approach is based on the empiricism that a person who discriminates unlawfully will rarely do so overtly and will not leave evidence of the discrimination within the complainant's power of procurement.

> Hence, the normal rules of evidence must be adapted in such cases so as to avoid the protection of anti-discrimination laws being rendered nugatory by obliging complainants to prove something which is beyond their reach and which may only be in the respondent's capacity of proof.[296]

The ESA uses the formula adopted under the relevant EU directives in that direct discrimination is less favourable 'on the ground' of age, disability and so on. In the 1990s the UK courts found that the equivalent phrase 'on grounds

---

[293] A court or tribunal can take into account evidence put forward by the respondent in deciding whether the complainant has established a *prima facie* case: *Dyflin Publications Ltd v Spasic* (ADE/08/7; EDA/08/23, 19 December 2008) (adopting the approach of Mummery LJ in *Madarassy v Nomura International plc* [2007] IRLR 246; applied in *Olaijde v Buck Properties Ltd*, DEC-S2010-021).

[294] See, for example, *Crawford v The Bootlegger Bar*, DEC-S2003-146/147, para 6.1; *Ross v Royal and Sun Alliance*, DEC-S2003-116, at para 7.1; and *A Nigerian National v A Financial Institution*, DEC-S2005-114, at para 7.1.

[295] *Glasgow City Council v Zafar* [1998] 2 All ER 953; approved by the High Court in *Davis v Dublin Institute of Technology* (High Court, Quirke J, unreported, 23 June 2000) and in *Iarnród Éireann v Mannion* [2010] IEHC 326. See also *Igen Ltd v Wong* [2005] 3 All ER 812 and *Madarassy v Nomura International plc* [2007] IRLR 246.

[296] *Ntoko v Citibank* [2004] ELR 116; applied in *McGreal v Clúid Housing*, DEC-S2011-004 and *Bisayeva v Westend Management Ltd*, DEC-S2011-030. See also the employment case of *Nevins & Others v Portroe Stevedores* [2005] ELR 282.

of' covers not just situations where someone deliberately treats a person in a less favourable manner because of a protected characteristic, but also situations where criteria based upon protected characteristics form the basis, or part of the basis, of the decision to treat an individual less favourably.[297] According to Goff LJ in *James v Eastleigh Borough Council*, this approach avoids 'complicated questions relating to concepts such as intention, motive, reason or purpose …'.[298]

The Equality Tribunal adopted the same position from the outset. For example, in a 2001 decision[299] the equality officer referred to the wording of the Equal Status Act 2000 and also considered the persuasive effect of the *James* case in finding that intention to discriminate was not a necessary condition to liability. This is not to say however that motive is irrelevant. As Bell (2007, p 233) points out:

> Often answering the question why someone was treated less favourably leads back in the direction of the respondent's motive. Where evidence of (for example) racial prejudice is present, this may indeed contribute to establishing the existence of direct discrimination. Nevertheless the absence of such proof, or alternatively proof of a non-prejudicial motive, should not be a stumbling block to a finding of direct discrimination.[300]

A respondent may even have perceived the discriminatory treatment as benign. For instance, in two disability ground cases the respondents reported that they were seeking to protect the complainant but were nonetheless found to have discriminated.[301]

In *McGreal v Clúid Housing* the equality officer found that a decision to evict a tenant raised a *prima facie* case of discrimination on the age ground because it followed an unsubstantiated complaint of elder abuse lodged by the complainant with other people.[302] It appears that the Tribunal is interpret-

---

[297] *James v Eastleigh Borough Council* [1990] 2 AC 751 and *Shamoon v Chief Constable of the RUC* [2003] 2 All ER 26.

[298] [1990] 2 AC 751, 774.

[299] *Collins v Bartra House Hotel*, DEC-S2001-015, citing *James v Eastleigh Borough Council* [1990] 2 AC 751. Intent is not required to establish discrimination either under the ECHR: *Jordan v United Kingdom* (2003) 37 EHRR 2, para 154.

[300] See also *R (E) v Governing Body of JFS and Anor* [2010] 2 AC 728, in which the UK Supreme Court found that an inquiry into a respondent's motive could assist in less obvious discrimination cases, but only for the purposes of finding out the ground of the treatment.

[301] *Cementwala v Colbert, Winters Property Management & Crescent Green Ltd*, DEC-S2005-184/186 and *A Complainant v An Irish Language College*, DEC-S2010-027.

[302] DEC-S2011-004.

ing 'on the ground' of age as including a decision that is based partly on a characteristic protected under the ESA. The relationship between the parties was 'extremely fractious' and a number of the respondent's employees were upset by their dealings with the complainant, but the eviction process was also influenced by the elder abuse allegation.

To summarise, the respondent need not have been motivated by prejudice or have intended to treat someone less favourably because of their gender, ethnicity and so on.[303] Furthermore, discrimination need not be the sole or even the principal factor behind the conduct complained of. It is enough that it is a significant influence.[304]

3.2.5 Rebuttal

Once a complainant has established a *prima facie* case the burden of proof shifts to the respondent. The respondent must rebut or counter the established inference of discrimination. In many cases the respondent tries to do so by supplying evidence which demonstrates that the treatment was not 'on' a discriminatory ground. A service provider might establish, for example, that all persons accessing the service in question were subject to similar treatment. They will usually do so by showing that standard practice was applied to any engagement with the complainant. Statistical evidence may also be introduced by service providers seeking to rebut a finding of discrimination. For example, in considering a claim of discrimination on the gender and marital status grounds in the allocation of housing the equality officer had regard to the patterns of decisions involving single men over the course of years:

> I note from the evidence adduced that the respondent has received 946 applications for housing during the period from 1997 to 2007

---

[303] See, for example, *Kearney v Budget Car and Van Rental*, DEC-S2007-090; *Lindberg v Press Photographers Association of Ireland*, DEC-S2011-041; *Nevins & Others v Portroe Stevedores* [2005] ELR 282; *Southern Health Board v A Worker* [1999] ELR 322 (citing *Dekker v VJV Centrum*, Case C-177/88, [1990] ECR 1-3941 and *Draehmpaehl v Urania Immobilienservice*, Case C-180/95, [1997] ECR 1-2195). See also the following UK cases: *R (European Roma Rights Centre) v Immigration Officer at Prague Airport* [2004] 2 AC 1; and *R (E) v Governing Body of JFS & Anor* [2010] 2 AC 728.

[304] See *McKeever v Board of Management, Knocktemple National School*, DEC-E2010-189, para 6.8; *A Construction Worker v A Construction Company*, DEC-E2008-048, para 5.6; *Nevins & Others v Portroe Stevedores* [2005] ELR 282; and *Lindberg v Press Photographers Association of Ireland*, DEC-S2011-041, para 4.4.4. In *Nagarajan v London Regional Transport* [1999] 4 All ER 65, Neill LJ interpreted the 'on grounds of' test as providing that if a protected characteristic 'had a significant influence on the outcome, discrimination is made out'. See also *Igen Ltd v Wong* [2005] 3 All ER 812 cited in *Ely Property Group Ltd v Boyle*, ADE/09/18; EDA/0920, 15 October 2009.

and that only 80 of these applicants have been allocated housing during this period. I also note that, of the 80 applicants that have been allocated housing during this period, a total of 14 applicants were single at the time of allocation (and of the same marital status to the complainant) and a further breakdown of this figure reveals that 10 of the 14 were single males (and of the same gender as the complainant) and the remaining 4 were female applicants. I am satisfied that these statistics demonstrate that the respondent does not operate a discriminatory policy against single male applicants.[305]

This evidence enabled the Council to rebut the inference of discrimination established by the complainant. His *prima facie* case relied to a great extent on the fact that a note stating 'single male not recommended' was included on the complainant's application following an assessment by a housing officer.

Respondents may also rebut an inference of discrimination by availing of a defence or an exemption. Treatment that would ordinarily amount to direct discrimination may fall within one of the numerous exemptions provided for under the ESA (Chapters 2.5–2.6).

Where a complainant fails to attend the hearing of his/her complaint a *prima facie* case will not be established and so the Tribunal will find in favour of the respondent.[306]

3.3 Case Law

3.3.1 Age

Age discrimination can take many forms. It might for example involve the application of numeric age limits or brackets, e.g. 'over 35s only'. Less favourable treatment may also be related to general life stages (e.g. older, younger or middle-aged people) or to bio-medical criteria (e.g. fertility, puberty or menopause).

Section 3(2)(*f*) does not provide guidance on the boundaries of age-based comparison; it just states that the complainant and comparator must be 'of different ages'. As a result the type of comparison to be drawn will very much depend on the facts. An eighteen-year-old man who was refused service in a pub because of negative behaviour on the part of other eighteen-year-olds in the past won a discrimination case in 2005.[307] The comparators were his

---

[305] *Mr X v A Town Council*, DEC-S2008-042, at para 4.4. See also *Cleary v Dublin City Council*, DEC-S2009-028 and *Cleary v Waterford City Council*, DEC-S2010-003.
[306] See, for example, the Director's finding to that effect in *A Named Individual v A Named Detective Garda Immigration Office, An Garda Síochána, Limerick*, DEC-S2004-187.
[307] *Madden v Quinlan's Public House*, DEC-S2005-113. A difference in age of two days

nineteen-year-old friends who were allowed into the pub. In that case the age criterion was used openly and communicated to the complainant, and so he had little difficulty in establishing that he was treated less favourably than someone of a different age. In many cases service providers will not use age-related factors overtly, but an individual may still believe that the treatment they experienced was related to their age. In those types of cases the age difference between the complainant and comparator may have to be sizeable in order to demonstrate that age was an operative reason for the detrimental treatment. In an employment case, *Superquinn v Freeman*,[308] the Labour Court found that an age gap of three years was not significant enough to establish a presumption of discrimination in the absence of other facts supporting that inference. Eight years was considered a 'significant' disparity in another Labour Court case, which also involved procedural irregularities at an interview including the destruction of interview notes.[309]

Children cannot refer direct discrimination complaints on the age ground, and several other exceptions allow age-based differences in treatment (Chapter 2.6.2.2). Section 5(2)(*j*) sanctions the use of an age requirement for eligibility as an adoptive or foster parent, where the requirement is reasonable having regard to the needs of the child or children concerned. There is no statutory upper age *limit* for adoptive parents, but the applicants' ages is a factor that the Adoption Authority must take into account in making an adoption order or in recognising an inter-country adoption.[310] In practice, many adoption agencies apply an upper age restriction (Department of Health and Children, 2005, pp 38–42) and it would seem that such a criterion is saved by the exception under the ESA provided it is not applied rigidly and takes account of the individual circumstances of the child or children in question.

Third level educational establishments are free to reserve places for mature students, that is, students who are 23 years of age or over in the year they apply for a place.[311]

Access to licensed premises, such as pubs and nightclubs, has featured in a number of age ground cases, with the complainants usually representing the upper and lower ends of the age spectrum.[312] It is not discriminatory to apply a minimum age threshold (other than the legal minimum of eighteen)

---

was adequate in a case concerning an age threshold for a voluntary retirement scheme: *Perry v The Garda Commissioner*, DEC-E2001-029.

[308] AEE/02/8, DEE02/11 (Labour Court, 14 November 2002).

[309] *Reynolds v Limerick County Council* (ADE/03/14; EDA/048, 31 May 2004).

[310] Section 34(*b*) Adoption Act 2010.

[311] Section 7(3)(*e*). See section 2 of the Local Authorities (Higher Education Grants) Act 1992.

[312] See, for example, *Scanlon and Ryan v The Russell Court Hotel*, DEC-S2001-013; *Madden v Quinlan's Public House*, DEC-S2005-113; *O'Reilly v Q Bar*, DEC-S2002-013;

in relation to selling alcoholic drinks, e.g. an over 21 only policy, provided that a notice to that effect is displayed in a prominent place and the policy is implemented in good faith.[313] A remark made by a doorman to the effect that the complainants, a 29-year-old and a 36-year-old, were 'too old' to gain entry to a bar and restaurant amounted to less favourable treatment on the age ground.[314] The case establishes that implementing a preference for clientele consisting of, for example, 'younger women and older men' is not acceptable under the ESA. It should be noted that complaints about discrimination on or at the point of entry to licensed premises must be referred to the District Court (Chapter 12.2).

One of the most significant cases on the age ground to date is that of *Ross v Royal & Sun Alliance Insurance plc*[315] The equality officer found that a company's 'across the board' policy of refusing motor insurance to persons aged over 70 was unlawful. Mr Ross was 77 when he sought and was refused a quote. He established a *prima facie* case of direct discrimination on the age ground and the insurance company tried to rebut the presumption by relying on an exemption under section 5(2)(*d*) for differences in treatment related to actuarial or statistical data (see Chapter 2.6.4.4). The equality officer explained that in order to avail of the exemption the respondents had to show that the treatment of Mr Ross was:

(1) 'effected by reference to actuarial or statistical data' which was 'obtained from a source on which it is reasonable to rely' AND 'is reasonable having regard to the data or other relevant factors' OR (2) 'is effected by reference to other relevant underwriting or commercial factors' AND 'is reasonable having regard to the data or other relevant factors'. In order to fall within the Section 5(2)(d) exemption, I consider that the respondents must show that they fully satisfy either test (1) or test (2) above (para 7.7).

Similarly, in *Fahey v Ulster Bank*[316] the complainant, a long-standing customer of the respondent bank, was not granted a car loan on the basis that she was over 65. Ulster Bank denied that Ms Fahey was informed by any of its officials that it operated such a policy. However, the equality officer determined that the complainant's account of the telephone conversation in question was

---

Duggan v The Castle Inn, Rathfarnham, DEC-S2003-142; and *Thornton v Turner's Cross Tavern*, DEC-S2004-142.

[313] Section 15(4). This exception was introduced by section 25 of the Intoxicating Liquor Act 2003.

[314] *Crawford v The Bootlegger Bar*, DEC-S2003-146/147.

[315] DEC-S2003-116.

[316] DEC-S2008-049.

more accurate. He was satisfied that Ms Fahey had been left in no doubt that her application for a loan was declined on the basis of her age. The equality officer found that the respondent did not adhere to its standard loan application procedures and Ms Fahey was not invited for an interview to discuss her application. Compensation of €2,000 was awarded. Niall Crowley, in his capacity as Chief Executive of the Equality Authority, welcomed the finding and observed:

> This case presents a challenge to financial institutions to review their policies and practices so as to eliminate any discrimination under the Equal Status Acts. Allegations of discrimination by financial institutions accounted for 10% of Equality Authority casefiles under the Equal Status Acts in 2007 (33 out of 328 casefiles). This is the sector with the highest level of such allegations, outside of the public sector.[317]

As with all cases of less favourable treatment, age ground complaints may fail where age was not an operative factor underlying the treatment concerned. For example, in *Murphy v Champion Lettings*[318] the complainant was not permitted to lease a property because it was withdrawn from the rental market and not because of his status as an old age pensioner. Exceptions may also protect the application of age-related criteria, such as in *Dalton v Limerick City Council*,[319] which concerned a local authority's refuse charges. The Council charged householders a set fee for weekly collection of refuse contained in a standard size bin provided by the Council. People aged over 65 (provided they lived alone, or with only one other person who was also aged over 65) could avail of a preferential rate if they used a smaller size bin. Mr Dalton wanted to use the smaller bin and maintained that he should be entitled to the preferential rate even though he was aged under 65. He argued that the Council's failure to extend the rate to him amounted to discrimination on the age ground. The equality officer was satisfied that the exception under section 16(1)(*a*) of the Equal Status Act applied to this practice. It provides that 'imposing or maintaining a reasonable preferential fee, charge or rate' regarding persons in a specific age group does not constitute discrimination (see further Chapter 8.2).

The fact that direct discrimination is limited to relative treatment of people linked to a ground and does not confer a right to a particular service is apparent

---

[317] See press release dated 28 August 2008 on the Authority's website: <http://www.equality.ie/>.

[318] DEC-S2010-041.

[319] DEC-S2004-042.

from *Cronin v Health Service Executive*.[320] Discrimination on the age ground was not established where a fitness to drive test availed of by an older man was not covered by the respondent's medical card scheme. There was no discriminatory treatment as all medical card holders had to pay for such a service; the question of whether the requirement to obtain a certificate of fitness in the first place was contrary to the ESA could not be investigated as the HSE was not responsible for that policy.

McGreal v Clúid Housing[321] examined several allegations of discriminatory treatment encountered by an older man in accessing the services provided by a voluntary housing association. While many of the reported instances of less favourable treatment were not proven, the Tribunal found that the eviction of a tenant without giving reasons for the decision and inviting the complainant to respond amounted to direct discrimination. The respondent maintained that the decision was not influenced by the complainant's age but was taken because he was extremely difficult to deal with and had upset staff consistently. The equality officer accepted that the relationship between the complainant and staff was very poor but concluded that a younger person would not have been treated in the same manner. The procedure adopted was 'extraordinary' and at variance with standard practice in social housing. It also followed a complaint of elder abuse made by the complainant and other tenants. For those reasons the equality officer concluded that the respondent had 'been unable to demonstrate that their actions were untainted by discrimination on the grounds of age' (para 4.4).

Echoing studies from other countries, research carried out by the National Council on Ageing and Older People (2005) uncovered significant evidence of discriminatory treatment of older people in the health and social services context.[322] The study comprised a literature review as well as interviews and focus groups with a substantial number of older people and staff. Participants reported several practices that could amount to direct discrimination, including dismissive attitudes on the part of healthcare professionals, upper age limits for certain treatments and a lack of referrals for specialist services.

The Equality Authority was involved in the resolution of a complaint in 2008 concerning the Motorised Transport Grant operated by the HSE (Equality Authority, 2009a, p 24). A woman was refused payment because she did not satisfy the criteria that set a maximum age limit of under 66 years. Significantly, the upper age limit was removed following correspondence

---

[320] DEC-S2009-080.

[321] DEC-S2011-004.

[322] UK literature on ageism in healthcare and social services includes Healthcare Commission (2009) and Mental Health Foundation (2009). See Filinson (2008) on the need for appropriate legislation.

between the Authority, the HSE and the Department of Health and Children (the Department had set the criteria). This settlement was relied upon by the Ombudsman in support of her finding that the 'upper age limit applying to Mobility Allowance is illegal and has been since the commencement of the Equal Status Act in October 2000' (Office of the Ombudsman, 2011a, p 14).

Access to medical treatment may well arise in future age ground cases. For example, programmes such as breast cancer screening are limited to those falling within a specified age group.[323] Where the age condition is not set out in law it would be open to challenge under the ESA. The Health Service Executive (HSE) or other service provider may try to avail of the exception concerning the exercise of a clinical judgment in connection with the diagnosis of illness or medical treatment (Chapter 2.6.4.5). However, it would seem from the wording of the provision that the exception applies to an individual and not to an entire class of people. According to the Equality Authority (2005a, p 10) it should apply on 'a case by case basis and cannot be used to justify a general practice, policy or approach'. Depending on how broadly it is interpreted, the clinical judgment exception could still prove an impediment where healthcare decisions are not based on express age limits.

3.3.2 Disability

Many of the successful cases to date on this ground involve discrimination as between persons with different disabilities.[324] When a claim of direct discrimination on the disability ground is raised it is standard practice for the investigating equality officer to also consider the application of the reasonable accommodation provision (Chapter 6).

Amongst other issues, *Maughan v The Glimmer Man Limited*[325] involved an initial refusal to serve a man with a guide dog in a pub. The equality officer recognised that a case of direct discrimination could be sustained where a respondent failed to treat persons differently (as did the Labour Court in *Rasaq*; see Chapter 3.2.3).

> I am satisfied that if a person brought a dog, which was not a guide dog, into the respondent's premises they would not have been served in line with the respondent's no dogs policy. On the face of it, therefore, the complainant was not treated less favourably because he

---

[323] <http://www.breastcheck.ie/>.
[324] In addition to those cases discussed here see also *Ms A (on behalf of her sister Ms B) v Aer Lingus*, DEC-S2009-038 and *A Complainant v A Local Authority*, DEC-S2007-049, which is considered in Chapter 6.4.4.3.
[325] DEC-S2001-020.

was treated the same as anyone else with a dog would have been treated. However, because of his visual impairment the complainant was not in the same circumstances as someone else with a dog who was not visually impaired. This difference is important and to quote the European Court of Justice ruling in the case of *Gillespie and others v Northern Health and Social Services Boards and others* (Case no. C-342/93) 'discrimination involves the application of different rules to comparable situations, or the application of the same rules to different situations'. This principle is supported by the ruling in the US Supreme Court case of *Jenness v Fortsom* (403 US 431 (1971)) and the rulings in the Irish Supreme Court cases of *O'Brien v Keogh* 1972 IR 144) and *de Burca v Attorney General* (1976 IR 38) (para 9.7).

The equality officer went on to suggest that the duty to reasonably accommodate under section 4 was a particular application of that general principle. On the facts the Tribunal found that there was no direct discrimination on the disability ground or breach of section 4. Once the complainant advised the bar staff that the dog was a guide dog and showed them a card on access produced by the Irish Guide Dogs for the Blind the usual policy was not applied. As discussed further in Chapter 6, denial of services to people accompanied by guide dogs will usually amount to a failure to afford reasonable accommodation.

Kelly v Kelly's Lounge[326] also involved a pub customer. In that case a young man with Down syndrome was discriminated against on the disability ground. A bar manager removed the complainant's drink and told him that he would have to sit with his mother if he wished to remain in the pub. This incident was apparently prompted by the complainant calling the bar manager several times. At the hearing of the complaint the manager acknowledged that he would not have treated a non-disabled customer in the same manner.

We now turn to look at two complaints concerning transport. Cases involving social welfare allowances are then reviewed followed by a discussion of important education cases on the disability ground.

Kearney v Budget Car and Van Rental[327] concerned a refusal to rent a car to a disabled man. The complainant's disability visibly affected his hands and feet but he worked in the motor industry and had a full driving licence for approximately 30 years. Nonetheless, when he arrived at the respondent's desk to collect a car he had booked online the company would not release the vehicle to him and suggested that his girlfriend hire the car instead. At the hearing

---

[326] DEC-S2003-161.
[327] DEC-S2007-090.

the respondent argued that the decision was made because the employee on duty at the time was unable to obtain clarification from its insurers that the complainant was covered to drive the vehicle. The Tribunal accepted that the employee did not intentionally set out to discriminate and was acting in good faith. However, his concerns were 'totally ill-founded and misconceived, and were at variance with the standard requirements that the respondent imposed on a person in order to hire a car' (para 5.2). The respondent was required to pay the complainant €4,500 in compensation and to have all staff trained in the terms and application of the ESA.

Safety concerns were raised in *Twomey v Aer Lingus*.[328] The complainant, a wheelchair user, had requested seating in the bulkhead area of an aircraft in advance of a flight. However, upon arrival at the check-in desk she discovered that she was to seated in a section that would have required two transfers (over an armrest and then across the adjacent seat) for her to use the toilet facilities or, if required, to evacuate the plane in the case of an emergency. Aer Lingus maintained its policy was not discriminatory but mandated by safety regulations, which stipulated that reduced mobility passengers should not occupy seats near emergency exits. However, the equality officer noted that the respondent's policy was inconsistent: the bulkhead area was occupied by passengers with infants who might cause an obstruction in the event of an emergency evacuation. The complainant had also been allocated a seat in that area on previous occasions. He concluded that the bulkhead area was not in fact located near an emergency exit but was used as a priority seating area for certain passengers. This conclusion was reinforced by the fact that the respondent had revised its seating policy following Ms Twomey's complaint so that reduced mobility passengers could be accommodated in the bulk-head area. The complaint of direct discrimination on the disability ground was upheld and the complainant was awarded €1,000 compensation for that element of the case.

Noonan v Price, Appeals Officer, HSE South[329] illustrated a point made in the introduction to this book, that is, the ESA is concerned with the relative treatment of individuals as opposed to granting people substantive rights to a particular good or service.[330] Because of a mobility impairment the complainant required taxis to travel to and from the doctor and to bring her shopping. Prior to the introduction of the Mobility Allowance by the HSE she was able

---

[328] DEC-S2009-079.

[329] DEC-S2007-076.

[330] Similarly, a complaint about the suitability of a care package to meet the complainant's needs was not amenable to review under the ESA in the absence of evidence of *discriminatory* treatment: *Kilduff v Health Service Executive*, DEC-S2009-019. On the age ground see *Cronin v Health Service Executive*, DEC-S2009-080.

to claim refunds for her taxi journeys through her Supplementary Welfare Allowance. Her application for the Mobility Allowance was refused and the respondent upheld this decision on appeal. She claimed that the decision was discriminatory because the HSE did not take the severity of her condition into account. The HSE pointed out that the test for qualification involved two criteria: a means test and a medical examination. Ms Noonan's condition did not satisfy the medical criteria. The equality officer found that there was no *prima facie* case of discrimination on the disability ground. However, she found that the medical criteria set out in the test for qualification for the Mobility Allowance were very narrow. She made a non-binding recommendation to the HSE that Ms Noonan be accommodated in any future applications she might make, given that her condition was progressive in nature.

By contrast, *Quigley v Health Service Executive*[331] involved a successful claim of direct discrimination in relation to the operation of the Mobility Allowance scheme. The complainant was affected by schizophrenia, agoraphobia and depression in such a manner that he was unable to use public transport and relied on two taxi drivers he was personally familiar with to travel to outpatient services. He contended that he was treated less favourably than a person with a different form of disability would be treated when his application for the Mobility Allowance was refused. The equality officer agreed:

> Having considered the wording of the actual Circular and the evidence in relation to the assessment process, I note that there is an obvious failure to assess the intellectual and/or psychological capacity of the applicant in relation to their mobility. I find that the current clinical assessment does not, in its current format, allow for assessment that is compatible with the broad definition of disability as set out in the Equal Status Acts. The concept of mobility in the circular is construed in such a narrow manner that it fails to recognise that in some severe cases a person's intellectual and/or psychological health may restrict their mobility as effectively as some physical disabilities do. I find that this is a clear omission and it is obvious that the Mobility Allowance has not been updated to comply with the requirements set out in the Equal Status Acts (enacted in October 2000). The complainant, in order for him not to have been less favourably treated than a person with a physical disability, should have had his psychological ability in relation to his mobility assessed. This ability should be assessed alongside the physical assessment procedures based on the clinical judgment of a medical officer (para 5.7).

---

[331] DEC-S2009-012.

Mr Quigley was awarded €1,500 for the effects of the discrimination and the equality officer further ordered that the HSE re-assess his application in light of the broad definition of disability set out under the ESA. On appeal the Circuit Court overturned the Tribunal's decision, but the HSE did not dispute the finding of disability discrimination as such. Instead the appeal addressed a technical matter, that is, whether the HSE had acted as agent for the Department of Health in applying the terms of a Department of Health circular (Chapter 7.2.3).[332]

In a similar 2009 decision the equality officer also found in favour of the complainant.[333] She distinguished *Noonan v Price* essentially on the basis that the case before her did not concern assessment findings in relation to a physical disability provided for under the Department of Health circular in question. Rather it challenged the omission from the scheme of an intellectual disability that could have a similar impact on a person's mobility as the physical conditions listed under the circular. Again, the equality officer found that the definition of 'disability' in issue was not broad enough to ensure non-discrimination as between persons with different forms of disability. Following an appeal it was agreed by the parties that the Tribunal's decision should not stand given the outcome of the *Quigley* case (Office of the Ombudsman, 2011a, p 11). Although both complaints were ultimately unsuccessful the interpretation of disability discrimination holds and may be used by complainants in similar cases. Indeed, the Ombudsman relied on the Tribunal's findings in an investigation of a complaint about the upper age limit used in the Mobility Allowance scheme (Office of the Ombudsman, 2011a, p 11). She found that confining eligibility to people aged under 66 ran counter to the ESA and recommended that 'the Department of Health completes its review of the Mobility Allowance scheme and, arising from that review, revises the scheme so as to render it compliant with the Equal Status Act 2000' (Office of the Ombudsman, 2011a, p 23). As of July 2012 it appears that both the age restriction and the limited mobility criteria remain in place.[334]

As discussed further in Chapter 6.7, complaints of disability discrimination involving failure to provide reasonable accommodation feature at all levels of the education sector. *Mrs Kn (on behalf of her son Mr Kn) and Others v The Minister for Education and Science*[335] is a highly significant finding of direct discrimination on the disability ground. Four complaints were referred about

---

[332] *Health Service Executive v Quigley* (Circuit Court Dublin, Linnane J, unreported, 26 April 2010).

[333] *A Complainant v Health Service Executive (South)*, DEC-S2009-011.

[334] See <http://www.hse.ie/eng/services/Find_a_Service/entitlements/Disability_Services/Mobility_Allowance.html>.

[335] DEC-S2009-050.

a Department of Education policy which required students attending so-called 'special schools' to leave school at the end of the year in which they reached their eighteenth birthday. Because of that requirement the complainants had taken various steps to ensure that they would be able to complete their Leaving Certificates by the age of eighteen. Some had spent less time than was needed at primary level, while others had skipped a year of their second level education. The equality officer identified the appropriate comparator in each case as being someone without a disability or with a different disability who attends a mainstream secondary school and is also pursuing an accredited programme of education (i.e. the Junior Certificate or the Leaving Certificate/Applied Leaving Certificate). The requirement as to school-leaving age was only imposed on students attending special schools and meant that the complainants were treated less favourably than those comparators. One of the complainants, Mr Kn, was in a position to provide a direct comparator. His twin sister, who did not have a learning disability and attended a mainstream school, had started primary school on the same day as her brother. Whereas Kn had to skip a year to complete his second level education, his twin sister was due to complete her second level course at age nineteen without restriction. The Department of Education was ordered to pay compensation totalling €10,000 and to review its policy accordingly. It has appealed the Tribunal's decision to the Circuit Court.

Another complaint about the same policy was not successful: *Mrs Cr (on behalf of her daughter Miss Cr) v The Minister for Education and Science.*[336] The equality officer made a distinction between students who are undertaking an educational programme leading to accreditation and those who are not. He accepted the Department's rationale for the policy in the case of the complainant as she was pursuing an educational programme that was designed to meet her individual requirements:

> The respondent's evidence was that the policy which requires the complainant to leave the special school at this juncture was based on sound, reasonable and rational considerations involving the interests of the pupil, the other pupils in the special schools, other children with special educational needs and resource implications. I have also noted that the Minister has determined that the most appropriate and efficient way to use resources is to provide for education in special schools up to the age of eighteen and then to provide for ongoing education, if necessary or appropriate, through the Department of Health and Children/HSE. I accept that this policy may be entirely appropriate in the situation of a student at a special school who has

---

[336] DEC-S2009-051.

reached the age of eighteen years and who is not pursuing an accredited course of education such as the Leaving Certificate Applied. In
such cases it may well be beneficial and in the best interests of that
particular student (depending on their individual circumstances) to
transfer from the special school to adult services at the end of the year
in which he/she has reached the age of eighteen years (para 6.10).

In effect, the equality officer found that the complainant in this case was not in
a comparable situation to that of students in mainstream schools: participants
in non-accredited courses of education are not subject to the same requirements in terms of having to complete a course of education within a defined
period of time. The decision illustrates the difficulties with pursuing discrimination claims faced by people who access goods or services in a segregated
environment (Woulfe, 2010, p 70).

The admissions policy of an Irish language school was challenged in a
2010 case.[337] A young woman with dyslexia was refused access to a course
on the basis that her disability would preclude her effective participation. The
college contended that it was not in a position to put in place the supports that
would enable the complainant to undergo the studies in question. However, the
complainant had consistently reiterated that she did not require any assistance
or supports. The equality officer found that the college had directly discriminated on the disability ground by forming an opinion as to the complainant's
capacities that was unsubstantiated by any evidence.

Finally, *A Post-Leaving Certificate Student v An Educational Institution*[338]
is another significant case concerning an educational establishment. A college
tried to rely on section 7(4)(*b*) to justify the exclusion of a disabled student
from certain classes and his placement on an individualised programme.
Section 7(4)(*b*) provides that the discrimination prohibition does not apply 'to
the extent that compliance with any of its provisions in relation to a student
with a disability would, by virtue of the disability, make impossible, or have a
seriously detrimental effect on, the provision by an educational establishment
of its services to other students' (Chapter 2.6.2.5). Evidence was presented
to the effect that the complainant's demeanour was hostile and disruptive.
The equality officer found that the actions taken by the respondent amounted
to less favourable treatment since the alternative programme was of lesser
duration and the student's progress had been affected. He was satisfied that
the decision to exclude was clearly influenced by the complainant's disability (Asperger syndrome) and that a student with no disability (or a different
disability) would have been given access to disciplinary or other procedures

---

[337] *A Complainant v An Irish Language College*, DEC-S2010-027.
[338] DEC-S2009-043.

and so afforded the chance to have the matter resolved in a formal manner. When considering whether the less favourable treatment was saved by the exception, the equality officer said that as 'instruments of social legislation, the Equal Status Acts must be interpreted in a purposive way. That is to say that, in the current context, any exemptions must be construed narrowly in light of the purposes of the Acts, whose primary purpose is the prevention of discrimination' (para 5.10). The evidence put forward by the respondent was scrutinised carefully. For instance, little weight was attached to letters that had been written by teachers *after* the discrimination complaint was referred. The equality officer also noted that no other students had made formal complaints, that no action had been taken following an allegation of physical intimidation directed at a teacher and that the allegation had not been put to the student. He accepted that the student's behaviour had been disruptive and that some action to deal with it was warranted. But he concluded that the respondent was 'unable to provide any convincing evidence that the complainant's behaviour was so serious and was having such a detrimental impact on the education of other students that it was obliged to take the discriminatory action …. As the onus is on the respondent to show that it was left with no choice but to avail of the provisions of Section 7(4)(*b*), it has therefore failed in that regard' (para 5.12).

3.3.3 Family Status

The definition of 'family status' refers to three distinct categories of people:

1. Those who can be classified as 'being pregnant'

2. Parents of children and people acting *in loco parentis*

3. Parents or the resident primary carers of people with a disability who require care or support on a continuing, regular or frequent basis

It is clear from the formulation of the ground under section 3(2)(*c*) that comparisons may be drawn across those sub-categories. A pregnant woman could, for example, compare the treatment she was afforded by a service provider with that of a parent of a child. Comparisons may also be made between a person with family status and a person without such a status. The ground is defined as 'that one has family status and the other does not or that one has a different family status from the other'. However, it is not clear whether comparators can be drawn from *within* the same category used in the definition. For example, could a grandparent acting *in loco parentis* base a discrimination complaint on the fact that he is not afforded a social welfare benefit that is available to the child's father or mother? Both sets of people fall within category 2 above. The decisions in *Twomey v Aer Lingus*[339] and *A Separated Complainant v A Hospital*[340] suggest that such comparisons are not possible.[341] The matter may instead have to be pursued under the ECHR Act 2003. Discrimination as between different categories of foster parents was examined in a UK case under the Human Rights Act 1998. The Court found that the local authority practice of lower payment rates for kinship carers than foster carers was unlawful discrimination.[342]

Much of the case law on the ground to date involves access to service providers' premises. *Shanahan v One Pico Restaurant*[343] involved refusal to admit a family with a baby to a restaurant. The discriminatory action was not saved by arguments that the restaurant was unsuitable and catered mostly for corporate clients (Chapter 2.6.4.3).[344] A number of successful cases on the ground have involved the admission of people accompanied by children to pubs.[345] However, the Intoxicating Liquor Act 2003 introduced amendments to the ESA so that the exercise of a licensee's discretion not to permit a person under fifteen accompanied by parent or guardian to be in a pub shall not of itself constitute discrimination.[346]

A complaint was referred by a woman who was refused admission to an auctioneer's premises because she was accompanied by her five-year-old

---

[339] DEC-S2009-079, para 6.10.

[340] DEC-S2010-046, para 5.4. See also *A Separated Father v A Community School*, DEC-S2010-049, para 6.2.

[341] But see *Flanagan Talbot v Casino Cinemas Limited t/a Killarney Cineplex Cinema*, DEC-S2008-053, where a person with family status because she was caring for her two-year-old child could compare her treatment with someone whose child was over two (para 4.7).

[342] *R (L and others) v Manchester City Council* [2002] 1 FLR 43.

[343] DEC-S2003-056. See also *Curtis v Lotamore Ltd t/a The Barn Restaurant*, DEC-S2003-154.

[344] See also *Keogh v Finegan's Bar and Lounge Carlow*, DEC-S2007-061.

[345] See, for example, *Maughan v The Glimmer Man Limited*, DEC-S2001-020; *Travers and Maunsell v Ball Alley House*, DEC-S2003-109/110; *Barry v Richardsons Pub*, DEC-S2004-020; *Reddin and Gilroy v Ryan's Bar and Restaurant*, DEC-S2004-194/195; *James v Stanalees Services Ltd t/a The Traders Pub, Dublin*, DEC-S2004-208; and *Callanan v O'Driscoll's Public House, Wicklow*, DEC-S2006-011.

[346] See section 25 of the 2003 Act. Section 14 of that Act prohibits persons under eighteen from entering licensed premises. However, under subsection (2), a licensee can permit a child aged under fifteen to be in the bar *before 9 p.m.* if accompanied by a parent or guardian. Subsection (4) gives licensees discretion to allow a person aged fifteen to seventeen or a child accompanied by a parent or guardian to be in the bar after 9.00 p.m. on the occasion of a private function at which a substantial meal is served to persons attending the function, e.g. a wedding reception. For a discussion of the exact dates on which the new provisions came into force see *Grogan v Crocketts on the Quay, Ballina*, DEC-S2009-001. See Crowley (2006, pp 102–106) on the political history of these changes.

son.[347] The respondent successfully availed of the defence available under section 15(1), which permits service providers to deny access where there is a substantial risk of damage to property or of disorderly conduct, etc. (see Chapter 3.4). The equality officer emphasised that the facts were exceptional and that the admittance of a young child to the showrooms posed a substantial risk to its merchandise that could not be avoided. She acknowledged that Ms Goldman was a responsible parent but found that it was unreasonable to expect the respondent to decide which children would be adequately supervised. The equality officer also pointed out that the respondents had provided facilities for the care of children while the adults accompanying them viewed the goods on sale.

In *De Burca and Fernandez v Homelocators*[348] the equality officer found that a letting agency had discriminated on the family status ground. A message was left by the agency on the complainants' phone to the effect that 'the landlord's wife isn't really that pushed about having children in the apartment' and so a viewing appointment was cancelled.

Accommodation provision also arose in *Cassidy and Wesemann v Doherty*,[349] which involved the element of the family status ground that refers to 'being pregnant'.[350] A heterosexual couple were asked to leave their rental accommodation shortly after the second complainant moved in while pregnant. The complainants' baby was born a few months later, and some four weeks following the birth, the couple were issued with a notice to quit. The equality officer found that the complainants had established a *prima facie* case of discrimination on the gender and family status grounds, but the respondent landlords successfully rebutted this. According to the respondents, the house usually accommodated three people, who had separate bedrooms and shared a common bathroom, kitchen and living room. Previously, tenants had been allowed to move their partners in by temporary arrangement while awaiting new accommodation. However, Ms Wesemann had moved in without the landlords' agreement. In accordance with the respondents' usual practice, the couple had been asked to leave but did not do so. Subsequently, an alternative, larger room had been offered to the couple but discussions about this broke down because of a dispute about furniture. The equality officer was satisfied that requests to leave were issued in accordance with the respondents' usual

---

[347] *Goldman v The Proprietor, Mullen's Auctioneers, Dublin*, DEC-S2004-048.

[348] DEC-S2004-030/031.

[349] DEC-S2003-040/041.

[350] See section 2(1). People cannot claim protection under the family status ground by virtue of the fact that they have been discriminated against because they are members of a particular family: *Browne & Devers v Joyce's Stores*, DEC-S2002-134/135. For a parallel finding on the marital status ground see *Morrell v Hogan's Bar, Ballina*, DEC-S2003-001.

practice concerning the suitability of the premises, and because of the first complainant's conduct, and were not based on the discriminatory grounds.

Pregnancy was at issue too in *Kelly v Panorama Holiday Group Ltd*[351] Twenty-eight weeks into her pregnancy the complainant travelled by air outside of the country on a holiday, having been certified to do so by her doctor. At check-in for the return flight airport staff advised Ms Kelly that she would need certification from a local health clinic that she was fit to fly. As a consequence of complying with that request the family missed their flight. The complainant argued that she was directly discriminated against on the family status ground. She maintained that the respondent tour operator had not informed her that written confirmation from a doctor would be required in order to board the return flight. The equality officer noted that the complainant's mother had initially mistakenly advised the airline staff that her daughter was 34 weeks pregnant. This, she found, raised issues about the safety of the complainant, her unborn child and the passengers and crew on the flight. Medical clearance was not demanded on the basis of pregnancy *per se* but because of the supposed advanced stage of pregnancy with its attendant safety and welfare risks. The equality officer found that the complainant had not established a *prima facie* case because someone in a comparable situation would have been treated in the same manner: 'I am satisfied that the respondent and/or airline carrier would take similar precautions in a range of situations involving potential medical difficulties' (para 6.2). In concluding her investigation the equality officer issued a non-binding recommendation that the respondent should make it clear in the literature it issues to clients that documentation of a very specific nature may be required by airline carriers in circumstances such as those encountered by the complainant.

Following the advent of the Gender Goods and Services Directive arguably a comparator should not be required in cases of pregnancy discrimination. By analogy with CJEU case law in the employment area, adverse or unfavourable treatment of a woman on the grounds of pregnancy should be a substantive wrong without any requirement for comparison with the treatment afforded another person.[352]

The application of an airline's policy was raised in a 2010 family status ground complaint. Staff of the respondent told the complainant and his family immediately prior to boarding a flight that they could not travel with British Midland unless they could produce either photographic identification or the birth certificate for their infant daughter.[353] The equality officer was satisfied

---

[351] DEC-S2008-007.

[352] See *R (Equal Opportunities Commission) v Secretary of State for Trade and Industry* [2007] ICR 1234.

[353] *A Complainant v British Midland Airways Ltd*, DEC-S2010-050.

that there was no direct discrimination on the facts because all passengers, irrespective of age or family status, were obliged to produce photographic identification in accordance with the company's policy: 'I am satisfied from the evidence that all customers regardless of their family status are required to carry appropriate identification for all persons travelling with them. I am satisfied therefore, that the complainant has not established that he was treated less favourably on the family status ground than another person with a different family status or a person with no family status was treated or would have been treated in similar circumstances' (para 4.5).

3.3.4 Gender

To date many of the cases on the gender ground have involved differences in treatment related to personal appearance. For example, in *Gallagher v Merlin's Night Club*[354] a man was refused admission to a nightclub because of his footwear. The woman who accompanied him was also wearing sandals but was admitted. His complaint of discrimination on the gender ground was upheld. A similar complaint failed in *Gallagher v the Kazbar*[355] as the equality officer found that there was a material difference between the complainant's footwear and that of his female comparators. While these one-off incidents seem trivial, cases involving clothing and personal appearance in schools reveal the serious impact such issues can have on the education of younger people.

The 2009 decisions in *Knott v Dunmore Community School*[356] and *A Male Student v A Secondary School*[357] addressed the discriminatory treatment of second level students on the gender ground. The two young men involved in the complaints had been asked to cut their hair in accordance with the school's dress code. Mr Knott was ultimately suspended for failing to comply with the request, while the complainant in the second case complied very reluctantly. The equality officer who investigated both claims had regard to a number of UK judgments as well as decisions of the Labour Court. He did not follow the reasoning employed by the High Court of Northern Ireland in a case that also concerned a school's dress and appearance policy.[358] The comparison drawn by the judge in that case between boys not being allowed to wear long hair and girls not being allowed to wear school trousers was not an appropriate one according to the equality officer: girls are free to wear trousers outside

---

[354] DEC-S2002-133.
[355] DEC-S2002-132.
[356] DEC-S2009-008.
[357] DEC-S2009-010.
[358] *An Application by Robert McMillen, Chairman of the Board of Governors of Ballyclare High School, for Judicial Review* [2008] NIQB 21.

school time while boys cannot change the length of their hair at the end of the school day. The equality officer preferred the approach adopted by the Labour Court in the employment field. In a number of decisions it had recognised the right of individuals to determine their own appearance and had noted the impact that rules relating to clothes and grooming had on employees outside of work.[359] An interesting feature of the decisions is the assessment of less favourable treatment. The Tribunal was of the view that males and females did not need to be subject to the same rules; rather the overall test was whether they were treated equally. In other words, different treatment (here based on gender norms) is permissible provided it does not have a detrimental effect. On the facts of these cases the respondents' actions had a detrimental impact on male students, as compared with female students, and so amounted to direct discrimination on the gender ground.

Irwin v Duiske College[360] dealt with different rules for secondary school boys and girls, this time as to hair colour. The respondent's code of conduct specified that boys' hair was to be 'kept tidy and of its natural colour', whereas no equivalent rule applied to girls (para 5.2). While noting that schools did not have to treat all pupils the same, the equality officer found that by only regulating male hair Duiske College had engaged in direct discrimination on the gender ground.

A school's dress policy for a Catholic Holy Communion ceremony was at the centre of *Carr v Gaelscoil Mhainistir Na Corann*.[361] A Labour Court precedent[362] was again availed of by the equality officer in concluding that while boys wore school uniforms and girls Communion dresses there was no less favourable treatment overall. Both sets of pupils were subject to a dress code that required them to wear specific clothing. The Tribunal's decision also appears to have been influenced by the fact that there was some flexibility in the application of the rules:

> Finally, I do note that both boys and girls have deviated from the dress code policy in the past, as did the complainant in this case, and I note that the respondent has not prevented those children from making their Holy Communion. Accordingly, I am satisfied that the dress code is nothing more than a guideline for the children who are making their Holy Communion, and that there are no adverse conse-quences for the children who fail to observe it. Under section 3(1)

---

[359] *Pantry Franchise Ireland Ltd v A Worker* [1994] ELR 8 and *O'Byrne v Dunnes Stores* [2004] ELR 96.
[360] DEC-S2012-009.
[361] DEC-S2009-023.
[362] *O'Byrne v Dunnes Stores* [2004] ELR 96.

of the Acts, discrimination shall be taken to occur where a person is treated less favourably than another person is, has been or would be treated in a comparable situation on any of the discriminatory grounds. I have not been presented with any evidence in the present case from which I could conclude that the complainant has been subjected to a policy of less favourable treatment by the respondent on the gender ground (para 5.10).

The Labour Court cases relied on in this series of decisions appear to condone a degree of stereotyping (Flynn, 1995). In *O'Byrne v Dunnes Stores*,[363] for example, the Court stated, 'In considering whether a dress code operates unfavourably with regard to one or other of the sexes, the conventional standard of appearance is the appropriate criterion to be applied.' Arguably different considerations should apply in the services, accommodation and education context since commercial factors are not relevant to the same extent. However, the equality officer drew a direct analogy between the two fields in the 2009 case of *A Complainant v A Secondary School*.[364] The complaint revolved around a series of incidents related to a boy's refusal to remove an earring at the request of the school authorities. Under the respondent's dress code boys, but not girls, were barred from wearing earrings (the policy was subsequently amended). In deciding whether the difference in treatment was less favourable the equality officer distinguished the Tribunal decisions on hair length as there was no equivalent effect on the students' appearance outside of school hours. Both genders were subject to restrictions and the overall impact of the policy was not discriminatory on the gender ground. The revised rules permitted boys and girls to wear two earrings and the equality officer did not accept the complainant's argument that this policy was discriminatory as it failed to take account of the convention that males tend to wear only one earring. She concluded that the school was entitled to formulate its own uniform codes and that there was a legitimate expectation that these rules would be followed (para 5.7).

It is also worth noting that the Equality Authority has been involved in the resolution of several cases concerning school uniform policies. For instance, its 2001 Annual Report (2002, p 43) notes that there were 'a number of claims resolved relating to the ban on trousers on female students in schools. A number of schools also voluntarily changed their rules on uniforms.' Following intervention by the Equality Authority in 2003 a policy prohibiting the wearing of earrings by boys was altered (2004, p 38).

---

[363] [2004] ELR 96.
[364] DEC-S2009-074, relying on *An Application by Robert McMillen, Chairman of the Board of Governors of Ballyclare High School, for Judicial Review* [2008] NIQB 21.

In *MacMahon v Department of Physical Education and Sport, University College Cork*[365] the complainant maintained that his unsuccessful application for a sports scholarship was due to gender discrimination. He said that the respondent had a policy of gender balancing its awards and of positively discriminating in favour of females. The equality officer found no evidence that the processes involved in assessing the application were gender biased, and in so doing had regard to statistics on the number of males and females who were awarded scholarships over the course of three years. Consequently the complainant failed to establish a *prima facie* case of discrimination. The equality officer did, however, strongly recommend that the respondent enhance the transparency of its procedures (no written notes had been maintained indicating how decisions had been reached in each case).

A Patient v Health Service Provider and a Hospital[366] addressed a complaint of gender discrimination referred by a female patient at a mental health institution. The complainant maintained that the facilities in the hospital's only female unit were inferior to those available to male patients. That unit catered for widely differing needs in relation to clinical care and in terms of risk and security status. In contrast, male patients are able to avail of a number of therapeutic units with differing security levels (including access to an external hostel). The equality officer accepted that there were differences in treatment between men and women, but found that those catalogued by the complainant did not amount to less favourable treatment overall. A number of the matters fell within the clinical judgment exception and the Tribunal considered that there was insufficient evidence to support other assertions of less favourable treatment.

To date there is no ESA case law involving the gender reassignment aspect of the gender ground (Chapter 2.3.6). In 2007 a case taken by a transsexual person against the State Examinations Commission was settled prior to hearing with the assistance of the Equality Authority. The Commission re-issued the complainant's Intermediate Certificate and Leaving Certificate in her new name as changed by deed poll to reflect her gender identity (Equality Authority, 2008a, pp 28–29). Two further cases were settled prior to hearing in 2009 (Equality Authority, 2010b, pp 34–35). Both concerned records held by a government department, including those relating to the complainants' Personal Public Service Numbers. The complainants were undergoing gender reassignment and had acquired passports that reflected their gender and new names.[367] The Department initially informed the complainants that they were not allowed to change the records in order to align them with the passports but

---

[365] DEC-S2009-014.
[366] DEC-S2010-053.
[367] See section 11 of the Passports Act 2008.

agreed to do so in settlement of complaints referred to the Tribunal. In 2011 a settlement was agreed with a hospital concerning the treatment of a transgender woman. The case was taken through the pro bono scheme operated by the Public Interest Law Alliance.[368] Staff had refused to address the complainant as female on the basis that her passport identified her as male. The hospital agreed to train its staff on transgender issues and to amend its policies.

It should be noted that transsexual people might also wish to lodge complaints under the disability ground. An individual who has been diagnosed as having gender dysphoria or gender identity disorder has a condition that falls within the section 2 definition of disability.[369] The benefit of using that ground is that it triggers the reasonable accommodation duty (Chapter 6). Both grounds were used in the first Tribunal decision involving a transsexual person under the EEA: *Hannon v First Direct Logistics Limited*.[370] Ms Hannon alleged that her employer treated her less favourably over a considerable period of time while she was undergoing a gender reassignment process. Significantly, the equality officer found that several of the respondent's actions amounted to direct discrimination on the gender ground and on the disability ground. The respondent's requests that the complainant work from home and that she revert to a male identity when meeting clients were two such actions. In relation to the gender ground, the equality officer decided that had the complainant remained in her male identity she would not have been asked to work at home (para 4.7).[371] Overall, it seems that the Tribunal adopted a flexible approach to the appropriate comparator: the treatment of Ms Hannon is compared with that which would have been afforded someone (male or female) who had not undergone gender assignment. Ultimately Ms Hannon had sought employment elsewhere and the Tribunal found that because her

---

[368] The Public Interest Law Alliance was established in 2009 and is a project of the Free Legal Advice Centres. Through various activities it aims to enhance the use of law to benefit marginalised and disadvantaged people. A summary of the case is available here: <http://www.teni.ie/news-post.aspx?contentid=289>.

[369] For a critique of the categorisation of gender identity disorder as a mental disorder see Council of Europe Commissioner for Human Rights (2009, pp 23–25).

[370] DEC-E2011-066.

[371] In this instance the equality officer followed the approach of the CJEU in *P v S and Cornwall County Council*, Case C-13/94, [1996] ECR 1-2143, at para 21: 'Where a person is dismissed on the ground that he or she intends to undergo, or has undergone, gender reassignment, he or she is treated unfavourably by comparison with persons of the sex to which he or she was deemed to belong before undergoing gender reassignment.' The CJEU has since revised this choice of comparator. In a subsequent case it compared the treatment of a transsexual woman with a female who had not undergone gender reassignment: *Richards v Secretary of State for Work and Pensions*, Case C-423/04, [2006] ECR 1-3585, para 29. In other words, the comparator is a woman or man of the same gender as the complainant whose identity is not the result of gender reassignment.

work conditions were intolerable she was constructively dismissed, again on both the gender and disability grounds. In reaching that conclusion the equality officer referred to the respondent's statutory duty to reasonably accommodate people with disabilities.

Since protection under EU law is linked to the process of gender reassignment, the gender ground does not adequately protect all transgender people (McIlroy, 2009). The Council of Europe Commissioner for Human Rights (2009, p 6) has pointed out that in referring only to transsexual persons many legal frameworks leave 'out a decisive part of the community'. Future cases may test the extent to which gender stereotypes permit differences in treatment. The reasoning used in the school uniform decisions may not fully protect people whose gender identity or gender expression differs from conventional expectations.

The UK judgment considered above, which includes the denial of valuable choices as a form of less favourable treatment, could be applied in this context (Chapter 3.2.3), as might the US Supreme Court decision in *Price Waterhouse v Hopkins*.[372] There the Court found that gender discrimination could stem from the imposition of stereotypes. A woman was denied partnership at a large accounting firm because, it was said, she should 'walk more femininely, talk more femininely, dress more femininely, wear make-up, have her hair styled, and wear jewelry'.[373] The firm's action was based on 'sex stereotyping', which was unlawful because '[i]n forbidding employers to discriminate against individuals because of their sex, Congress intended to strike at the entire spectrum of disparate treatment of men and women resulting from sex stereotypes.'[374] Applying similar analysis, a transgender individual is discriminated against if they suffer adverse treatment for failing to adhere to social stereotypes attached to their sex as ascribed at birth. In any event, amending the ESA to include discrimination on the grounds of gender identity and gender expression would enhance the protection afforded transgender people.

3.3.5 Civil Status

The Civil Partnership Act 2010 entered into force on 1 January 2011, replacing the marital status ground with that of 'civil status'. Civil status 'means being

---

[372] 490 US 228 (1989). See Kirkland (2006) for a discussion of the case in the context of transgender rights. See also *Smith v City of Salem*, 378 F.3d 566, 572–573 (6th Cir. 2004) (concluding that a transgender plaintiff can advance a gender stereotyping claim) and *Barnes v Cincinnati*, 401 F.3d 729, 737 (6th Cir. 2005) (affirming *Smith*). Stereotyping was also recognised as a form of direct (race ground) discrimination in *R (European Roma Rights Centre) v Immigration Officer at Prague Airport* [2005] 2 AC 12.
[373] 490 US 228, at p 235.
[374] 490 US 228, at p 251.

single, married, separated, divorced, widowed, in a civil partnership within the meaning of the Civil Partnership and Certain Rights and Obligations of Cohabitants Act 2010 or being a former civil partner in a civil partnership that has ended by death or been dissolved'.[375] A person alleging discrimination under this ground compares the treatment in question with that of someone with a different civil status. So, for example, a divorced person may claim that she has been treated less favourably than a single person. Under the new civil status ground a civil partner can compare a service provider's treatment of them *vis-à-vis* a married individual. It should therefore apply to situations such as those addressed in a 2011 English case, which found that the owners of a hotel discriminated in refusing to accommodate a gay couple who had entered into a civil partnership.[376] The couple had booked a room by telephone but when they arrived at the hotel the proprietors told them that because of their religious beliefs double rooms were only provided to married partners. Bristol County Court found in favour of the complainants. The distinction made between married couples and civil partnership couples was direct discrimination on the ground of sexual orientation. Under the ESA, complainants in that situation could lodge complaints under both the sexual orientation and civil status grounds.

Since the changes brought about by the civil partnership law only came into force on 1 January 2011 most of the case law discussed here concerns the original marital status ground. 'Marital status' was defined as 'being single, married, separated, divorced or widowed' under section 2. To date there are relatively few cases but two significant decisions concerning discrimination against separated fathers were issued in 2010 and are discussed below.

A Student's Mother v A Local Authority is a notable successful complaint.[377] A local authority treated a student's mother less favourably when she was required to swear an affidavit in relation to her marital status and financial means when her son's application for a higher education grant was being considered. Married parents were simply asked to sign the grant application form. According to the equality officer the policy of requiring affidavits should have applied 'across the board'.

---

[375] Section 103(2)(*a*) of the Civil Partnership and Certain Rights and Obligations of Cohabitants Act 2010. The definition of 'near relative' under section 2 is also amended to include civil partners. But that change seems unnecessary since the term 'near relative' only appeared in subsections of the 2000 Act (section 6(2)(*b*) and (*d*)), which were repealed by section 49 of the Equality Act 2004.

[376] *Hall & Anor v Bull & Anor* [2011] EW Misc 2 (CC). Upheld on appeal to the UK Court of Appeal: *Bull & Bull v Hall & Preddy* [2012] EWCA Civ 83.

[377] DEC-S2004-086.

The complainant in *A Parent v A Primary School*[378] did not establish a *prima facie* case. A series of events that led to her daughter's removal from school was not related to her status as a divorced woman but because of ongoing conflict with the school authorities over the education of the child.

The 2010 decision in *A Separated Complainant v A Hospital*[379] raised significant questions about parental consent for medical treatment of children. A man who was separated from his spouse referred a complaint when he discovered that his child, Z, had undergone an operation at the respondent hospital without his prior knowledge or approval. The complainant argued that in failing to obtain his consent to the procedure the respondent had discriminated on the family status and marital status grounds. There was no discrimination on the family status ground, according to the equality officer, because all people in the same or similar circumstances would also have a child: 'By definition, then, the complainant could not have been discriminated against on the family status ground vis-à-vis such a comparator as they would have the same family status as the complainant' (para 5.4). The man was not treated less favourably on the marital status ground either. Consent was sought from one parent in all situations irrespective of the marital status of that parent, even where both parents were present. In other words, single, married, divorced and widowed parents were treated the same as separated parents.

A further aspect of the complaint related to a request the complainant made for information about Z's admission and operation. In response to that request a hospital employee advised the complainant that the records would be released only through a solicitor. The Tribunal found that this 'heavy-handed approach' amounted to direct discrimination on the marital status ground (para 5.16). If the complainant had not been separated he would have been granted the information without any difficulty once he had presented evidence of his identity. The respondent tried to argue that its actions were necessary to ensure compliance with data protection laws and to establish that the father was the child's guardian. However, it could not point to any provision of the Data Protection Acts that required the course of action it had adopted and a request for Z's birth certificate would have resolved the guardianship issue. The case is an example of less favourable treatment comprising the application of relatively harsh procedures to someone protected by a discriminatory ground.

It should be noted that the Health Service Executive (2009a) has issued a protocol for dealing with parental consent for non-emergency medical treatment. It recommends that where one of a child's guardians is not living with the child the wishes of that guardian to be informed about treatment or care

---

[378] DEC-S2003-135.
[379] DEC-S2010-046.

should be sought and recorded on a consent form. The protocol also underlines that where a child has two guardians both must consent to medical treatment unless they have waived that right or are not contactable.

A Separated Father v A Community School[380] dealt with the practices of a secondary school. The complainant (Mr M) had separated from his spouse and moved out of the family home, which was occupied by his children and their mother. He was concerned about his children's education and in particular absenteeism. He initiated a series of meetings and entered into correspondence with the respondent with a view to discussing the matter. Despite several requests for his children's attendance and absenteeism records, and apparent agreement by school officials to release them to Mr M, the records were not forthcoming. Ultimately the school principal sought legal evidence that he was the students' father. It also emerged that during part of the period in question the school had liaised with the mother of the children about the issues Mr M had raised. He referred a complaint on the gender, family status and marital status grounds.

The gender ground complaint did not succeed. It was standard practice for the school to deal directly with the parent or parents who had custody of a child. The equality officer was satisfied that the respondent would have liaised with Mr M if the children had been living with him. In other words, the complainant's gender was not the reason for any differences in treatment. The family status ground could not be relied upon because Mr M had the same family status as all other parents of children attending the community school in that they all had responsibility as parents in relation to persons who had not attained the age of eighteen years. There was direct discrimination on the marital status ground, however. The consistent failure to release the information sought by Mr M and in particular the letter sent by the principal seeking legal evidence that he was the children's father was 'a clear indication that he was being treated differently to other parents of children in the school with a different marital status' (para 6.3). In addition to paying compensation, the school was directed to revise its guidelines for dealing with parents to ensure that communications treated all parents in a fair and equitable manner irrespective of their marital status.

In a previous case, a separated father had also referred a complaint about his dealings with a school.[381] The school offered separated parents the option of attending two distinct parent–teacher meetings. The complainant maintained that the facility amounted to discrimination on the gender and marital status

---

[380] DEC-S2010-049. For practical guidance as to how school authorities should liaise with unmarried, separated or divorced parents of pupils see Binchy (2008).

[381] *A Complainant v A Primary School*, DEC-S2009-040. See also *A Complainant v A School*, DEC-S2012-003.

grounds. He had not been invited to a meeting with teachers that the child's mother had attended. In essence he argued that both parents should be invited to every meeting and so treated the same as parents who were not separated. In response the school said it could not force parents to meet one another and supplied details of the policy it had put in place to facilitate separated parents, explained its rationale and how it had operated in the complainant's situation:

> The school agrees that it offered Mr A and Ms B different parent/ teacher meeting appointments once it was made known to it that Ms B would not agree to attend a meeting with Mr A. It accepts that this treatment is different but they claim it is reasonable in the circumstances and it does not amount to less favourable treatment. The school claims that had its policy been the reverse, namely if it had not facilitated a separate meeting, the child could conceivably claim that he had been treated less favourably by not facilitating each of his parents with a meeting with his teacher. It claims that such an approach would constitute less favourable treatment and be detrimental to the child and the parents. It maintains that it has developed this policy to facilitate both parents to meet with the teachers for the benefit of the children (para 4.2).

At the hearing the school principal said the meetings were structured so that the same material would be discussed with both parents. The Tribunal agreed that the respondent's policy was responsive to the position of separated parents and did not involve less favourable treatment on either the gender or marital status grounds. In relation to the gender discrimination complaint, the school provided the same information and facilities to male and female parents. Its practice of offering two meetings actually benefited separated parents and their children. Indeed the equality officer observed that had the respondent not agreed to provide separate meetings it could have infringed the ESA.

A complaint of discrimination on the civil status, gender and race grounds was the subject of *Fizel v Health Service Executive*.[382] The complainant applied for rent supplement and objected to the manner in which a community welfare officer dealt with her when he was visiting her home. The equality officer found, however, that the official was entitled to ask questions about the complainant's living arrangements and other matters connected with her civil and family status:

> A person who has a different civil status (formerly marital status) than the complainant may be treated differently in such assessments

---

[382] DEC-S2012-001.

than a person who is residing alone. Such different treatment cannot be construed as less favourable treatment as one is not comparing two identical realities. Equally, it ought to be clear that it would be highly irrelevant to ask a person with a different family status from the complainant, that is, a person who is not pregnant nor has a responsibility as a parent of a child, about maintenance payments. Such an approach is not less favourable treatment, it is different treatment necessitated by the protected ground (para 5.5).

The equality officer was satisfied that while the complainant was treated differently than a person of a different family or civil status would have been treated, she did not experience less favourable treatment in relation to any aspect of her claim.

Morrell v Hogan's Bar, Ballina[383] established that a complaint would not succeed where a person is treated less favourably because they are married to a given individual. The equality officer stated:

Having considered the above definition, it appears clear to me that the marital status ground, as defined in the Equal Status Act 2000, relates specifically to a situation where a person is treated differently than another person because their marital status is different from that other person. Therefore, for a married person to claim that they were discriminated against on the 'marital status' ground, it must be shown that the treatment afforded them was different to the treatment a single, separated, divorced or widowed person would have received in similar circumstances (para 7.7).

Having considered Mr Morrell's complaint, I find that he is not alleging that he was treated differently than a single, separated, divorced or widowed person. Instead, he is claiming that he was treated differently because of his marriage to a member of a family, members of whom had caused trouble previously in Hogan's Bar. Having deliberated on this issue, I find that I cannot accept that Mr Morrell's interpretation of the 'marital status' ground falls within the definitions contained in the Equal Status Act 2000 (para 7.8).

---

[383] DEC-S2003-001. This reasoning can be contrasted with the broader approach to the definition adopted by the Canadian Supreme Court. In *B v Ontario (Human Rights Commission)* [2002] 3 SCR 403; 2002 SCC 66, the Court found that the grounds of marital and family status set out in the Ontario Human Rights Code were broad enough to cover situations where discrimination results from the particular identity of the complainant's spouse or family member.

3.3.6 Race, Colour, Nationality, Ethnic or National Origins

Several exceptions apply to the 'nationality' element of the race ground. These concern grants, entry requirements and payment of fees for accessing third level education. Certain immigration and asylum matters are also exempt; these complex provisions are addressed at the end of this section.

There are several Tribunal decisions involving refusal of service. For example, *Maphosa v Dublin Bus*[384] concerned the provision of public transport. The complainant argued that a bus driver had seen him waiting at a bus stop but did not pick him up apparently because he was black. There was a direct conflict of evidence since the driver denied that the incident had occurred or that she would have behaved in such a manner and there were no independent witnesses. Based in part on the consistency and credibility of the complainant's evidence, the equality officer concluded on the balance of probabilities that the discriminatory incident had occurred. He awarded the complainant €1,200 compensation for humiliation and distress.

An Azerbaijani national who was denied entry to a pub brought a successful race discrimination claim in *Sajjadi v The Turk's Head*.[385] Mr Sajjadi was asked for identification and when he produced his student card it was not accepted. There was evidence that two younger Irish men had been admitted without being asked for proof of their identity. The equality officer concluded that the complainant was subjected to a tougher screening process than usual because of his ethnic origin. He awarded €1,500 compensation for distress, humiliation and loss of amenity.

Sabherwal v ICTS (UK) Ltd[386] was decided in 2008. Mr Sabherwal maintained that security agents acting for the respondent at Shannon Airport treated him less favourably. The ground staff in question had insisted that the complainant produce alternative proof of identification with a residential address in addition to his passport. At the time Mr Sabherwal was queuing for check-in and claimed that as the only non-white person in the queue he was singled out because of his skin colour. In upholding the claim the equality officer found:

> I accept that any air carrier must operate a security programme and that, for a variety of reasons, certain persons are selected for further

---

[384] DEC-S2004-189.

[385] DEC-S2002-101. See also *Buckley v Joy's Niteclub*, DEC-S2006-031: the Equality Tribunal found that a woman was denied access to nightclub because she was black. The decision was appealed and a settlement was reached out of court; and *Axinte v Q-Bar Dublin*, DEC-S2004-188: a man of Romanian origin was unlawfully denied access to a pub.

[386] DEC-S2008-037.

questioning. However, while making this decision I must acknowledge that the respondent has not submitted any tangible evidence to rebut the complaint. The respondent's evidence at the hearing states: 'Due to the fact that the Complainant presented a passport that was not Irish, the security procedures then required Mr Long to obtain a secondary form of identification which showed Complainant's place of residence.' This evidence was subsequently confirmed in writing by the respondent. The only conclusion which I can draw from the statement is that the complainant's nationality was the substantive reason why the complainant was selected for further questioning. I find this statement as an admission that the complainant's nationality was the reason why he was expected to show secondary form of identification. This additional requirement that was imposed on the complainant because of his citizenship constitutes direct discrimination as defined by section 3(1) of the Acts (para 5.12).

She then noted that unlike the prohibition on indirect discrimination contained in section 3(1)(c) of the Acts, direct discrimination could not be objectively justified by a legitimate aim (para 5.12).

The manner in which an application for rent supplement was processed was the subject of an ESA complaint in *Baziz v Health Service Executive – Community Welfare Services*.[387] Mr Baziz was of Algerian origin, had lived in Ireland since 1997 and held an Irish passport. Before the community welfare officer in question, Ms C, visited the complainant's home she spoke with his wife on the phone. In the course of that conversation it emerged that Mr Baziz was originally from Algeria and Ms C changed the nationality from Irish to Algerian on the form that he had submitted. Upon her visit she asked to see the complainant's identification and when the complainant produced his Irish passport Ms C apparently asked how he had obtained it. He replied that the Department of Justice, Equality and Law Reform had issued it. Following further questions he showed Ms C his marriage certificate as evidence of citizenship by marriage. Ms C acknowledged that she had changed the entry on the application form because it was standard practice to enter the original nationality of applicants on the HSE's computer system. She conceded that she had asked for evidence of identity but again claimed that this was routine and also accepted that she may have asked further questions about Mr Baziz's citizenship. The equality officer accepted that the rationale behind the change to the form was non-discriminatory but found that the respondent's questions

---

[387] DEC-S2007-050; *Fizel v Health Service Executive*, DEC-S2012-001 also involved the processes involved in assessing eligibility for rent supplement.

regarding Mr Baziz's citizenship constituted less favourable treatment on the race ground.

Access to banking facilities has featured in a number of race ground cases. When the complainant in *Mr F v A Financial Institution*[388] tried to open a bank account on three occasions the respondent sought additional documentation to that furnished by him. Mr F contended that the bank's requests amounted to less favourable treatment on the race ground, as it would not have treated a person of Irish ethnicity in a similar manner. He pointed out that demands made of him went beyond the requirements set out in the bank's marketing and promotional literature relating to the product in question. The respondent maintained that the requirements did not stem from discrimination but were necessary to counter increased fraudulent activity at the branch and to comply with its duties under the Criminal Justice Act 1994. It argued that the enhanced security requirements were applied to all customers regardless of their race or nationality. The equality officer accepted that the requests made were standard and routinely applied to all customers and so the complainant had failed to establish a *prima facie* case of discrimination on the ground of race.

Compliance with the Criminal Justice Act 1994 was also at issue in *A Nigerian National v A Financial Institution*.[389] The complainant was refused a number of banking facilities over a fifteen-month period and alleged that the respondent's actions amounted to discrimination. The equality officer found that several of the incidents involved were exempt because the processes concerned were necessary to comply with the 1994 Act. A number of other incidents such as the refusal of an overdraft facility and a Laser card were in line with standard bank procedures and did not involve less favourable treatment. However, an application for a term loan was refused although the complainant met the applicable criteria. This raised an inference of discrimination on the race ground that was not rebutted by any evidence presented by the respondent. The complainant was awarded €500 compensation. In the course of the investigation the equality officer uncovered a number of 'administrative failings' and he recommended that the bank review its internal procedures to ensure greater transparency and adequate record keeping.

Immigration and asylum law and policies obviously affect people who are not Irish citizens and so raise direct discrimination on the race ground. Decisions about people's immigration status or on asylum applications fall outside the material scope of the ESA because those decisions are government functions as opposed to services. Additionally, several rules mandating different

---

[388] DEC-S2008-003. See also *Moriarty v Rabo Direct*, DEC-S2010-051: a US citizen was treated less favourably on the nationality element of the ground when he could not open a savings account with the respondent.

[389] DEC-S2005-114.

treatment of non-Irish nationals are set out in law and so immune from challenge through an equal status complaint. The ESA also includes specific exceptions aimed at the spheres of immigration and asylum. However, as discussed above, those exceptions have yet to be tested in case law. It seems that the day-to-day operation of the direct provision system, for example, is not outside the reach of the ESA (Chapter 2.6.2.4).

It is open to individuals affected by discrimination that does fall outside the scope of the ESA to rely on other sources of law including the ECHR Act 2003. The Free Legal Advice Centres (2009) have catalogued a range of practices within the direct provision system that appear to breach Convention and other human rights standards. The Convention's non-discrimination prohibition (article 14) explicitly refers to 'national or social origin' as a ground on which adverse treatment may be challenged.

There have been a number of cases in which free primary and second level schooling has been denied to the children of foreign students studying in Ireland (Irish Council for Civil Liberties, 2008). Such practices would appear to violate both the ESA and the European Convention on Human Rights. In *Timishev v Russia*[390] the applicant's children were refused access to school on the basis that he was not registered as being resident in the area. There was no suggestion that alternative education was available. According to the European Court of Human Rights:

> [T]he Convention and its Protocols do not tolerate a denial of the right to education. The Government confirmed that Russian law did not allow the exercise of that right by children to be made conditional on the registration of their parents' residence. It follows that the applicant's children were denied the right to education provided by domestic law. Their exclusion from school was therefore incompatible with the requirements of Article 2 of Protocol No 1 (para 66).

3.3.7 Religion

To date the religion ground has generated very little case law. As noted in Chapter 2.3.8, should the Draft Goods and Services Directive come into effect the definition of the ground will have to be extended to encompass 'belief'.

Sheeran v The Office of Public Works[391] is a distinctive case on the religion ground. The complainant, a humanist, objected to the ringing of the Angelus

---

[390] (2007) 44 EHRR 37.
[391] DEC-S2004-015. The right to freedom of thought, conscience and religion under article 9 ECHR also protects the rights of persons with no religious beliefs: *Grzelak v Poland*, Application No. 7710/02, 15 June 2010.

bells[392] in a state-owned church building maintained by the Office of Public Works. Although the equality officer felt there was some doubt as to whether humanism could be regarded as a religion, the ground could still be invoked as the complainant was covered by virtue of his lack of religious belief *vis-à-vis* the Catholic beliefs inherent in the Angelus bells. She dismissed the direct discrimination claim in the following terms:

> The complainant's main difficulty was not with the Angelus bell being rung, but with who was ringing it. His argument was vehemently for the separation of Church and State. In this regard, the Equal Status Act, 2000 relates to services which may be discriminatory. It does not provide for services which are perceived to be discriminatory only when offered by a particular service provider. The complainant is arguing that public bodies, as emanations of the State, must adopt a strictly secular approach. This would preclude the respondent from being involved in any traditions connected with the buildings in its charge where those traditions had even remote religious associations. This could be perceived as directly contrary to its constitutional obligation to honour religion. This obligation must be understood as requiring the State to respect and honour a diversity of religious viewpoints. The complainant has not shown that the respondent treats some religious traditions less favourably than others in this context. Nor has he shown that the ringing of the Angelus bell represents anything other than a minimal intervention, if any, into his own lack of religious belief.

Another complaint on the religion ground in *A Parent on Behalf of a Child v A National Youth Work Organisation*[393] was also unsuccessful. The equality officer concluded that, on the facts, the initial refusal of a place on a programme aimed at young people was based on factors other than the child's religion.

The 2007 Annual Report of the Equality Authority (2008a, p 41) records a settlement reached in a case involving a secondary school pupil with no religious beliefs. The student had been required to attend religious instruction and subsequently to sit in the corridor outside the principal's office for the duration of the classes. Following correspondence from the Authority the school arranged for supervision of the pupil in a classroom environment. A similar outcome issued from a 2004 case (Equality Authority, 2005b) where a child

---

[392] Catholic, and some other Christian, churches sound the Angelus bells at given times each day to coincide with a particular form of prayer or devotion.
[393] DEC-S2008-030.

of a different religious background was obliged to leave the school premises while religion classes were underway.[394]

Any ban on religious symbols or dress in educational establishments could give rise to a claim of direct discrimination on the religion ground, since a person could assert that they were treated less favourably than someone with no religious beliefs (e.g. a student who wears symbols associated with a political belief). It is far more likely, however, that a student would encounter discrimination related to a religious belief as a consequence of a neutral practice, such as a school uniform policy. A practice may be neutral in the sense that it does not refer explicitly to religion but it may nonetheless disadvantage students from certain religious backgrounds and so be challenged as indirectly discriminatory. This issue is discussed further in Chapter 4.4.

Denominational schools are permitted to distinguish between prospective students on the basis of their religious background. They are also entitled to refuse admission to a child who is not of that denomination where it is *essential* to maintain the ethos of the school (Chapter 2.6.2.3). These provisions have yet to be tested in case law but are likely to be interpreted restrictively. A court may have to assess the constitutionality of the provision and perhaps too its compliance with the Racial Equality Directive. Religion and ethnicity are closely intertwined for some groups such as Sikhs and Jews. And so a decision to refuse admission to a Jewish child on the basis that her presence would in some way compromise the ethos of the school could amount to direct discrimination on both the race and religion grounds. A UN committee has called on the Government to revise the legislative exception, especially in light of the dominance of Catholic schools in education provision at primary level (United Nations Committee on the Elimination of Racial Discrimination, 2005, para 18, 2011, para 26).[395]

---

[394] Section 30(2)(*e*) of the Education Act 1998 provides that students are not required 'to attend instruction in any subject which is contrary to the conscience of the parent of the student or in the case of the student who has reached the age of 18 years, the student'. See also Article 44.2.4° of the Constitution and the Supreme Court decision in *Crowley v Ireland* [1980] IR 102 (Whyte, 2010). In *Zengin v Turkey* (2008) 46 EHRR 44 the European Court of Human Rights held the right to education was violated by a refusal to exempt a state school pupil whose family was of the Alevi faith from mandatory lessons on religion and morals. The Court has provided some guidance as to the acceptability of alternatives to religious instruction (Mawhinney, 2010).

[395] See also the concluding observations of the Human Rights Committee on Ireland's report under the International Covenant on Civil and Political Rights (United Nations Human Rights Committee, 2008, para 22). Several experts suggest that Ireland is not complying with the ECHR at primary school level by supporting the integrated curriculum within the 97 per cent of national schools that adhere to a religious ethos, and by failing to provide non-denominational alternatives (see, for example, Daly, 2008; Irish Human Rights Commission, 2010; Mawhinney, 2010; Temperman, 2010).

The Minister for Education has initiated two processes that should result in reform of this area. A Forum on Patronage and Pluralism in the Primary Sector was established in April 2011. Under the direction of a Forum Advisory Group a series of public working sessions were convened and written submissions sought on the question of divesting some Catholic schools of patronage. The report of the Advisory Group (Coolahan, Hussey and Kilfeather, 2012) recommends that change of patronage should happen in a phased, incremental way. An envisaged preliminary phase would include examining provision in 43 towns and 4 Dublin areas. This process would involve examining some 250 schools of which approximately 50 might be divested. The Department of Education and Skills (2011) commenced a consultation process on school enrolment with the launch of a discussion paper in June 2011. Submissions from interested parties were sought over the following five months and a final report is pending as of July 2012.

3.3.8 Sexual Orientation

There are very few Tribunal decisions on the sexual orientation ground. To date most of the direct discrimination complaints have concerned the hospitality sector. A number have failed for technical reasons.[396] In *O'Regan v The Bridge Hotel, Waterford*[397] the equality officer found that the complainant was discriminated against when asked to leave a hotel because he was gay. *A Female v A Publican*[398] concerned a refusal to serve a lesbian woman in a pub. In both cases the respondents had maintained that the individuals were denied access to services for reasons other than their sexual orientation. However, on the basis of the total evidence considered by the Tribunal, including witness statements, the equality officer in each case was satisfied that the complainants were treated less favourably on the sexual orientation ground.

The version of events presented by the complainant and respondent were diametrically opposed in a case concerning a bisexual's man treatment in a fast food outlet.[399] Based to a large extent on the credibility of the parties and the witnesses, the equality officer found that no *prima facie* case was established. Likewise, a gay student on an adult education programme who

---

[396] *Woodhead and Sparkes v Swinford Garda Station*, DEC-S2008-064: the complainants were not accessing a service because the complaint involved the investigation of a crime by the Gardaí (see Chapter 2.4.4). A complaint about the treatment of a gay and lesbian choir failed because a case could not be referred by an association: *Gloria – Ireland's Gay and Lesbian Choir v Cork International Choral Festival Ltd*, DEC-S2008-078 (Chapter 12.3.2).

[397] DEC-S2004-037.

[398] DEC-S2005-026.

[399] *A Complainant v A Fast Food Franchise*, DEC-S2008-036.

complained about the behaviour of staff did not produce evidence of discriminatory treatment.[400] The Tribunal found the respondent's accounts of events to be more credible and consistent. Many of those accounts were backed up by contemporaneous notes and written records of problems with the complainant's behaviour.

McGuffin and Harte v Eyre Square Hotel[401] involved the cancellation of social functions by a hotel, which the complainants argued was attributable to sexual orientation discrimination. During meetings with hotel management, the complainants said they were advised that the ultimate decision had come from the respondent owner, who did not want his property to be used for gay events. The respondent denied that he objected to the complainants' sexuality and argued that financial considerations were the reason for the cancellation, as the bar had not been profitable at previous events run by the complainants. While the equality officer accepted that such a rationale could be advanced she found that the alleged losses were not large enough nor frequent enough for a reasonable person to accept that they were so alarming as to justify the respondent's actions. The fact that the hotel had sent a member of its staff to remove posters advertising one of the events and that the manager told the complainant that this was done at the proprietor's insistence established a *prima facie* case of discrimination. The complainants were awarded €1,500 each for the effects of the discrimination and the respondent was ordered to implement an equal status policy and appropriate training.

3.3.9 Traveller Community

Complaints on the Traveller community ground have challenged outright refusal of service,[402] as well as less favourable conditions in accessing education, accommodation, social welfare, transport and so on. Some decisions relate to accommodation that is used exclusively by Travellers and so involves a comparison with provision of housing to settled people 'in a comparable situation'. In many decisions the Tribunal has had little difficulty in drawing an analogy between the two forms of accommodation. It has used both actual and hypothetical comparators in establishing whether the treatment was less favourable in such cases. In some instances, however, the complainants were unable to establish that their accommodation situation was similar to that of settled people.

---

[400] *A Student v An Educational Establishment*, DEC-S2009-084.

[401] DEC-S2008-051.

[402] See, for example, *Ward v Paddy Keane Auctioneers*, DEC-S2008-119 (failure by estate agent to transact with a Traveller) and *Twelve Complainants v Digger Jay's Pub*, DEC-S2008-040 (respondent refused to allow a group of women enter a concert venue because they were members of the Traveller community).

In *O'Brien v Iarnród Éireann*[403] the complainant was a Traveller who was accused of stealing a bag in the course of a train journey. The ticket collector had accepted the word of another passenger that she was implicated in the theft, on the basis that two other passengers had speculated that her children had been involved. He called the Gardaí without attempting to identify or interview those passengers. The complainant was not informed of the allegation before she was taken off the train and had her luggage searched by a Garda in view of other passengers. She was allowed back on the train when nothing was found, but received no apology from Iarnród Éireann. The equality officer concluded that the woman had been treated less favourably on the Traveller community ground: if a non-Traveller had been accused of theft, it was reasonable to expect that the ticket collector would at least have asked to speak to the two witnesses before contacting the Gardaí. Additionally, the failure of the ticket master to inform the complainant of the allegation against her, and the fact that she had not been offered an apology, indicated that standard procedures had not been adopted in relation to the incident. This case involved the use of a hypothetical comparator, i.e. the complainant was treated less favourably that a settled person *would have* been treated.[404]

Deviations from standard practice also featured in the equality officer's assessment of the facts in *Faulkner v St Ita's & St Joseph's School, Tralee*.[405] The complainant was subjected to direct discrimination in the course of contact with the principal of a 'special needs' school about her son's application for admission. In effect the principal had ignored the admission request, which was based as standard on a psychologist's assessment, and was also rude in his dealings with the complainant. Similarly in *Mrs K (on behalf of her son) v A Primary School*[406] a complaint of direct discrimination was upheld where the respondent board of management took over four months to process an enrolment application. In deciding whether the delay was attributable to the complainant's membership of the Traveller community, the equality officer had regard to the respondent's statutory obligation to respond to a request for enrolment within 21 days.[407] In the absence of any explanation for the delay the equality officer did not 'accept that it would have taken the respondent

---

[403] DEC-S2003-029.

[404] See also *O'Brien v The Canada House Shop*, DEC-S2002-002/003: staff approached two members of the Traveller community on arrival in a shop and the door to the premises was locked after they had entered. In the absence of an actual comparator the equality officer found that a non-Traveller would not have been treated in the same way. For example, she stated: 'if a non-Traveller was involved, it is reasonable to expect that the respondents would at least have let them browse for a few minutes …'.

[405] DEC-S2006-037.

[406] DEC-S2011-003.

[407] Section 19(3) of the Education (Welfare) Act 2000.

such a period of time to make a decision on an application for enrolment, in similar circumstances, from a member of the settled community' (para 4.9). A further aspect of complaint was not upheld. The Tribunal found that the boy was not allowed to commence school following an offer of a place not because of discrimination but because of failure to comply with school regulations.

A further decision of major significance on the ground is the 2007 case of *Reilly v Health Service Executive*.[408] Mr Reilly was informed that he could not access his Supplementary Welfare Allowance at a local health centre but instead was obliged to attend a Dublin city centre location that processed such payments to Travellers exclusively. The equality officer concluded that the complainant was treated less favourably than a non-Traveller in the provision of a service, namely the payment of Supplementary Welfare Assistance (SWA): 'Specifically, the complainant must travel to the central unit for payment while all non-Traveller recipients of SWA can elect to have it paid locally or via a number of alternative outlets.' The redress ordered comprised the maximum award of compensation possible, a direction that Mr Reilly be paid at his local health centre or at any other alternative venues open to non-Travellers, and an order that the HSE arrange for payment of SWA to Travellers at all outlets at which payment is available to non-Travellers. In effect the decision led to the closure of the infamous Castle Street social welfare office (Fay, 2008).

Provision of segregated services also arose in *A Complainant v Dublin City Council*,[409] which involved a complaint about the maintenance service for people living in Traveller-specific accommodation. The equality officer distinguished the *Reilly* decision from the facts before her. The service provided in that case was clearly inferior to the one settled people enjoyed, but the maintenance service was not of a lesser standard. Accordingly the treatment in question while different was not less favourable. She went on to address a more general point:

> The issue of whether having separate service provision – in relation to any of the protected grounds – is in itself discriminatory is an interesting question. It is generally acknowledged that equality of opportunity cannot be achieved in circumstances where every person is treated the same and the legislation itself provides for a number of exemptions in relation to the right to maintain separate services in appropriate circumstances. I am satisfied that the service complained of is separate to best accommodate a distinct housing policy designed for Travellers. The Traveller Housing Act,

---

[408] DEC-S2007-059.
[409] DEC-S2012-006.

1998, necessitates the existence of such programmes and gives legal recognition to different housing needs of Travellers (para 5.6).

Segregation is not expressly prohibited under the ESA. The Tribunal suggests here that it may be acceptable, at least where there is a rationale for separate service provision and no evidence of less favourable conditions. As noted above, a UK court has found that the denial of a choice between options that are apparently of the same value can amount to less favourable treatment (Chapter 3.2.3).

Accommodation provision and associated services have featured in several further Traveller community ground cases. The complainant in *McCann v Dún Laoghaire–Rathdown County Council*[410] argued that the Council's Traveller unit treated him less favourably than a non-Traveller would have been treated in a similar situation by turning down his request for a key to a barrier restricting access to his home on a halting site. The key was necessary because of the height of Mr McCann's vehicle. As a preliminary matter, the equality officer reiterated that section 6(6) is a positive action measure and should not be used to sanction discriminatory treatment. In upholding the claim of direct discrimination she concluded:

> It is clear from the evidence presented to me that Mr McCann has not been given a key because he is a Traveller living in a residential halting site. If Mr McCann lived in standard local authority housing his movements would not be restricted in a similar manner. Firstly, there would be no barrier at the entrance and secondly, if there was some type of a protective measure in place, he would be given a key. I am certain that the reason why Mr McCann is not trusted with a key has nothing to do with his personal traits. I am satisfied that the treatment he received was entirely based on his membership of the Traveller community and a direct result of him choosing to live in Traveller specific accommodation (para 5.11).

Notably here persons living in residential halting sites were found to be in a similar position to people living in standard local authority housing. The case was subsequently settled on appeal to the Circuit Court.

The behaviour of a Traveller liaison officer (TLO) following the death of the complainant's daughter was the subject of a successful harassment complaint in a 2009 case (Chapter 5.4).[411] Another element of the complaint alleged that the respondent county council discriminated on the Traveller commu-

---

[410] DEC-S2008-004.
[411] *A Complainant v A County Council*, DEC-S2009-009.

nity ground by obliging the complainant to deal exclusively with the TLO while settled people could deal with housing officers. Here too the Tribunal considered settled people and Travellers as being in a comparable situation in relation to accommodation provision. The equality officer found that records presented by the respondent and maintained by the TLO in relation to the complainant's case compared unfavourably with those relating to the non-Traveller cases viewed by the Tribunal. The latter included precise details about the progress of requests for housing transfers, while no 'such traceability existed in respect of the complainant's application to the respondent'. According to the Tribunal, the impact of the requirement on the complainant to deal with the TLO exclusively, in comparison with the treatment received by non-Travellers, amounted to less favourable treatment. In addition to ordering the maximum amount of compensation payable under the Acts, the equality officer issued a series of directions aimed at changing the manner in which the respondent dealt with the housing needs of Travellers.

In these decisions Travellers and settled people were considered to be in a comparable position. In other cases, however, complaints have failed in part because of the particular accommodation difficulties encountered by Travellers. For example, a complaint was referred by a number of individuals against Waterford City Council following their eviction from a halting site.[412] They claimed they were forcibly removed from their homes, and that the decision to evict and the way in which they were treated during and after the eviction was discriminatory. The Council argued that the complainants had no permission to be on the site, but had been provided with amenities nonetheless. It said that the eviction was a necessary measure aimed at regaining control of the site, which had become dangerous for health and safety reasons and because of criminal activity. The respondent accepted that none of the complainants had contributed to the disorder on the site. The equality officer appeared to regard the circumstances surrounding the eviction as distinctive, in that no analogy was drawn between the accommodation situation of the complainants and occupants of settled housing. Instead he noted that all other persons allowed to remain on the site were also members of the Travelling community (para 6.6). He concluded that the treatment of the complainants did not amount to less favourable treatment:

> I am of the view that on the balance of probabilities the reason the complainants were evicted from the Kilbarry site was that they were not assigned to a permanent bay on the site and that all those asked to leave were asked because the respondent wished to regain control

---

[412] *O'Reilly and Others v Waterford City Council*, DEC-S2010-018.

of the site and not because of their membership of the Traveller community (para 6.7).

Following the eviction a number of the complainants had no option but to live on the side of the road. Indeed, the respondent sought to remove one of the complainants from the roadside through a court order. However, the equality officer reviewed the evidence provided about contact between the parties about housing needs, as well as statistical information about the Council's available Traveller-specific accommodation. He accepted that the Council was constrained by available resources and in that light offers of temporary accommodation had been made to each complainant within a reasonable period of time (i.e. some three months following the eviction) (para 6.12). The experiences of the complainants in this case took place within a wider legal and policy context that makes a nomadic way of life extremely difficult. In 2002 the law was changed to make trespass on land a crime and 'in the absence of sufficient transient accommodation outputs as per statutory obligations, the Act has effectively curtailed Travellers' freedom to move as guaranteed in a number of different policy documents' (Coates, Kane and Treadwell Shine, 2008, p 52).

Arguably the complaint in *A Traveller v A Local Authority*[413] would have had a better prospect of succeeding under the European Convention on Human Rights Act 2003. The complainant maintained that she had been discriminated against on the Traveller community ground in not being granted a housing transfer by the respondent. Her request was related to her husband's violent conduct and associated health problems. These factors suggest that the complaint should also have been referred on the disability and gender grounds. Essentially, the case failed for technical reasons: the inter-personal violence and medical issues were not outlined in the written application for a housing transfer and so the local authority had acted within the terms of its scheme of letting priorities. However, after submitting the written application the complainant explained her situation to a local authority official at a meeting about her housing needs. Under the ECHR states have positive duties to protect victims of repeated inter-personal violence, and must take active steps to protect persons at risk.[414] A case could have been made that the local authority breached its duty under section 3 of the ECHR Act by failing to

---

[413] DEC-S2009-066.

[414] *Opuz v Turkey* (2010) 50 EHRR 28. In that judgment the Court found that a failure by a state to address gender-based violence can amount to discrimination under the Convention. It is also worth noting that, according to the High Court, housing authorities are obliged to inform people about their housing entitlements: *O'Reilly v Limerick County Council* [2006] IEHC 174.

take account of the violence experienced by the complainant in assessing her housing needs (Chapter 10.5).

3.3.10 Multiple Grounds

Alleged discriminatory treatment frequently implicates several of the grounds. For instance, less favourable treatment experienced by the carer of a disabled person could give rise to a claim of family status discrimination and discrimination by association on the disability ground. Transsexual people may, albeit reluctantly, base complaints on both the gender and disability grounds (Chapter 3.3.4). Thirty-one complaints of discrimination on multiple grounds were referred to the Tribunal in 2009. The figure for 2010 was twenty-two (Equality Tribunal, 2011a, p 9).

Where a complaint is referred on several of the ESA grounds it is investigated as a single case but a decision must be made on each of the claims.[415] This means that a complaint on each ground must be established separately and in practice the Tribunal tends to deal with the grounds in turn.[416] Even where a complaint succeeds on several grounds of discrimination the ceiling of €6,348.69 compensation applies (Chapter 12.6).

The family status and gender grounds featured in *Flanagan Talbot v Casino Cinemas Limited t/a Killarney Cineplex Cinema*.[417] When attempting to buy tickets for an afternoon screening of a film the complainant was informed that children under the age of two years were not allowed into the cinema. She was with three children, one of whom was seven months old. The respondent said the policy had been put in place in response to numerous complaints from customers about the presence of babies. When queried further, the respondent apparently referred to patrons' objections to breastfeeding. However, the respondent denied that its refusal to admit was related to breastfeeding, although it was mentioned as an example of the type of complaint received. The manager had apologised to the complainant for his remark about same, and she had accepted that apology. Instead the respondent argued Mrs Flanagan Talbot was subject to its general policy not to admit babies. That policy was based on health and safety grounds, as children could be harmed in the darkened environment of a cinema, as well as a concern for the enjoyment and comfort of other customers.

---

[415] Section 25(1A).

[416] See, for example, *Maughan v The Glimmer Man Limited*, DEC-S2001-020 and *Superquinn v Freeman* (AEE/02/8; DEE/0211, 14 November 2002). But see *O'Brien v Computer Scope Ltd* (DEC-E2006-030): an equal pay case on the age and gender grounds, in which the grounds were treated in a holistic way. This may have been due to the fact that the actual comparators were both of a different gender and a different age to the complainant.

[417] DEC-S2008-053.

Having reviewed the evidence offered by both parties, the equality officer was satisfied that the respondent did not operate discriminatory practices against mothers who wished to breastfeed and so the complainant failed to establish a *prima facie* case of discrimination on the gender ground. He then looked at the respondent's policy of refusing admittance to children under the age of two years and whether it was discriminatory on the family status ground. The complainant established a *prima facie* case on that ground as she was denied entry in her role as the parent of a child aged under two. She was treated less favourably than someone without family status or with a different family status (e.g. someone accompanied by a child aged over two) would have been in seeking admission to the cinema. In terms of the respondent's attempt to rebut that *prima facie* case, it did not refer to any specific legislative requirements apart from section 12 of the Safety, Health and Welfare at Work Act 2005. Section 12 provides that:

> Every employer shall manage and conduct his or her undertaking in such a way as to ensure, so far as is reasonably practicable, that in the course of the work being carried on, individuals at the place of work (not being his or her employees) are not exposed to risks to their safety, health or welfare.

The equality officer did not accept that this provision made it necessary to impose a blanket ban on the admittance of children under the age of two years, when accompanied by a parent or adult, to an afternoon screening of a children's film. Other policies in place were adequate to cover situations where some patrons were disruptive and the respondent was obliged to employ adequate staff to fulfil its duty of care to customers. He awarded the complainant the sum of €750 in compensation and ordered that the respondent review its admissions policy.

Denial of planning permission to build a home was at issue in *O'Donoghue v North Tipperary County Council*.[418] The complainant argued that the negative decision was based on her membership of the Traveller community and made reference to objections lodged by members of the local community. She also claimed that she was discriminated against by association on the disability ground because the respondent council failed to take her son's disability into account when arriving at its decision. The Council acknowledged that an objection to the applicant's planning application was received from a large group of local residents; however, it submitted that the submission did not make any reference to the complainant's membership of the Traveller community and that it was valid and in accordance with the relevant planning regulations.

---

[418] DEC-S2008-097.

It argued that the decision to refuse the complainant's application was based on established planning policies contained in the County Development Plan 1998 and in accordance with applicable laws. The equality officer was satisfied that the application was processed in compliance with the respondent's legal obligations under the Planning and Development Acts 2000–2002 (and all relevant subsequent regulations). On the facts, the equality officer found that the complainant had not established that she had been treated less favourably than a non-Traveller would have been treated in terms of the manner in which the application was processed. As for discrimination by association on the ground of disability, the equality officer noted the respondent's uncontested evidence that it had no problem with the internal design of the house, which was drafted to meet the special needs of the complainant's son. Accordingly, the equality officer held that the complainant had failed to establish a *prima facie* case of discrimination on both grounds. Notably, the respondent did not contest that the planning process was a 'service' within the terms of section 2 ESA (see Chapter 2.4.4).

No provision of the ESA explicitly allows for a *combination* of grounds to be examined and, as we have seen, different exceptions apply to the various grounds. As a consequence the phenomenon of intersectional discrimination is difficult to address under the current statutory framework. Intersectional discrimination arises from the interaction of grounds, so that the influence of various grounds cannot be disentangled (Hannett, 2003; McColgan, 2007a; Solanke, 2009).[419] As Malik (2008, p 5) explains, using the example of an African woman who experiences discrimination, the sex and race ground elements of her case cannot easily be distinguished:

> It could be argued that the presence of both these categories at the same time transforms the grounds of both sex and race: i.e. she experiences discrimination as a woman in a way that is distinct from other women who are not African; and she experiences discrimination as an African in a way that is distinct from other Africans who are not women. Where an individual falls within more than one

---

[419] In the UK case of *Bahl v The Law Society* [2004] IRLR 799, an Asian woman alleged that she had been discriminated against on the grounds of her race and gender. The Employment Tribunal held that she could compare her treatment with that accorded a white man. But the Court of Appeal held that each claim had to be established separately. The case determines then that under UK law a black female complainant who alleges racial and gender discrimination must first compare her treatment with that which a white woman would have received (to establish race ground discrimination) and then compare her treatment with that which a black man would have received (to establish gender discrimination). Similar restrictions do not seem to apply in indirect discrimination cases: *Ministry of Defence v DeBique* [2010] IRLR 471.

protected group, and where there is a qualitative change in the nature of the discrimination, we can call this *intersectional discrimination* [emphasis in the original].

In a limited number of EEA cases equality officers have recognised 'compound discrimination'.[420] 'Additive' or 'compound' discrimination entails discrimination on multiple grounds where the role of the different grounds can still be differentiated (Makkonen, 2002, pp 10–11; Schiek, 2009, pp 12–13). In such cases gender or race discrimination, for example, is compounded or reinforced by discrimination on, say, the age ground. *Lindberg v Press Photographers Association of Ireland*[421] appears to recognise intersectional discrimination, however. In that case the Tribunal found that less favourable treatment arose because of a *combination* of the complainant's race and gender. Ms Lindberg applied for membership of the respondent association on a number of occasions. Despite meeting the applicable criteria her applications were unsuccessful. The equality officer concluded that the respondent's decisions were based on a perception that the complainant would not 'fit in'. She found that the complainant's outsider status was related to the gender and race grounds:

I find the combination of the complainant's circumstances in this case is significant. She is both female and non-national and is attempting to join an association, whose membership is predominantly Irish male. While this is not discriminatory per se and in fact it is more likely that it simply reflects the industry itself, it means in practice that the complainant is automatically outside the group in certain ways. The complainant does not fit into the respondent association because the combination of her race and gender automatically put her into a very small minority (para 4.4.4).

The equality officer appears to suggest that the grounds interacted with each other simultaneously so that they were inseparable. This seems therefore to be a case of intersectional discrimination; it is not clear that a case of direct discrimination on either ground would have succeeded if analysed separately. It remains to be seen how the case law on multiple discrimination will develop. A legislative amendment could explicitly allow for a flexible approach by specifying that dual or even multiple grounds could be applied with reference to a single hypothetical comparator.[422]

---

[420] See *Luzak v Sales Placement Ltd*, DEC-E2011-010 and *McDermott v Connacht Gold Cooperative Society Ltd*, DEC-E2011-147.

[421] DEC-S2011-041.

[422] See, for example, section 3.1 of the Canadian Human Rights Act 1998 (MacKay and

3.4 Defences under Section 15

In addition to the exceptions outlined above (Chapters 2.5 and 2.6), section 15 of the ESA allows for two defences to claims of discrimination that have proved controversial. According to Crowley (2006, p 101) these were introduced as a result of lobbying by vintners' organisations. The defence provided for in subsection (1) was roundly criticised by various human rights NGOs at the time the 2000 Act was introduced. A primary objection was that the exception was too broad and could, in effect, protect discriminatory behaviour and attitudes.[423] It permits a provider of goods, property, services or accommodation to decline service:

> [I]n circumstances which would lead a reasonable individual having the responsibility, knowledge and experience of the person to the belief, on grounds other than discriminatory grounds, that the [provision of the goods, services, etc.] ... to the customer would produce a substantial risk of criminal or disorderly conduct or behaviour or damage to property at or in the vicinity of the place in which the property or services are sought or the accommodation or land is located.

Although the defence is not limited to cases where the person alleging discrimination is responsible for the criminal or disorderly conduct, reference to action being taken 'on grounds other than discriminatory grounds' tempers its application to an extent.[424] Without that clause it could mean that if a shopkeeper or publican could demonstrate that the presence of for instance, a black person, in the shop or pub would lead to disorderly conduct by other customers he/she could refuse to serve that person. Such a scenario arose in *Mongan v The Firhouse Inn, Dublin*,[425] which concerned two Travellers who were refused service because of the hostile reaction of other patrons to their presence in the pub. There had been ongoing disputes between local settled and Traveller people about an official halting site. The complainants were innocent of any

---

Piper, 2009, pp 76–81). Section 14 of the UK Equality Act 2010 made provision for a direct discrimination complaint on two *combined* grounds, e.g. race and gender, or disability and age. However, in 2011 the UK Government decided that the provision would not be brought into effect (HM Treasury and BIS, 2011, p 53).

[423] See further 162 *Seanad Debates* Col 559 (Second Stage).

[424] For example in *McDonagh v Heatons*, DEC-S2011-024, the respondent was entitled to refuse access to its store because the complainant had been found removing security tags from items on a previous occasion. In light of that incident and other evidence about her behaviour during subsequent attempts to gain access to the shop, the equality officer concluded the decision to exclude was made 'on grounds other than discriminatory grounds'.

[425] DEC-S2003-034/035.

wrongdoing, but the equality officer agreed that the reaction of other patrons gave rise to a substantial risk of imminent violence while the complainants remained on the premises. Travellers were served in the pub before and after the incidents in question. The equality officer found that the refusal of service was not made on a discriminatory ground but was in accordance with section 15(1). It is to be hoped that this decision is confined to its particular facts, as otherwise persons who are the most vulnerable to stigma and exclusion could enjoy the least protection in this context. Liability for harassment could be imposed on a service provider where customers subject other customers to an intimidating, hostile, degrading, humiliating or offensive environment (Chapter 5, Chapter 7.3). To avoid such a finding the service provider would have to show that it had taken such steps as were reasonably practicable to prevent the harassment.

According to Crowley (2006, p 101) section 15(1) has 'the effect of placing an onus on complainants in cases where the exemption is used as a defence to establish their good character and that of their family and friends'. It appears from the cases heard to date that equality officers will generally scrutinise quite closely any attempts to raise the defence. The word 'substantial' means that there must be more than a reasonable risk of criminal or disorderly conduct and so on (Redmond, 2002, p 21).[426] In *A Complainant v A Supermarket*[427] the Tribunal underlined that the exception sets a 'high bar' for respondents and that allegations must be substantiated (para 5.3).

The damage to property aspect of the defence was availed of successfully in *Goldman v The Proprietor, Mullen's Auctioneers, Dublin.*[428] The equality officer emphasised that the facts were exceptional and that the admittance of a five-year-old to the respondent auctioneer's premises posed a substantial risk to its merchandise that could not be averted.

A further defence, set out under section 15(2), allows holders of licences to sell alcohol to refuse service on the basis that the action was taken in good faith to comply with the Licensing Acts. It can be used to exclude people who are intoxicated, violent or abusive, for example.[429] According to the Equality Tribunal in *Moorehouse v Ayleswood*,[430] this defence imposes a less severe test for the respondent than the section 15(1) defence, since it does not require a 'substantial degree of risk'. Actions taken in 'good faith' are made honestly with no underlying ulterior motive and so cover genuine instances of mistaken

---

[426] *Conroy v Carney's Public House*, DEC-S2001-002. See also *Flanagan Talbot v Casino Cinemas Limited t/a Killarney Cineplex Cinema*, DEC-S2008-053, at para 4.11.
[427] DEC-S2010-013.
[428] DEC-S2004-048.
[429] See, for example, *O'Reilly v Dragon Inn*, DEC-S2002-017.
[430] DEC-S2001-009.

identity, for example.[431] The defence will not succeed where a decision to exclude is influenced by the complainant's membership of a group covered by the discriminatory grounds.[432] It should be noted that cases of alleged discrimination occurring on or at the point of entry to licensed premises are heard by the District Court (Chapter 12.2).

The Irish Human Rights Commission (2004b, p 10) has called for the removal of both section 15 exceptions on the basis that they 'run counter to the Race Directive' and 'cannot be justified on any objective grounds'.

3.5 Victimisation

Persons who bring, or assist in, discrimination law proceedings are afforded some protection from retaliatory actions under section 3(2)(j). The victimisation ground covers situations where someone has in good faith applied for redress under the legislation, acted as a witness or given evidence in any ESA proceedings, opposed (by lawful means) any unlawful conduct under the Acts, or indicated an intention to do any of these things.

The criteria to be satisfied in order to establish a *prima facie* case of victimisation were outlined in *Collins v Campions Public House*.[433] The complainant must show:

1. That he/she applied in good faith for redress under the Act, indicated an intention to do so or otherwise satisfied section 3(2)(j)

2. That he/she was subjected to specific acts of treatment by the respondent after he/she did so and

3. That this treatment was less favourable than would have been afforded to a person in similar circumstances who had not taken the action at 1 above

In that case Ms Collins had been barred from a pub and notified the owner of her intention to make a complaint of discrimination. On a subsequent visit

---

[431] See further *Osborne and Killeen v Skelly's Pub*, DEC-S2004-190/191 (exclusion of children was a measure taken erroneously but in good faith to ensure compliance with the terms of a pub licence). See also *Delaney v Jamesons Hotel*, DEC-S2002-102; *Dooley and Boyne v The Grand Hotel*, DEC-S2002-015/016; *O'Reilly v Fowler's Pub*, DEC-S2003-134; and *Hanrahan v Cuckoo's Nest Off Licence*, DEC-S2007-048.

[432] See, for example, *Griffin v Mary B. Public House*, DEC-S2001-023 (upheld on appeal to the Circuit Court); *Collins v Drogheda Lodge Pub, Finglas*, DEC-S2002-097/100; *McDonagh v Patrick Powers Pub*, DEC-S2002-114/115; and *McCarthy v O'Looney's Bar*, DEC-S2003-075.

[433] DEC-S2003-071.

to the pub she was asked whether she was the person who had made a claim and was then told to leave. A number of other people who had been barred at the same time were also present but allowed to remain. The respondent maintained that the fact of the complaint was just used as a means of identifying the complainant, but the equality officer found this unconvincing in the circumstances and concluded that the respondent's actions were based on Ms Collins' use of the ESA.

Persons who want to lodge a complaint with the Equality Tribunal are obliged to notify the goods or service provider in writing of the discrimination allegation and of their intention to take a case (see Chapter 12.3.4). Respondents sometimes react to notification in a way that amounts to victimisation. For example, in a 2007 case a solicitor's letter threatening defamation proceedings was sent in response to a stated intention to make a complaint under the ESA.[434] That act amounted to victimisation and attracted an award of €4,000 in compensation. A statement to the effect that the complainant would be barred from the respondent's pub, also sent in response to notification of a possible referral, breached the ESA in *Griffin v Mary B. Public House*.[435]

Victimisation was established in *A Post-Leaving Certificate Student v An Educational Institution*,[436] where a written agreement reached with a disabled student as to the terms of his continued participation on a course included an undertaking not to proceed with a discrimination complaint.

Mrs A (on behalf of her son, B) v A Primary School[437] concerned discrimination in access to education for a child on the disability and Traveller community grounds. Mrs A had lodged a complaint under the ESA against another primary school and then sought to enrol her son in the respondent school. The chairperson of the board of management at the time was also chair of the board of the previous school attended by the boy. On the basis of the evidence supplied the equality officer was satisfied that the enrolment decision was influenced by the previous events. She found that the school victimised B and awarded the maximum amount of compensation allowed under the Acts.[438]

In *Curran v Total Fitness*[439] the equality officer examined in some detail the meaning of various elements of the victimisation provisions under the ESA and EEA. She concluded that the reference to opposing 'unlawful' conduct could include opposition to an incident that the complainant reasonably believed to

---

[434] *Cantwell v Giles & Co., Tralee*, DEC-S2007-010.

[435] DEC-S2001-023.

[436] DEC-S2009-043.

[437] DEC-S2007-003.

[438] See Equality Authority (2005b, pp 28–29) for a discussion of the successful Circuit Court appeal from the decision in *Salmon v Para Equestrian Ireland*, DEC-S2004-002.

[439] DEC-S2004-164. See also *Barrett v Department of Defence*, DEC-E2009-053.

be unlawful and need not be something which has been established as such by a court or tribunal:

> Looking back at the inception of this wording in the Employment Equality Act, those whose protection may have been intended by this wording might include union representatives. If they, the union representatives, were to be afforded protection only when a case was decided in their client's favour, the operation of trade union business in respect of equality would be seriously hampered. Another example would be the victimisation of representatives assisting complainants under the Equal Status Act, 2000, particularly at local level. A respondent could resolve a complaint with the complainant, be they employee or person availing of a service, and then treat the representative less favourably with impunity because of the assistance rendered by them in opposing what was perceived to be an unlawful act. To suggest that these, and others, are only afforded protection when they have successfully represented a complainant in a case under either of the Acts is, in my view, an unacceptable diminution of the spirit of the Acts. I am satisfied, given the construction of the subsection, that the intention was not to restrict protection but to afford it and therefore that the act complained of need not be found unlawful for the subsection to apply. I am satisfied that it would apply in situations where a person, given the gender equality provisions, would reasonably consider the act unlawful (para 4.2).

Mr Curran had queried why a portion of a gym was reserved for use by females. During a telephone conversation with the director of the company he asked what would happen if men sought access to that area. He had asked the question with a view to referring a gender discrimination complaint to the Tribunal. On subsequent visits to the gym he did not use the females-only facility. His membership of the gym was terminated, apparently because the company director mistakenly assumed that Mr Curran was going to breach one of the gym's rules by using the female section. The equality officer concluded that the complainant had opposed by lawful means conduct which he thought was unlawful under the ESA. She noted that the practice of reserving a female-only space might be permissible under the Acts because of the exception under section 5(2)(g) for situations where 'embarrassment or infringement of privacy can reasonably be expected to result from the presence of a person of another gender' (Chapter 2.6.2.1). But as that issue had not been dealt with in case law, it was not clear whether the gym's policy was actually 'unlawful' gender discrimination. It was sufficient, however, that Mr Curran believed it was. Having assessed all of the evidence, including information provided about other terminations of membership, the equality officer found that the complainant was treated less favourably on the victimisation ground.[440]

The finding of victimisation in *Twomey v Aer Lingus*[441] attracted an award of €3,000 in addition to orders directing the respondent to review its staff training in relation to people with disabilities and its communication procedures concerning customer complaints. In that case the equality officer concluded that Ms Twomey's treatment at check-in for a flight amounted to victimisation. The Tribunal concluded that following her requests for reasonable accommodation, in the form of being seated in a particular area of the aircraft, she was victimised by being allocated an even more unsuitable seat. Here too then, victimisation arose where someone opposed an act that was unlawful under the ESA.

It should be noted that the unlawful act in question must be connected to the rights protected under the ESA.[442] So for instance a customer who complained about compliance with food hygiene regulations and was subsequently barred from a restaurant could not invoke the victimisation ground.

O'Brien v Dunnes Stores, Tralee[443] entailed a finding of discrimination by association on the victimisation ground. A Traveller man was refused access to a store some weeks after his brother had been asked to leave and had indicated an intention to lodge an equal status complaint (Chapter 3.1.2). A case of discrimination by association on the Traveller and victimisation grounds did not succeed in *Smyth v Regdale Limited t/a 79 Inn, Dublin*.[444] The complainant was asked to leave a pub following a conversation with a member of staff about a discrimination complaint that was being pursued by Traveller friends of hers. Ms Smyth was inquiring whether the staff member had witnessed the incidents in question with a view to supporting the case against the respondent. The Tribunal found that the complainant was not treated less favourably than someone else would have been in similar circumstances. Even though the manager was aware of the topic of the conversation, the equality officer accepted that he had ejected Ms Smyth because the staff member was visibly upset. The equality officer was satisfied that another person who had upset a staff member would also have been asked to leave.

Under section 25(1A) a separate decision must be issued on the outcome of an investigation on the victimisation ground and compensation levels tend

---

[440] For a discussion of similar findings under the EEA see Curran (2008). An incident that occurred prior to the entry into force of the ESA is not unlawful and therefore cannot ground a victimisation complaint: *Hennessy v Network Catering/Iarnród Éireann*, DEC-S2009-029.

[441] DEC-S2009-079

[442] *Moriarty v Dúchas*, DEC-E2003-013.

[443] DEC-S2007-038.

[444] DEC-S2003-047.

to be relatively high. In principle, a separate award of compensation up to the €6,348.69 limit can be issued for a finding of discrimination on the victimisation ground, in addition to any award for other instances of discrimination or harassment.[445]

The framing of victimisation as a ground of discrimination is awkward and arguably does not meet EU law requirements (Connolly, 2009a). The Racial Equality Directive obliges member states to 'introduce into their national legal systems such measures as are necessary to protect individuals from any adverse treatment or adverse consequences as a reaction to a complaint or to proceedings aimed at enforcing compliance with the principle of equal treatment'.[446] There is no comparator requirement under the Directive, i.e. the requirement that a complainant show that they were treated in a less favourable manner than another person would have been in a similar situation. Under the UK Equality Act 2010 it is no longer necessary to draw comparisons (section 27). Instead persons must establish that they suffered a detriment because they had done a protected act, or because the service provider believed that they had done a protected act.

By analogy with discrimination law in the employment field, protection against victimisation should apply to conduct that occurs outside the services setting and should extend after a relationship between a service provider and recipient has ended.[447] So that, for example, a university lecturer should not refuse to give a former student a reference because they undertook any action set out in section 3(2)(*j*).

3.6 Conclusion

It is not clear whether the direct discrimination prohibition can be used in a preventative way. Section 3(1)(*a*) states that 'discrimination shall be taken to occur ... where a person is treated less favourably than another person is, has been or would be treated' on any specified ground which exists, existed or may exist in the future. The issue was raised in two 2009 decisions: *Mrs Cr (on behalf of her daughter Miss Cr) v The Minister for Education and Science*[448] and *Mrs Kn (on behalf of her son Mr Kn) and Others v The*

---

[445] Section 27(3).

[446] Article 9; recital 20 states: 'The effective implementation of the principle of equality requires adequate judicial protection against victimisation ...'. See also article 10 and recital 23 of the Gender Goods and Services Directive.

[447] See the Labour Court decision in *Panuta v Watters Garden World Ltd* [2010] 21 ELR 86, applying the CJEU judgment in *Coote v Granada Hospitality Ltd*, Case C-185/97, [1998] ECR 1-5199.

[448] DEC-S2009-051.

Minister for Education and Science.[449] As outlined above, the parents of children in so-called 'special schools' lodged a set of complaints. The children had been notified that under the terms of a Department circular they would be compelled to leave school upon reaching eighteen years of age. The respondent argued that the complaints were premature as all of the students were currently being provided with an education and no discriminatory act had actually taken place. In other words, the Minister maintained that section 3(1) (*a*) does not cover a situation of apprehended discrimination or apply to an act that may occur at some point in the future. The equality officer concluded that the Department's policy was already having an impact on the education of each child because all had taken steps, such as spending less time at primary level, to offset the effects of the exit requirement. As a result it was not necessary to decide whether the section applies to apprehended discrimination (the substance of the Tribunal's decisions in these important cases is considered in Chapter 3.3.2).

Similar questions arise in the context of indirect discrimination and are discussed in Chapter 4. Notably, the Australian High Court has found that an indirect discrimination ban should apply to policies that have yet to be implemented.[450] Further support for that position could be taken from the CJEU's judgment in the employment case of *Firma Feryn*.[451] The Court found that liability for direct discrimination under the Racial Equality Directive could arise even where there was no identifiable victim. It noted that the aim of the Directive, as stated in recital (8) of the Preamble, is 'to foster conditions for a socially inclusive labour market'. This, the Court observed, would be hard to achieve if the scope of the Directive was to be limited only to those cases where an unsuccessful candidate for a post brought legal proceedings against an employer. On the basis of this reasoning it could similarly be argued that the effectiveness of the equality directives would be undermined unless they can be applied to prevent the future application of an existing policy with discriminatory effects. In the alternative, the CJEU decision clearly allows the Equality Authority to use its power to refer cases of discrimination in situations like that encountered by the students in *Mrs Kn* and *Mrs Cr* (Chapter 11.3).

The next chapter examines indirect discrimination, a type of anti-discrimination measure that seeks to address disadvantage that stems from group membership, and is therefore distinguished from the individual harms tackled by direct discrimination. Indirect discrimination is also usually aimed at supposedly neutral measures, whereas direct discrimination is generally

---

[449] DEC-S2009-050.
[450] *Waters v Public Transport Corporation* [1991] HCA 49.
[451] *Centrum voor Gelijkheid van Kansen en voor Racismebestrijding v Firma Feryn NV*, Case C-54/07, [2008] ECR 1-1587.

based explicitly on a protected ground. However, it is difficult to maintain a boundary between direct and indirect discrimination in some cases. These difficulties typically arise in cases of segregation or other situations where a rule or measure applies exclusively to members of a protected group. In *Maruko* the CJEU established that direct discrimination is the appropriate provision in the latter situation.[452] That approach was also adopted by the equality officer in *Mrs Cr (on behalf of her daughter Miss Cr) v The Minister for Education and Science*[453] (para 6.5) and *Mrs Kn (on behalf of her son Mr Kn) and Others v The Minister for Education and Science*[454] (para 6.12). A major distinction between the two forms of discrimination as provided for in law is that indirect discrimination can be objectively justified whereas as we have seen direct discrimination cannot.[455]

---

[452] *Maruko v Versorgungsanstalt der Deutschen Buhnen*, Case C-267/06, [2008] ECR 1-17571. See further Tobler and Waaldijk (2009).

[453] DEC-S2009-051.

[454] DEC-S2009-050.

[455] Both direct and indirect discrimination can be justified under the European Convention on Human Rights.

4

Indirect Discrimination

4.1 Introduction

As discussed in Chapter 3, direct discrimination takes place *on* a discriminatory ground. There is a direct link between the less favourable treatment and the protected status or characteristic. By contrast, indirect discrimination involves treatment that arises from the application of neutral provisions. For example, a policy that requires loan applicants to have a permanent address appears neutral but that requirement may exclude Travellers. The idea is that while no open distinction is made between given groups or individuals, in practice rules or standards may have an adverse effect on certain people. The concept is valuable because it looks beyond the formal picture to focus on the *effects* of provisions.[456]

Because it examines the impact of service provision practices indirect discrimination can unearth institutional discrimination. Institutional discrimination consists of policies, practices and patterns of behaviour that are embedded in the systems and structures of an organisation, and which have the effect of disadvantaging some categories of people relative to others. These policies and so on may appear to be unobjectionable but have an exclusionary impact (see, for example, Barnes, 1991; Conaghan, 1986; McCrudden, 1982; Ontario Human Rights Commission, 2005; Tobler, 2005a). Generally there is no intention to exclude or discriminate behind such provisions; they simply

---

[456] The concept was first applied by a court in *Griggs v Duke Power Co.* 401 US 424 (1971). The US Supreme Court struck down reliance on general ability testing and high school diplomats as job requirements because of the disproportionate negative impact these had on black workers. The test and qualifications were not sufficiently related to ability to perform the jobs in question. Subsequently, the concept of 'disparate impact' discrimination, as it is termed in the US, was recognised in the legal systems of other countries under EU law (Tobler, 2005a; Schiek, 2007, pp 333–359). Indirect discrimination is also prohibited under the ECHR. See, for example, *Hoogendijk v Netherlands* (2005) 40 EHRR SE22 and *DH v Czech Republic* (2007) 47 EHRR 3.

reflect 'how things are done' in an organisation.[457] As Day and Brodsky (1996, p 472) note, seemingly neutral rules 'are typically descriptions of the practices that suit an institution's traditional participants'.

Identifying a provision that disadvantages people covered by a discriminatory ground is not enough to succeed in an indirect discrimination claim. Under Irish and EU law the claim will not be successful if the measure in question can be justified as a proportionate means of achieving a legitimate aim. As we will see from the case law considered in this chapter much depends on how the justification test is applied.

Indirect discrimination was prohibited under the Equal Status Act of 2000, but the definition was overhauled in 2004 to bring Irish law into line with the Racial Equality Directive.[458] This chapter will focus on the revised definition and so much of the case law discussed dates from 2008 on.

4.2 Definition of Indirect Discrimination

According to the ESA indirect discrimination occurs 'where an apparently neutral provision puts a person referred to in any paragraph of section 3(2) at a particular disadvantage compared with other persons, unless the provision is objectively justified by a legitimate aim and the means of achieving that aim are appropriate and necessary'.[459]

The prohibition then has two basic elements. First, an apparently neutral provision puts a person covered by the grounds at a particular disadvantage compared with other persons. 'Provision' is broadly defined as 'a term in a contract or a requirement, criterion, practice, regime, policy or condition affecting a person'.[460] Second, an indirect discrimination complaint can be defeated if it is established that the 'provision is objectively justified by a legitimate aim and the means of achieving that aim are appropriate and necessary'.[461]

---

[457] A practice that is couched in a neutral way but is intended to discriminate against a particular group should be considered a form of direct discrimination as it is based on a discriminatory ground (Bamforth et al., 2008, p 156).

[458] Section 3(1)(*c*) Equal Status Act 2000. The main Tribunal decisions that consider the original definition of indirect discrimination are *Ogunlade and Oyefeso v Michael Guiney Ltd*, DEC-S2003-016/017; *McDonagh v Navan Hire Ltd*, DEC-S2004-017; *Tsourova v Trinity College Dublin*, DEC-S2004-162; *Ward and Kavanagh v Sacred Heart Secondary School Tullamore*, DEC-S2005-019/020; *Hassan v Western Union Financial Services*, DEC-S2006-004; and *A Student v City of Dublin Vocational Education Committee*, DEC-S2007-089.

[459] Section 3(1)(*c*).

[460] Section 2.

[461] Section 3(1)(*c*).

The ESA definition replicates to a large extent the wording of the relevant EU directives. For example, article 2(2)(*b*) of the Racial Equality Directive provides:

> [I]ndirect discrimination shall be taken to occur where an apparently neutral provision, criterion or practice would put persons of a racial or ethnic origin at a particular disadvantage compared with other persons, unless that provision, criterion or practice is objectively justified by a legitimate aim and the means of achieving that aim are appropriate and necessary.

There are two points of divergence. First, the Irish legislation refers to 'a person' covered by a discriminatory ground whereas the directives refer to 'persons'. This suggests that under the ESA a complainant must just demonstrate that she or he personally is disadvantaged by an apparently neutral provision, while EU law also requires that the wider group she or he is part of is so affected. In an employment equality case the UK Court of Appeal examined a similar provision and found that a complainant must show that the group in question is put at a disadvantage (Hatzis, 2011).[462] The uniform policy of Ms Eweida's employer did not allow the visible display of jewellery including her necklace, which depicted a Christian cross. According to the Court she was unable to establish that the visible display of the cross was a requirement of the Christian faith. Because she could not show that Christians generally were placed at a disadvantage by the uniform rule there was no group disadvantage and her case failed. It is possible that the Irish definition will allow cases of individual disadvantage to succeed. However, in the existing Tribunal decisions the complainants have produced evidence of group disadvantage and the main case suggests that such an impact is necessary.[463] It remains to be seen what is required under the Racial Equality Directive (Barnard and Hepple, 2000, pp 568–569; Schiek, 2007, pp 330–331; Tobler, 2005a, p 287).

Second, the ESA applies to a provision that 'puts' a person at a particular disadvantage. Article 2(2)(*b*) of the Racial Equality Directive refers to 'an apparently neutral provision, criterion or practice that *would put* persons of a racial or ethnic origin at a particular disadvantage compared with other persons' (emphasis added). This difference in wording could have two sets of

---

[462] *Eweida v British Airways* [2010] ICR 890. The law in issue was Regulation 3 of the Employment Equality (Religion or Belief) Regulations 2003, which implements the indirect discrimination prohibition on the grounds of religion or belief under the Framework Directive.

[463] *Stokes v Christian Brothers' High School, Clonmel and Department of Education and Skills*, DEC-S2010-056.

implications. One relates to proof of disadvantage. The EU standard appears to be lighter because it does not require the complainant to show that a provision actually generates a disadvantage, but just that it is liable to have that effect (Tobler and European Network of Legal Experts in the Non-Discrimination Field, 2008, p 40).[464] This matter is revisited below.

The other question raised by the use of the word 'puts' is whether indirect discrimination applies to measures that have not yet been applied in practice. The EU formula, it seems, does not require that a disadvantage has already arisen (Finlay, 2003, p 149). Viewed from another angle, does the word 'provision' used in the ESA include a proposal to implement a discriminatory policy at a future date? In *Waters v Public Transport Corporation*[465] the Australian High Court found in favour of the complainants who had argued that the removal of conductors from trams and the introduction of a scratch ticket system indirectly discriminated on the disability ground by imposing a condition or requirement that disadvantaged them (Patmore, 1999). Each of the nine complainants was affected by a disability that would make the proposed ticket system difficult or impossible to use (including cerebral palsy, intellectual disability and visual impairment). The practical outcome of the case was the discontinuance of the scratch ticket system, but not the reinstitution of tram conductors. Significantly, the case involved a decision to make changes to a public transport system that had yet to be implemented.

4.3 Establishing Indirect Discrimination

4.3.1 Introduction

This section examines the steps involved in establishing a case of indirect discrimination under the ESA. To prove indirect discrimination, a complainant must identify a provision and demonstrate that it puts him or her, as a person covered by one of the protected grounds, at a particular disadvantage compared with other persons. In line with the ESA rules on the burden of proof, the onus is on the complainant to prove on the balance of probabilities that the measure has that effect:

> 38A(1) Where in any proceedings facts are established by or on behalf of a person from which it may be presumed that prohibited conduct has occurred in relation to him or her, it is for the respondent to prove the contrary.

---

[464] The wording used in the Directive reflects the standard first set out by the CJEU in *O'Flynn v Adjudication Officer* [1998] ICR 608, at para 20.
[465] [1991] HCA 49.

(2) This section is without prejudice to any other enactment or rule of law in relation to the burden of proof in any proceedings which may be more favourable to the person.

The usual rules on *locus standi* apply to indirect discrimination cases (Chapter 12.3.2) and so a complainant must show that they have been personally affected by a neutral provision (or possibly will be so affected in the future). For that reason in *Fahey v Ulster Bank*[466] a claim of indirect discrimination on the age ground was defeated because the provision (working in full-time employment) had not been applied to the complainant's application for a personal loan.

4.3.2 Apparently Neutral Provision

The complainant must point to the apparently neutral provision or provisions that form the basis of the complaint.[467] 'Provision' is broadly defined as 'a term in a contract or a requirement, criterion, practice, regime, policy or condition affecting a person'.[468] Taken together the words 'practice' and 'regime' would cover informal measures or procedures that are not written down. For example, a school might adopt the practice of holding parent–teacher meetings in part of a school building that is not wheelchair accessible, putting certain disabled people at a particular disadvantage compared with non-disabled people. In a 2011 case the Tribunal seemed to accept that a practice of failing to verbally explain the terms and conditions of an insurance contract could amount to a 'provision'. It found on the facts, however, that the respondent did not operate such a policy.[469] A 'criterion' will usually mean a standard or principle on which a decision is based. Decisions to extend loans, award grants or offer insurance coverage, for example, are often based on multiple criteria. Many standard criteria such as a secure employment status, a track record of saving money and so on appear to be neutral but when applied in practice they could operate so as to disadvantage younger and older people.

A 2006 case illustrates that a wide range of practices are subject to the indirect discrimination prohibition. In *Hassan v Western Union Financial Services*[470] the Equality Tribunal found that a financial services institution

---

[466] DEC-S2008-049; see also *Walsh v Ryanair*, DEC-S2010-054.

[467] Indirect discrimination complaints will fail where the complainant cannot identify any relevant provision: *Dalton v Department of Health and Children*, DEC-S2010-033, para 5.6 and *Comerford v Trailfinders Ireland Ltd*, DEC-S2011-013, para 6.12.

[468] Section 2, ESA.

[469] *Mongan v FBD Insurance plc*, DEC-S2011-016.

[470] DEC-S2006-004. See also *Secretary of State for Trade & Industry v Rutherford (No.2)* [2006] ICR 785, at para 47.

had indirectly discriminated against the complainant on the religion ground. While the actual decision to freeze payment of a money transfer pending a security check was required by EU law and so exempt under section 14(1)(*a*), the *manner* in which the EU security regulations were implemented was at the discretion of the company. The processes involved were onerous and affected substantially more persons with Muslim names than people with non-Muslim names. The equality officer was satisfied that the requirements were arbitrarily imposed and that the respondent's obligations could have been carried out by alternative means. Consequently the requirements imposed on Mr Hassan could not be objectively justified.

As discussed below, various service provision practices have been tested in ESA indirect discrimination complaints, including criteria for accessing bank loans, conditions imposed by public transport providers, school admission criteria and conditions in insurance policies.

4.3.3 Particular Disadvantage

The complainant must establish that they are covered by a discriminatory ground, and then show that they (and according to case law, also persons sharing that status) are put at a particular disadvantage compared with other persons.

The term 'particular disadvantage' is not defined under Irish or EU law. 'Disadvantage' may be read in two ways. It could be applied in a qualitative sense to describe the type of harm or detriment experienced by the complainant. For example, would a provision that just inconveniences someone (and their group) amount to a disadvantage or do they have to establish a more serious harm? This question has not been probed in the ESA decisions issued to date. Once-off and repeat economic losses have amounted to a particular disadvantage,[471] as have requirements to acquire and queue for a train ticket on each day of travel.[472] In a case about a school dress code the UK Court of Appeal found that the 'adverse consequences' do not have to 'reach a particularly high threshold'.[473] A fact-sensitive decision should be reached in each

---

[471] *Martin v Esplanade Hotel*, DEC-S2010-034 and *Fitzgerald v Dairygold Co-Operative Society Ltd*, DEC-S2009-083.

[472] *Thompson v Iarnród Éireann*, DEC-S2009-015 and *O'Connor v Iarnród Éireann*, DEC-S2010-048.

[473] *R (Watkins Singh) v Governing Body of Aberdare Girls' High School* [2008] ELR 561, at para 52. In *Shamoon v Chief Constable of the Royal Ulster Constabulary* [2003] 2 ALL ER 26 the House of Lords found that there could be a 'detriment' in the employment context where a reasonable worker would or might take the view that he had thereby been disadvantaged in the circumstances in which he had thereafter to work and that, although an unjustified sense of grievance could not amount to a 'detriment, it was not necessary to demonstrate any physical or economic consequence'.

situation as to whether the disadvantage experienced by the complainant amounted to a particular disadvantage.[474] In a subsequent judgment the same court found that 'the adjective "particular" is obviously intended to indicate that what is recognised is more than a disadvantage – that would apply if a person was unable to act in a way in which he or she wished to act ....' More than a denial of choice is therefore required; the matter must be of 'particular importance'.[475] It should be noted that because both individual and group disadvantage must be established (Chapter 4.2) a provision that just results in a personal detriment for the complainant would be inadequate.

The second meaning that attaches to the phrase 'particular disadvantage' concerns the level of impact on the complainant's group *relative to* the level of impact on the comparator group of other persons. This has not been contentious in the existing ESA case law because the successful complainants were able to demonstrate substantial comparative levels of disadvantage. In other words, a substantially larger proportion of their group was disadvantaged by the provision.[476] It is clear that not all members of the complainant's group have to be put at a particular disadvantage by the provision in question.[477]

The High Court, however, has found that the term 'particular disadvantage' bears a third meaning.[478] According to McCarthy J the word 'particular' means a complainant must show that the disadvantage in question is one that

---

[474] *R (Watkins Singh) v Governing Body of Aberdare Girls' High School* [2008] ELR 561, at para 56A. In that case the court had to decide whether a girl suffered a particular disadvantage when she was precluded from wearing a religious bangle (the Kara) at school. According to Silber J there was both a subjective and objective element to establishing a particular disadvantage, which aligns with the requirement that there be a personal and group impact: 'On the facts of this case, I believe that there would be a "*a particular disadvantage*" or "*detriment*" if a pupil is forbidden from wearing an item when (a) that person genuinely believed for reasonable grounds that wearing this item was a matter of *exceptional* importance to his or her racial identity or his or her religious belief and (b) the wearing of this item can be shown objectively to be of *exceptional* importance to his or her religion or race, even if the wearing of the article is not an actual requirement of that person's religion or race' [emphasis in original] (para 56B). Compare *G v St Gregory's Catholic Science College* [2011] EWHC 1452, paras 37–38.

[475] *G v St Gregory's Catholic Science College* [2011] EWHC 1452, para 37.

[476] The exception here is perhaps the level of disadvantage established in *Stokes v Christian Brothers' High School, Clonmel and Department of Education and Skills*, DEC-S2010-056 (discussed in Chapter 4.4). That case was about a Traveller boy's prospects of gaining admission to a secondary school. The Tribunal found that the difference between a 70 per cent chance of getting a place before the application of the impugned provision and 55 per cent afterwards was sufficient.

[477] *R (Bailey) v London Borough of Brent* [2011] EWCA Civ 1586, para 44; *G v St Gregory's Catholic Science College* [2011] EWHC 1452, para 32.

[478] *Stokes v Christian Brothers High School Clonmel* (High Court, McCarthy J, unreported, 6 February 2012).

is 'peculiar or restricted to' the complainant's group. It is submitted that the High Court's approach in *Stokes* is out of sync with established discrimination law principles. Indirect discrimination under the ESA was originally concerned with comparing the relative proportions of two groups that could comply with a condition applied by a service provider. Now it is a question of whether people sharing a characteristic protected by a discriminatory ground are placed at a particular disadvantage compared to those who do not share it. The term 'particular disadvantage' then refers to the respective impact of a provision on the two comparator groups at issue in the case (Tobler and European Network of Legal Experts in the Non-Discrimination Field, 2008, p 31). The fact that other persons not sharing the complainant's characteristic are also adversely affected by the provision is irrelevant. What matters is that the complainant's group is disproportionately affected. The *Stokes* case is discussed further in Chapter 4.4.

We have seen that discrimination law is concerned with the relative treatment of people. Comparisons of individuals and groups across the discriminatory grounds are, therefore, an inevitable part of discrimination complaints. Indirect discrimination is more complicated than direct discrimination on this front, because the comparisons are made between groups and it is difficult to identify how the two groups should be constructed. Neither EU law nor the ESA specify how the pools of comparison should be drawn. In other words, there is no guidance as to who the 'other persons' are who must be compared with the complainant's group. It is just clear that they must not belong to the same element of the discriminatory ground as the complainant.

For the purposes of making the comparison a complainant must first look to the definition of the discriminatory ground(s) in question. So, for example, a person with a particular disability can compare her position with persons with other disabilities or people without disabilities. A wheelchair user could argue that her group (people with mobility impairments) is put at a particular disadvantage by a provision compared with persons without mobility impairments or persons with a different disability.

But the question still remains as to what pool of 'other persons' are relevant. For example, in a case of an indirect gender discrimination complaint advanced by a woman is the comparator group all males in the population at large, all males who avail of the same service as the complainant or a sub-set of males who use the same service? As we will see from the case law considered below, the appropriate pool of comparison will depend on the facts of the case.[479] Generally speaking it will depend on which section of

---

[479] In *Grundy v British Airways plc* [2008] IRLR 74, Sedley LJ reflected on the difficulty of selecting the right pool for comparison: 'One of the striking things about both the race and sex discrimination legislation is that, contrary to early expectations, three decades of

the public is likely to be affected by the provision.[480] So that where *access to a service* is in issue the relevant pool will generally be the population at large without the complainant's status or characteristic. In cases that involve provisions applied in the course of using a service, undergoing an educational programme or living in accommodation, the applicable pool will usually be other service users.[481]

4.3.4 Proving Disadvantage

The ESA and relevant EU directives do not specify *how* disadvantage is to be established. Before the definition was revised under EU law statistical evidence was often required to support a claim of indirect discrimination.[482] The particular disadvantage test gets around the need to produce statistics and allows other evidence to be taken into account.

Such developments were occurring at any rate under the 2000 Act. *McDonagh v Navan Hire Ltd*[483] is a notable case on the Traveller community ground. The Tribunal found that the requirement of having a permanent address to hire a sander had a disparate impact on Travellers and could not be objectively justified. Since the equality officer dealt at some length with the form of proof required in indirect discrimination cases her reasoning is worth quoting in some detail:

> [T]he respondent imposed a condition (that is being able to provide a permanent address which is not a halting site address) which substantially fewer Travellers than non-Travellers would be able to satisfy. While the complainant has not produced any statistical evidence to support this contention it is obvious that halting sites are specifically designed for Travellers and that Travellers are substantially more likely to live on halting sites than non-Travellers.

---

litigation have failed to produce any universal formula for locating the correct pool, driving tribunals and courts alike to the conclusion that there is none', at para 27.

[480] *London Underground Ltd v Edwards (No. 2)* [1998] IRLR 364.

[481] In a recent case about the equality impact of proposed library closures Pill LJ considered it was legitimate to take the pool of library users rather than that of the entire borough population: *R (Bailey) v London Borough of Brent* [2011] EWCA Civ 1586, para 82.

[482] 'Disproportionate impact' was the original legislative formula used at EU level and it gave rise to problems in practice. Statistical evidence was frequently required to establish such impact, but it was often difficult or impossible for complainants to source (Curtin, 1989). Under the ESA 2000 it was necessary to establish that 'substantially more people outside the category than within it' were able to comply with a condition imposed by a service provider: section 3(1)(c), Equal Status Act 2000.

[483] DEC-S2004-017.

In considering this point concerning statistical evidence, I have referred to the Labour Court decision in an employment case, *NBK Designs Ltd v Inoue* ED/02/34 Determination No. 0212. In this Decision, the Labour Court held that an expert tribunal like the Labour Court could take account, even in the absence of specific evidence, [of] matters such as risk of disparate impact on a protected ground under the Act which are well established and are obvious from its specialist experience. In *Inoue*, the Labour Court held that it was obvious that measures impacting on part-time workers, or on those caring for small children, would impact disproportionately on women. It would be reasonable therefore to infer from this rationale that an expert tribunal, such as the Equality Tribunal, can similarly take account of matters such as the number of Travellers living on halting sites in comparison to the number of non-Travellers, matters which are obvious from the Tribunal's specialist experience (para 7.2).

The decision confirms that a court or tribunal can rely on common knowledge, obvious facts or matters within its specialist expertise to ease the eviden-tial burden associated with indirect discrimination complaints (Tobler and European Network of Legal Experts in the Non-Discrimination Field, 2008, p 40).[484] However, since such matters will be obvious or well established through case law, complainants who raise novel issues will still have to source proof of disadvantage.

Section 3(3A) provides that statistics are admissible for the purpose of determining whether discrimination has occurred. The Central Statistics Office and other statutory bodies collect data and issue reports on many of the groups covered by the ESA, but reliable data on some grounds such as sexual orientation and race is very difficult to source (Bond, McGinnity and Russell, 2010; Tobler, 2005a, pp 291–292). The disability ground may also present difficulties. People covered by that ground are an eclectic group who cannot easily be classified for the purposes of statistics:

> There are many different forms of disabilities, each demonstrating large variations as to their nature and severity and this is further compounded by the existence of multiple disabilities. As a result,

---

[484] The Labour Court decision in *NBK Designs Ltd v Inoue* [2003] ELR 98 is frequently applied in support of that approach. In addition to the *McDonagh* case see, for example, *O'Brien v Cork University Hospital*, DEC-E2008-021 and *Lazar v Dublin Bus*, DEC-E2010-150. See also the UK case of *London Underground Ltd v Edwards (No. 2)* [1998] IRLR 364.

some people with disabilities would have great difficulty in identifying a particular group that is disadvantaged by the relevant provision, criterion or practice in the same manner and to the same extent as they are (Whittle, 2002, p 309).

Since the ESA allows comparisons between 'a person' with a disability and other persons (who may have no disability or a different form of disability), it is possible to compare people with particular types of conditions (e.g. dyslexia or depression). EU law also allows an 'individual to establish a claim by reference to tightly defined sub-groups within the larger ground of "disability"' (Whittle, 2002, p 309). A complainant from such a 'sub-group' will probably not have access to appropriate statistics. In these and other cases other forms of evidence will be crucial. Relevant evidence could potentially include sociological studies or reports issued by bodies with expertise on the experiences of the group in question.[485] As discussed below, in an age ground case the complainant successfully relied on statistics as well as research conducted by an NGO into computer usage by older people.[486] Despite these developments, several complainants have not been able to source adequate evidence to satisfy the particular disadvantage test (Chapter 4.4).

4.3.5 Objective Justification

Once the complainant has established a *prima facie* case – in this context that (1) they are covered by a discriminatory ground and (2) that a provision puts them at a particular disadvantage compared with other persons – the onus shifts to the respondent to rebut the inference of discrimination. A service provider will seek to do so by establishing that the provision was objectively justified.

---

[485] That type of evidence may be especially useful in situations where the provision is an informal one, and so there would be no rules as such to measure and compare. In the first indirect discrimination case under the ESA a shop denied access to the complainant, a black woman, apparently on the basis that she had behaved aggressively towards staff on a previous occasion: *Ogunlade and Oyefeso v Michael Guiney Ltd*, DEC-S2003-016/017. The respondent denied that it had directly discriminated on the race ground and in effect sought to avail of the defence under section 15(1). The complainants contended, however, that it was a case of mistaken identity, which in turn amounted to indirect discrimination because the indigenous white population has greater difficulty in distinguishing between black people than other white people. The equality officer found that the complainants had not discharged the burden of proof because they had not supplied any evidence to support the suggestion that it is substantially easier for a white person to be recognised by other white people.

[486] *Martin v Esplanade Hotel*, DEC-S2010-034.

A complaint will not succeed if a service provider can establish that the 'provision is objectively justified by a legitimate aim and the means of achieving that aim are appropriate and necessary'.[487]

To satisfy the first limb of the defence a service provider must show that the provision in question pursues a legitimate aim. In ESA cases a 'legitimate aim' is usually interpreted widely to include, for example, an organisation's commercial interests and administrative efficiency.[488] Fostering a 'community spirit' amongst pupils was accepted as a legitimate aim in a UK case on school uniforms,[489] while for the Irish Circuit Court a school admission criterion that gave preference to children of past pupils pursued the legitimate aim of supporting a family ethos.[490] Respondents generally have little difficulty in showing that a provision pursues a legitimate aim.[491]

The second limb of the test is more difficult to satisfy. A service provider must show that the provision was both an appropriate and necessary means of pursuing the legitimate aim. It is not sufficient that the provision is convenient or desirable (Tobler and European Network of Legal Experts in the Non-Discrimination Field, 2008, p 35).[492]

The word 'appropriate' means that the measure is suitable for achieving the aim in question. Mere generalisations are not sufficient; the service provider

---

[487] Section 3(1)(*c*). The previous test required a service provider to establish that the condition was 'justified as being reasonable in all the circumstances of the case': section 3(1)(*c*) (iv), Equal Status Act 2000.

[488] On commercial interests as a legitimate aim see the discussion below of *Jordan v Marsh Ireland Ltd*, DEC-S2008-054; *Martin v Esplanade Hotel*, DEC-S2010-034; and *Fitzgerald v Dairygold Co-Operative Society Ltd*, DEC-S2009-083. Under the EEA the following have been accepted as legitimate aims: payment of a fee to have an examination exemption considered pursued the legitimate aim of ensuring that applicants seeking to enter a profession have a minimum standard of relevant education: *Nowak v Law Society of Ireland*, DEC-E2010-051; rostering arrangements pursued the legitimate aim of maintaining industrial relations harmony: *O'Donnell and Others v Health Service Executive (North West Area)*, DEC-E2006-023.

[489] *R (Watkins Singh) v Governing Body of Aberdare Girls' High School* [2008] ELR 561.

[490] *Christian Brothers High School Clonmel v Stokes* [2011] IECC 1.

[491] It should be noted that EU law on sex discrimination distinguishes between the legitimate aims that can be relied upon by employers as opposed to member states. Employers must show that the aim corresponds to a real need on the part of the undertaking, whereas member states are entitled to rely on social policy goals. In either case the aim must be unrelated to any discrimination on grounds of sex (Tobler and European Network of Legal Experts in the Non-Discrimination Field, 2008, p 32). It remains to be seen how such a distinction will apply in the goods and services context.

[492] According to Mummery LJ in a UK case, 'it is necessary to weigh the need against the seriousness of the detriment to the disadvantaged group. It is not sufficient that [the party discriminating] could reasonably consider the means chosen as suitable for attaining the aim': *R (Elias) v Secretary of State for Defence* [2006] 1 WLR 3213 at p 3249.

must show that the provision in fact advances the aim (Fredman, 2011, p 194; Tobler and European Network of Legal Experts in the Non-Discrimination Field, 2008, p 35). A provision will be 'necessary' where there are no alternative, less discriminatory ways of advancing the respondent's aim.[493] The burden is on the respondent to establish each element of the objective justification defence. Usually there must be evidence that at the time of applying the provision the service provider had considered whether there were other less discriminatory ways of achieving the aim (Fredman, 2011, p 195).

According to the CJEU and the Equality Tribunal in employment equality cases cost, in itself, is not justification.[494] By analogy, it would appear that a service provider cannot simply argue that it is cheaper to discriminate; it must point to additional factors in order to avail of the defence.

4.4 Case Law

This section reviews the decisions on indirect discrimination in chronological order. It focuses on the case law that has emerged since 2008 on the definition introduced under the Equality Act 2004. Because there are relatively few decisions to date there is an amount of uncertainty about its operation. Equality officers and judges tend not to rely on EU law or to draw on the body of case law developed under the EEA. However, this can be expected to change when decisions emerge from the CJEU on the indirect discrimination prohibition under the Racial Equality Directive and the Gender Goods and Services Directive.

Jordan v Marsh Ireland Ltd[495] involved a discriminatory condition in an insurance policy. When he broke his wrist Mr Jordan made a claim under a policy he had taken out with the respondent. He was informed that he had not been eligible for the plan at the time he had entered into the contract since he did not meet the criterion of being in 'good health'. The complainant had a disability as a result of a car crash and maintained that the person in Permanent TSB who sold him the insurance was satisfied that he was eligible to sign up for the scheme. In assessing the terms of the insurance contract the equality officer had regard to a Supreme Court judgment which specifies that any ambiguity in such a contract should be read against the person who prepared

---

[493] According to the Labour Court in an employment discrimination case: 'This would normally require the Respondent to establish that alternative means of achieving the objective were considered and rejected for cogent reasons': *National University of Ireland, Maynooth v Buckley* [2011] ELR 324.

[494] See, for example, *McGarr v The Department of Finance*, DEC-E2003-036, *Catholic University School v Dooley* [2010] IEHC 496 and *Kutz-Bauer v Freie und Hansestadt Hamburg*, Case C-187/00, [2003] ECR 1-2741.

[495] DEC-S2008-054.

it. She noted that the term 'good health' was not defined on the policy form and that the complainant had not sought to conceal his disability from the person who had sold him the insurance. The equality officer accepted that Mr Jordan could subjectively consider himself to be in 'good health', noting that he 'like many other people with disabilities, manages his condition and goes about his everyday life' (para 5.8).

She then went on to consider whether the policy condition was indirectly discriminatory on the disability ground. In *Bilka-Kaufhaus v von Hartz*,[496] a gender discrimination employment case, the CJEU set out three criteria that must be met to avail of the objective justification defence. An employer must demonstrate that the impugned provision:

- Corresponds to a real need on the part of the undertaking
- Is appropriate with a view to achieving the objective pursued and
- Is necessary to that end

Applying that test to the facts before her the equality officer concluded:

> 1. Insurers do have a real need to make commercially advantageous decisions when taking on customers;
>
> 2. The insurer, and an agent acting on their behalf, has a right to treat people differently in relation to the assessment of risk in accordance with the defences set out in section 5(2)(d) of the Acts;
>
> 3. It may be essential to limit insurance cover or the conditions of the insurance where reliable actuarial data, statistical data, relevant underwriting or commercial factors [affect] the commercially advantageous decisions (para 5.14).

She noted that there was no relationship between the wrist injury incurred and the pre-existing disability. The 'good health' condition amounted to a blanket ban on any person with a disability qualifying for the plan in question. The complaint of indirect discrimination on the disability ground succeeded:

> If I were to accept the current wording, and the respondent's interpretation of them, I would be accepting a condition that excludes any person who lives with a chronic condition, that is, a health related concern that can be managed[,] from any insurance at all. This condition, which may appear to be neutral, puts a person, such as

---

[496] Case 170/84, [1986] ECR 1607.

the complainant, at a particular disadvantage compared with persons who live without his condition. I do not find that the provision is objectively justified by a legitimate aim as the insurer has clearly indicated that it refuses to insure any person, regardless of data or any other relevant factors, with any health issues at all (para 5.16).

Thompson v Iarnród Éireann[497] gave rise to a finding of indirect discrimination on the disability ground, as well as a failure to afford reasonable accommodation under section 4 of the ESA (the reasonable accommodation element of the decision is dealt with in Chapter 6.4.3). The visually impaired complainant used a free travel pass to get to work. He claimed that the requirement to queue for a travel ticket every day, a condition not imposed on customers without a travel pass, breached the ESA. The Tribunal found that the apparently neutral provision in question – the obligation to acquire a new ticket each day – put the complainant as the holder of a free travel pass and a person with a disability (and other persons within this category) at a disadvantage compared to other customers of the respondent without a disability who do not avail of the pass. An inference of indirect discrimination was therefore raised and in accordance with section 38(A) it then fell to the respondent to rebut that inference. According to the equality officer, Iarnród Éireann failed to demonstrate that the provision was objectively justified by a legitimate aim and that the means of achieving that aim were appropriate and necessary. It had sought to argue that the restrictions imposed were necessary to counter fraudulent practices but no evidence was offered in support of that contention. Alternative means of preventing fraud, such as requiring pass holders to present identification, were open to the respondent. The equality officer ordered the respondent to review its policy on free travel pass holders to ensure its compliance with the terms of the ESA.

A similar decision was issued in *O'Connor v Iarnród Éireann*, this time on the age ground.[498] The complainant also held a free travel pass, which he was entitled to because he was over 66 years of age. He argued that the requirement to obtain a ticket on the day of travel, and other related conditions such as the absence of an online booking facility, put him at a particular disadvantage compared to younger persons. The equality officer found that the conditions for members of the Free Travel Scheme fell within the definition of 'apparently neutral provisions'. She also found that the provisions put older persons and disabled people at a particular disadvantage: 'I find that the Free Travel Scheme members are predominantly aged over 66 or disabled or both, and therefore the imposition of these unfavourable conditions has a disproportion-

---

497 DEC-S2009-015.
498 DEC-S2010-048.

ate effect on these groups' (para 4.4). As with the *Thompson* decision, because a *prima facie* case of indirect discrimination was established the outcome rested on whether the respondent could rebut that inference by establishing that the provisions were objectively justified. The equality officer accepted that the prevention of fraud was a legitimate aim and then considered whether the measures taken to realise that aim were appropriate and necessary. She found that the respondent had given minimal consideration to the operation of the Free Travel Scheme (para 4.6.1) and concluded that, 'the measures which are currently in place go beyond what is appropriate and necessary. I find them to be disproportionate restrictions on a very significant group of passengers, rather than a targeted solution to a specific problem' (para 4.7).

Fitzgerald v Dairygold Co-Operative Society Limited[499] concerned the bonus share scheme operated by an agricultural cooperative. Bonus shares were only allocated to the A1 category of members, which comprised those who had traded with the respondent in the year prior to the allocation. Mr Fitzgerald, a retired farmer, maintained that this practice amounted to indirect discrimination on the age ground. Since he had ceased trading with the respondent he belonged to a membership category that was not allocated bonus shares and as a result the overall value of his shareholding in the cooperative was diluted. From the available statistical evidence supplied by the respondent the equality officer concluded that the vast majority of farmers in the A1 category were under 65 years of age. He was satisfied that the requirement to conduct trade with the cooperative in order to obtain and keep A1 category membership was an apparently neutral provision which placed an older farmer at a particular disadvantage compared to a younger farmer. The complainant, therefore, succeeded in raising an inference of indirect discrimination.

However, the provision was objectively justified. Allocating shares provided members with an incentive to continue trading with the respondent and pursued the legitimate aim of enhancing its profitability. The means of implementing the aim were also appropriate and necessary:

> In the present case, the means by which the respondent achieves the aim of rewarding members for their trade and of providing an incentive to continue to trade with it is by way of distributing its net surplus and reserves among shareholders at the end of a trading year (which manifests itself through the issue of bonus shares to A1 members). It is only the members in the A1 category that contribute towards the generation of the net surplus and reserves through the trade which they have conducted with the respondent in the previous trading year. I am therefore satisfied that it is entirely appropriate

---

[499] DEC-S2009-083.

and totally legitimate for an industrial and provident society such as the respondent to reward these members (in accordance with the rules of the society) by distributing any net surplus by means of an allocation of bonus shares (para 6.5).

The age ground also featured in *Martin v Esplanade Hotel*.[500] The respondent's method of offering discounted room rates was challenged. Mr Martin claimed that the practice of offering cheaper rates only through the online booking system put him as an older person at a particular disadvantage compared with younger service users. He sought to establish that disadvantage by supplying evidence to the effect that older people were less likely to have access to computer facilities and have information technology skills. The evidence in question was gathered from Central Statistics Office reports as well as from research conducted by an NGO, Age Action Ireland. The respondent hotel accepted that less expensive rates were available through its online booking system. It was able to offer those rates because there was no advertising and labour costs involved and those savings could be passed on as a discount to customers.

Mr Martin established a *prima facie* case of indirect discrimination. The equality officer was satisfied that the documentary and statistical evidence presented showed that he and persons of his age group were put at a particular disadvantage by the requirement to transact online. The comparator group in question was 'persons of a different (younger) age' (para 5.6). However, the Tribunal found that the hotel could justify the provision. It pursued a legitimate aim, that of increasing occupancy. Using the internet as a sales tool was a 'well-established and effective business practice' and it was not necessary for the hotel to show that the aim was successful (i.e. that the online booking facility actually increased occupancy) (para 5.8). As to whether the provision was appropriate and necessary to achieve the stated aim, the equality officer first noted that other methods of booking rooms were available to the complainant. He then reached the following conclusion:

> The policy in question was to provide discounts to persons who availed of the respondent's services by using the internet rather than other methods of booking. Providing the same rates through other methods as through the internet would make a nonsense of the strategy required to implement this policy. Therefore, it is perfectly reasonable and necessary for the respondent not to offer the discounts in question to other customers in such circumstances as this, and where it has already been established that the aim in question was legitimate (para 5.10).

---

[500] DEC-S2010-034.

In essence then the provision was objectively justified because inducing people to use the online facility was legitimate: it resulted in lower costs for the hotel and it was justifiable to confine the benefit of those lower costs to persons availing of that facility.

In the 2010 case of *O'Keeffe v Irish Life and Permanent plc*[501] the complainant unsuccessfully argued that the manner in which applications for credit cards were assessed was indirectly discriminatory on the gender ground. Her request for a Visa card was turned down on the basis that she was not in permanent employment. She maintained that fewer women could satisfy the criterion of being in permanent employment since a significant proportion of temporary, agency and contract workers were female. The respondent countered that the complainant offered no evidence to support her claim and the Tribunal accepted that she could not establish an inference of indirect discrimination. This case illustrates the considerable difficulties faced by some complainants in accessing appropriate statistics.[502]

The complaint in *Murray v Irish Life and Permanent TSB*[503] also failed because a particular disadvantage could not be established. Mr Murray was undergoing treatment for cancer and had obtained provisional approval for a HSE grant to enable him to buy a car. He required the car to travel from his home to hospital. Under the terms of the grant Mr Murray was required to purchase the car and he could then recoup 75 per cent of the price up to a value of €5,020. He planned to use approximately €1,500 of his own funds and applied to Permanent TSB for a loan of €5,000 to cover the rest of the cost pending the payment of the grant. In support of the loan application he provided information about the provisional grant approval, including advice that the grant would be paid within two to three weeks of receipt of the relevant documentation, and the name and contact number of a HSE finance officer who could confirm those details. Mr Murray also provided evidence of his disabled status and of his record as a customer of the bank for over six years.

His loan application was refused and the reasons for that refusal were not communicated to Mr Murray. He referred a complaint of disability ground discrimination to the Tribunal. Before the Tribunal the respondent maintained that the loan was declined for reasons that had nothing to do with the complainant's disability. The bank's confidential lending criteria were given to the Tribunal for the purposes of the hearing. It emerged that the bank refused the loan application on the basis that the complainant was a tenant with an

---

[501] DEC-S2010-001.

[502] Data of the sort required by the complainant on male and female employment patterns does not appear to be available from the Central Statistics Office, through its analysis of the Live Register and surveys on men and women in Ireland: <http://www.cso.ie/>.

[503] DEC-S2010-004.

income below the level indicated and had not been in continuous employment for a specified number of years. He, therefore, fell outside the lending criteria that were authorised at branch manager level. The equality officer concluded that the decision to refuse the application was based on those 'neutral' lending criteria and was not taken on the ground of Mr Murray's disability (i.e. it was not a case of direct discrimination).

The complainant was unrepresented and did not raise the question of indirect discrimination. The Tribunal did not engage in any detailed consideration of that form of discrimination, revealing perhaps the limits of the Tribunal's capacity to operate as an investigative forum where the burden of proof rests on the complainant to establish a *prima facie* case (Chapter 12.5.4). In the absence of other data the equality officer accepted the respondent's contention that there was no evidence that disabled people are more or less likely to be tenants, to be in receipt of an income below the threshold, or to be in continuous employment for less than three years (para 3.5). In this particular case the complainant was not given *any* reasons for the refusal of his loan application (para 3.2). He could not, therefore, be expected to gather the data required to establish a *prima facie* case of indirect discrimination. Had the Tribunal pursued the question of indirect discrimination further, it arguably could have found that the lending criteria (or at least those relating to employment and income) were *liable* to disadvantage disabled people. Reports based on national survey data have found that chronic illness and disability have a major impact on employment rates and hence on income levels (Gannon and Nolan, 2005; National Disability Authority, 2005a).[504] The *Murray* case was one that seemed to involve a failure to reasonably accommodate a person with a disability as required by section 4, but that element of discrimination under the ESA was not addressed in the decision. It is discussed further in Chapter 6.4.4.3.

A Separated Complainant v A Hospital[505] involved a complaint about the respondent's practice of obtaining consent from one parent only when their child was undergoing surgery. The complainant could not establish that the policy put him at a disadvantage as a separated parent. The equality officer found that the provision impacted those with various custodial arrangements and so did not concern the marital status ground (now the civil status ground) *per se*. There was no detailed explanation of the steps that led to that finding. It seems the Tribunal reasoned that separated parents as a group could not suffer a particular disadvantage compared with, say, married parents because 50 per cent of separated parents (i.e. one of a child's parents) would have

---

[504] See also the analysis of the *National Disability Survey* issued by the Central Statistics Office (2010).
[505] DEC-S2010-046.

custody of a child at any given time, and that this was not adequate to estab-lish a particular disadvantage. Had the complaint been lodged on the gender ground as well, interesting questions would have arisen as to the intersection between the gender and marital (now civil) status grounds. The complainant could have argued that the provision put separated men, and perhaps even men irrespective of marital status, at a particular disadvantage compared with married women or simply women generally.[506] In order to do so the complain-ant would have had to show that a significantly higher proportion of men were unlikely to have custody, that is day-to-day care, of their children.

Stokes v Christian Brothers' High School, Clonmel and Department of Education and Skills[507] is perhaps one of the most significant ESA cases to date. The complainant argued that a provision in a school's admission policy indirectly discriminated on the Traveller community ground. Mr Stokes had applied for admission to a secondary school and was unsuccessful in the first and second round allocations of places. In assessing first round applications the school selected boys who fulfilled all of the following essential criteria:

The application is made on behalf of a boy:

- whose parents are seeking to submit their son to a Roman Catholic education in accordance with the mission statement and Christian ethos of the school;

- who already has a brother who attended or is in attendance at the School, or is the child of a past pupil, or has close family ties with the School

- who attended for his primary school education at one of the schools listed in Schedule Two, being a school within the locality or demo-graphic area of the school (para 3)

The complainant satisfied two of the three essential criteria. Both he and his parents were Catholics and he had attended a feeder school to the Christian Brothers' High School (i.e. one of the schools listed in Schedule Two). He did not meet the other criterion since his father had not attended the school and he

---

[506] The definition of indirect discrimination under section 3(1)(*c*) should permit complaints on multiple grounds because it refers to 'a person referred to in any paragraph of section 3(2)'. In such a case the comparator group would be persons who do not fall under the same elements of the grounds as the complainant. In a UK case, *Ministry of Defence v DeBique* [2010] IRLR 471, the Employment Appeal Tribunal considered the effect of a provision on men and women of Vincentian national origin and British national origin, i.e. the disadvan-tage suffered by the complainant was assessed with reference to her combined sex and race.
[507] DEC-S2010-056.

was the eldest of seven children. The boy did not, therefore, have maximum eligibility under the first round. In accordance with the admission policy his application was placed in the second round lottery. He did not secure a place in that round either and referred a case of indirect discrimination in relation to the admission criterion he did not fulfil.

The Director of the Equality Tribunal found that the impugned criterion had four elements:

1. Has a brother who attended the High School in the past, or

2. Has a brother who is currently in attendance in the High School, or

3. Is the child of a past pupil, or

4. Has close family ties with the High School (para 9)

He considered the fourth element, which referred to children of staff, irrelevant because no applicants had benefited from it in the year in question.

The Director first assessed the elements relating to siblings (criteria 1 and 2 above) together. He noted that Travellers were statistically less likely to enter or remain in post-primary education than their settled counterparts. However, the 2006 Census revealed that Traveller family size is on average double that of the general population. Giving priority to brothers of existing or former pupils could therefore operate to the detriment or to the benefit of Travellers as a group. The Director concluded that the complainant did not establish a *prima facie* case on that element of the admission policy.

Giving priority to the sons of former pupils did put members of the Traveller community at a particular disadvantage compared with non-Travellers. Proof of group disadvantage was established through statistical evidence, which demonstrated that Travellers of the complainant's father's generation were far less likely to have progressed to second level education than the settled population. The Director then considered whether Mr Stokes was personally put at a particular disadvantage by the admission criterion. He found if that criterion had not been used to assess applications the complainant's prospects of being admitted to the school would have increased by some 15 per cent. Mr Stokes was therefore able to demonstrate both individual and group disadvantage on the Traveller community ground.

The school was unable to justify use of the provision in question. It claimed that the criterion strengthened family loyalty to the school by rewarding fathers who supported the school in various ways. The Director accepted that this aim was a legitimate one. However, giving a blanket priority to children of former pupils was not an appropriate or necessary means of advancing that aim for the following reasons:

> 1. The priority applies to the children of all past pupils, irrespective of the actual level of current engagement of the father with the school. In many cases therefore, the means would not achieve the aim.

> 2. There are other ways of achieving this aim which would not disadvantage children whose fathers did not attend the school, such as organising a past pupils' union, by the activities of a parents' association etc.

> 3. The impact on Travellers is disproportionate to the benefit of the policy (para 11)

The respondent school appealed the Tribunal's decision to the Circuit Court. That appeal was upheld.[508] Teehan J found that while the parental admission criterion generated a particular disadvantage it was objectively justified. The criterion pursued the legitimate aim of supporting a 'family ethos' within education and was also in keeping with the characteristic spirit of the school (para 17). Teehan J's reasoning as to whether the rule was appropriate and necessary diverged from that of the Equality Tribunal. He had regard to the history of the admissions policy and noted that a number of priority rules had been adopted in previous years in an attempt to manage the shortfall in places. None had proved entirely satisfactory and, in light of the many relevant considerations the board of management had to weigh up, the parental rule balanced competing considerations and was, therefore, appropriate.

As to whether the criterion was necessary, the school pointed out that there was an active past pupils' union which incentivised high achievement by pupils: former students had provided mentoring, sports bursaries and financial assistance to the sons of impoverished parents. According to the school principal's evidence, the activities of such former students provided critical funding to the school. He believed that these activities 'would most probably be considerably less were such strong bond[s] not in place' (para 19). Teehan J concluded that these matters were:

> [M]anifestly important considerations in the formulation of school policies. In the light of all this (and, in particular[,] the highly important issue of funding) I find – and not without hesitation – that the inclusion of the 'parental rule' was a necessary step in creating an admissions policy which is proportionate and balanced (para 19).

---

[508] *Christian Brothers High School Clonmel v Stokes* [2011] IECC 1.

The Circuit Court then adopted a less stringent approach to the question of whether the provision was appropriate and necessary than the Tribunal had.

An appeal on a point of law to the High Court resulted in a judgment which generates uncertainty about the indirect discrimination prohibition under the ESA.[509] Unlike the Tribunal and the Circuit Court, McCarthy J found that the complainant failed to establish a particular disadvantage. He said it was insufficient to demonstrate disadvantage; the complainant was obliged to 'go further' and show that the disadvantage is 'particular' (para 22). Drawing on a dictionary definition of the word 'particular' he concluded:

> I do not believe that the disadvantage suffered by [T]ravellers (in common with all other applicants who were not the sons of past pupils) pertains or relates to 'a single definite person … or persons as distinguished from others' or 'distinguished in some way among others of the kind: more than ordinary; worth notice, marked, special'. The disadvantage relates to persons in addition to [T]ravellers and is not peculiar or restricted to [T]ravellers, and does not distinguish them among others of the kind (i.e. applicants for admission) and cannot be said to be 'more than ordinary', 'worth notice', 'marked', and 'special' because, of course, there are others in the same position as they are (para 25).

McCarthy J did not draw on principles established in Irish, EU or ECHR case law in formulating this test.[510] Such principles do not require that the disadvantage be 'peculiar or restricted to' the complainant's group. The High Court appears to suggest that either the disadvantage must accrue exclusively to Travellers or that the *type* of detriment experienced must be related in some way to the Traveller community ground.[511] Leading EU discrimination law experts point out that:

> Typically, the group of the disadvantaged does not exclusively, but only predominantly, consist of persons [who] are protected by the discrimination ground in question. Accordingly, they are 'merely' disproportionately represented in the disadvantaged group (Tobler

---

[509] *Stokes v Christian Brothers High School Clonmel* (High Court, McCarthy J, unreported, 6 February 2012).

[510] No finding was made by McCarthy J on the issue of whether members of the Traveller community are covered by the Racial Equality Directive. The case was dealt with as a matter solely of domestic law. It is unfortunate that CJEU precedents were not addressed since the wording used in the ESA is derived from the relevant EU directives.

[511] Arguably a provision which had such effects would be directly discriminatory instead (Tobler and European Network of Legal Experts in the Non-Discrimination Field, 2008, pp 48–50).

and European Network of Legal Experts in the Non-Discrimination Field, 2008, p 48).

Moreover, in a recent case the UK Court of Appeal underlined there is no need for there to be an intrinsic link between the relevant protected characteristic and the particular disadvantage suffered.[512]

The meaning of 'particular disadvantage' under the ESA will obviously be revisited in future decisions and ultimately, I would argue, ought to be realigned with domestic and international standards.

4.5 Conclusion

At this juncture indirect discrimination is one of the least developed aspects of the ESA. Apparently neutral provisions that could put persons covered by the grounds at a particular disadvantage include conducting transactions or providing education exclusively through the medium of the English language (raising indirect discrimination on the race ground and for Deaf people on the disability ground).[513] Residency requirements for accessing goods or services implicate the race ground.[514] Conditions for renting property such as a requirement that one is not in receipt of rent allowance could create a particular disadvantage on the family status and disability grounds (Ontario Human Rights Commission, 2007). Dress codes for accessing particular premises raise indirect discrimination on the religion and race grounds. A dress code in a restaurant might for example require all patrons to remove headwear. Sikh and Jewish males would be placed at a particular disadvantage by that condition, as would Muslim females, and the question then would be whether the restaurant could justify the condition.

As we have seen above, a provision in a school admissions policy did not violate the indirect discrimination provision on the Traveller community ground.[515] It is submitted, however, that the High Court's reasoning is open to question and does not seem to conform to established Irish and EU law

---

[512] *R (Bailey) v London Borough of Brent* [2011] EWCA Civ 1586.

[513] The term 'Deaf' signifies people with hearing impairments who use sign language and so constitute a linguistic minority. For examples of successful indirect discrimination cases taken by Deaf students within the Australian education system see *Catholic Education Office v Clarke* [2004] FCAFC 197 and *Hurst v State of Queensland* [2006] FCAFC 100.

[514] See *Tsourova v Trinity College Dublin*, DEC-S2004-162.

[515] Exclusionary provisions appear to be commonplace. A Department of Education and Science (2007) audit found that many schools used restrictive admissions policies, which operated to exclude certain categories of students, including those with special needs and the children of immigrants. See also Smyth, Darmody, McGinnity and Byrne (2009, pp 59–67).

principles (Chapters 4.4.3 and 4.4). Such admissions policies may also generate disadvantage on many of the other grounds covered by the ESA. Indirect discrimination on the race ground in particular may arise given that many migrants will have not been resident in the country for equivalent periods of time to their Irish national counterparts. Preferences for siblings or parents, a requirement that one has been resident in the catchment area for a substantial period or even the practice of putting applicants on a waiting list for a number of years could have an exclusionary effect on non-Irish nationals. The religious preference criteria in admissions provided for under section 7(3) (c) may also be tested in the future for compatibility with the Racial Equality Directive. Refusing admission to a Jewish or Sikh child could amount to direct discrimination on the race ground, should the CJEU follow UK case law on the definition of an ethnic group. A child from another minority ethnic group who is refused access to a Catholic school on the basis that they are not Catholic could assert that the section indirectly discriminates on the race ground. The 2006 Census found that 92 per cent of Irish nationals were Roman Catholics compared with 50.8 per cent of nationals of other countries (Central Statistics Office, 2007b). For some nationalities, such Chinese and Germans, those statistics appear to establish a particular disadvantage on the race ground and the question would then be whether the law could meet the objective justification test. However, it should also be borne in mind that any such challenge would depend on the extent to which the EU has competence over national education policies and would also be interpreted in light of the other fundamental rights at stake. It remains to be seen whether the review of school enrolment instigated by the Department of Education and Skills (2011) will result in changes to school admissions policies (Chapter 3.3.7).

School uniform policies have come under scrutiny before the UK courts in cases on the race and religion grounds.[516] *Mandla v Dowell-Lee*[517] concerned a Sikh boy who was refused admission to a private school on the basis that wearing a turban would breach the school's uniform rules. Significantly, the House of Lords found that Sikhs were an ethnic group for the purposes of the Race Relations Act 1976. No attempt was made to justify the policy and it was held that the school indirectly discriminated on the race ground. A Sikh

---

[516] Litigants have also relied on the Human Rights Act 1998 to challenge such policies but with little success. See, for example, *R (Begum) v Governors of Denbigh High School* [2006] UKHL 15. See also *R (X) v Headteachers and Governors of Y School* [2007] HRLR 20. The Human Rights Act gives further effect to the European Convention on Human Rights in UK law, and so its application in that jurisdiction offers some guidance as to how the ECHR Act 2003 might operate in the Irish context. For reviews of relevant decisions see Barnett (2008), Daly (2009), Gold (2009), Hickey (2009) and Mullally and O'Donovan (2011).

[517] [1983] AC 548.

teenager who was excluded from school for refusing to remove a religious bangle, the Kara, won a discrimination case in 2008.[518] Under its uniform policy the school did not permit students to wear jewellery other than wristwatches and ear studs. Mr Justice Silber found that wearing the Kara was objectively of exceptional importance to the applicant's religion and ethnicity, even though it was not an actual religious requirement. While promoting a school identity and fostering a community spirit amongst pupils was a legitimate aim, refusing to grant an exemption from the no jewellery policy was a disproportionate means of advancing that aim. In considering whether the school's actions were objectively justified Silber J had regard to various factors, including the fact that the Kara was small and barely visible. The school's actions therefore amounted to unlawful indirect discrimination on the race ground (Race Relations Act 1976) and on the ground of religion (Equality Act 2006).

Following consultation with relevant stakeholders the Minister for Integration prepared a guidance note for schools on school uniform policies which focuses on the *hijab* (Department of Education and Science, 2008).[519] The recommendations suggest that schools are responsible for formulating their uniform policy at local level and that 'no uniform policy should act in such a way that, in effect, excludes pupils of a particular religious background from seeking enrolment or continuing their enrolment in a school.' Schools are also requested to consult widely when drafting a uniform policy and to take account of their obligations under the ESA and the Education Act 1998. However, the guidelines suggest that the 'wearing of clothing in the classroom which obscures a facial view and creates an artificial barrier between pupil and teacher' may not be acceptable as 'such clothing hinders proper communication'. According to Glendenning (2008b, p 290) the guidelines may not satisfy the requirements of international human rights law and in particular the ECHR. She suggests that the guidelines should be placed on a statutory footing and ought to be formulated with a greater degree of precision.

The guidelines on intercultural education drawn up by National Council for Curriculum and Assessment (2006) should assist schools in eliminating institutional practices that may discriminate. For example, the guidelines suggest that admissions criteria requiring residence in the area may discriminate against nomadic families (National Council for Curriculum and Assessment, 2006, p 9), which would include Traveller and Roma families for the purposes of the ESA. The guidelines suggest that schools should consider whether students will have 'specific requirements concerning food, jewellery or clothing (for example, the range of tastes catered for by the school canteen ...)' (National Council for Curriculum and Assessment, 2006, p 45).

---

[518] *R (Watkins Singh) v Governing Body of Aberdare Girls' High School* [2008] ELR 561.
[519] See Hickey (2009) for a critical assessment of the guidelines.

5

Harassment and Sexual Harassment

5.1 Introduction

In order to ensure that goods and services are accessed in an environment that respects people's dignity the ESA prohibits harassment and sexual harassment.[520] The harm to an individual's psychological well-being caused by such practices also 'has a social and collective aspect: it reflects, and perpetuates, patterns of subordination' (Bamforth et al., 2008, p 470). By outlawing harassment, discrimination law aims to tackle some types of subordination, or the exercise of power and dominance, that are linked to the discriminatory grounds.

Recognition of sexual harassment as a legal harm first occurred in the United States and ultimately found its way into European legal systems. Its development was heavily influenced by feminist writing and activism, which demonstrated the effects such practices had on female workers (Epp, 2010, Chapter 8). Irish law on sexual harassment stems from the 1985 case of *A Garage Proprietor v A Worker* (Bolger and Kimber, 2000, p 258).[521] During the 1970s US courts also recognised harassment on the grounds of race as a form of discrimination (Bacik, 2003; McColgan, 2007b, Chapter 4.2). Ireland and the EU followed suit. Principles developed in case law were eventually set out in legislation. The Employment Equality Act 1998 and the Equal Status Act 2000 explicitly prohibited harassment in the discrimination law context for the first time across all nine grounds.

---

[520] Sexual harassment, and harassment more broadly, has been the subject of extensive academic debate. On Irish law see Bacik (2003), Bolger and Kimber (2000, Chapter 8, 2009, pp 421–436) and Quill (2005). Samples of writing from other jurisdictions include Barmes (2007), Conaghan (1999), Dine and Watt (1995), Eichhorn (2002), Halley (2002), MacKinnon (1979), Mason (2002), McColgan (2007b), Smith and Kimmel (2005) and Thornton (2002). On harassment on the religion ground see Uccellari (2008) and Vickers (2006).
[521] EEO/02/1985.

Harassment first evolved as a form of direct discrimination, which meant that complainants had to show that they had been treated less favourably than a relevant comparator. Significantly, the 2000 Act made harassment a distinct form of prohibited conduct, which does not depend on demonstrating less favourable treatment. One of the main benefits of this approach is that the law directly tackles manifestations of ageism, transphobia, sexism, racism and so on. It avoids the need for a complainant to establish that she or he is covered by one of the discriminatory grounds. As we saw in Chapter 3, the comparator requirement in direct discrimination complaints is especially problematic for some groups of people. A transgender person, for instance, faces considerable difficulties because the gender ground has been defined to include only transgender people who intend to, are undergoing or have undergone gender reassignment procedures. For the purposes of harassment law the complainant's particular identity or status does not matter, what matters is whether prohibited conduct related to a ground occurred.

This chapter examines the provisions on harassment set out in the ESA. But it should be noted that outside of discrimination law, civil and even criminal law could also provide a remedy for harms caused by harassment depending on the context (Bacik, 2003; Campbell, Kilcommins and O'Sullivan, 2010, Chapter 17; Ward, 2010).[522]

5.2 Definitions of Harassment and Sexual Harassment

5.2.1 Overview

According to section 11(5)(*a*) of the Equal Status Acts, harassment is 'any form of unwanted conduct related to any of the discriminatory grounds', while sexual harassment is 'any form of unwanted verbal, non-verbal or physical conduct of a sexual nature', and is conduct which in either case 'has the purpose or effect of violating a person's dignity and creating an intimidating, hostile, degrading, humiliating or offensive environment for the person'. The section on harassment then goes on to supply examples of unwanted conduct: 'acts, requests, spoken words, gestures or the production, display or circulation of written words, pictures or other material'.[523] Various forms of communication have been the subject of harassment

---

[522] Public bodies also have positive obligations under the ECHR Act 2003 to protect people from harassment, in particular where it may amount to inhuman and degrading treatment under article 3 of the ECHR. A case lodged with the European Court of Human Rights was settled in 2011: *X, Y & Z v United Kingdom* [2011] ECHR 1199.

[523] Section 11(5)(*b*).

complaints under the ESA and EEA, including text messages,[524] graffiti[525] and website content.[526]

These definitions stem from the Equality Act 2004, which came into force on 19 July 2004 and applies to events that took place after that date.[527] Because of the considerable delays in hearing cases, the Tribunal harassment decisions issued until 2008 apply the original definitions. Two basic changes occurred in the 2004 Act.

First, conduct must now be 'related to' a discriminatory ground, whereas previously the unwanted conduct had to be conduct 'which in respect of the victim is based on any discriminatory ground'. 'Related to' seems to be a less onerous standard for the complainant, in that the connection between the ground and the conduct would appear to be looser, but there is no significant shift in the decisions following the amendment (Chapter 5.4.2). Additionally, as discussed in Chapter 5.2.2, the previous definition suggested that the victim had to belong to the category of persons covered by the ground. That is no longer the case under the revised definition, so that, for example, people harassed because of their association with a person who falls within a ground can lodge harassment complaints.

Second, the original definitions included an objective element in that the conduct had to be both unwelcome from the complainant's perspective and be capable of being *reasonably regarded* as offensive, humiliating or intimidating to him or her.[528] Under the subjective test now applicable, it appears that the yardstick is the complainant's understanding of the behaviour in question. But it is not clear whether this shift will have a measurable impact in practice; even where it is established that the conduct complained of actually occurred equality officers do not always accept that it constituted harassment (Chapter 5.4.3).

Neither harassment prohibition requires a comparator but it must be shown that the unwanted conduct was 'related to' at least one of the discriminatory grounds, or was of a 'sexual nature' if sexual harassment is in issue. A person of the same gender as the complainant may commit sexual harassment, so a man could sexually harass another man. A person covered by the same element of the ground as the complainant can perpetrate harassment on that ground,

---

[524] *A Female Employee v A Recruitment Company*, DEC-E2008-015; *Merriman v O'Flaherty's Ltd t/a Reads Print Design and Photocopying Bureau*, DEC-S2011-049.

[525] *Boyle v Ely Property Group Ltd*, DEC-E2009-013; *Ely Property Group Ltd v Boyle*, ADE/09/18; EDA/0920, 15 October 2009.

[526] *Dalton v Aspire*, DEC-S2009-062.

[527] The revised definitions were designed to bring Irish law into line with the Race and Equal Treatment Amendment Directives. On the latter and sexual harassment see Samuels (2004).

[528] See, for example, *Cassidy and Wesemann v Doherty*, DEC-S2003-040/041.

e.g. a woman could harass another woman on the gender ground. In such cases the respondent(s) might try to claim that because the alleged harasser shared the identity of the claimant the behaviour at issue was just general bad conduct and not 'related to' the ground in question. Any such arguments should be probed carefully.[529]

5.2.2 The Complainant in Harassment Cases

The ESA prohibits unwanted conduct related to a discriminatory ground or of a sexual nature outright. A complainant does not need to demonstrate that she or he falls under one of the discriminatory grounds. As a result, the personal scope of the harassment provisions is broader than that of the other forms of discrimination prohibited under the ESA.

The Framework Directive covers people subjected to harassment because of their association with an individual 'belonging to' one of the grounds: *Coleman v Attridge Law*.[530] This case established that someone could be harassed on a given ground even where he/she does not fall into the category of persons that comprise the ground. It is to be expected that the other equality directives will be interpreted in a similar manner. As noted above, the Racial Equality Directive and the Gender Goods and Services Directive overlap with the coverage of the ESA. In any event, harassment 'by association' was established in the Irish decision of *Kane v Eirjet Ltd*,[531] which is discussed further in Chapter 5.4.2.

It is clear that harassment may occur where the perpetrator imputes membership of a social group to a person and then engages in 'unwanted conduct' as described in the ESA. The UK case of *English v Thomas Sanderson Ltd*[532] dealt with another dimension to the nature of protection in this area (Connolly, 2009b). At issue was whether a claim of harassment 'on the grounds of' sexual orientation could be sustained where the treatment in question was unrelated to a particular person's sexuality.[533] The complainant, a heterosexual man, was subjected to homophobic comments over a protracted period and ultimately resigned from his position. However, the

---

[529] *Ms M v R – A Named Organisation*, DEC-E2007-066: in assessing the complainant's credibility the equality officer appeared to attach some weight to the fact that both the alleged perpetrator of harassment on the sexual orientation ground and the complainant were lesbian women. NGOs could perhaps usefully make submissions on phenomena such as intra-ground harassment to assist the Tribunal in suitable cases. See further Chapter 10.4.

[530] Case C-303/06, [2008] ECR 1-5603; [2008] ICR 1128.

[531] DEC-S2008-026.

[532] [2009] 2 All ER 468.

[533] See the Employment Equality (Sexual Orientation) Regulations 2003 (SI 2003/1661).

colleagues who had engaged in the impugned conduct were aware of the fact that he was not gay. The harassment complaint was successful. Sedley LJ stated: 'If ... tormenting a man who is believed to be gay but is not amounts to unlawful harassment, the distance from there to tormenting a man who is treated as if he were gay when he is not is barely perceptible ...' (para 38). He went on to explain that this finding advanced the overall objectives of the legislation since otherwise a person would be obliged to declare his sexual orientation in order to establish whether abuse was 'on grounds of sexual orientation'.[534]

Similar situations to that encountered in *English* have not been addressed in this country but it seems that the formula used in the ESA would apply in an equivalent way. Furthermore, it could perhaps be invoked by a witness of harassment, provided it was possible to establish that the treatment of another person violated the complainant's dignity *and* created an intimidating, hostile, degrading, humiliating or offensive environment.[535] This is because under section 11 the behaviour complained of need only be 'related to any of the discriminatory grounds'. Likewise, article 2(3) of the Racial Equality Directive refers to 'an unwanted conduct related to racial or ethnic origin', while leaving the precise definition of harassment to the law of the member states. By contrast the relevant provision in the Gender Goods and Services Directive is arguably narrower since it comprises 'an unwanted conduct related to the sex *of a person*' (article 2(*c*), emphasis added). At any rate the apparently more generous Irish definition prevails since the Directive sets down minimum requirements (recital 26).

5.2.3 Extent of Liability for Harassment

Section 11 describes the context in which the harassment provisions apply and the circumstances in which liability can be imposed. Service providers are legally responsible for the discriminatory actions of their employees and agents under the vicarious liability principle set out under section 42 (Chapter 7). Harassment and sexual harassment are included under that general provision, but section 11(2) goes further in obliging service providers to protect people from harassment or sexual harassment committed by other third parties, subject to a defence (section 11(3)).

---

[534] See also the judgment of the British Columbia Court of Appeal in *School District No. 44 (North Vancouver) v Jubran* (2005) BCCA 201.

[535] That understanding of the Gender Equal Treatment Directive's sexual harassment provision was adopted by the UK Court of Appeal in *R (Equal Opportunities Commission) v Secretary of State for Trade and Industry* [2007] ICR 1234.

Section 11 provides:

(1) A person shall not sexually harass or harass (within the meaning of *subsection (4)* or *(5)*) another person ('the victim') where the victim—

(*a*) avails or seeks to avail himself or herself of any service provided by the person or purchases or seeks to purchase any goods being disposed of by the person,

(*b*) is the proposed or actual recipient from the person of any premises or of any accommodation or services or amenities related to accommodation, or

(*c*) is a student at, has applied for admission to or avails or seeks to avail himself or herself of any service offered by, any educational establishment (within the meaning of *section 7*) at which the person is in a position of authority.

(2) A person ('the responsible person') who is responsible for the operation of any place that is an educational establishment or at which goods, services or accommodation facilities are offered to the public shall not permit another person who has a right to be present in or to avail himself or herself of any facilities, goods or services provided at that place, to suffer sexual harassment or harassment at that place.

(3) It shall be a defence for the responsible person to prove that he or she took such steps as are reasonably practicable to prevent the sexual harassment or harassment, as the case may be, of the other person referred to in *subsection (2)* or of a category of persons of which that other person is a member.

Harassment is only prohibited in defined contexts: a customer or client of a service provider is protected from both forms of harassment in the course of accessing goods or services under section 11(1)(*a*). A recipient of property, accommodation or related services or amenities is similarly protected under section 11(1)(*b*), as is any student, prospective student or person seeking to use any service offered by an educational establishment (section 11(1)(*c*)).

The reference to a person 'in a position of authority' in the education context (section 11(1)(*c*)) could mean that those responsible for running educational establishments would not be liable for harassment as between students (unless the student engaging in harassment is in a position of authority).[536] Vicarious

---

[536] Currently EU law in the field of education only prohibits harassment on the race ground; the Gender Goods and Services Directive does not apply to this area. But it should be

liability for harassment of a boy by other pupils at a school was, however, considered but not proven in *Two Complainants (a mother and her son) v A Primary School.*[537] And in *A Student v An Educational Establishment*[538] the Tribunal investigated harassment of a gay student by his classmates on an adult education programme. It would seem, therefore, that the duty placed on 'responsible persons' under subsection (2) is of a general nature and not strictly confined to the situations outlined in subsection (1).

Notably, protection from harassment is not afforded to members of registered clubs, but actions that might usually constitute harassment may also be considered a form of less favourable treatment (see Chapter 5.4.4; Chapter 9). Sexual harassment in employment was first recognised as direct discrimination on the gender ground (Bolger and Kimber, 2000, Chapter 8; Flynn, 1995) and a complainant in an equal status case should be able to rely on that vein of case law. Seeking protection under the direct discrimination prohibition is more limited because liability can only be attached to a club for the acts of its employees or agents (Chapter 7).[539]

5.3 Establishing Harassment or Sexual Harassment

The general rules on the burden of proof apply to cases of harassment and sexual harassment. Under section 38(A) a person making a complaint of discrimination must establish facts from which it may be presumed that prohibited conduct has occurred in relation to him or her. This is known as establishing a *prima facie* case. To establish a *prima facie* case of harassment a complainant must supply evidence that determines on the balance of probabilities:

- That the alleged incident(s) actually took place, and

- That the incident(s) was related to the ground(s) in question or was of a sexual nature in a sexual harassment complaint, and

---

remembered that EU law does provide protection from discrimination on the grounds of gender, age, disability, sexual orientation, religion or belief in access to vocational guidance, vocational training, advanced vocational training and retraining, including practical work experience: Framework Directive (article 3(1)(*b*)); Recast Directive (article 14(1)(*b*)).

[537] DEC-S2006-028.

[538] DEC-S2009-084.

[539] The Oireachtas debates indicate that the extension of an express prohibition on harassment to registered clubs was ruled out because of concerns that it would be too draconian (particularly were it to cover harassment as between members) and could give rise to constitutional difficulties: 162 *Seanad Debates* 25, Cols 1724–1727 (Equal Status Bill 1999: Committee Stage (Resumed)); 514 *Dáil Debates* 4, Cols 818–820 (Equal Status Bill 1999: Report Stage (Resumed)); Select Committee on Justice, Equality, Defence and Women's Rights, 4 November 1999 (Equal Status Bill 1999: Committee Stage (Resumed)).

- That it had the purpose or effect of violating his/her dignity *and* creating an intimidating, hostile, degrading, humiliating or offensive environment for him/her

Where there is a direct conflict of evidence between the parties and little or no independent verification of what transpired the complainant will find it difficult to meet the burden of proof.[540] The equality officer will examine all of the surrounding circumstances, including the behaviour of the parties after the event(s) in question. The lodgement of a complaint or a contemporaneous note of the incident(s) is useful in that regard. For example, in *Cantwell v Giles & Co., Tralee*[541] the equality officer observed that there was a direct conflict between the parties as to whether a derogatory comment was made by an employee of the respondent. She found, however, that the complainant's version of events was supported by the fact that he had sent a letter of complaint the day after the incident in question, which had not been replied to.

Each element of establishing a *prima facie* case is discussed in the next section of this chapter. For now it should be noted that the words 'purpose or effect' used in the statutory definitions mean that the perpetrator need not have intended to harass.[542] A complainant does not therefore have to put forward any evidence as to motive or intent.

Where a complainant establishes a *prima facie* case the onus shifts to the respondent to rebut the inference of harassment. At that juncture the defence set out under section 42(3) and, if applicable, section 11(3) is considered.[543] Section 42 details the circumstances in which employers can be held responsible for the acts of their employees and agents 'in any proceedings' brought under the ESA. Under section 11(3) it is a defence for the 'responsible person' (i.e. service or goods provider) to prove that they took reasonably practicable steps to prevent the harassment or sexual harassment of the victim or of any category of persons which includes the victim. Employers and service providers' liability and the applicable defences are examined in Chapter 7.

---

[540] See, for example, *Mr A v Mr Y, a Solicitor*, DEC-S2009-058; *A Male Student v A Secondary School*, DEC-S2009-010; and *Ms C v TMD*, DEC-E2007-057.

[541] DEC-S2007-010.

[542] *Brooks v BRC Shooting Club*, DEC-S2010-042, para 5.8. In an EEA case the equality officer found that it was immaterial whether racially derogatory remarks were 'made in fun': *Valaithan v Martin Quigley (Nenagh) Ltd t/a Quigley's Café & Bakery*, DEC-E2009-050, para 4.3.

[543] *O'Donnell and Madden v Premium Distribution Limited*, DEC-E2007-032, para 5.8.

5.4 Case Law

5.4.1 Introduction

The bulk of harassment complaints referred to date have concerned 'spoken words' or words in combination with physical gestures. Harassment complaints have been lodged under each of the nine grounds. There have been no successful complaints of sexual harassment under the ESA. A table of the cases heard to date by the Equality Tribunal is set out below (Table 2).

The remainder of this section examines how the various elements of the harassment definitions have been applied in case law. First it looks at the requirement that the unwanted conduct is related to a discriminatory ground, or is of a sexual nature in the case of a sexual harassment complaint (Chapter 5.4.2). Then it explores how the Tribunal decides whether that conduct had the purpose or effect of violating the complainant's dignity and creating an intimidating, hostile, degrading, humiliating or offensive environment for him or her (Chapter 5.4.3).

Table 2: Harassment Cases under the ESA[544]

Decision	Ground(s)	Central Findings
Two Customers v A Retail Outlet, DEC-S2002-008/009	Gender Sexual harassment	Complaint of harassment comprising physical gestures upheld; no evidence of sexual harassment
McDonagh v Patrick Powers Pub, DEC-S2002-114/115	Traveller community	Complaint of harassment involving hostile and unwelcoming attitude upheld
Cassidy and Wesemann v Doherty, DEC-S2003-040/041	Gender and family status	No *prima facie* case established on the facts: insufficient evidence that events complained of occurred
Hennessy v Dublin Bus, DEC-S2003-046	Disability	No *prima facie* case established on the facts: comments made did not amount to harassment

(Continued)

---

[544] This table does not include cases that were unsuccessful because the complainant failed to attend the hearing.

Table 2: (*Continued*)

Decision	Ground(s)	Central Findings
Kamal Khan v United Travel, Dublin, DEC-S2004-062	Race and religion	No *prima facie* case established on the facts
O'Shea v Hennessy Salon Supplies Ltd, Cork, DEC-S2004-092	Age	Complaint of harassment involving disparaging comments upheld
Campbell v Bus Éireann, DEC-S2005-197	Disability	No *prima facie* case established on the facts; incidents not related to the disability ground
Two Complainants (a mother and her son) v A Primary School, DEC-S2006-028	Traveller community and disability	Complaint of harassment involving presence of Garda at parent–teacher meeting upheld
Belton v Dún Laoghaire–Rathdown County Council, DEC-S2006-067	Disability	No *prima facie* case established on the facts: material in question not related to the ground
A Customer v The Licensee, A Bar, Dublin, DEC-S2007-006	Sexual harassment Age, gender, marital status, race, religion and sexual orientation	No *prima facie* case: insufficient evidence to support claim
Cantwell v Giles & Co., Tralee, DEC-S2007-010	Disability	Finding of direct discrimination on the disability ground
King v Dublin Bus, DEC-S2008-019	Disability	Complaint of harassment involving comments and physical gestures upheld
Wellard v Killester College, DEC-S2008-024	Disability	No *prima facie* case: no evidence of harassment supplied
Woodhead and Sparkes v Swinford Garda Station, DEC-S2008-064	Sexual orientation and race	Complaint outside scope of the Acts

(Continued)

Table 2: (*Continued*)

Cases in which revised definitions of harassment were applicable following entry into force of Equality Act 2004

Decision	Ground(s)	Central Findings
Kane v Eirjet Ltd, DEC-S2008-026	Disability	Complaint of harassment involving insensitive treatment by staff and resultant disparaging comments by other customers upheld
Stevens v The Helix Theatre, DEC-S2008-033	Family status	No *prima facie* case: comments did not have effect of violating complainant's dignity or creating an intimidating environment, etc.
Dalton v Glynn, DEC-S2008-082	Disability and gender	Failed to establish *prima facie* case: incidents not related to the ground
Cash and O'Brien v Tesco Ireland Ltd, DEC-S2008-114	Traveller community	No *prima facie* case established: insufficient evidence to support claim
A Complainant v A County Council, DEC-S2009-009	Traveller community	Complaint of harassment involving disparaging remark upheld
A Male Student v A Secondary School, DEC-S2009-010	Gender	No *prima facie* case established: insufficient evidence to support claim
Chawla v Irish Wheelchair Association, DEC-S2009-024	Victimisation	Failed to establish *prima facie* case: incidents not related to the ground
Kent v Iarnród Éireann, DEC–S2009-026	Disability	Failed to establish *prima facie* case: unrelated to ground

(*Continued*)

Table 2: (*Continued*)

Decision	Ground(s)	Central Findings
Hennessy v Network Catering/ Iarnród Éireann, DEC-S2009-029	Disability	Complaint of harassment involving disparaging comments and physical gestures upheld
Ms A v A Library, DEC-S2009-060	Age	Respondent successfully availed of defence in relation to harassment comprising comments made by other service users
Dalton v Aspire, DEC-S2009-062	Disability	Failed to establish *prima facie* case re: website content: written material did create an intimidating, etc. environment Respondent successfully availed of defence in relation to post by third party to online discussion forum
Husband and Wife v A Voluntary Housing Association, DEC-S2009-071	Traveller community	Failed to establish *prima facie* case: unrelated to ground
A Complainant v A Secondary School, DEC-S2009-074	Gender	Failed to establish a *prima facie* case: unrelated to ground
A Student v An Educational Establishment, DEC-S2009-084	Sexual orientation	Respondent successfully availed of defence in relation to comments by students
McGrath v University of Dublin, Trinity College, DEC-S2010-006	Disability	Failed to establish *prima facie* case: unrelated to ground

(*Continued*)

Table 2: (*Continued*)

Decision	Ground(s)	Central Findings
O'Brien v Kerry County Council, DEC-S2010-015	Traveller community	No *prima facie* case established on the facts: inadequate evidence that events complained of occurred
O'Brien v Health Service Executive South, DEC-S2010-016	Traveller community	No *prima facie* case established on the facts: inadequate evidence that events complained of occurred
O'Reilly and Others v Waterford City Council, DEC-S2010-018	Traveller community	Failed to establish *prima facie* case: unrelated to ground
Olaijde v Buck Properties Ltd, DEC-S2010-021	Race and gender	Failed to establish *prima facie* case: unrelated to grounds
Mr and Mrs X (on behalf of their son Mr Y) v A Post Primary School, DEC-S2010-024	Disability	Failed to establish *prima facie* case: unrelated to ground
Williams v DSG Retail Ireland Ltd t/a Currys Superstore Limerick, DEC-S2010-029	Race	No *prima facie* case established on the facts: inadequate evidence that events complained of occurred
Ennis v Navan O'Mahony's Football Club, DEC-S2010-031	Disability	Failed to establish *prima facie* case: unrelated to ground
Doherty v Letterkenny Institute of Technology, DEC-S2010-039	Disability	Failed to establish *prima facie* case: unrelated to ground
Brooks v BRC Shooting Club, DEC-S2010-042	Gender	Complaint of harassment involving disparaging comments upheld

(Continued)

Table 2: (*Continued*)

Decision	Ground(s)	Central Findings
A Student v Galway–Mayo Institute of Technology, DEC-S2010-047	Disability	No *prima facie* case established: no evidence of behaviour amounting to harassment
Mrs Z (and on behalf of her three children) v A National School, DEC-S2010-055	Traveller community	No *prima facie* case established in relation to two complainants: one incident did not amount to harassment; insufficient evidence that other incidents occurred and if so that related to ground
Mrs K (on behalf of her son) v A Primary School, DEC-S2011-003	Traveller community	No *prima facie* case established; inadequate evidence to support claim
McGreal v Clúid Housing, DEC-S2011-004	Age	Failed to establish *prima facie* case: unrelated to ground
A Parent (on behalf of her son) v A Supermarket, DEC-S2011-015	Disability	Complaint of harassment involving aggressive behaviour and comments upheld
Smyth v Dublin Bus, DEC-S2011-017	Age and disability	No *prima facie* case established; comments did not amount to harassment
Duyn v Aer Arran Group, DEC-S2011-023	Disability	No *prima facie* case established; conduct did not amount to harassment
McDonagh v McHale, DEC-S2011-025	Traveller community	Failed to establish *prima facie* case: unrelated to ground

(*Continued*)

Table 2: (*Continued*)

Decision	Ground(s)	Central Findings
Burke v Kerry County Council, DEC-S2011-032	Traveller community	No *prima facie* case established; inadequate evidence that events complained of occurred
Parker v Federal Security Ltd, DEC-S2011-036	Race and gender	No *prima facie* case established; comments did not amount to harassment
Payne v City of Dublin VEC, incorporating Pearse College and Trinity College Dublin, DEC-S2011-038	Age, disability and race	Failed to establish *prima facie* case: unrelated to grounds
A Hotel Guest v A Dublin Hotel, DEC-S2011-040	Sexual orientation	Complaint of harassment involving comments upheld
Burke v Kerry County Council, DEC-S2011-043	Traveller community	No *prima facie* case established: no evidence of behaviour amounting to harassment
Stralkowski v Dublin City Council, DEC-S2011-046	Race	No *prima facie* case established; remark did not amount to harassment
Merriman v O'Flaherty's Ltd t/a Reads Print, Design and Photocopying Bureau, DEC-S2011-049	Sexual orientation Sexual harassment	Complaint of harassment concerning content of text message upheld No *prima facie* case of sexual harassment; messages were not of a sexual nature
Oladapo v Irish Citylink ComfortDelgro Ltd, DEC-S2011-063	Race	No *prima facie* case established; conduct did not amount to harassment

(*Continued*)

Table 2: (*Continued*)

Decision	Ground(s)	Central Findings
Fizel v Health Service Executive, DEC-S2012-001	Civil status, family status and race	No *prima facie* case established; conduct did not amount to harassment; inadequate evidence that events complained of occurred
Baziz v Noonan Services Group, DEC-S2012-008	Race	No *prima facie* case established; inadequate evidence to support complaint

5.4.2 Unwanted Conduct Related to a Ground or of a Sexual Nature

As the table set out above illustrates, complainants often cannot establish the first element of a *prima facie* case, i.e. that the alleged incidents actually took place. Where that is established complainants must go on to demonstrate that the incidents were 'related to' the grounds in question or were of a sexual nature in a sexual harassment complaint. This section examines significant Tribunal decisions about this second necessary component of a *prima facie* case. A complaint will not succeed if there is no link between the ground and the conduct in question; harassment does not include general poor conduct or ill treatment. The case law demonstrates, however, that a link can be established even where there is no explicit reference to a characteristic associated with a ground.

The first ESA harassment complaint, *Two Customers v A Retail Outlet, Dublin*,[545] concerned the gender ground. Two female customers had objected to the behaviour of a male shop manager when one of them was seeking to return a product bought previously in the store. The equality officer referred to the complainants' evidence 'that the manager of the respondent premises stood in such close proximity to them that they had to strain back away from him which was physically and psychologically uncomfortable for, and intimidating to, them. They gave equally credible evidence that the words and tone used by the said manager to them was rude and hostile and caused offense and loss of dignity to both of them' (para 8.7). She concluded that, 'a male customer would not be treated in such a manner, because there exists a perception that a female is more likely to be intimidated and cowed by the type of behaviour experienced

---

[545] *Two Customers v A Retail Outlet, Dublin*, DEC-S2002-008/009. For an example of gender-related harassment in the form of physical intimidation in the employment field see the Labour Court decision in *A Worker v A Hotel* [2010] ELR 72.

and less likely than a male to physically retaliate' (para 8.7). The conduct in question amounted to harassment on the gender ground. Notably, while the manager did not refer to the complainants' gender, his general demeanour and body language was (perhaps unconsciously) influenced by the complainants' gender and so was 'related to' that discriminatory ground.

A complaint of sexual harassment was not substantiated on the facts (para 8.6), presumably because the manager's behaviour was not of a 'sexual nature'. There are dozens of established cases of sexual harassment under the EEA. From those decisions we can assume that conduct of a sexual nature includes inappropriate physical contact with sexual overtones as well as verbal remarks or written words with a sexual content.[546]

In some cases the relationship between the unwanted conduct and the grounds will be overt or obvious. For example, age-related harassment was established in *O'Shea v Hennessy Salon Supplies Ltd, Cork*.[547] The Tribunal was satisfied that derogatory remarks made to a customer about the suitability of products for someone of her age and the respondent's reference to her as 'an aul wan' breached section 11. A series of incidents involving members of a club was the subject of a gender ground harassment complaint in *Brooks v BRC Shooting Club*.[548] Over the course of a number of years a male club member dealt with the female complainant in a hostile and aggressive manner. He also made a number of gender-specific comments, which the complainant found offensive. The Tribunal found that the response to her complaint of harassment was inadequate, as discussed further in Chapter 7.3.

Many of the successful harassment complaints referred to date are on the Traveller community ground and the disability ground. A selection of these cases is now reviewed.

Traveller community ground harassment occurred in *McDonagh v Patrick Powers Pub*.[549] As with the *O'Shea* case, remarks made and the general demeanour of the proprietor were the subject of the complaint, but no abusive comments about the two complainants' Traveller identity were made. According to the equality officer it was clear 'that Mr. Power's behaviour and attitude towards the complainants and the tone of his response to them could reasonably be regarded as offensive, humiliating and intimidating' (para 6.1).

---

[546] See, for example, *A Complainant v A Contract Cleaning Company*, DEC-E2004-068 (crude and sexually offensive remarks and a slap on the buttocks amounted to sexual harassment); *A Female Employee v A Printing Company*, DEC-E2008-022 (a kick did not amount to sexual harassment); and *A Female Employee v A Recruitment Company*, DEC-E2008-015 (sexually explicit text messages constituted sexual harassment).

[547] DEC-S2004-092. On the sexual orientation ground see *A Hotel Guest v A Dublin Hotel*, DEC-S2011-040.

[548] DEC-S2010-042.

[549] DEC-S2002-114/115.

The behaviour of a Traveller liaison officer (TLO) following the death of the complainant's daughter was the subject of a harassment and victimisation complaint in a 2009 case.[550] According to the complainant's written account of his exchanges with the TLO:

> On the 8th of October 2004 you sent your Traveller Liaison Officer to visit me. I told him that I needed a transfer out of the site to [Town X]. I told him that my daughter had just died and he replied 'that's water under the bridge'. I was very upset by this remark as my daughter was found in the river. He went on to say 'I know you all my life you're a rogue'.

The respondent denied that its employee had made those statements, but the Tribunal considered the complainant's evidence to be more credible. The equality officer found that the remark about 'water under the bridge' was an unfortunate and inappropriate choice of words, which had greatly disturbed the complainant. However, it did not constitute harassment on the Traveller community ground. The 'rogue' comment did amount to harassment. According to the Tribunal it was:

> … a comment that might be said to Travellers and non-Travellers alike. However, in the circumstances of this case, uttered by the TLO who is a person in a specialised role dealing with only Travellers I am satisfied that the comment affronted the complainant's dignity and created an offensive environment for him leading to the TLO being asked to leave.

The decision illustrates that comments which may on the surface appear inoffensive can amount to harassment in a particular context. Likewise, the use of 'xxx' in text messages constituted harassment on the sexual orientation ground in a 2011 case.[551] According to the equality officer:

> It is clear that this dispute progressed to an unfortunate climax where the respondent sent inappropriate texts to the complainant that clearly had the intention of intimidating and/or undermining him because he was gay. It is clear that this was done in the context of the commercial dispute and it is in this context that I consider the texts 'xxx' had that effect on the complainant. It should be said that,

---

[550] *A Complainant v A County Council*, DEC-S2009-009.
[551] *Merriman v O'Flaherty's Ltd t/a Reads Print, Design and Photocopying Bureau*, DEC-S2011-049.

while the literal meaning of those texts, on their face, may normally be a sexual or benign one, I am satisfied that, in all the circumstances of the present complaint, the intended meaning of these words was to undermine the complainant (and his masculinity) on the basis of his sexual orientation (para 5.6).

The disability ground has generated a number of successful complaints, many of which happened in the course of accessing public transport. In *King v Dublin Bus*[552] a bus driver and the complainant, who was a wheelchair user and blind, were involved in an altercation on two separate occasions. The equality officer summarised the facts in the following terms:

On 29 March 2003 the driver of the bus in question left his cab, again in contravention of the respondent's own policy in this regard, and followed the complainant down the bus while verbally haranguing him. I note that the complainant swore at the driver because of the latter's actions. However, I am satisfied that the driver would not have left his cab or followed an able bodied male passenger down the bus while verbally haranguing them in this manner. In any event, the entire dialogue between the complainant and the driver arose on foot of the complainant's disability, specifically his use of a wheelchair.

On 17 May 2003 the same driver stated to the complainant that he was 'not his minder'. The driver then left the cab of the bus and loudly related his version of the previous incident to all of the passengers on board (para 7.2).

The respondent maintained that the words used by the bus driver were not related to the disability ground but were based on personal differences between the driver and the complainant. However, the Tribunal found that the actions of the driver on both occasions constituted harassment. As can be seen from the extract quoted above, the statement 'I am not your minder' was related to the disability ground.

A post to an online discussion forum by another service user amounted to harassment on the disability ground in *Dalton v Aspire*.[553] The following statement was made in response to material posted by the complainant on the thread in question:

I apologise to anyone else who may think this is harsh, but really, you do not come across very well in your writings. If this is the way

---

[552] DEC-S2008-019.
[553] DEC-S2009-062.

you deal with the professionals and agencies then I am not surprised that you are making no headway with them. Perhaps it is a lack of understanding or skill in communicating with others – I don't know. All I can say, though, that I would be horrified if my DS becomes this way. I hope I will have thought [sic] him better (para 5.7).

The respondent voluntary organisation was, however, entitled to avail of the section 11(3) defence because it had responded effectively to the complaint (Chapter 7.3).

Hennessy v Network Catering/Iarnród Éireann[554] involved the adverse treatment by staff of a regular passenger in the respondent's dining car. The equality officer accepted that the complainant was subjected to ongoing and continuous harassment, which consisted of both physical acts such as banging the dining car trolley against the complainant's wheelchair and verbal abuse and ridicule.

In *Kane v Eirjet Ltd*[555] a passenger with Down syndrome was asked to vacate an aircraft seat located in an emergency exit row. He was travelling with his mother, who also referred a complaint, and other relatives. The equality officer found that the actual request was covered by the section 14(1) (*a*) exemption since it was required under applicable safety regulations (see Chapter 2.5). However, the manner in which the airline staff carried out their duties amounted to harassment on the disability ground. There was uncontested evidence that prior to take-off a member of the cabin crew approached the area where the complainants were sitting, pointed at Mr Kane and stated in an abrupt manner that 'this young man will have to move'. No explanation was offered at that juncture. After inquiring into the rationale for the request the complainants moved seats. As they were doing so they were subjected to unpleasant comments from other passengers and it was argued that the incident was portrayed as if they had been causing trouble. The equality officer was satisfied that the complainants' evidence was very credible. He accepted that they felt intimidated by the atmosphere on the flight surrounding the incident and that the upset, humiliation and embarrassment experienced was as a direct consequence of the treatment they were afforded by the members of respondent's cabin crew. As no evidence was presented on behalf of the respondent it failed to rebut the allegation. Notably, both complainants were harassed on the disability ground even though only of one them was a person with a disability for the purposes of the ESA. Moreover, it appears that the respondent was found liable both for the conduct of its staff and for that of the other passengers on the flight, since the equality officer suggested that the

---

[554] DEC-S2009-029.
[555] DEC-S2008-026.

harassment stemmed from the cumulative effects of the behaviour of both sets of people. Each complainant was awarded €1,000 for the effects of the harassment.

Kane, *King* and several of the other decisions issued to date demonstrate that behaviour can amount to harassment where there is no explicit reference to a characteristic associated with the ground in question.[556] When considering whether the impugned conduct is 'related to' a ground, equality officers often in effect use hypothetical comparators but assessing the relative treatment of complainants is not a legal requirement.[557] The technique employed is perhaps an attempt to get around what Barmes (2007, p 460) has called the 'wrongfulness riddle': that is 'the riddle of how to determine when conduct is plain harassment, outside the scope of the discrimination legislation (although potentially unlawful on other grounds) and when it is discriminatory harassment. In other words, what link between unwanted conduct and a protected ground should be sufficient to push harassment over the discrimination boundary?'

Comparators were used as an evidential device in a novel way in a multiple ground EEA harassment case: *Nyamhovsa v Boss Worldwide Promotions*.[558] The complainant, a black woman, worked in a commission-based sales role and referred a number of interrelated complaints against the respondent. When she left her identification card in her car one day the owner of the company said to her, 'You will be on the field for seventy gazillion years', while her trainee listened. The equality officer concluded that the comment amounted to harassment on the gender and race grounds:

> In terms of how the respondent's remark is connected to the complainant's race and gender, I wish to note that in general, blatantly racist and sexist remarks appear to be declining, as public awareness of their offensiveness increases. However, I find that the remark of the respondent is directly connected to the complainant's race and gender in that it links to longstanding, persistent stereotypes of black people as being less intelligent than white people, and similarly, of women being less intelligent than men.

---

[556] See also *Two Customers v A Retail Outlet*, DEC-S2002-008/009 and *Two Complainants (a mother and her son) v A Primary School*, DEC-S2006-028.

[557] See, for example, *McDonagh v McHale*, DEC-S2011-025, para 5.11 and *Nyamhovsa v Boss Worldwide Promotions*, DEC-E2007-072. In some early ESA cases equality officers considered harassment to be a form of less favourable treatment and so used comparators to assess the conduct in question: *Two Customers v A Retail Outlet, Dublin*, DEC-S2002-008/009 and *Two Complainants (a mother and her son) v A Primary School*, DEC-S2006-028, para 5.4.

[558] DEC-E2007-072.

I am satisfied that the respondent would not have made such an undermining remark to a white, Irish man in front of a trainee. I am further satisfied that while the respondent might have commented on such a man's forgetfulness, he would have been conscious of not undermining that man's authority in front of a subordinate (paras 5.27–5.28, footnote omitted).

Significantly here a hypothetical comparator of a different ethnic origin *and* gender is used to determine whether the unwanted conduct in question is related to the race and gender grounds.

Several harassment complaints have failed where the equality officer was satisfied that the conduct in question was not 'related to' the ground in question. Complainants have been upset and offended by behaviour or comments, but their cases were unsuccessful because what occurred was not considered discriminatory.

For example, in *Olaijde v Buck Properties Ltd*[559] the equality officer found that a series of exchanges between the parties, including an accusation that the complainant had stolen property, were not related to the gender and race grounds. There was insufficient evidence that the respondent's behaviour was linked to the grounds; some of the unwelcome and unpleasant conduct described took place because the respondent was trying to recover arrears in rent.

Likewise, in *Chawla v Irish Wheelchair Association*[560] the complainant claimed that the respondent harassed him on the victimisation ground through letters in which he was instructed to stop contacting certain employees of the Association. The letters were sent after Dr Chawla had referred a complaint to the Tribunal. The equality officer accepted that the respondent sent the letters in response to inappropriate contact that the complainant had initiated with two workers. The actions of the Association did not amount to harassment, but were considered reasonable in light of the distress caused to one employee in particular. In other words, the correspondence was not related to the discrimination complaint (and therefore the victimisation ground), but was aimed at protecting the welfare of employees.

In *Kent v Iarnród Éireann*[561] the complainant referred a complaint of discrimination and harassment on the disability ground when she was exposed to obnoxious drunken behaviour on the part of other passengers on a train journey. It was accepted that the conduct of the group in question was unacceptable and frightening but the respondent successfully argued that it was not

---

[559] DEC-S2010-021.
[560] DEC-S2009-024.
[561] DEC-S2009-026. See also *Campbell v Bus Éireann*, DEC-S2005-197; *Dalton v Glynn*, DEC-S2008-082; and *O'Reilly and Others v Waterford City Council*, DEC-S2010-018.

connected to the disability ground:

> I note that it was accepted by both parties that the complainant and her carer were situated in the same carriage as a group of youths who were engaging in inappropriate behaviour whilst on a train journey from Dublin to Waterford on the date in question. However, I also note that the complainant has not adduced any evidence to suggest that this inappropriate behaviour was directed personally against her on the grounds of her disability or that she was in any way singled out by the group of youths on the basis of her disability. I fully accept the complainant's evidence that she felt intimidated and vulnerable because of this inappropriate behaviour and that as a result she had to endure a very unpleasant experience after the group of youths had boarded the train. However, I am of the view that the experience and exposure to the inappropriate behaviour to which the complainant was subjected in the present case would have been unpleasant and intimidating to any passenger who might have travelled on the train regardless of whether or not they had a disability (para 5.1).

The reasonable accommodation aspect of the complaint had a better prospect of success since Ms Kent was a wheelchair user and had no option but to remain in the carriage occupied by the group in question since it was the only accessible area of the train. However, on the facts the Tribunal found that the respondent's employees had done all that was possible in the circumstances to deal with the situation and had therefore complied with section 4 (see generally Chapter 6.).

A number of incidents were outlined in a 2006 complaint.[562] The case was about the conduct of school authorities towards a woman and her son, M, who was attending the school in question. In relation to the parent the incidents were:

> (i) inviting a Garda into the parent teacher meeting, (ii) the refusal of the respondent principal to make a timely apology to her in relation [to] the Garda presence and only did so after a telephone call from the Department of Education, (iii) constantly being called to meetings in the school, (iv) successive allegations of bullying by M and complaints about minor infringements (para 5.1).

The equality officer found that first item amounted to harassment on the Traveller community ground. She was satisfied that it was reasonable for

---

[562] *Two Complainants (a mother and her son) v A Primary School*, DEC-S2006-028.

the complainant to find the presence of a Garda at the parent–teacher meeting to be intimidating and for her to feel humiliated by the experience (para 5.4). The incident would not have happened if the complainant were a settled person; it was therefore related to the ground. The other matters were not related to the complainants' Traveller identity. In those situations, staff were dealing with disciplinary issues in line with Department policy and the school's code of behaviour (para 5.5).[563]

5.4.3 Impact of Unwanted Conduct

In addition to showing that unwanted conduct of a sexual nature or conduct related to a ground took place, the complainant must present evidence which establishes that the conduct had the purpose or effect of violating their dignity *and* of creating an intimidating, hostile, degrading, humiliating or offensive environment for him or her.

The word 'unwanted' as well as the reference to conduct which 'has the purpose or effect of violating *a person's* dignity and creating an intimidating, hostile, degrading, humiliating or offensive environment *for the person*' [emphasis added] suggest that the primary reference point should be the complainant's perspective (Bolger and Kimber, 2009, pp 422–424). However, objective criteria are also employed to assess the impugned behaviour or material in the Tribunal's decisions.[564] So while the question of whether the act was 'unwanted' is entirely subjective, and perhaps too the element concerning the violation of the complainant's dignity,[565] equality officers use some form of reasonableness standard in deciding whether an intimidating, etc. environment was created.

In most of the cases where unwanted conduct related to a ground occurred, the Tribunal also concluded that the conduct affected the complainants in the manner required under the ESA. For example, in a 2011 case a mother and her child were refused service in the respondent's shop because they had a guide dog with them.[566] A security guard assumed

---

[563] See also *A Complainant v A Secondary School*, DEC-S2009-074.

[564] In *Parker v Federal Security Ltd*, DEC-S2011-036, the equality officer noted that the revised definition of harassment was more subjective but found 'there must still be an element of reasonableness in the analysis; otherwise the effect would be that it would be impossible for a respondent to defend themselves and I believe that this could not have been intended by the legislators' (para 4.3).

[565] Although in *Stevens v The Helix Theatre*, DEC-S2008-033, the equality officer found that comments made by a staff member did not have the purpose or effect of violating the complainant's dignity (para 5.11). See also *Stralkowski v Dublin City Council*, DEC-S2011-046, paras 5.7–5.8.

[566] *A Parent (on behalf of her son) v A Supermarket*, DEC-S2011-015.

that since neither of them was blind the dog was not an assistance dog and he behaved aggressively in asking them to leave the premises. The equality officer was satisfied that his behaviour, which involving shouting abuse and calling the complainant's mother a liar, violated the complainant's dignity and created an intimidating and hostile environment. The woman referred the complaint on behalf of her son and so the decision addressed his rights under the ESA. It is evident from the facts, however, that both customers were subjected to harassment related to the disability ground (as in the *Kane* decision; see Chapter 5.4.2).

The Tribunal does not always accept, however, that the unwanted conduct created an intimidating and hostile environment.[567] In *Stevens v The Helix Theatre*[568] the complainant was told that she would have to purchase a theatre ticket both for herself and for the baby she was breastfeeding at the time. When talking to an employee of the respondent (Ms Q) about its admission policy the complainant inquired as to what she could do and by way of response the employee suggested that she could express milk and leave the baby at home. The complainant pointed out that she was admitted with her baby without a second ticket on a previous occasion. Ms Q suggested that the male employee who dealt with her on that occasion was probably embarrassed. The equality officer accepted that the comments were made, but found that there was no harassment on the gender or family status grounds:

> While Ms Stevens was upset by these comments, and while they may be viewed as inconsiderate, I do not consider it reasonable that the comments could be regarded as creating a hostile, degrading, humiliating or offensive environment for the complainant. Nor do I believe that these comments had the effect of violating the complainant's dignity (para 5.11).

Dalton v Aspire[569] involved a complaint of harassment in relation to website content. The respondent is a voluntary organisation that provides support to people with Asperger syndrome and their carers. Ms Dalton complained that the manner in which various sections of its website presented Asperger syndrome was inaccurate, derogatory, unbalanced and unduly negative. The equality officer assessed the complaint of harassment on the disability ground as follows:

---

[567] See, for example, *Walsh Toolan v Board of Management of Coláiste Bride Secondary School*, DEC-E2007-058; *Dalton v Aspire*, DEC-S2009-062; *Duyn v Aer Arran Group*, DEC-S2011-023; *Parker v Federal Security Ltd*, DEC-S2011-036; *Oladapo v Irish Citylink ComfortDelgro Ltd*, DEC-S2011-063.
[568] DEC-S2008-033.
[569] DEC-S2009-062.

Using everyday language to interpret the supplied quotes from the website I am satisfied that they clearly express individual points of view – described as case notes – that I construe as such. Any opinion of a person – when expressed as such – is simply an opinion. These quotes do not say to me 'all persons with Asperger need full time care' or that 'no person with Asperger can have a successful relationship'. These comments simply suggest that, in individual circumstances, these events may occur to a person with Asperger syndrome or indeed, to any person (para 5.6).

She went on to find that although the complainant might not have agreed with the issues and opinions presented on the website that material did not create an intimidating, hostile, degrading, humiliating or offensive environment (para 5.6). Significantly, the Tribunal seemed to accept that material could ground a harassment complaint where it is not directed at a particular person, as was the case here, but at the public at large. A previous decision that addressed material in general circulation appeared to suggest the opposite. Information literature about refuse collection methods did not breach section 11 as it was 'issued automatically to all registered households and … not directed at the complainant in particular, or in any way related to his disability'.[570]

5.4.4 Harassment and Direct Discrimination

Two Complainants (a mother and her son) v A Primary School[571] raised allegations of direct discrimination and harassment on the disability and Traveller community grounds. As to the harassment, the equality officer found that it was reasonable for the first complainant to find the presence of a Garda at a parent–teacher meeting to be intimidating and for her to be humiliated by the experience. The equality officer did not elaborate as to how this constituted harassment on the Traveller community ground but reasoned that a settled person would not have been treated in the same way (para 5.4). The decision to invite a Garda to the meeting was also less favourable treatment within the meaning of section 3(1)(*a*). Similarly, a pub owner's general demeanour towards two customers amounted to both direct discrimination and harassment on the Traveller community ground in a 2002 case.[572] The equality officer found that the respondent had behaved in an 'intentionally provocative, rude and unwelcoming manner' and that such conduct could

---

[570] *Belton v Dún Laoghaire–Rathdown County Council*, DEC-S2006-067, para 4.5.
[571] DEC-S2006-028.
[572] *McDonagh v Patrick Powers Pub*, DEC-S2002-114/115.

reasonably be regarded as offensive, humiliating and intimidating to them (paras 6.1–6.2).

These cases illustrate that there is considerable overlap between the concepts of direct discrimination and harassment given that harassment related to one of the nine grounds will also typically constitute less favourable treatment on that ground. As of yet the interplay between these provisions has not been probed in Tribunal decisions. In *Mongan v Kenny's Public House, Galway*[573] the equality officer declined to deal with a harassment allegation that had not been raised in the notification or referral of the complaint, partly because she was satisfied that the actions in question had been dealt with fully under the direct discrimination heading.

Several other decisions have given rise only to findings of direct discrimination although the facts also implicated harassment. In *Kudryavitsky v Ballyfermot Resource Centre*[574] it was accepted that racist remarks were directed at the complainant and that he found them to be highly offensive. Yet the equality officer held that the conduct in question amounted to less favourable treatment on the race ground, presumably because the complaint was referred under section 3. Similarly, the facts in *Osemwegie v Grove Car Sales*[575] might also have amounted to harassment but the Tribunal issued a finding of direct discrimination. The complainant, a Nigerian national, was treated less favourably when he visited a garage to inquire about buying a car. An employee of the respondent (Mr A) made a number of offensive and derogatory comments to Mr Osemwegie. According to the complainant, upon approaching Mr A he was told, 'we have no cheap cars here'. Mr Osemwegie asked how he would know whether or not he wanted a cheap car. Mr A responded, 'Some of your friends came here before with no intention to buy. If you are looking for a car to drive, you can try that one over there.' The complainant understood the reference to 'your friends' as meaning black people in general. He expressed offence at Mr A's behaviour and since no change in attitude or apology was forthcoming, he left the showroom and indicated that he would make a complaint. Neither the respondent nor his representative attended the hearing. The equality officer found in favour of the complainant and awarded €500 in compensation for the effects of the discrimination. Likewise, the finding of direct discrimination on the disability ground in *Cantwell v Giles & Co., Tralee*[576] stemmed in part from the complainant being called 'a stupid useless cripple'.

---

[573] DEC-S2006-014/015, at para 4.2.
[574] DEC-S2008-079.
[575] DEC-S2008-103. For a further example on the race ground see *Wang v Yo Yo Paris Angel*, DEC-S2010-025.
[576] DEC-S2007-010.

5.5 Conclusion

Many issues remain unexplored in the general area of harassment. For instance, in the education context it could be argued that the harassment prohibition extends to teaching materials that depict minority sexual orientations or different family forms in a negative light. This may be a particular issue in schools with a religious ethos that promotes marriage and heterosexual relationships. As cases come before the ordinary courts the definition of harassment will be applied in the light of the relevant ECHR case law on the article 10 right to freedom of expression, as well the constitutional guarantee contained in article 40.6.1.i.[577] The Charter of Fundamental Rights (article 11) will also be relevant in cases on the grounds currently covered by EU law, that is, gender and race. Some grounds, such as those concerning sexual orientation, civil status and family status, directly implicate the teachings of various religions and so raise the right to freedom of religion and belief protected under the Constitution and article 9 of the ECHR as well.[578] Bell (2010a, pp 15–16) notes that the relationship between harassment and freedom of speech and religion is one of the 'sticking points amongst the Member States' in negotiations about the Draft Goods and Services Directive.

A further question arises as to the role of customer choice in relation to some potential forms of harassment. It may be argued, for example, that people who object to the display of materials by a service provider are not subjected to an intimidating, etc. environment if they are free to access similar services elsewhere.[579]

---

[577] The European Court of Human Right's judgment in *Vejdeland v Sweden* [2012] ECHR 242 appears to be the most relevant to the ESA to date.

[578] In a judicial review of the harassment provisions of the Equality Act (Sexual Orientation) Regulations (NI) 2006 the Northern Ireland High Court suggested that the provisions could be interpreted and applied in a manner which respected both Convention rights: *Re The Christian Institute* [2007] NIQB 66. See the discussion of this and other relevant cases by McGlennan (2010).

[579] The idea of 'contracting out' has been applied in cases concerning freedom of religious expression under the Human Rights Act 1998 and seems to be supported by the ECtHR. It essentially means that a court will not readily find an interference with the right to manifest one's religious belief where a person has other means open to them for practising their religion without undue hardship or inconvenience (e.g. by re-locating to another school). See *R (Begum) v Governors of Denbigh High School* [2006] UKHL 15 and *R (Playfoot) v Millais School* [2007] 3 FCR 754.

6

Reasonable Accommodation

6.1 Introduction

In discrimination law, 'reasonable accommodation' refers to an obligation to adjust rules, standards, policies or physical environments to meet the specific needs of people covered by a protected ground. It involves removing barriers, and often treating people differently, in order to secure equality of opportunity. Unlike most other elements of discrimination law, reasonable accommodation obliges service providers to take a protected characteristic into account when providing access to education, housing and so on.

Reasonable accommodation first evolved in the United States as a means of adjusting work practices to facilitate the religious beliefs of employees. Common adjustments include the introduction of flexible working hours to enable worship (Kelly, 2008). Subsequently the duty was extended to the disability ground.[580] Reasonable accommodation was introduced to Irish discrimination law under the Employment Equality Act 1998 and extended to the field of goods and services in the Equal Status Act 2000. Mirroring the position under EU law, it only arises in relation to people with disabilities.

Efforts to accommodate are generally required up to the point where the organisation attempting to provide accommodation would suffer 'undue hardship' or be subject to a 'disproportionate burden' by doing so. For instance, article 2 of the UN Convention on the Rights of Persons with Disabilities defines reasonable accommodation as 'necessary and appropriate modification and adjustments not imposing a disproportionate or undue burden, where needed in a particular case, to ensure to persons with disabilities the enjoyment or exercise on an equal basis with others of all human rights and fundamental freedoms.' A nominal cost threshold applies under the ESA. As we will see, the use of such limits means that obligations are not open-ended and also that

---

[580] The Rehabilitation Act 1973 is a federal law that covers public bodies, while the Americans with Disabilities Act 1990 extended protection from disability discrimination (including the reasonable accommodation duty) to the private sector.

the standards required vary depending on the capacity and resources of the organisation.

At present, EU reasonable accommodation law is confined to employment and vocational training. Article 4 of the Draft Goods and Services Directive requires service providers to make appropriate modifications or adjustments so as to enable disabled people to access housing, transport and other services, goods, social security, and social, healthcare and education services.[581] Modifications and adjustments are subject to a 'disproportionate burden' threshold, which is arguably more onerous than the 'nominal cost' ceiling currently applicable under the ESA. Assuming the draft Directive becomes legally binding the ESA will have to be amended accordingly.[582]

6.2 Definition of Reasonable Accommodation

Under Irish law the reasonable accommodation duty only arises with respect to people who are covered by the definition of 'disability' under section 2 (Chapter 2.3.4). Unlike the direct discrimination prohibition, it cannot be invoked by people associated with a disabled person or by people who have a disability imputed to them by a service provider (Chapters 3.1.2–3.1.3).[583]

Section 4 of the ESA provides:

> (1) For the purposes of this Act discrimination includes a refusal or failure by the provider of a service to do all that is reasonable to accommodate the needs of a person with a disability by providing special treatment or facilities, if without such special treatment or facilities it would be impossible or unduly difficult for the person to avail himself or herself of the service.

---

[581] The European Disability Forum (an NGO funded by the European Commission) has campaigned for the enactment of comprehensive disability rights legislation at EU level. See <http://www.edf-feph.org/>.

[582] ECHR law in this area appears to impose less onerous standards than the ESA. For a critical assessment of the limits and potential of relevant cases see De Schutter (2005b) and Lawson (2008, pp 36–49).

[583] This is also the position under EU law. In *Coleman v Attridge Law*, Case C-303/06, [2008] EC 1-5603; [2008] ICR 1128, the CJEU contrasted the areas of direct discrimination and harassment with other aspects of EU disability law that can only apply where the claimant has a disability. Referring to the reasonable accommodation obligation in article 5 and the provision for positive action in article 7(2), the Court stated: '[T]he measures in question are intended to accommodate the needs of disabled people at the workplace and to adapt the workplace to their disability. Such measures are therefore designed specifically to facilitate and promote the integration of disabled people into the working environment and, for that reason, can only relate to disabled people and to the obligations incumbent on their employers and, where appropriate, on the Member States with regard to disabled people' (para 42).

(2) A refusal or failure to provide the special treatment or facilities to which *subsection (1)* refers shall not be deemed reasonable unless such provision would give rise to a cost, other than a nominal cost, to the provider of the service in question.

Subsections (3) to (5) of section 4 clarify the extent of the duty to reasonably accommodate further. They provide for some exceptions and set out the relationship between reasonable accommodation and other provisions of the ESA, as well as its interaction with other laws. These provisions are discussed in Chapter 6.6.

Briefly, the duty entails 'providing special treatment or facilities, if without such special treatment or facilities it would be impossible or unduly difficult for the person to avail himself or herself of the service'. It applies to all of the fields covered by the ESA, that is, to goods and services, accommodation and premises, and educational establishments.[584] The types of treatment or facilities involved vary widely, but could include changes to practices (for example, allowing additional time for completing an examination), the use of assistive technology or changes to the physical environment (Chapter 6.4.2). 'Providing' includes making provision for 'or allowing such treatment or facilities'.[585] This means that the service provider must enable the use of facilities or treatment that come from other sources (including those supplied by the person seeking reasonable accommodation, like a guide dog). In the education sector, for example, the facilities in question might be provided by the Department of Education and Skills as opposed to a school.

A service provider must 'do all that is reasonable' in providing treatment or facilities, meaning that it must address a range of options. Case law establishes that section 4 is not simply concerned with whether treatment or facilities are delivered but also with *how* the service provider deals with the complainant, if at all. In order to comply with its obligations the service provider must engage in a process of consultation with the disabled person. As we will see from the decisions discussed below, the term 'reasonable' also limits the duty, in that a service provider is not expected to undertake very burdensome measures. Additionally, special treatment or facilities need not be provided where they would give rise to more than a 'nominal cost'. In other words, restrictions are placed on the obligation both by the term 'reasonable' and by the nominal cost ceiling.[586]

---

[584] Section 4(6).
[585] Section 4(6).
[586] Technically an accommodation that incurs more than a nominal cost is not 'reasonable' (section 4(2)). However, since the nominal cost threshold is usually assessed only after a

In order to establish a *prima facie* case, as required by section 38, the complainant must establish:

- That they have a disability as defined under section 2, and

- That the respondent did not do all that was reasonable to provide special treatment or facilities, without which it was unduly difficult or impossible to access the service in question

As discussed in Chapter 2.3.4, the definition of 'disability' under section 2 includes a wide range of conditions and impairments, whether permanent, temporary or episodic. An individual who has been diagnosed as having gender dysphoria or gender identity disorder will have a condition that falls within that definition (Chapter 3.3.4). Transsexual people may therefore lodge complaints about failure to reasonably accommodate.

From the case law to date it is not clear to what extent a complainant must demonstrate that the respondent's actions were not 'reasonable' as part of establishing a *prima facie* case.[587] As discussed below, the evidence put forward frequently does not meet the required threshold, since the Equality Tribunal often accepts that respondents have taken adequate steps where access to a service is technically possible albeit in less than ideal conditions from a disabled person's perspective.

Once the complainant has established a *prima facie* case the burden of proof shifts to the respondent. In other words, the respondent must then rebut the inference of discrimination. The nominal cost ceiling (Chapter 6.5), or one of the defences available under section 4 (Chapter 6.6), may be open to a service provider where a *prima facie* case of failure to reasonably accommodate has been established.

6.3 Reactive Operation of the Duty

In the employment context the duty to reasonably accommodate operates in a highly individualistic fashion. It does not apply to the workforce at large but is triggered by the actual situation of a given employee. That approach is logical since the nature of the adjustments to work practices, etc. required

---

complainant has established a *prima facie* case, it is referred to as a 'defence' and is dealt with separately in this book.

[587] But it should be noted that the Tribunal may take evidence put forward by the respondent into account in deciding whether the complainant has established a *prima facie* case: *Dyflin Publications Ltd v Spasic* (ADE/08/7; EDA/08/23, 19 December 2008) (adopting the approach of Mummery LJ in *Madarassy v Nomura International plc* [2007] IRLR 246, applied in *Olaijde v Buck Properties Ltd*, DEC-S2010-021).

will be specific to the job, the employee and the employment environment in question. However, the same cannot arguably be said of the service and goods provision context. Equivalent UK laws recognise this distinction (Gooding and Casserley, 2005, pp 151–154; Hepple, 2011, pp 76–77; Lawson, 2008, Chapter 3.3).[588] Parts III and IV of the Disability Discrimination Act 1995 imposed anticipatory duties in the arena of goods, services, facilities, premises and education whereas employers 'are under no obligation to make adjustments prior to being confronted with a particular individual whose disability results in the need for such an adjustment ...' (McColgan, 2005, p 590). That approach is retained in the Equality Act 2010. As Gooding and Casserley (2005, p 151) explain, the anticipatory nature of the duty in Britain is regarded as 'a major driver in encouraging service providers to think in advance about removing barriers experienced by disabled customers or potential customers. It helps to avoid a situation in which a provider claims that, because they did not know in advance that an adjustment was required, it was not reasonable to provide one.' They cite as an example the onus on conference organisers to ask delegates in advance about what adjustments they require.

Irish law can be differentiated from its UK counterpart in that section 4 does not refer to 'disabled people' or 'people with disabilities' but to 'the needs of a person with a disability.' The wording used suggests that the duty is triggered on a case-by-case basis and the decisions issued to date reflect that. For instance in a 2008 decision concerning public transport the equality officer stated:

> The duty to provide reasonable accommodation arises when a service provider becomes aware of the need to provide special treatment or facilities to a person with a disability. In this case I am very mindful of the fact that the complainant never told anyone working with Bus Eireann that she had a disability nor requested information or assistance from such a person.[589]

The Equality Authority's Annual Report for 2005 (Equality Authority, 2006b, pp 50–51) details a Circuit Court judgment on the nature of the duty to reasonably accommodate. The complainants' case had been successful before the Equality Tribunal but the outcome was overturned on appeal. The Circuit Court stipulated that the duty is only triggered when there is actual or constructive knowledge of the service user's disability. According to the report of the

---

[588] See the judgment of the UK Court of Appeal in *Roads v Central Trains Ltd* (2004) 104 Con LR 62.
[589] *Garcia-Rodriquez v Bus Eireann*, DEC-S2008-077, at para 5.5. See also *Carroll v Midleton Cabs*, DEC-S2010-010.

case, the judge held 'that where a person seeks reasonable accommodation under the Acts, he must prove that the service provider had actual or implied knowledge of the disability and disregarded such knowledge either intentionally or unintentionally in order to succeed in a claim' (Equality Authority, 2006b, p 51).

It remains to be seen how constructive knowledge of a disability will be inferred from the facts in any given case.[590] A direct discrimination complaint failed because the staff and management of a supermarket were unaware of the complainant's disability.[591] The equality officer concluded that a decision to exclude him could not, therefore, have been on the disability ground. The complainant had disclosed his disability to a Mr X who worked for the respondent. However, since Mr X was not present during the incident in question and had not discussed the matter with other staff his actual knowledge of the complainant's disability was irrelevant. The complainant argued that because he had been a customer for approximately twenty years the respondent would have become aware of his disability (clinical depression and anxiety). The equality officer addressed the argument about constructive knowledge of disability as follows:

> I am also satisfied that the complainant has established that a person who became reasonably acquainted with him, but who hadn't been told by him directly that he had a disability, nonetheless might reasonably become aware of his disability over time, through observation and/or inquiry of third parties. Conversely, I am satisfied, based on all the evidence presented to me regarding the present complaint that, in general, a person whose contact with the complainant was infrequent and/or only in passing would not necessarily conclude that he had a disability (para 5.6).

On the facts he concluded that the complainant failed to establish that the 'respondent's staff would have known him frequently enough and/or well enough to have become aware of his disability in the context outlined in the previous paragraph' (para 5.7). It would seem by analogy that in the reasonable accommodation context constructive knowledge of a disability would be assessed in light of all the circumstances, which should include the level of contact between the parties and the degree to which the disability is apparent or obvious.[592]

---

[590] Cases under the EEA do not seem to place a heavy onus on employers. See, for example, *Flynn v Emerald Facility Services*, DEC-E2009-065.

[591] *A Complainant v A Supermarket*, DEC-S2010-013.

[592] In *Two Complainants (a mother and her son) v A Primary School*, DEC-S2006-028, the

To sum up, the duty to provide special treatment or facilities must be triggered in the course of an encounter, or series of encounters, between a person with a disability and a service provider. Service providers' obligations to the public at large are instead found in the law and policy concerning general accessibility standards. A brief note on those standards is set out below (Chapter 6.8). It should be noted that the reasonable accommodation provision of the Draft Goods and Services Directive if enacted in its current form would establish an anticipatory duty. But, as Bell (2009, p 10) notes, the general provisions on enforcement will limit its potential since an individual complaint will be required to trigger the obligations.

Despite the reactive operation of section 4, its application can have effects beyond an individual case. In Canada, significant advances have been achieved through expansive readings of the duty to accommodate. Under the Canadian Human Rights Act 1995 the duty operates to qualify the defences available in cases of direct or indirect discrimination.[593] Courts have applied the general duty so that it requires an employer to re-structure the workplace in a manner that accommodates the needs of all employees, not just the particular claimant in issue (Sheppard, 2001; Vizkelety, 2008). Equivalent standards apply in the service provision arena.[594] The ESA has the potential to deliver similar knock-on effects because the Equality Tribunal and courts have the power to issue orders directing changes to a service provider's practices in general (Chapter 12.6). And of course the changes brought about to service provision because of a successful case improve the situation for other persons with similar needs including perhaps employees of the respondent (Emens, 2008).

6.4 Components of the Duty

6.4.1 Introduction

This section looks at the interrelated elements of reasonable accommodation under section 4. The nominal cost defence open to service providers is considered in Chapter 6.5. Chapter 6.6 examines other qualifications of the duty and some education cases are reviewed in Chapter 6.7.

---

respondent school claimed it did not know that the pupil had a disability. However, he had been placed on a list of pupils who were to be referred to an educational psychologist and the equality officer was satisfied from the evidence of staff that the school was aware that he had ADHD (para 6.9).

[593] There is no free-standing right to accommodation under the Canadian Human Rights Act: *Moore v Canada Post Corporation* (2007) CHRT 31.

[594] See *British Columbia (Superintendent of Motor Vehicles) v British Columbia (Council of Human Rights)* [1999] 3 SCR 868 (known as *Grismer*).

In practice the reasonable accommodation duty revolves around the process of engagement entered into by a service provider once they become aware that a service recipient has a disability. According to the Tribunal, 'a service provider cannot be deemed to be providing "reasonable accommodation" unless they have taken proper account of the needs and views expressed by the person with the disability, who obviously has [firsthand] knowledge of their condition.'[595] Failure to give *any* consideration to measures that could assist a complainant will certainly breach section 4.[596] The form of dialogue the service provider must engage in with a disabled person is considered further below (Chapter 6.4.4.3).

The Tribunal has underlined that the duty to provide special treatment or facilities is mandatory and distinct from the optional positive action measures permitted under other provisions of the ESA (Chapter 8):

> The purpose of reasonable accommodation is to provide for a situation where people with disabilities can avail of the service on an equal footing with those who have no disabilities. It is to remove a disadvantage rather than confer an advantage. It is to allow them to take part on a level playing field while allowing for their disability.[597]

The case in question here involved the annotation of certain disabled students' Leaving Certificates and as the subsequent appeals illustrate, judges and equality officers may disagree as to whether a particular measure provides a 'level playing field' or confers an unfair advantage (Chapter 6.7).

6.4.2 Special Treatment or Facilities

The type of special treatment or facilities required to access a service logically depends on the particular situation. In Irish case law to date there have been several complaints that entailed minor changes to service provision practices. For instance, in *Maguire v Bob's News and Deli*[598] the established failure to reasonably accommodate Ms Maguire, who was a wheelchair user, involved discontinuance of a practice whereby staff collected her groceries. The complainant in *Kenny v Sufi's Café*[599] was a regular customer whose visual impairment had been accommodated on several occasions by providing additional lighting. The café manager withdrew that facility on the date in

---

[595] *Maguire v Bob's News and Deli*, DEC-S2004-025, at para 7.10.
[596] See, for example, *Barnes v John Adams*, DEC-S2003-121, at para 6.3.
[597] *Two Named Complainants v Minister for Education and Science*, DEC-S2006-077.
[598] DEC-S2004-025.
[599] DEC-S2008-029.

question and because the respondent failed to attend the hearing no reasons were established as to why Ms Kenny was refused the special treatment she had originally received. An award of €250 compensation was made. *Golden v Just Beds*[600] is another straightforward example of failure to provide special treatment or facilities: a shop owner could have afforded the customer in question reasonable accommodation by simply inquiring as to whether she required assistance.

Denial of services to people accompanied by guide dogs has been interpreted as a failure to afford reasonable accommodation in several cases.[601] The guide dog should be registered, otherwise a respondent may be entitled to refuse access on health and safety grounds.[602] *Moloney v Park House Hotel*, for example, dealt with the unlawful refusal to allow a guide dog to accompany its owner in accessing overnight accommodation.[603] In *A Parent (on behalf of her son) v A Supermarket*[604] the complainant and her son were asked to leave the respondent's shop because he was accompanied by a guide dog. The boy in question had autism and the dog provided him with assistance under a scheme operated by Irish Guide Dogs for the Blind. His mother, who referred the complaint on her son's behalf, had the identification necessary to establish that the dog was a registered assistance dog. The equality officer reasoned as follows:

> From the evidence, I am satisfied that it would have been unduly difficult for the complainant's son to go to the shops with his mother without the assistance of his guide dog. I am satisfied therefore that the respondent in asking that the guide dog be removed from the shop failed to provide reasonable accommodation to the complainant's son. For the foregoing reasons I find that the respondent did unlawfully discriminate against the complainant by refusing to provide reasonable accommodation to a person with a disability in accordance with Section 4 of the Equal Status Acts when she was asked to remove the guide dog from the shop (para 4.4.).

There are several findings of discrimination where taxi drivers have refused to take guide dogs in their vehicles.[605]

---

[600] DEC-S2007-064.

[601] See, for example, *Roche v Alabaster Associates Ltd t/a Madigans*, DEC-S2002-086; *Leacy v Viart Ltd t/a Centra*, DEC-S2007-082; *McDaid v China Gold Restaurant*, DEC-S2011-021.

[602] *Wellard v Killester College*, DEC-S2008-024, para 8.1.

[603] DEC-S2008-073.

[604] DEC-S2011-015.

[605] See, for example, *A Complainant v A Taxi Driver*, DEC-S2009-025, and *Kealy v*

When the treatment or facilities sought extend beyond such modest changes the precise requirements of section 4 are more complex. Complainants have sought a variety of measures, including wheelchair-accessible public transport and premises (as well as parts of buildings); written materials in accessible formats; sign language interpretation services; and adjustments to assessment and disciplinary procedures in the education context. The 'special treatment or facilities' required to avail of a service then can range from changes to the built environment to modifications of how service providers communicate with people. As discussed below, each case is assessed with reference to a number of factors. A complainant must establish that access to the service would be impossible or unduly difficult without the provision of special treatment or facilities and a number of cases fall at that hurdle (Chapter 6.4.3). Even where it is established that access would be so impeded, the respondent may have done all was reasonable to accommodate the complainant's needs (Chapter 6.4.4). When these factors are combined with the fact that a nominal cost ceiling applies and the duty is a reactive one, we will see that the ESA requires little in the way of significant infrastructural change.

6.4.3 Availing of Service Impossible or Unduly Difficult

A service provider's duty to provide special treatment or facilities arises only if without such special treatment or facilities it would be impossible or unduly difficult for the disabled person to avail of the service. The terms 'impossible' and 'unduly difficult' are not defined under the ESA but decisions of the Tribunal provide some guidance as to the applicable thresholds.

The complainant in *Harrington v Cavan Crystal Hotel*[606] failed to establish a *prima facie* case of discrimination in relation to the leisure facilities at a hotel. According to the equality officer Ms Harrington could have been lifted in and out of the swimming pool in question by hotel staff and was therefore technically in a position to access that facility. The complainant had argued that installation of a hoist would have enabled autonomous use of the pool. The decision arguably indicates the need for a purposive approach to interpretation of the phrase 'unduly difficult' (see Chapter 1.6). In cases where access to services would be technically possible but compromise a person's dignity the question of reasonable accommodation could instead be decided on the nominal cost issue. A code of practice issued by the Disability Rights Commission on similar provisions which applied under UK law advised that in assessing whether 'services are unreasonably difficult for disabled people to use ... service providers should take account of whether the time,

---

Orayinyin, DEC-S2010-014.
[606] DEC-S2008-117. See also *A Minor v Dublin City Council*, DEC-S2011-039.

inconvenience, effort, discomfort, anxiety or loss of dignity entailed in using the service would be considered unreasonable by other people if they had to endure similar difficulties' (Disability Rights Commission, 2006, p 56). The code took into account factors such as a person's dignity, which inform the rationale for discrimination law. The 2011 decisions in *Duyn v Aer Arran Group*[607] and *Doherty v Bus Èireann*,[608] discussed below, reflect that rationale.

In *A Complainant v Marks and Spencer plc*[609] an offer to assist a visually impaired person in collecting groceries was adequate to discharge the supermarket's obligations. Because the complainant had not taken up that offer she could not establish that the service was impossible or unduly difficult to access. There was therefore no duty to alter a lighting system that rendered shopping independently impossible for the complainant. That decision was applied in *Connolly v Hughes and Hughes*[610] in which a regular visitor to a book store found that following renovations part of the premises had been rendered inaccessible to wheelchair users. Again the equality officer found that an offer to assist the complainant, in this case by bringing books to him, was adequate to meet the requirements of section 4. The offer of assistance meant that Mr Connolly could have accessed the service in question without undue difficulty. In reaching that conclusion the equality officer had regard to an observation of the Circuit Court to the effect that different treatment was not necessarily less favourable treatment.[611]

In *Wellard v Tesco Ireland*[612] the equality officer assessed the respondent's efforts to ensure that Ms Wellard had access to information on its club card system. The complainant had sought that information in Braille format and the equality officer accepted that the cost of doing so, at €180 per statement, would not be more than nominal relative to the respondent's resources. Nevertheless he found that the respondent had fulfilled its obligations under section 4. The complainant was provided with access to the information she sought over the telephone within a reasonable time. While the complainant's experience of that system 'had not been ideal', she was not 'entitled to perfection' and access to the service in question was not unduly difficult (para 5.6). As a result she failed to establish a *prima facie* case.

The complainant in *Walsh v Health Service Executive*[613] also could not establish that it would be 'unduly difficult or impossible' for him to access

---

[607] DEC-S2011-023.

[608] DEC-S2011-052.

[609] DEC-S2009-005.

[610] DEC-S2009-064.

[611] *Minister for Education and Science v Hollingsworth* (Circuit Court Dublin, Hunt J, unreported, 19 October 2007).

[612] DEC-S2009-047.

[613] DEC-S2008-014.

the services in question. Mr Walsh referred a complaint concerning several aspects of the HSE's dental treatment policies and processes, including the fact that appointments were not available on Fridays and could be accessed only at defined times at a particular hospital. The HSE claimed that its service delivery arrangements were necessary on health and safety grounds and that all people accessing various services were inevitably inconvenienced at times. In her assessment of the evidence the equality officer concluded that the HSE had not breached its duty to reasonably accommodate the complainant. She found that Mr Walsh could have accessed the service by adjusting his work commitments and the hours his personal assistant (PA) worked:

> I do not accept it is impossible or unduly difficult for Mr Walsh to allocate one day's allowance for his healthcare. PA hours are designed to enable the person with a disability to achieve maximum independence in his/her daily living by providing assistance in all areas of personal and domestic need and by acting as an escort and aide in the social and day-to-day activities. The role is [dependent] on the particular needs of the person being assisted and a certain degree of flexibility is a requirement of the PA job. I believe that Mr Walsh could, if he so wished, request that his PA start his/her day earlier on the day of his treatment (para 5.6).

A refusal to allow a guide dog to accompany a visually impaired person in a respondent's premises will generally make it unduly difficult or impossible to access the services in question.[614] The final four cases reviewed in this section provide examples of proven undue difficulty and impossibility.

The conditions imposed on persons using free travel passes on rail and DART services came under scrutiny in a 2009 case: *Thompson v Iarnród Éireann*.[615] As a holder of such a pass Mr Thompson was obliged to queue to obtain a ticket each day, whereas persons with regular tickets could obtain weekly or monthly cards. The equality officer considered whether the respondent did all that was reasonable to accommodate the needs of the complainant, as a visually impaired person, by providing special treatment or facilities:

> I have noted the complainant's evidence that the restrictions imposed upon him, as the holder of a Free Travel Pass, result in a considerable amount of hardship in terms of the travelling time that it takes

---

[614] See, for example, *Roche v Alabaster Associates Ltd t/a Madigans*, DEC-S2002-086, and *Moloney v Park House Hotel*, DEC-S2008-073.

[615] DEC-S2009-015. The indirect discrimination element of this case is considered in Chapter 4.3.

him to get to and from work and that this is exacerbated by the nature of his visual disability. I am satisfied that these restrictions result in a significant degree of inconvenience and difficulty to him as a regular commuter on the respondent's DART services, and as a person with a disability, who is dependent on this mode of public transport in order to travel to and from work. In the circumstances, I am of the view that the restrictions imposed upon the complainant make it excessively and 'unduly' difficult on him to avail of the respondent's DART service (para 4.7).

Mr Thompson had raised these difficulties on a number of occasions. Iarnród Éireann conceded that it had afforded other customers some flexibility in applying the impugned policy and the equality officer concluded that it could have done so in relation to the complainant and so afforded him reasonable accommodation.

In a 2009 decision the equality officer upheld a complaint of disability discrimination that involved appropriate toilet and bathing facilities during a hospital stay.[616] Contrary to medical advice the complainant, a wheelchair user, had to use a catheter for a period of 37 days because no accessible toilets were available. A facility that had been designated for wheelchair users was locked and used for storage. She also had to wash at a sink in the ward. The respondent acknowledged that the complainant had been unable to access the facilities in question and outlined steps it had taken since then to ensure that those facilities were upgraded and made available for use by patients. The Tribunal found that the treatment of the complainant breached section 4. In relation to bathing, the respondent's staff had not done all that was reasonable to enable the complainant to avail of appropriate washing facilities. In light of the severity and impact of the unlawful conduct on the complainant the equality officer awarded her the maximum amount of €6,348.69 in compensation. She also ordered the respondent to develop and implement an equal status policy and to ensure that accessible toilets are not restricted by keypads and/or locks and remain reasonably accessible in all wards.

An airline company refused to carry the complainant's mobility scooter on its aircraft in *Duyn v Aer Arran Group*.[617] It maintained that its actions were required by safety regulations. The Tribunal did not, however, accept that argument as discussed in Chapter 6.6.3. In the course of her decision the equality officer made a significant finding as to the meaning of the term 'unduly difficult', which took account of the importance of accessing services in an independent manner.

---

[616] *A Patient v Mater Misericordiae University Hospital*, DEC-S2009-057.
[617] DEC-S2011-023.

I accept the complainant's contention that the respondent's continued refusal to carry the battery in her mobility scooter makes it
unduly difficult for her to avail of its flight service. Without the use
of her mobility scooter the complainant is obliged to use a manual
wheelchair requiring somebody else to push her wheelchair. While
I appreciate that the respondent provides an assistance service for
passengers with disabilities, I can also understand the complainant's
desire to be independent, where possible (para 4.6).

Finally, *Doherty v Bus Éireann*[618] involved access to the respondent's bus
service on the Derry to Dublin route between April 2010 and April 2011. Mr
Doherty, a wheelchair user, 'had to drag himself on the steps of the bus "on
his bum", which he submitted was clearly unhygienic, degrading, humiliating
and very embarrassing to him' (para 3.2). Bus Éireann maintained that the
physical assistance given by its employees in boarding the bus satisfied its
obligations under the ESA. The Tribunal found, however, that it was 'unduly
difficult' for the complainant to avail of the service (para 5.4). The equality
officer clearly took account of the indignity Mr Doherty was subjected to.

6.4.4 Reasonableness

6.4.4.1 Overview

A service provider must 'do all that is reasonable to accommodate the needs
of a person with a disability' who seeks access to special treatment or facilities in order to avail of a service. This aspect of the duty has two components:
(1) a substantive element which concerns the level of treatment or facilities
required, including consideration of the nominal cost threshold, and (2) a
procedural requirement which relates to the process of engagement between
the service provider and recipient. Since the question of nominal cost generally arises after a complainant has established a *prima facie* case it is dealt
with separately in Chapter 6.5.

The obligation to do all that is 'reasonable' is assessed objectively. So
while a complainant may not have been satisfied with the measures taken by
the service provider the Tribunal will independently evaluate whether those
measures comply with section 4. Similarly, a service provider's assessment
of the treatment it provided and the steps it undertook might not correspond
with the Tribunal's.

In *Wellard v Killester College*[619] the equality officer stated that the
'complainant seems to confuse the concept of reasonable accommodation as

---

[618] DEC-S2011-052.
[619] DEC-S2008-024.

envisaged by the Equal Status Act with what she personally terms reasonable' (para 8.1). The Circuit Court adopts a similar approach. In a case about the provision of suitable housing Hunt J found that 'the housing authority is not obliged to submit to every wish expressed by a disabled person in the context of an application for facilities …. All that it is commanded to do by the equality legislation is to devise a "reasonable" solution to a problem, not to achieve perfection and not to give in to every demand that is made of it ….'[620]

According to the Circuit Court, 'reasonableness must be judged according to the context of the individual case.'[621] The case law suggests that what is reasonable for a respondent to do depends, among other factors, on its size and nature, and on the type of goods, facilities or services it provides.[622] The nature of the relationship between the parties is also taken into account. The standards expected in once-off service provision are generally lesser than those applicable where relationships between service providers and disabled people are likely to extend over a period of time and involve considerable levels of interaction.

6.4.4.2 Substantive Requirements

Kilduff v The Horse and Jockey Inn[623] involved a single transaction between a service provider and a potential service user. The complainant had made a reservation in the Horse and Jockey Inn, which is advertised as being wheelchair friendly. About one week prior to his stay, Mr Kilduff telephoned to request a

---

[620] *Dublin City Council v Deans* (Circuit Court Dublin, Hunt J, unreported, 15 April 2008), at p 34. Hunt J's interpretation of this aspect of the duty has been applied by the Tribunal in a number of subsequent cases, such as *Mr and Mrs X (on behalf of their son Mr Y) v A Post Primary School*, DEC-S2010-024 (reasonableness of measures taken by a school to accommodate a student's learning difficulties); *Mr X v A Town Council*, DEC-S2008-042 and *Cleary v Waterford City Council*, DEC-S2010-003 (operation of the respondents' housing lists); *Neary v Dublin Airport Authority*, DEC-S2010-036 (airport parking facilities); *Hennessy v Network Catering/Iarnród Éireann*, DEC-S2009-029 (accommodation of a wheelchair user on the respondent's transport service); and *Fogarty v Employment Appeals Tribunal*, DEC-S2009-087 (measures taken to ensure that the complainant could participate in an employment rights hearing).

[621] *Dublin City Council v Deans* (Circuit Court Dublin, Hunt J, unreported, 15 April 2008), at p 34.

[622] In *Seifu v Irish Wheelchair Association* (DEC-S2010-005) the equality officer took into account the nature of the facility provided in assessing the respondent's obligations under section 4. She noted that a driving licence would have an impact on the complainant's independence and quality of life. There was, therefore, 'a heavy burden' on the respondent to do all that was reasonable to accommodate the complainant (para 3.4). See also *Percy v Board of Laois Independent Living Association Company Ltd*, DEC-S2008-118.

[623] DEC-S2007-088.

bed with legs to facilitate his using a hoist to get in and out of bed. He cancelled his reservation upon being told that there were no such beds available. The respondent argued that prior to the complainant's request it was unaware of the necessity for a bed to have legs in order to use a hoist; guidelines on equipping a hotel for wheelchair use did not refer to that necessity. It had since purchased a suitable bed but could not acquire one in time to accommodate Mr Kilduff. The equality officer accepted that given the time constraints the hotel did all that was reasonable to accommodate the complainant.[624]

The respondent in *Hallinan v Moy Valley Resources*[625] operated a large resource centre that provided facilities for development and training programmes to the community at large. When attending a training session at the respondent's premises Mr Hallinan had no option but to use a bathroom in a nearby building. It transpired that the bathroom was not in fact accessible; because it could not accommodate the complainant's wheelchair he was forced to leave the door open. Upon inquiring as to whether the bathroom facilities had been upgraded and being told that they had not Mr Hallinan was unable to avail of subsequent courses. In assessing the duties imposed by section 4 the equality officer noted that the respondent was an organisation that provided services to the community at large. She stated:

> While I appreciate that it may not be reasonable to presume that providers of goods and services have an expert understanding of all types of reasonable accommodation issues that may arise, the fact is that it is reasonable to assume that a facility serving the wider community would have considered such basic needs as an accessible toilet facility (para 5.8).

Here the Tribunal factors in both the type of services and facilities provided by the respondent, as well as the essential nature of the facility required.

Fogarty v Employment Appeals Tribunal[626] dealt with the provision of sign language interpretation by an employment rights body (the EAT). The

---

[624] See also *Hallinan v Mayo Education Centre*, DEC-S2008-063: the respondent provided reasonable accommodation to the complainant who was attending a meeting at its premises, even though the meeting room and the toilet facilities were inaccessible. 'As all of the matters complained of by the complainant refer to structural changes such as ramps, resizing of the lift and refitting the toilet door, it is not reasonable, within the meaning of this Act, to presume that they could have been rectified then and there. I also find that it is not reasonable to presume that a service provider has the relevant experience to assess accessibility for all. In this case, it is clear that the respondent did all that was reasonable on the day' (para 5.7).

[625] DEC-S2008-025.

[626] DEC-S2009-087.

complainant explained that the respondent knew he was Deaf approximately five months prior to the hearing of his case. On the day of the hearing his representative again notified the EAT that he communicated through sign. An oral hearing went ahead with the parties agreeing that Mr Fogarty and his representative would write notes to one another. The complainant argued that his ability to participate in the proceedings was compromised because although he understood the messages from his representative he could not follow the hearing and communicate directly with the EAT. The respondent agreed that it knew about the complainant's language requirements prior to the hearing but pointed out that a sign interpreter was not requested at any stage. It was satisfied that since Mr Fogarty's representative was an experienced union official the complainant's interests would be adequately represented. Furthermore, the parties agreed on the procedures to be adopted on the day of the hearing. The equality officer was not, however, satisfied that the EAT had afforded Mr Fogarty reasonable accommodation. She concluded that the respondent had not devised 'a reasonable solution' in the context of the case:

> In my view it was the duty of the respondent to ensure that there was no impediment to the complainant's full participation and understanding of the hearing. From the evidence of both parties it would appear that the complainant was not asked if he required the services of a sign language interpreter. The non-availability of a sign language interpreter was an impediment to the [complainant's] participation in the hearing and was in breach of his right to … fair procedures and natural justice and his right to be heard. As sign language is the complainant's first language and his primary means of verbal communication, I am satisfied that without the special facilities of a sign language interpreter it was both impossible and unduly difficult for him to fully participate in his appeal hearing before the respondent …. I am of the view that a reasonable solution in the context of this case would have been for the respondent to adjourn the EAT hearing to a new date and to provide the facilities of a sign language interpreter for the complainant (para 5.3).

The Tribunal's decision in *Fogarty* was appealed to Nenagh Circuit Court and was due to be heard in March 2012. At the time of writing no information is available as to the outcome of those proceedings.

The Tribunal's assessment of what is reasonable may take account of an organisation's other legal obligations. For example, a crèche was not obliged to permit a child to be dropped and collected from its premises by taxi in order to accommodate the child's mother who was temporarily unable to drive.[627] Its insistence on dealing with a named individual, as opposed to several taxi drivers, was not unreasonable given the respondent's obligations to safeguard the health, safety and welfare of children attending the service under the Child Care Act 1991 and associated regulations.

Access to the built environment is mainly controlled by Part M of the Building Regulations, entitled 'Access for People with Disabilities' (Chapter 6.8). As to the relationship between Part M and the ESA, equality officers have no authority to assess compliance with the regulations.[628] Those standards are monitored instead by the building control officers of local authorities. What this means is that a reasonable accommodation case cannot succeed on the basis that a respondent's premises does not comply with Part M and also that compliance cannot provide a defence to a claim of discrimination under section 4.[629] Nonetheless, the building regulations can be taken into account in evaluating whether a service provider did all that was 'reasonable' in a given case. In *Harrington v Cavan Crystal Hotel*[630] the equality officer considered the guidelines in establishing whether the respondent should have provided the complainant with a wheelchair-accessible shower. The hotel in question was constructed following the enactment of Part M and the respondent conceded that its architects had failed to implement those guidelines when designing the building. The hotel was made aware of the complainant's disability when the room was booked. The equality officer was satisfied that the hotel failed to provide special treatment or facilities:

> [I]n all the circumstances of this complaint, it was reasonable to expect the respondent to have been aware of the need to provide level access showers for disabled customers and it was therefore reasonable for the complainant to expect that her needs in relation to the provision of bathroom facilities in the room in question should have been met (para 5.5).

Nolan v Bettystown Court Hotel[631] also involved a complaint about hotel facilities. The complainant was staying in a room that was wheelchair acces-

---

[627] *Banjoko v Mellon t/a Dolmen Nursery & Montessori School*, DEC-S2009-020. See also *Murphy-Madigan v Peter Mark*, DEC-S2010-023: a respondent who seeks to rely on health and safety concerns has no automatic defence to a reasonable accommodation complaint but must demonstrate that those concerns are well founded (para 5.3).

[628] See *Hallinan v Mayo Education Centre*, DEC-S2008-063, and *Nolan v Bettystown Court Hotel*, DEC-S2009-042.

[629] *A Patient v Mater Misericordiae University Hospital*, DEC-S2009-057, at para 5.10.

[630] DEC-S2008-117. See also *Kilduff v The Horse and Jockey Inn*, DEC-S2007-088.

[631] DEC-S2009-042.

sible but when using the bathroom a handrail came away from the wall and he was injured. He alleged that the respondent had breached its duty under section 4 in not providing special facilities and referred in support to Part M of the Building Regulations. The respondent argued that the incident did not comprise discrimination but instead could have given rise to a personal injuries claim. Applying *Hallinan v Mayo Education Centre*[632] the equality officer emphasised that he had no power to assess compliance with Part M and found that there was no failure to reasonably accommodate:

> [I]t is critical to note that the respondent, in order to ensure its compliance with the Acts, had only to do all that was reasonable in providing suitable facilities to the complainant. I consider that it was perfectly reasonable for the respondent to rely on the written assurances regarding the safety of the hotel in general, including the special facilities in question, that it received from its architects when the building was complete (para 5.4).

6.4.4.3 Procedural Requirements

A service provider who refuses or fails to consider whether special treatment or facilities could be put in place will breach section 4. However, where the service provider does enter into a process of consultation the question remains as to what form that process should take. Decisions that address this procedural aspect of the obligation to 'do all that is reasonable to accommodate the needs of a person with a disability' are examined in this section.

It should be borne in mind that the person seeking accommodation must communicate his or his needs to the service provider and otherwise keep them informed about relevant developments.[633] Where a service provider seeks medical evidence or other certification and the service recipient chooses not to comply with that request it may relieve the service provider of their duty to reasonably accommodate.[634] For both parties, maintaining a written record of dialogue about accommodations is advisable. Several complainants have been unable to establish a *prima facie* case because they could not demonstrate

---

[632] DEC-S2008-063.

[633] See, for example *Mrs C (on behalf of her daughter J) v Mrs L, the Proprietor of a Montessori School*, DEC-S2008-031; *Carroll v Midleton Cabs*, DEC-S2010-010; *Byrne v Miami Café*, DEC-S2010-019; *McGrath v University of Dublin, Trinity College*, DEC-S2010-006; *A Student v Galway–Mayo Institute of Technology*, DEC-S2010-047; and *Ryan v Dublin Institute of Technology*, DEC-S2011-057.

[634] See, for example, *A Student v Galway–Mayo Institute of Technology*, DEC-S2010-047, at para 5.12.

that requests for accommodation had been made at all or in the manner they described at the hearing.[635]

The procedural aspect of the reasonable accommodation duty can address flawed decision-making processes. Adherence to fair procedures and explanation of the reasons for decisions are central to the Tribunal's findings in several recommendations aimed at public service providers. For example, in a 2006 decision the equality officer applied standards developed in the employment arena to a housing authority's treatment of a couple's application to buy a house under the terms of a Shared Ownership Scheme: *Gallagher and Wilson v Donegal County Council*.[636] He found that the respondent failed to comply with the duty to reasonably accommodate, as it did not take into account all material facts when assessing their application. In particular the council did not adequately consider the Disability Allowance payable to the applicants. When assessing the obligations inherent in section 4 the Tribunal relied on the test set out by the Labour Court in the employment case of *A Health and Fitness Club v A Worker*,[637] which stressed that an employer must at a minimum possess all the material facts concerning the employee's condition.

A Complainant v A Local Authority[638] involved an application for a grant to fund an extension to a house in order to meet the needs of an autistic boy. The equality officer found several flaws with the manner in which the application was processed, including the following:

- The child's specific circumstances and needs were not properly considered by the local authority. Staff processing the mother's application were not qualified in any respect to reach a number of stated conclusions in relation to the son's disability and they did not seek the expertise of a person suitably qualified to assess the nature of the child's disability. Recommendations of a number of qualified external professionals in favour of the complainant's application were ignored.

- Staff of the local authority compared the disability of the claimant's son less favourably with physical disabilities.

---

[635] See, for example, the different recollections of the contents and outcomes of conversations about students' needs in *Kwiotek v National University of Ireland, Galway*, DEC-S2004-176; *A Mature Student v A College*, DEC-S2010-007; and *McGrath v University of Dublin, Trinity College*, DEC-S2010-006.

[636] DEC-S2006-060; see also *Buckley v Tipperary Town Council and Tipperary Town Clerk*, DEC-S2007-066.

[637] ED/05/29; EED/037, 18 February 2003. The decision was upheld on appeal to the Circuit Court: *Humphries v Westwood Fitness Club* [2004] ELR 296.

[638] DEC-S2007-049.

She concluded that the respondent directly discriminated against the complainant by arbitrarily comparing her son's disability less favourably with physical disabilities under a scheme which was stated to cater for persons with either a physical or mental disability. This is an example of direct disability discrimination as between people with different disabilities (see Chapter 3.3.2). The local authority had also failed to afford the complainant reasonable accommodation in light of several procedural flaws, including those alluded to above. Furthermore, the nominal cost defence could not be used, since no evidence was supplied as to how much the extension would cost and given that any such work would only amount to a small proportion of the overall housing budget funded by Government.

Ms D (a tenant) v A Local Authority[639] concerned an application for a larger housing unit on the part of a disabled woman. Her application was supported by medical evidence, which outlined the nature of her condition and the specific needs she had for space as well as the benefits the additional space would have for her. The authority's medical referees on the other hand did not recommend her for the allocation of a larger apartment, and had reached that conclusion without meeting Ms D or assessing the extent of her disability. The sole criterion for allocations of housing units was family size and all single occupants, such as Ms D, were provided with similar-sized units. In the opinion of the equality officer the decision-making process did not meet the standards required by section 4:

> At the very least it would appear that reasonable accommodation for Ms D should include a full and proper assessment of Ms D and her application for special facilities, particularly where the outcome of the application is to contradict the substance of the medical references provided by Ms D in support of her application (para 3.9).

The case was appealed and while the aspects of the decision concerning Ms D's particular situation were upheld, the Circuit Court set aside a broader order concerning the local authority's general housing policy.[640] Hunt J agreed that the respondent failed to adequately consider or evaluate the material submitted by the complainant. The equality officer had directed that the council revise its scheme of priority in relation to disabled persons to take further account of medical reports and applicants' particular disabilities. Hunt J found that the order interfered unduly with the city council's discretion in maintaining and operating its housing plan. The ESA obliged the council to devise a reasonable solution to an individual's housing needs in light of its obligations

---

[639] DEC-S2007-057.
[640] *Dublin City Council v Deans* (Circuit Court Dublin, Hunt J, unreported, 15 April 2008).

to the community as whole. As a result 'it cannot be forced to make more than a modest or nominal departure from its carefully constructed allocation scheme to meet the needs of any particular individual and its obligations to the disabled must be seen in that context.'[641]

The Circuit Court's approach aligns with that of the Tribunal in *Jones v Dún Laoghaire–Rathdown County Council*,[642] which established that the reasonable accommodation duty does not give rise to an obligation to maintain a separate housing list for disabled people. The duty was fulfilled by other measures undertaken, including an assessment of the complainant's disability and the allocation of medical points in accordance with the respondent's scheme of letting priorities.[643]

The procedural requirements of section 4 also apply to private sector bodies. For instance, in *Percy v Board of Laois Independent Living Association Company Ltd*[644] Mr Percy's right to reasonable accommodation was not respected when his personal assistance service was withdrawn in a manner that did not adhere to fair procedures. The respondent removed the service at short notice pending an investigation into claims of bullying and harassment made against the complainant. According to the equality officer, while the service provider was obliged to investigate the claims and to protect its employees, the service was crucial to Mr Percy and it would have been reasonable to at least explore the provision of temporary cover for the complainant.

In *T (on behalf of his son D) v R, SAMBA Soccer School*[645] a child with cerebral palsy was denied a place on a summer soccer camp apparently because the respondent's insurance policy would not cover his participation. However, the boy's father was not provided with any evidence to that effect. Essentially no attempt had been made to provide any treatment or facilities to the complainant to allow him to avail of the service in question. SAMBA Soccer was directed to pay the complainants €750 and to examine the criteria for accepting children on its programmes with the aim of accommodating children regardless of their ability or disability where possible.

A series of cases involving the manner in which several car rental companies dealt with requests for modified vehicles also illustrate the need for written procedures and adequate training on the ESA. Each of the respondents,

---

[641] *Dublin City Council v Deans* (Circuit Court Dublin, Hunt J, unreported, 15 April 2008), pp 34–35.
[642] DEC-S2004-081.
[643] See also *Compagno v Kinsale Town Council*, DEC-S2009-052, at paras 4.10–4.11; *Cleary v Waterford County Council*, DEC-S2009-085, at paras 4.11–412; and *Cleary v Waterford City Council*, DEC-S2010-003, at paras 4.10–4.12.
[644] DEC-S2008-118.
[645] DEC-S2007-009.

bar one, had refused service without engaging in any or adequate efforts to facilitate the complainant's request, e.g. by referring him to a specialist in the field.[646] In a number of those decisions the equality officer suggested that reasonable accommodation could have been afforded to the complainant by modifying a vehicle and then seeking to recoup some or all of the costs from the customer.[647] The complainant did not establish a *prima facie* case in *Goulding v Ryan's Investments Limited t/a Hertz Rent a Car*[648] because the respondent successfully demonstrated that it had offered to supply a modified car within four days. Mr Goulding apparently failed to take up that offer and the respondent also reported that it was willing to absorb the cost involved, which was estimated at €130 plus VAT.

Reasonable accommodation was not addressed in *Murray v Irish Life and Permanent TSB*[649] but it seems to be exactly the type of situation in which standard procedures should be adjusted to take account of a person's disability. Mr Murray had obtained approval for a HSE grant to purchase a car. He needed the vehicle to travel the considerable distance between his home and the hospital at which he was undergoing treatment for cancer. The grant was to be paid following purchase of the car and Mr Murray applied for a bank loan to enable him to do so. The complainant's loan application provided detailed information about the terms of the grant, including details of the contact person within the HSE who could verify the conditions that had to be met. Mr Murray also provided evidence of his disabled status and of his record as a customer of the bank for over six years. The bank was clearly on notice that the complainant was a person with a disability for the purposes of the ESA. Despite those circumstances the respondent bank applied its lending criteria in a rigid manner and did not give the complainant any reasons for declining his application.

He referred a complaint of disability ground direct discrimination to the Tribunal. Before the Tribunal the respondent maintained that the loan was declined for reasons that had nothing to do with the complainant's disability. The bank's confidential lending criteria were given to the Tribunal for the

---

[646] *Goulding v Murray's Rent a Car t/a Sixt Rent a Car*, DEC-S2009-054; *Goulding v Enterprise Rent-a-Car, Ireland Ltd*, DEC-S2009-049; *Goulding v Johnson & Perrott Rent a Car Ltd t/a Avis Rent a Car*, DEC-S2009-056; *Goulding v Flynn Bros Rent a Car Ballygar t/a Budget Car Rental*, DEC-S2009-070; *Goulding v Irish Car Rentals Limited (Formally Argus Car and Van Rentals Limited)*, DEC-S2009-068; and *Goulding v Centre Point Rent a Car Limited t/a Car Rental (Formally National Car Rental)*, DEC-S2009-055.
[647] *Goulding v Irish Car Rentals Limited (Formally Argus Car and Van Rentals Limited)*, DEC-S2009-068, at para 5.7; *Goulding v Centre Point Rent a Car Limited t/a Car Rental (Formally National Car Rental)*, DEC-S2009-055, at para 5.7.
[648] DEC-S2009-067.
[649] DEC-S2010-004.

purposes of the hearing. It emerged that the bank refused the loan application on the basis that the complainant was a tenant with an income below the level indicated and had not been in continuous employment for a specified number of years. He, therefore, fell outside the lending criteria that were authorised at branch manager level. The equality officer inquired whether the manager had any discretion in applying those criteria and was advised that an application could be sent to the bank's external lending unit if the manager believed there were strong reasons for doing so. In his evidence to the Tribunal the manager insisted that the provisional grant approval did not warrant a referral; the current lending environment was extremely risk averse and payment of the grant depended on the complainant satisfying conditions over which the bank had no control. It is regrettable that the equality officer did not use her discretion to consider section 4 even though the complainant had not raised that form of discrimination in his submission to the Tribunal (Chapter 12.5.4). Indeed, it is arguable that reasonable accommodation ought to have been included in the investigation since section 4(1) provides that for 'the purposes of this Act discrimination *includes* a refusal or failure by the provider of a service to do all that is reasonable to accommodate the needs of a person with a disability ...' (emphasis added). Given this wording, equality officers in a significant proportion of disability ground complaints automatically examine compliance with section 4.[650] The facts did not reveal any attempt to consider special treatment or facilities to enable Mr Murray to access the loan facility.

The respondents in *Harrington v The National Concert Hall*[651] had complied with the procedural obligations inherent in the reasonable accommodation duty. Ms Harrington referred a claim of discrimination on the disability ground: as a season ticket holder she could not attend pre-concert receptions since these were held in an inaccessible part of the respondent's building. The equality officer concluded that the respondent had done all that was reasonable to accommodate the complainant's needs. It had replied to correspondence from her outlining the constraints that affected its ability to install a lift facility in the building and/or to hold events in an accessible room. In deciding what constitutes 'reasonable accommodation' the equality officer noted that a high standard of consultation was required under the EEA, drawing in particular on the Labour Court decision in *A Health and Fitness Club v A Worker*.[652] While the standard of reasonable accommodation required in an employment

---

[650] See, for example, *A Complainant v A Choir*, DEC-S2012-004, para 5.2.
[651] DEC-S2008-048. See also *Kent v Iarnród Éireann*, DEC-S2009-026, discussed in Chapter 5.4.2.
[652] ED/05/29; EED/037, 18 February 2003. The decision was upheld on appeal to the Circuit Court: *Humphries v Westwood Fitness Club* [2004] ELR 296.

context may be higher, the duty to consult should also apply in the goods and services field.[653]

Similarly, the respondent in *Wellard v Eircom*[654] had engaged in an extensive process of consultation with the complainant. On foot of those communications it had put in place a range of measures that enabled access to its bills in accessible formats, including the translation of bills into Braille, access to speech synthesiser software via its website and the appointment of a dedicated contact person to deal with queries from the complainant. It had outsourced the production of other documents in Braille format to the National Council for the Blind of Ireland, and the turnaround time for those materials was approximately three weeks. A delay of three weeks in accessing written material other than bills was not excessive, according to the equality officer. The Tribunal concluded that the respondent had complied fully with, and even went beyond, its obligations to reasonably accommodate the complainant.

From the case law to date it is not clear to what extent the duty to do 'all that is reasonable' includes an obligation to avail of grant aid and schemes that are available to service providers. That may not be the position for many sectors given the reactive nature of the duty. However, where there is an ongoing relationship between the parties, as in the education setting, different standards ought to prevail.[655] Tribunal decisions seem to follow that logic. For example, in *Two Complainants (a mother and her son) v A Primary School*[656] the Tribunal found that it was incumbent upon a school to apply for available educational supports in order to satisfy its obligations under section 4. In another education case the equality officer stated:

> [T]he provision of special treatment or facilities in the context of Section 4 of the Act would have placed an obligation on the respondent to provide all reasonable assistance to Mrs. C in her attempts to obtain or source the services of an SNA [special needs assistant] to assist J in her Montessori school, and in circumstances where sanction was obtained for the appointment of such a person, there would also be an obligation on the respondent to facilitate the appointment and integration of this person into her school so that the appropriate assistance could be provided for.[657]

---

[653] See also *A Student v Galway–Mayo Institute of Technology*, DEC-S2010-047, at para 5.11.

[654] DEC-S2008-098; see also *Murphy-Madigan v Peter Mark*, DEC-S2010-023.

[655] In *Hallinan v Moy Valley Resources*, DEC-S2008-025, the equality officer found that the respondent could not rely on an assertion that no grant aid was available as a defence because it provided no evidence that it has endeavoured to secure such aid (para 5.7).

[656] DEC-S2006-028.

[657] *Mrs C (on behalf of her daughter J) v Mrs L, the Proprietor of a Montessori School,*

The reasonable accommodation duty is often read in conjunction with the obligations of primary and second level schools under the Education Act 1998 (Chapter 6.6.4; Chapter 6.7).

Where funding is available upon application by the service recipient, as is the case in the third level education sector, it would seem that the service provider should meet its procedural obligations by facilitating students to apply for such aid.[658]

6.5 Nominal Cost

Owing to a Supreme Court judgment reasonable accommodation is subject to a 'nominal cost' ceiling. The 'undue hardship' threshold set out in a parallel employment discrimination law bill was declared unconstitutional because, according to the Court, it would undermine the constitutional rights of employers to earn a livelihood.[659] As a result both laws were re-drafted and the nominal cost limit was adopted in place of the offending provision. A 'dispro-portionate burden' threshold now applies under the Employment Equality Acts 1998–2011 because the Framework Directive mandated such a change, but it deals with employment and vocational training. The Draft Goods and Services Directive purports to extend EU law on reasonable accommodation to the field of goods and services. It too employs the 'disproportionate burden' standard and if that Directive comes into force the nominal cost limit will change under the ESA.

Section 4(2) states:

> A refusal or failure to provide the special treatment or facilities to which *subsection (1)* refers shall not be deemed reasonable unless such provision would give rise to a cost, other than a nominal cost, to the provider of the service in question.

Since the nominal cost ceiling effectively operates as a defence, once the complainant establishes a *prima facie* case the onus generally rests on the respondent to demonstrate that the costs involved are more than nominal.[660]

DEC-S2008-031, para 4.11. See also *Mrs X (on behalf of her son, Mr Y) v A Post-Primary School*, DEC-S2010-009, which is discussed in Chapter 6.7.

[658] See, for example, the Special Fund for Students with Disabilities administered by the Higher Education Authority: <http://www.hea.ie/en/node/1125>. See generally: <http://www.assistireland.ie/eng/Information/Education/Education_Bodies_and_Services/>.

[659] *Article 26 of the Constitution and the Employment Equality Bill 1996, Re* [1997] 2 IR 321.

[660] In *Hallinan v Moy Valley Resources*, DEC-S2008-025, the equality officer suggested that the nominal cost issue should be addressed following the establishment of a *prima*

The Equality Authority has consistently argued that the provision should be read in a way that maximises its potential. For example, in its publication on the duties of schools under the ESA it states:

> The meaning of 'nominal cost' will depend on the circumstances such as the size of and resources available to the organisation. A large and well-resourced organisation is more likely to be able to afford a higher level of cost in making reasonable accommodation than a small one is. As most schools are funded by the State, this would suggest the 'nominal cost' exemption may not be very significant in practice. If the State provides grants or other resources for assisting in providing special treatment or facilities, there may be an onus on the school to avail of these (Equality Authority, 2005c, p 10).

That approach is supported by the Oireachtas debates on the Equal Status Bill 1999. The Minister for Justice advised, 'the issue of nominal costs may vary, according to the nature of the service and the circumstances of the service provider. In other words, what might be regarded as a nominal cost for a service provider with a large turnover might not be a nominal cost for a small business.'[661]

Because there are relatively few ESA cases dealing specifically with the issue, it is not yet clear how this understanding of nominal cost as a relative concept will play out in practice. In *A Complainant v Marks and Spencer plc*[662] the equality officer made some observations on the question of nominal cost although it was not in issue in the case before her:

> Service providers must be cognisant of the fact that every nominal cost issue will be assessed depending very much on whether the requested special treatment and/or facility is a necessary and reasonable request from the complainant, the size of the organisation in question, its resources and whether grants, etc. are available (para 5.6).

It is clear nevertheless that because the duty centres on accommodation of the actual complainant, the ESA will not generate significant infrastructural

---

facie case: 'While the legislation deems any special action required from any service provider not reasonable if it creates more than a nominal cost, the onus is on the organisation to demonstrate how the provision of a special treatment or facility would create more than a nominal cost to it' (para 5.6). But see *Regan v Old Bawn Community School*, DEC-S2010-043, in which the complainant did not establish a *prima facie* case even though the outcome rested on the nominal cost issue.

[661] 162 *Seanad Debates* Col 589 (Equal Status Bill 1999: Second Stage).

[662] DEC-S2009-005.

changes. In a 2003 decision the complainant *Hennessy v Dublin Bus*[663] could not board a wheelchair-accessible bus because the access ramp was out of order. According to the equality officer the bus driver 'had a responsibility and a duty to … make every reasonable effort to assist the complainant' and was satisfied on the evidence that he had gone to considerable lengths to do so. Although it was not pivotal to the outcome of the case the equality officer went on to consider the general duties imposed on public transport providers. According to evidence submitted by Dublin Bus each accessible vehicle cost in the region of €150,000. The equality officer noted that there was no specific requirement under the Equal Status Act that public buses should be wheelchair accessible and that the general duty to provide reasonable accommodation was subject to a limit of nominal cost. The respondent gave evidence that it was progressively making the entire Dublin Bus fleet accessible and had trained all drivers to operate the wheelchair ramps. By the date of hearing, the route in question had become wheelchair accessible. The equality officer accepted that provision of an entirely wheelchair-accessible fleet of buses would far exceed nominal cost to the respondent. She relied on provisions in the ESA (since repealed by the Disability Act 2005), which specified that the Minister could make regulations on accessible transport as support for the proposition that such an extensive obligation was not envisaged under the Act.

In a more recent decision, also involving the accessibility of public transport, the Tribunal reiterated that the ESA required the accommodation of individual service users and did not impose wider accessibility obligations. The complainant used a motorised wheelchair and the aisles of the respondent's trains were too narrow to accommodate it. As a consequence his wheelchair was stored during journeys and he was obliged to transfer to a manual wheelchair, which could only be placed in the dining car because of space restrictions. The equality officer concluded that the measures taken to accommodate the complainant were adequate to satisfy section 4 and went on to observe that in any event the provision of adequate access for motorised wheelchairs would be likely to exceed the nominal cost ceiling.[664]

Harrington v The National Concert Hall[665] involved the accessibility of premises to a wheelchair user. With respect to the question of nominal cost, the equality officer accepted that the work required to install a lift would exceed the threshold, since the evidence presented to the Tribunal indicated that such work could only be undertaken within the context of a larger development that would cost approximately €10 million.

---

[663] DEC-S2003-046.
[664] *Hennessy v Network Catering/Iarnród Éireann*, DEC-S2009-029, at paras 4.19–4.21.
[665] DEC-S2008-048.

The defence was also availed of successfully by a financial institution in *Wellard v The Educational Building Society and Allied Irish Banks.*[666] According to the Educational Building Society (EBS), the production of automated teller machine (ATM) pin numbers in Braille would compromise existing security arrangements and require the introduction of an entirely new encryption system at 'huge expense'. The equality officer accepted this evidence, apparently without reference to any actual figures, and in deciding that the accommodation sought exceeded the nominal cost appeared to be swayed by the fact that no other customer had requested a similar accommodation (para 7.5). The Equality Authority has queried such an approach to the question of nominal cost in its discussion of the *Kwiotek* case (see below).

On the other hand, in *Wellard v Tesco Ireland*[667] exact figures for the cost of producing a clubcard statement in Braille were provided. The Tribunal found that a sum of €180 per statement was nominal given the resources of the respondent (para 5.5). As discussed above, however, the complaint did not succeed because the equality officer was satisfied that the respondent had provided alternative means of accessing the information sought, which complied with the reasonable accommodation requirement.

A stringent approach to nominal cost was adopted in some decisions concerning public housing authorities. *A Complainant v A Local Authority*[668] addressed grant aid to fund an extension to a house in order to meet the needs of an autistic boy. According to the equality officer, the nominal cost defence could not avail the respondent because it provided no evidence as to how much the extension would cost and any such work would only amount to a small proportion of the overall housing budget funded by Government. She referred to a 2002 employment case, decided when the same threshold applied under the EEA. In that decision the Tribunal found that 'nominal cost' should assessed according to the size and resources of the employer whether in the public or private sector.[669]

> The respondent has never determined the actual cost of an extension to the complainant's residence. I note that, at the time of the initial application by the complainant, the Scheme operated by

---

[666] DEC-S2005-093.

[667] DEC-S2009-047.

[668] DEC-S2007-049.

[669] *An Employee v A Local Authority*, DEC-E2002-004. In reaching that conclusion the equality officer considered the Dáil debates on the Bill as well as the decision in *Article 26 of the Constitution and the Employment Equality Bill 1996, Re* [1997] 2 IR 321. See also the Labour Court decision in *A Motor Company v A Worker*, ED/01/40; EED/026, 2 July 2002: the provision of equipment costing €450 by a small company with a large turnover did not exceed the threshold.

the respondent was two thirds funded by the Department of the Environment, Heritage and Local Government. This meant that only one third of the cost would have to be borne by the respondent at that time. Subsequently all such extensions became fully funded by the Department.

The respondent has failed to establish any cost figure for the extension in question. In light of this and taking into consideration all of the figures provided by the respondent subsequent to the Hearing of this complaint which indicate that overall expenditure by the respondent on extensions under the Scheme amounted to a small proportion of overall housing budget, which is now fully funded by the Department, I am unable to properly consider or determine whether the construction of an extension to the complainant's property would amount to more than nominal cost. In the circumstances I am satisfied that the respondent has failed to demonstrate that the construction of an extension to the complainant's residence would constitute more than nominal cost (paras 7.3.2–7.3.4).

Likewise, in *Ms D (a tenant) v A Local Authority*[670] the equality officer found that the complainant was not afforded reasonable accommodation in the context of an application for a larger housing unit. The nominal cost issue was dealt with as follows:

[I]t is common case that the local authority would be providing Ms D with an apartment in any event and the additional cost arising would be that involved in providing her with the larger apartment she says she needs. As no costings have been given on the difference in cost between different sized units I consider that if there is a differential in the unit cost, the difference could be no more than nominal in the context of the overall budget of 3 billion Euro available to the council for the scheme and of the total budget available to the local authority (para 3.14).

Budgetary considerations also arose in *Mr X v Health Service Executive.*[671] The complainant was undergoing treatment for schizophrenia and claimed that by not providing access to a psychologist the HSE had failed to offer reasonable accommodation. Such treatment was the most effective means of treating him and he had requested that the services of a psychologist be made available

---

[670] DEC-S2007-057.
[671] DEC-S2008-112.

through the National Treatment Purchase Fund. The HSE argued that Mr X was treated in accordance with the prognosis of a medical team, who initially considered that medication was the appropriate form of treatment. This aspect of the complaint fell within the clinical judgment exception and so could not be challenged as discriminatory (Chapter 2.6.4.5). Subsequently, the doctor treating Mr X decided that he would benefit from seeing a psychologist but those services were not provided for some nine months because of budgetary constraints. The equality officer was satisfied that the inability of the HSE to provide timely access to those services was an administrative issue. However, it is submitted that the delay in affording appropriate treatment might instead have been dealt with under the nominal cost defence.

Very few cases have failed solely on the nominal cost issue. The two main examples concern educational establishments. *Mrs A (on behalf of her son, B) v A Childcare Facility*,[672] concerned the admission of the complainant's child (B) to a crèche. She was informed that a place would not be available unless the boy was accompanied by a full-time personal assistant, a requirement which the respondent maintained was necessary due a combination of factors. The respondent referred to its obligations concerning child–staff ratios under childcare regulations and to the fact that due to a disability B was unable to physically move on his own without assistance (Chapter 2.6.2.5). HSE funding was available to provide five hours of assistance per week for the child and so the respondent could only accommodate B by employing another childcare worker. The Tribunal accepted that the costs involved went beyond what was required under section 4. Hiring an additional staff member in a private crèche that catered for some 30 children would have amounted to more than a nominal cost in an organisation of that size. In *Regan v Old Bawn Community School*[673] the Tribunal found that the provision of sign language interpretation facilities by a community college would also have exceeded the nominal cost ceiling. As discussed further below, the college's budget was very limited (Chapter 6.7).

6.6 Additional Qualifications of the Duty

6.6.1 Introduction

Section 4 sets out several other qualifications to the reasonable accommodation duty:

> (3) A refusal or failure to provide the special treatment or facilities to which *subsection (1)* refers does not constitute discrimination

---

[672] DEC-S2009-041.
[673] DEC-S2010-043.

if, by virtue of another provision of this Act, a refusal or failure to provide the service in question to that person would not constitute discrimination.

(4) Where a person has a disability that, in the circumstances, could cause harm to the person or to others, treating the person differently to the extent reasonably necessary to prevent such harm does not constitute discrimination.

(5) This section is without prejudice to the provisions of sections 7(2) (*a*), 9(*a*) and 15(2)(*g*) of the Education Act, 1998, in so far as they relate to the functions of the Minister for Education and Science, recognised schools and boards of management in regard to students with a disability.

Each of these exceptions is now considered in turn.

6.6.2 Other Exceptions under the ESA

Essentially, subsection (3) clarifies that exemptions and exceptions set out under other provisions of the ESA also apply to the question of reasonable accommodation.

On occasion service providers charged with failure to reasonably accommodate have tried to avail of the defence for any action required by law under section 14(1)(*a*) (Chapter 2.5). For example, in *Roche v Madigans*[674] the equality officer held that a pub failed to provide reasonable accommodation to a visually impaired man when it required him to leave his registered guide dog outside before entering the premises. The Food Hygiene Regulations 1950–1989, which the respondent cited in its defence, were not sufficiently clear to constitute a *requirement* for the guide dog's exclusion under section 14. The equality officer found that the Regulations did not specifically apply to the complainant's guide dog as she was on a leash and in any event Department of Health circulars provide that guide dogs can be exempted from the Regulations.

Murphy v Spawell Centre[675] involved a refusal to admit a man on crutches to a club because the doorman observed that his movement was unsteady. The equality officer accepted that in such a situation there were legitimate health and safety concerns that could give rise to a defence under the Act:

> I am satisfied that having arrived at the conclusion that Mr. Murphy was lacking some control of his crutches, it was reasonable to refuse

---

[674] DEC-S2002-086.
[675] DEC-S2004-036.

admission on the basis of the Occupiers' Liability Act 1995. It may also be appropriate to consider Section 7 of the Safety, Health and Welfare at Work Act 1989. Section 14 of the Equal Status Act, 2000 provides a defense for a service provider who attempts to ensure compliance with these or any other legislative provisions. However, I am satisfied that where safety issues arise in accordance with the legislation mentioned above that are in respect of a disability, they must be considered in tandem with Section 4 of the Equal Status Act, 2000.

The complaint was unsuccessful. The equality officer concluded that while people with mobility impairments were entitled to enjoy a spontaneous night out 'it must be questioned whether the entire burden of impromptu access must be placed with the service provider. In the circumstances of this case I am satisfied that it would not have been an unreasonable imposition for the complainant to phone ahead, had it occurred to him.' As discussed in Chapter 6.3, the duty to provide reasonable accommodation is a reactive one.

The respondent also raised health and safety concerns in *O'Riain v H.M.V. Ireland,*[676] which involved a series of incidents involving the accessibility of a music store to Mr O'Riain, a wheelchair user. On several visits to the HMV shop goods were blocking the entrance to the lift and a space had to be cleared inside; as a result it took some time before the complainant could travel between floors. A member of staff accompanied him in the lift for health and safety reasons. On another occasion access to the lift was refused. According to the respondent the lift had been upgraded to ensure it was accessible to disabled people. However, an independent consultant had advised HMV that an emergency phone ought to be installed and a decision was made to use the lift solely for the purposes of transporting goods until a phone was fitted. At the time of the incidents, staff would have been informed that the lift was not to be made available to any member of the public but the respondent's health and safety officer conceded that there might have been some confusion amongst staff as to the availability or not of the lift. The equality officer first addressed the occasion when Mr O'Riain was denied access to the lift and a friend had pushed and pulled the wheelchair up and down the stairs step-by-step, unaided by any member of staff. HMV claimed that the installation of a lift discharged its reasonable accommodation duty and argued that access was denied for health and safety reasons. But the equality officer regarded the evidence presented on the health and safety concerns as 'inconsistent and quite often, indeed, conflicting' (para 5.8). He pointed to the fact that the complainant was permitted to use the lift on other occasions and concluded

---

[676] DEC-S2008-034.

that the training of staff was inadequate. Affording the complainant reasonable accommodation in the form of suitable staff training, as well as providing assistance in accessing products (as staff had done on some of Mr O'Riain's other visits), would not have imposed more than a nominal cost. HMV was ordered to pay €2,500 as redress for the effects of failure to provide reasonable accommodation.

6.6.3 Risk of Harm

According to the terms of section 4(4) treating a person differently will not constitute discrimination where their disability could cause harm to themselves or to others, and the difference in treatment is reasonably necessary to prevent such harm. In *Duyn v Aer Arran Group*[677] an airline refused to carry the complainant's mobility scooter on board its aircraft on the basis that the type of battery used in the device was unsafe. The equality officer examined the safety regulations in question and noted that comparable airlines did not apply such a policy. She found that the regulations encouraged the carriage of mobility devices by air operators and provided detailed guidance as to how those devices should be stored safely (para 4.13). In light of that evidence the respondent was not entitled to avail of the defence under section 4(4).

The defence was also considered in *Connery v Coiste an Asgard*[678] and *A Post-Leaving Certificate Student v An Educational Institution.*[679] In *Connery* because he had type 1 diabetes the complainant was excluded from serving as a crew member of a sailing training vessel on open sea voyages. The equality officer determined that the respondent's decision fell within section 4(4) and did not, therefore, constitute discrimination on the disability ground. Evidence had been provided of a previous incident involving a very experienced crew member who was also diabetic and had become ill on a voyage. Taking into account that evidence the equality officer was satisfied that the safety of the complainant, the ship, other crew members and air and sea rescue personnel could be compromised by efforts to tend to the complainant.

The other case addressed the exclusion of a disabled student from certain classes. The equality officer stated that 'the onus is on the respondent to show that i) it had reasonably formed the opinion that the complainant could cause harm to himself or others; ii) the cause of the prospect of such harm was the complainant's disability; iii) the actions it took to prevent such harm were reasonable and necessary' (para 5.15). Having reviewed the evidence he concluded that the onus was not met. Testimony to the effect that the student

---

[677] DEC-S2011-023.
[678] DEC-S2006-034.
[679] DEC-S2009-043.

had banged his head against a classroom wall was considered unconvincing. The equality officer also noted that the delay between that incident and the removal of the complainant from class indicated that the respondent did not consider there to be any significant danger of harm being caused to anyone.

In educational establishment cases the risk of harm exception is often raised along with section 7(4)(b), which provides that the bar on discrimination does not apply 'to the extent that compliance with any of its provisions in relation to a student with a disability would, by virtue of the disability, make impossible, or have a seriously detrimental effect on, the provision by an educational establishment of its services to other students' (Chapter 2.6.2.5). A selection of relevant cases is reviewed in Chapter 6.7.

6.6.4 Education Act 1998

Section 4(5) provides that the reasonable accommodation provision 'is without prejudice to the provisions of sections 7(2)(a), 9(a) and 15(2)(g) of the Education Act, 1998, in so far as they relate to the functions of the Minister for Education and Science, recognised schools and boards of management in regard to students with a disability'. It is evident from the Dáil debates that the purpose of the subsection was to ensure that the ESA would not dilute the obligations incurred by service providers under the Education Act.[680]

According to section 7(2)(a) of the Education Act 1998, one of the Minister's functions is 'to provide funding to each recognised school and centre for education and to provide support services to recognised schools, centres for education, students, including students who have a disability or who have other special educational needs, and their parents, as the Minister considers appropriate and in accordance with this Act'. It should be noted, however, that the availability of resources is one of the factors that delimits the Minister's statutory duties.

Section 9(a) of the 1998 Act states that recognised schools should: 'Ensure that the educational needs of all pupils, including those with a disability or other special needs, are identified and provided for.' Section 15(2)(g) addresses the functions of school boards of management and provides that such boards shall 'use the resources provided to the school from monies provided by the Oireachtas to make reasonable provision and accommodation for students with a disability or other special educational needs, including, where necessary, alteration of buildings and provision of appropriate equipment'.

Section 9(a) in particular obliges service providers to be proactive, since they must identify and then provide for the educational needs of students. It

---

[680] 513 *Dáil Debates* Cols 940–944 (Equal Status Bill 1999: Report Stage (Resumed)).

was taken into account in a 2010 decision on a school's duty to reasonably accommodate a student with ADHD:[681]

> I cannot accept that the respondent's offer to provide him with only 5 hours of resource teaching per week, without further access to the normal standard of full-time education provided to other students, would have been adequate to address his educational needs and thereby comply with [its] obligations under section 9(a) of the Education Act, 1998. Furthermore, I am not satisfied that the respondent's offer in this regard would have been in any way sufficient to cater for the special educational requirements that arose as a result of his disability (para 4.14).

Here the Tribunal uses section 4(5) to shed light on the reasonableness standard applicable in second level education. This decision is discussed further in Chapter 6.7. In another case the Tribunal rejected an argument put forward by the Department of Education and Skills to the effect that section 4(5) rules out consideration of reasonable accommodation in relation to educational support services. The equality officer adopted a purposive approach to interpreting the provision and concluded that such an exemption would have been explicitly provided for. On appeal, however, the Circuit Court suggested that section 4(5) could operate to effectively exempt the Minister for Education from the terms of the ESA.[682] Since the case was decided on other grounds the judge's observations are not binding on the Tribunal or other courts. The Tribunal's approach is preferable because, as noted above, it appears to correspond with the intention of the Oireachtas.

6.7 Education Cases

There have been a number of significant cases in the education field. Under the principle of vicarious liability (Chapter 7), legal responsibility for the conduct of individual teachers, lecturers and other staff might be attributed to an educational establishment.[683]

Education cases tend to be complex because the relationship between the student and the service provider often extends over a considerable period of

---

[681] *Mrs X (on behalf of her son, Mr Y) v A Post-Primary School*, DEC-S2010-009.

[682] *Two Named Complainants v Minister for Education and Science*, DEC-S2006-077; *The Minister for Education and Science v Hollingsworth* (Circuit Court Dublin, Hunt J, unreported, 19 October 2007).

[683] See, for example, *McGrath v University of Dublin, Trinity College*, DEC-S2010-006, at para 5.4.

time and involves multiple activities. Furthermore, primary and second level educational establishments have additional duties under the terms of the Education Act 1998, the Education (Welfare) Act 2000 and the Education for Persons with Special Educational Needs Act 2004.[684] Cumulatively those Acts oblige schools to adopt a proactive approach to identifying and putting in place measures that enable the participation of disabled students in education (Chapter 6.4.4.3). Cases involving schools are dealt with first in this section; we then turn to examine third level and other forms of adult education.

Two Complainants (a mother and her son) v A Primary School[685] dealt with a number of interrelated instances of discriminatory treatment. The equality officer decided that in the case of a student diagnosed as having ADHD reasonable accommodation could have been afforded the child by prioritising him for assessment with an educational psychologist and requesting educational supports from the Department of Education to meet his needs. She ordered the respondent school to put in place a system facilitating early identification of students who have disabilities or learning difficulties with the aim of directing these students to the appropriate educational services quickly in order to ensure that they maximise the benefit of their participation in formal education. In determining what was 'reasonable' the equality officer had regard to Department policies which emphasised that schools should refer children with emotional difficulties for psychological assessment and counselling without delay (para 6.10).

Similarly, in a 2010 decision a secondary school's response to the needs of a pupil with ADHD was considered to be inadequate.[686] Mr Y had behavioural difficulties and a very poor attendance record. His mother referred a complaint on the Traveller community, disability and race grounds. In relation to the reasonable accommodation aspect of the case, it was agreed that the respondent had taken several steps to accommodate Mr Y's needs, including providing access to a full-time SNA and one-to-one tuition in a number of different subjects. However, the school ultimately concluded that the student should not be educated in mainstream classes. In order to deal with his behavioural and educational problems he was to be provided with five hours teaching per week instead. In deciding whether the respondent had complied with section 4, the equality officer took into account its obligations under other legislation concerning the educational rights of disabled students (para 4.6). The Tribunal found that the respondent failed to activate the full range of available structures and supports. For that reason it did not do all that was possible to

---

[684] See generally <http://www.citizensinformation.ie/en/education/the_irish_education_system/special_education.html>.

[685] DEC-S2006-028.

[686] *Mrs X (on behalf of her son, Mr Y) v A Post-Primary School*, DEC-S2010-009.

reasonably accommodate the complainant. For example, given the significant problems with Mr Y's attendance from the outset, the school should have complied with its statutory duty under the Education (Welfare) Act 2000 to notify the educational welfare officer of those difficulties, which in turn would have triggered further assistance for the student.

Schools' responses to behavioural difficulties have featured in several cases. Under section 7(2)(*d*) educational establishments cannot discriminate in relation to 'the expulsion of a student from the establishment or any other sanction against the student'. And section 4 obliges establishments to adjust codes of behaviour, disciplinary processes and sanctions to take account of the 'special needs' of students with disabilities. Boards of management are charged, under section 23 of the Education (Welfare) Act 2000, with ensuring that a code of behaviour is drawn up, applied in the school and kept under review. The code must adhere to the guidelines produced by the National Education Welfare Board (2008). The guidelines specify that codes should promote equality for all members of the school community, prevent discrimination and allow for appropriate accommodation of difference including special education needs, in line with the ESA. Sanctions must not be used in a manner that discriminates against students (National Education Welfare Board, 2008, p 53).

In cases about sanctions respondents often rely on the section 4(4) exception, which permits a school to treat a person differently where their disability could cause harm to themselves or to others, and the difference in treatment is reasonably necessary to prevent such harm. It is frequently invoked in tandem with section 7(4)(*b*), which provides that the bar on discrimination by educational institutions does not apply 'to the extent that compliance with any of its provisions in relation to a student with a disability would, by virtue of the disability, make impossible, or have a seriously detrimental effect on, the provision by an educational establishment of its services to other students' (Chapter 2.6.2.5).[687] Both exceptions featured in *Mrs A (on behalf of her son B) v A Boys National School*.[688] In this case the respondent's actions fell within the section 7(4)(*b*) exception. A child with autistic spectrum disorder and attention deficit disorder was suspended from school following a series of incidents, which included him striking an SNA and other pupils. The equality officer considered that the sanction had been invoked as an option of last

---

[687] This section is similar to section 2 of the Education for Persons with Special Educational Needs Act 2004, which provides: 'A child with special educational needs shall be educated in an inclusive environment with children who do not have such needs unless the nature or degree of those needs of the child is such that to do so would be inconsistent with – (*a*) the best interests of the child as determined in accordance with any assessment carried out under this Act, or (*b*) the effective provision of education for children with whom the child is to be educated.'

[688] DEC-S2009-031.

resort when all other alternative means of dealing with the complainant's behaviour had been explored and exhausted. He found that the school could avail of the exception:

> Based on the evidence adduced in the present case, I am satisfied that the extreme nature of the difficulties presented by the complainant's behaviour, especially in terms of the incidences of striking his teachers/SNA/peers and the disproportionate amount of time that it was necessary for his class teacher to dedicate towards the management of this behaviour, were having a seriously detrimental effect on the capacity of the respondent to provide educational services to both the complainant and the other students in his class (para 5.8).

The equality officer then considered whether the respondent had complied with its reasonable accommodation duty. There was a clear dispute between the parties about the effectiveness and appropriateness of the measures implemented by the respondent. The complainant maintained that the school failed to develop a proper educational and behaviour management plan as recommended by experts in the field. The Tribunal, however, was satisfied that the respondent had taken sufficient steps to satisfy the requirements of section 4. An individual education plan[689] was in place for the student and had been drawn up and revised in light of input from a wide range of professionals. The equality officer attached particular weight to the evidence of a psychologist from the National Educational Psychological Service (NEPS) who provided assistance to the complainant and felt the respondent had attempted to facilitate the complainant as best it could given the fact it was operating as a mainstream school. Ultimately, the equality officer was satisfied that the special measures and facilities adopted by the school were reasonable in the circumstances of the case. He found that the respondent's decision to suspend the complainant on two occasions did not amount to a refusal or failure to provide reasonable accommodation. Since the Tribunal found that the respondent had afforded the complainant reasonable accommodation, it was not necessary to consider the section 4(4) defence.

In *Clare v Minister for Education and Science*[690] the High Court found that the provision of separate tuition for a student with ADHD did not amount

---

[689] An individual education plan (IEP) is a written document which specifies the learning goals that are to be achieved by a student with special educational needs over a period of time. They are provided for under the Education for Persons with Special Educational Needs Act 2004. The National Council for Special Education (2006) has issued guidelines on planning an IEP.

[690] [2004] IEHC 350.

to discrimination, having regard to section 4(4). Smyth J also found that a secondary school did not discriminate against the boy, whose conduct was disruptive and violent on occasion, in expelling him. The decision to expel was taken following substantial efforts on the part of the school authorities to deal with the student's behavioural difficulties and the school was entitled to balance the rights of the student with that of other students under section 7(4)(*b*).

Two Named Complainants v Minister for Education and Science[691] is a salient and ultimately unsuccessful reasonable accommodation case concerning assessment. Leaving Certificate students with dyslexia complained that the annotation on their certificate to the effect that all parts of the subject were assessed except spelling and some grammatical elements amounted to disability discrimination. The Department of Education argued that the annotation was necessary to maintain the integrity of the examination system and that it was part of the 'special treatment' afforded to the complainants when sitting exams. In a robust recommendation the equality officer who heard the case at first instance found there was no evidence that the annotation advanced the integrity of the system. The Department could not claim that since it had afforded the students reasonable accommodation by exempting them from certain elements of the examination it was then entitled to impose an annotation. She recommended that the Department of Education implement individualised means of accommodating students.[692]

In October 2007 the Circuit Court overturned the Tribunal's decision (Equality Authority, 2008a, pp 41–42).[693] Hunt J held that the disclosure of a disability did not amount to direct discrimination and that there was no failure to comply with the reasonable accommodation duty. He noted that a difference in treatment was not synonymous with less favourable treatment. The Department was entitled to use the annotation because the students who availed of the exemption were not in a comparable position to those who were not granted a waiver. In doing so it preserved the integrity of the examination. The notation system did not breach the reasonable accommodation duty either:

> I do not think it would be reasonable to require the Department to provide waivers without annotation in the light of the evidence given

---

[691] DEC-S2006-077.

[692] The Tribunal's decision seems to accord with one delivered by a Cypriot equality body in 2006. See the case note in European Network of Legal Experts in the Non-Discrimination Field (2007, pp 63–64).

[693] *The Minister for Education and Science v Hollingsworth* (Circuit Court Dublin, Hunt J, unreported, 19 October 2007).

to me on this point; that this has not been done anywhere else in the world. The fact that the subsequent notation is invariably viewed as being inextricably linked to the earlier waiver is, to me, a constant, through time and throughout all jurisdictions.

I take the view that what the Claimants require of the Department in this respect would go beyond the concept of what constitutes a reasonable accommodation.[694]

He also stated that even if there had been discrimination, the provisions of section 5(2)(*h*) would have exempted the Department's system from the general prohibition on discrimination. Section 5(2)(*h*) exempts differences in treatment provided for the principal purpose of promoting, for a bona fide purpose and in a bona fide manner, the special interests of a category of persons (Chapter 2.6.4.3).

An appeal on a point of law to the High Court was dismissed.[695] DeValera J found that the Circuit Court had not erred in law.

The case illustrates the courts' approach to the boundary between reasonable accommodation and an impermissible form of positive discrimination (Chapter 8.1).[696] In effect, the Circuit Court suggests that failing to annotate would confer an unfair advantage on the complainants. DeValera J distinguished between various forms of reasonable accommodation afforded students sitting state examinations. Some accommodations, such as granting a student additional time or enabling the use of assistive technology would not require a notation because they would not affect the assessment of a fundamental skill such as spelling, grammar and punctuation. The notation in this case was, however, a necessary consequence of the waiver. The High Court had regard to internationally recognised practice and case law from other countries in concluding that the notation was not discriminatory but a measure that was required to preserve the integrity of the examination.

The net effect of the litigation is that the system of annotating Leaving Certificates to signal that a grammar waiver was applied should not be regarded as reasonable accommodation as provided for under the ESA. Failure to comply with the section 4 duty is expressly defined as a form of discrimination, and so ought not to be seen as a 'special' or exceptional measure to which conditions may be attached.

---

[694] *The Minister for Education and Science v Hollingsworth* (Circuit Court Dublin, Hunt J, unreported, 19 October 2007), at p 97.

[695] *Cahill v Minister for Education and Science* [2010] IEHC 227.

[696] On the distinction between positive discrimination and reasonable accommodation in third level education see the comments of the equality officer in *A Student v Dublin City University*, DEC-S2011-067, at para 5.2.

At first glance it may seem that the obligation to provide for a 'reason-able accommodation' is a particular form of positive action, as it provides for 'advantages' to individuals who fall within the group of persons with a disability. However, this impression is mislead-ing and the obligation to provide for a reasonable accommodation can better be characterised as a particular kind of non-discrimination legislative provision, related to, but not synonymous with, the established forms of direct and indirect discrimination (European Commission, 2009a, p 27) [footnotes omitted].

The bulk of reasonable accommodation cases have concerned children attend-ing 'mainstream' schools. In 2008 the Equality Authority was involved in the settlement of a case taken by a mother on behalf of her son (Equality Author-ity, 2009b, pp 28–29). The boy attended a so-called 'special school' but only two of his subjects were taught through his first language, namely, Irish Sign Language (ISL). As a consequence he had huge difficulties with the other subjects. His parent contended that the failure to provide an education through ISL amounted to discrimination on the disability ground. The case was settled on the second day of the hearing before the Tribunal and most of the terms of the agreement reached are confidential. However, the Authority reported that the Department of Education undertook to invite universities to tender for the provision of a professional development course aimed at providing teachers with the skills necessary for the design, implementation and evalu-ation of learning and teaching programmes for students learning through the medium of ISL. The school and the Department agreed to take reasonable steps to ensure that teachers of Deaf pupils had access to university education in ISL.[697]

Each year there are a number of complaints about third level and adult education but very few are successful. The predominant reasons are failure to disclose a disability at all or in sufficient time to enable appropriate 'special treatment or facilities' to be put in place.[698] It is therefore critical that students register with the disability support service where one is available or disclose their disability to the staff member responsible for coordination of the programme they are registered to. Keeping a written record of all conversa-tions about reasonable accommodation measures is also advisable so that both

---

[697] Australian courts have found that failing to provide an education in sign language can amount to indirect discrimination on the disability ground: *Catholic Education Office v Clarke* [2004] FCAFC 197; *Hurst v State of Queensland* [2006] FCAFC 100.

[698] See, for example, *Kwiotek v National University of Ireland, Galway*, DEC-S2004-176; *A Mature Student v A College*, DEC-S2010-007; *McGrath v University of Dublin, Trinity College*, DEC-S2010-006; and *Ryan v Dublin Institute of Technology*, DEC-S2011-057.

parties are clear about what has been agreed. Where medical evidence or a needs assessment is sought and the student decides not to comply with that request it may relieve the educational establishment of their duty to reasonably accommodate.[699] The booklet about disability disclosure produced by AHEAD (Association for Higher Education Access and Disability) is a useful resource for students and staff. For instance it advises students:

> You have a choice on what you say and a choice as to whether you say anything, just think about the consequences.
>
> When/where/how/what/if you disclose is your choice.
>
> Try to give useful, relevant information.
>
> Be specific. Every person is different; every person's disability affects them differently. If you aren't specific, people make presumptions based on what they know (AHEAD, nd, p 11).

Staff should be aware that information about a student's disability is confidential and should be managed in accordance with the requirements of the Data Protection Acts 1998–2003.

Most of the complaints concern access to a facility or a 'term or condition of participation'[700] covering issues like assessment procedures and accessible course material. Relevant decisions are set out below, but as a preliminary matter it is important to appreciate that cases involving vocational training should be lodged instead under the EEA (Chapter 2.4.2). Vocational training is 'any system of instruction which enables a person being instructed to acquire, maintain, bring up to date or perfect the knowledge or technical capacity required for the carrying on of an occupational activity and which may be considered as exclusively concerned with training for such an activity.'[701] To date the Tribunal has interpreted the definition narrowly so that most third level and university courses do not amount to vocational training. It has placed particular emphasis on the words 'exclusively concerned with' and it appears that the programme of training in question must be aimed at preparing participants for a specific occupation.[702] The nominal cost threshold does not apply; instead educational institutions running such courses are obliged to afford accommodations to the point of a disproportionate burden.[703] Compensation

---

[699] See, for example, *A Student v Galway–Mayo Institute of Technology*, DEC-S2010-047, at para 5.12.

[700] Sections 7(2)(*b*) and (*c*).

[701] Section 12(2) EEA.

[702] *Ngongban v Dublin Institute of Technology*, DEC-E2011-144.

[703] *Mr X v A Third Level Educational Establishment*, DEC-E2008-062: the respondent

awards may be higher under the EEA and there is no notification requirement (Chapter 12.3.4). However, as Woulfe (2010, p 67) notes, there is a delay of about three years in hearing EEA cases, while ESA complaints are dealt with in approximately twelve months (unless they are dealt with through mediation). This imbalance may shift, however, when the new infrastructure for hearing EEA and ESA cases is fully operative (see Part II).

Kwiotek v National University of Ireland, Galway[704] was one of the first ESA cases on reasonable accommodation in third level education. It concerned NUI Galway's response to the educational needs of a PhD student. The complainant unsuccessfully argued that she was discriminated against when the university failed to provide her with adequate Braille material. According to the equality officer, the respondent had discharged its duty to reasonably accommodate because once its employees were aware of the need for material exclusively in Braille extra resources were put in place to provide the service (including employment of a part-time library assistant). She found that the complainant had failed to communicate her specific requirements and this led to delays in obtaining appropriate material, as opposed to inefficiency or a systems failure on the respondent's part. Difficulties in reading the material in Braille supplied because of formatting problems were also dealt with adequately through obtaining external expert advice and providing additional training for library staff.

Although it did not affect the outcome of the complaint, the equality officer dealt with the nominal cost issue and found that the accommodation provided to the complainant exceeded the threshold required under the Act. In its commentary on the decision, the Equality Authority (2005b, pp 34–35) states that the case 'highlights the need for an adequate assessment of the need of a student with disabilities to be carried out at the outset'. It also points out that the expenditure figures relied on give only a partial picture of the issue:

> According to the recommendation, the budget of the Disability Liaison Office was €108,000, the total library budget was €3,978,000. However there is no indication in the recommendation of what the overall budget of the University is, how many students and employees have disabilities and what type of disabilities they have and how much of the overall budget it spent on the specific needs of people with disabilities. The averaging of the amount spent on all types of disabilities does not reflect the differing needs of students, some of whom will require no reasonable accommodation and others who

---

failed to provide reasonable accommodation to a student with ADHD, in the form of extra time and a quiet room, for the written exam component of the assessment process.
[704] DEC-S2004-176.

require significant reasonable accommodation (Equality Authority, 2005b, pp 34–35).

Provision of accessible course materials was also dealt with in *Wellard v Killester College*.[705] The complainant was not supplied with reading material that was made available to other students on the induction day for an educational programme. However, the Tribunal found that the respondent had gone to considerable lengths to accommodate Ms Wellard. It had arranged for the installation of assistive technology specifically for use by the complainant at a cost of approximately €10,000. According to the equality officer the college had done all that was reasonable to enable Ms Wellard to avail of its services:

> While reading material was not available to the complainant on the induction day there was no evidence to the effect that the material would not be available to the complainant subsequently to enable her to participate in her chosen course. It appears that the complainant was not merely seeking that the respondent would take reasonable measures to ensure that she could participate in her chosen course but was expecting, and indeed demanding, that the measures would be in place from the induction day onward. I do not find that the complainant's unreasonable expectation in this regard constitutes reasonable accommodation as envisaged by the legislation, particularly where all indications were that the respondent was going to great lengths and expense to accommodate her needs. Nor do I find it unreasonable that any education provider, including the respondent, would wait until the person for whom the assistive technology is required had already commenced the course to ensure that they would actually be availing of the technology and to avoid needless expenditure in the event that the prospective student had a change of heart and did not attend at the course (para 6.iv).

Regan v Old Bawn Community School[706] is one of the few reasonable accommodation complaints that failed because the nominal cost defence applied (Chapter 6.5). It concerned the provision of sign language interpretation to a student on an adult education course. The complainant's request for interpretation was turned down because the respondent did not have the resources to pay for the service. Instead the school arranged for a fellow classmate, who had studied sign language, to provide some assistance to the complainant. Ms Regan completed the course but the equality officer accepted that

---

[705] DEC-S2008-024.
[706] DEC-S2010-043.

her educational experience was 'unduly difficult' because of the respondent's failure to provide access to a qualified interpreter proficient in the skills required to communicate all aspects of the course work. The respondent claimed that it was instructed by the Department of Education to run all of its part-time adult education programmes on a self-financing basis. For the year 2007/2008 a surplus of €119.39 was generated from the entire adult education programme. Provision of a sign language interpreting service would have cost between €1,300 and €1,700. The equality officer accepted that evidence in finding that the school did not breach section 4 because the costs involved in providing the facility were more than nominal.

In a number of cases students were unable to demonstrate that they were denied access to special treatment or facilities that made accessing a service impossible or unduly difficult. For example, the complainant in *A Student v Dublin City University*[707] objected to the manner in which his examination script was marked. In particular he argued that the staff member in question had not followed the university guidelines on assessment of students with learning disabilities by including comments in red ink on his paper highlighting certain grammatical errors. He did not contest the actual grade awarded. The equality officer concluded that since the complainant had passed his exams, and did not object to the grade received, he could not point to anything which he found impossible or unduly difficult to do.

6.8 Accessibility Standards

A patchwork of laws and policies currently regulate accessibility. The controversial Disability Act 2005 is the primary source of domestic law (De Wispelaere and Walsh, 2007; Flynn, 2007, 2009; Irish Human Rights Commission, 2004c), while EU law governs access in some narrow fields.

The Disability Act 2005 only applies to public bodies and it has two core elements: the provision of needs assessment for people with disabilities[708] and

---

[707] DEC-S2011-067. See also *Ryan v Dublin Institute of Technology*, DEC-S2011-057 and *Doherty v Letterkenny Institute of Technology*, DEC-S2010-039.

[708] Part II of the Disability Act 2005 provides for the assessment of the health and educational needs of persons with disabilities. Persons aged over eighteen are covered but as of April 2012 this part of the Act has only been brought into force in relation to children under the age of five (Disability Act 2005 (Commencement) Order 2007 (SI 234/2007)). According to the High Court that age limit is based on the date the Act commenced (1 June 2007), rather than the age of the child at the time the application was made: *Health Service Executive v Dykes* [2009] IEHC 540. In essence, the Act confers a right on children to have their needs assessed, but no enforceable right to any of the services that may flow from such an assessment.

the accessibility of public services and premises.[709] The definition of 'disability' employed is more restrictive than that set out under section 2 of the ESA. It refers to 'a substantial reduction in the capacity of the person to carry on a profession, business or occupation in the State or to participate in social or cultural life in the State by reason of an enduring physical, sensory, mental health or intellectual impairment'.[710]

Access to the built environment is mainly controlled by Part M of the Building Regulations (2000), entitled 'Access for People with Disabilities'.[711] It does not apply to existing buildings unless they are being altered or refurbished, although under the Disability Act 2005 public areas of public buildings must be brought into compliance with Part M by 2015. The Regulations require all buildings to have wheelchair access and in the event that they trade on more than one floor there must be a wheelchair-accessible lift giving access between the floors. In addition, if stores are providing public toilets they must include at least one wheelchair-accessible toilet. A review conducted by the National Disability Authority (2005b) concluded that the regulations were deficient in several respects and compared poorly with the standards in force in other countries. Section 5 of the Building Control Act 2007 effected a modest improvement in providing for a Disability Access Certificate, which requires building control authorities to certify that designs comply with Part M *before* work commences.

Under Part III of the Disability Act six government departments are obliged to prepare 'Sectoral Plans' demonstrating how key disability issues are to be addressed.[712] Sections 32–40 of the Act supply general guidelines as to the areas that should be dealt with under each plan, specify that an internal complaints system should be established by all six departments, and provide an oversight role for the Ombudsman in relation to implementation of the plans and the related general accessibility measures contained in the remainder of Part 3.

---

[709] According to section 2 of the Disability Act 2005 'public body' includes government departments, local authorities and the Health Service Executive, as well as bodies or organisations (other than the Defence Forces) established by or under any enactment. The last category should include universities and a range of state and semi-state organisations.

[710] Section 52 of the Disability Act 2005 amends the definition of 'disability' set out under the Education Act 1998, so that it too refers to restrictions in capacity and conditions of an enduring nature.

[711] Building Regulations 1997 to 2010.

[712] The six departments are: 1) Communications, Marine and Natural Resources; 2) Enterprise, Trade and Employment; 3) Environment and Local Government; 4) Health and Children; 5) Social and Family Affairs; and 6) Transport. The inaugural plans were published in July 2006 and are available for consultation on the website of the National Disability Authority: <http://www.nda.ie/>.

The Ombudsman has the power to investigate complaints about compliance by public bodies with the Disability Act 2005 (Chapter 10.5).[713]

Public bodies are required to make their public buildings accessible by 2015, although a Minister may, after consultation with other Ministers and interested parties, make an order to exclude a public building from the scope of these requirements if satisfied that the building is being used as a public building on a temporary basis, will no longer be used as a public building after three years, or does not justify refurbishment on cost grounds having regard to the use of the building.[714]

Section 26 deals with access to services. It came into effect on 31 December 2005 and obliges public bodies to integrate, where practical and appropriate, their services for people with disabilities with those provided to other people. Access officers have been appointed in each public body to coordinate these arrangements. Public bodies are also obliged to ensure that goods or services purchased are accessible, unless it would not be practicable or justifiable on cost grounds or would result in an unreasonable delay.[715] Finally, section 28 deals with the accessibility of information provided by public bodies and their communications systems; again the obligations need only be met where practicable.

In all cases, duties are tempered by conditions of practicality or resource constraints without any requirement that efforts should be directed towards increasing practicality or funding. The National Disability Authority (2006) published a *Code of Practice on Accessibility of Public Services and Information Provided by Public Bodies*, which provides guidance on how public bodies can comply with their statutory duties under the 2005 Act.

The Equal Status Act 2000 contained two provisions concerning transport infrastructure. Section 17 dealt with the accessibility of road and rail passenger vehicles, and section 18 with the accessibility of bus and rail stations. Those provisions enabled the Minister for Justice, Equality and Law Reform to make regulations obliging operators of passenger services to ensure that new vehicles and stations were 'readily accessible to and usable by persons with a disability'. No such regulations were produced and the sections were repealed under section 57 of the Disability Act 2005. These matters now fall instead to be addressed under the Department of Transport's Sectoral Plan (2006). The National Disability Authority (2005c) has published *Recommended Accessibility Guidelines for Public Transport Operators in Ireland*, which focus on the whole experience of a journey, from information that is accessible,

---

[713] Section 40, Disability Act 2005.
[714] Section 25, Disability Act 2005.
[715] Section 27, Disability Act 2005.

vehicles and buildings that are accessible, to disability awareness training for staff, and consultation and communication with people with disabilities.

Section 19 of the ESA deals with the provision of kerb ramps by a road authority (in effect a local authority) and remains in place. It requires road authorities when altering or constructing any public pavement or footpath to take into account the needs of persons with impaired mobility by making provision for ramps, dished kerbs or other sloped areas. As discussed further below the Equality Authority has limited powers to enforce the ESA (Chapter 11.3.4). One instance provided for under section 23(1)(*b*) allows it to refer a case to the Director of the Equality Tribunal where it appears that 'a person has contravened or is contravening *section ... 19* or regulations made under *section 17* or *18* ....' It seems that the Disability Act 2005 impliedly repealed the latter part of this section, but the Authority may still refer a case about public footpaths.[716]

The European Union has introduced standards in the areas of telecommunications and transport. The regulations that apply to the airline industry should ensure that some disabled passengers will be able to access airports and flights with greater ease.[717] Air carriers are, for instance, obliged to carry recognised assistance dogs in the cabin subject to national regulations. The regulations also oblige airports and air carriers to provide free-of-charge assistance and information.[718] No reservation can be refused on the grounds of disability except for safety reasons or insufficient size of aircraft. Passengers with reduced mobility and disabilities travelling by rail transport are guaranteed assistance and information on accessibility. Responsibility for mobility equipment falls on carriers.

Arguably an amendment to the ESA is now required in order to clarify the relationship between the reasonable accommodation section and other laws that apply to services provided to disabled people.

---

[716] The Authority was involved in the settlement of a complaint about access to a public building in 2003, which entailed 'lower flagstones and leveling of access from road to pavement' (Equality Authority, 2004, p 37).

[717] Regulation (EC) No 1107/2006, which came into effect in July 2008, imposes legal obligations on airport operators, air carriers, their agents and tour operators. Within Ireland the Commission for Aviation Regulation acts as the enforcement body for Regulation 1107/2006 – European Communities (Rights of Disabled Persons and Persons with Reduced Mobility When Travelling By Air) Regulations 2008 (SI 299/2008). For further information see the European Disability Forum's web pages on the Regulations: <http://www.edf-feph.org/> and the European Commission's site on passengers' rights: <http://ec.europa.eu/transport/passengers/index_en.htm>.

[718] In *Ross v Ryanair* [2005] 1 WLR 2447 the UK Court of Appeal found that both an airline and an airport authority had discriminated under the Disability Discrimination Act 1995 by failing to provide a passenger with a wheelchair free of charge in order to access a flight.

7

Vicarious Liability and Instructions to Discriminate

7.1 Introduction

Vicarious liability refers to the allocation of legal responsibility to a party for legal wrongs committed by persons under its control, such as employees. The principle applies in several fields, but obviously we are concerned here with how it operates in the area of discrimination law. Vicarious liability was developed for a range of reasons (Lockwood, 2011), but for the purposes of this book it is important to appreciate that it makes the legislation more effective because it encourages good management practices. Writing about harassment, McColgan (2007b, p 536) comments: 'Unless liability can be pinned on employers … [they] will not be provided with incentives to prevent harassment occurring or continuing.'

Under the ESA, vicarious liability is imposed on service providers for the discriminatory conduct of an employee that occurs 'in the course of his or her employment', subject to a defence. As discussed further below, a prudent service provider should produce appropriate policies dealing with discrimination, ensure that employees are trained in same, and put in place complaints and disciplinary procedures. Service providers are also vicariously liable for discrimination perpetrated by agents acting on their behalf. There is no defence; a service provider is liable where the agent acted with its express or implied authority.

With respect to harassment and sexual harassment a further specific duty is placed on service providers (Chapter 5.2.3). The Acts oblige a person who is responsible for the provision of services and goods, education or accommodation not to permit a person who is availing or seeking to avail of any of these to be sexually harassed or harassed, subject to a defence that reasonably practical steps were taken to prevent the sexual harassment or harassment. In other words, liability extends beyond the conduct of employees and agents to include harassment committed by other third parties. These provisions are considered further in Chapter 7.3.

The final section of this chapter deals with 'instructions to discriminate'.

7.2 Case Law

7.2.1 Introduction

This section first considers how liability is attached to service providers in their capacity as employers (Chapter 7.2.2). It goes on to examine vicarious liability for agents of the service provider.

Section 42 sets out the vicarious liability principle that applies to all cases under the ESA:

> (1) Anything done by a person in the course of his or her employment shall, in any proceedings brought under this Act, be treated for the purposes of this Act as done also by that person's employer, whether or not it was done with the employer's knowledge or approval.
>
> (2) Anything done by a person as agent for another person, with the authority (whether express or implied and whether precedent or subsequent) of that other person shall, in any proceedings brought under this Act, be treated for the purposes of this Act as done also by that other person.
>
> (3) In proceedings brought under this Act against an employer in respect of an act alleged to have been done by an employee of the employer, it shall be a defence for the employer to prove that the employer took such steps as were reasonably practicable to prevent the employee —
>
> (*a*) from doing that act, or
>
> (*b*) from doing in the course of his or her employment acts of that description.

7.2.2 Liability for Employees

7.2.2.1 Overview

As is evident from the cases considered in this book, section 42 is regularly applied to make service providers legally responsible for the discriminatory conduct of employees. For example, shop owners are frequently held liable for the actions of managers and security staff. The employer need not have sanctioned or have been aware of the employee's behaviour. But liability is only incurred if the employee was acting 'in the course of his or her employment'. Even where the employee was so acting an employer may avoid liability by successfully invoking the defence provided for under subsection (3).

7.2.2.2 The 'Course of Employment' Test

Section 42 and its equivalent under section 15 of the EEA displaced the previous test for determining employers' liability (Ryan and Ryan, 2007). The primary High Court judgment on the original principles was that of Costello J in *A Health Board v BC and the Labour Court*.[719] In that case two colleagues subjected the plaintiff to a sexual assault. The Employment Equality Act 1977 did not make express provision for vicarious liability and the Court therefore applied the general common law test. Although the High Court found that the acts amounted to sexual harassment it reversed the Labour Court's finding on the issue of vicarious liability. It found that the assault did not fall within the scope of the employees' duties and so the health board was not legally responsible.[720] Following the judgment it appeared that employers could never be found liable as sexual harassment or similar objectionable behaviour would never amount to something done in 'the course of employment'.[721]

The Employment Equality Act 1998 filled that perceived gap by expressly providing for vicarious liability in relation to all discriminatory acts and the same provision was included in the 2000 Equal Status Act. It now seems that 'acting in the course of his or her employment' refers to the location at which the incident(s) occurred as opposed to the nature of the activity in issue.[722]

---

[719] [1994] ELR 27.

[720] *Jones v Tower Boot Co. Ltd* [1997] 2 All ER 406 involved racial harassment under the UK Race Relations Act 1976. The Court of Appeal considered whether a racially motivated serious assault on an employee could be regarded as 'done by a person in the course of his employment' and held that to take an unduly restrictive approach to the phrase would undermine the objectives of discrimination law. The Court found that the concept of vicarious liability under 1976 Act was wider than the concept of vicarious liability at common law. *Jones* was approved of by the Irish High Court in *Fanning v University College Cork* [2007] ELR 301, perhaps signalling that the Irish courts are now more receptive to a broader understanding of the common law test in employment equality cases.

[721] The Labour Court subsequently modified the test by holding employers vicariously liable where the employer had placed the employee against whom a complaint was made in a position of authority over other colleagues: *A Worker v A Company* [1994] ELR 202 and *A Worker v A Company* [1996] ELR 85. But see *A Worker v An Employer* [1996] ELR 65. For recent consideration of the common law vicarious liability principles see the Supreme Court judgments in *O'Keeffe v Hickey* [2009] 2 IR 302; [2009] 1 ILRM 490 and *Reilly v Devereux & Ors* [2009] 3 IR 660.

[722] To my knowledge, the contemporary case law on this issue, under both the EEA and ESA, deals with incidents occurring outside the workplace while employees are off duty.

Hennessy v Network Catering/Iarnród Éireann[723] is the only ESA case to date involving responsibility for an employee's conduct that occurred while they were off duty and not at the workplace. A disabled man, who was a regular user of the respondent's public transport service, referred a harassment complaint about several incidents. One of those incidents took place outside the workplace and for that reason the respondent sought to avoid liability. A staff member (Mr A) had approached the complainant in a threatening and aggressive manner when they met each other on a public street and made reference to a previous incident on the train. The equality officer was satisfied that the exchange as reported by Mr Hennessy had taken place and that the perpetrator was an employee of the respondent. The crux of the legal argument was whether Mr A was acting 'in the course' of his employment. Since the equality officer had already established that the respondent was vicariously liable for the actions of employees that occurred on the train she did not consider it necessary to decide on the specific point. But she did accept that the episode was 'closely connected' with the employment of Mr A, noting that the two men only knew each other through the train service provided by the respondent. The complainant's representative had pointed to a number of UK cases, which established 'that if an incident is so closely connected with the employment it should be regarded as having happened in the course of the employment' (para 4.14).[724] It remains to be seen how this aspect of vicarious liability under the ESA will develop.

7.2.2.3 The Statutory Defence

An employer will not be liable where it can prove that it took such steps as were reasonably practicable to prevent the employee from doing the act complained of, or from doing acts of that description in the course of his or her employment.[725]

See, for example, *Ms O'N v An Insurance Company*, DEC-E2004-052; *Ms Z v A Hotel*, DEC-E2007-014; and *Maguire v NE Health Board*, DEC-E2002-039.

[723] DEC-S2009-029.

[724] The cases in question were *Lister v Helsey Hall Ltd* [2002] 1 AC 215, *Mattis v Pollock* [2003] IRLR 603 and *Majrowski v Guy's and St Thomas' NHS Trust* [2006] UKHL 34. It is by no means certain that the positions adopted in those cases are relevant to liability under the ESA since they did not address discrimination law as such. In any event, there is considerable disagreement amongst Irish judges as to whether developments in UK law should be followed in this jurisdiction (D. Ryan, 2008).

[725] Section 42(3). Where liability in a harassment or sexual harassment complaint is in issue the Tribunal will also, or sometimes alternatively, apply section 11(3), which deals specifically with the employer's defence in such cases. The defence is effectively the same

The most detailed discussions of the defence tend to be found in the case law on harassment and sexual harassment. A code of practice on harassment at work was adopted in 2002 following consultation with the social partners.[726] Under section 56(4) of the EEA, the Code may be taken into account in legal proceedings under either the EEA or ESA where relevant.[727] It is obviously relevant, therefore, to the many cases under the ESA that address the liability of service providers for the conduct of their employees. The Code provides that employers are obliged to act in a 'preventative and remedial way', and supplies detailed guidance on what is required. It states that in order to rely on the defence 'employers would need to show that they have comprehensive, accessible, effective policies that focus on prevention and best practice and remedial action and an accessible effective complaints procedure.' While the Code deals specifically with harassment and sexual harassment, many of the general principles it sets out correspond with those applied in other discrimination cases.

Decisions under both the ESA and EEA illustrate that employers' policies are crucial to vicarious liability. Where a service provider has no equal status policy it will be difficult to avoid liability.[728] For example, in *De Burca and Fernandez v Homelocators*[729] the equality officer found that a letting agency had discriminated on the family status ground when a phone message was left to the effect that their client did not wish to rent premises to families with children. Homelocators was vicariously liable for the message left by the staff member because there was no evidence that it had taken any measures to ensure that its staff or clients were aware of the requirements of the ESA.

Failure to provide reasonable accommodation and disability-related harassment occurred in *A Parent (on behalf of her son) v A Supermarket*.[730] A mother and her child were refused service in the respondent's shop because they were accompanied by a guide dog that was assisting the boy. A security guard acted aggressively towards the two customers in asking them to leave

---

under both provisions as both involve the employer taking 'such steps' as were 'reasonably practicable to prevent' the employee from acting as she or he did.

[726] Code of Practice on Sexual Harassment and Harassment at Work made under the Employment Equality Act 1998 (SI 78/2002).

[727] See, for example, *Maguire v NE Health Board*, DEC-E2002-039 and *Persaud v The Shelbourne Hotel*, DEC-E2004-075. To my knowledge, the Code of Practice has not been taken into account in an ESA case. However, in *Doherty v Letterkenny Institute of Technology*, DEC-S2010-039, the equality officer advised the respondent to draw up a harassment policy in line with the Code.

[728] On the importance of adopting a policy under the EEA see, for example, *Ms A v A Gym*, DEC-E2004-011, and *A Worker v A Hotel* [2010] ELR 72.

[729] DEC-S2004-030/031.

[730] DEC-S2011-015.

the premises. The Tribunal had little difficulty in imposing liability on the respondent because the manager did nothing to diffuse the situation:

> I note that when the manager came on the scene he did not make any attempt to stop the abusive behaviour of the security guard and in fact the shouting and abusive treatment continued until the complainant and her son left the shop. I am satisfied that the manager took no steps to prevent the harassment of the complainant and I find therefore that the defence cited above does not apply (para 4.7).

Poor implementation and monitoring mechanisms will also expose the employer to a finding of vicarious liability. The complainants in *Ward v # 1 Bar*[731] were refused access to a pub by the doorman and the Tribunal found that the incident amounted to direct discrimination on the Traveller community ground. The equality officer accepted that the management of the pub did not operate a discriminatory policy and appeared to accept the respondent's evidence that it had provided training to staff, which addressed its duties under the ESA. She found, however, that the procedures in place did not absolve the employer of responsibility. There was inadequate monitoring of the door staff's behaviour on the occasion in question as evidenced by the fact that the decision to deny access was sanctioned by a regular staff member and not the manager of the bar.

Even where staff members have been trained in the requirements of the legislation, and procedures are in place to deal with incidents, an inadequate investigation may make the employer liable.[732]

King v Dublin Bus[733] and *Hennessy v Network Catering/Iarnród Éireann*[734] address vicarious liability for harassment in some detail. In *King* the demeanour of and remarks made by a bus driver on two separate occasions amounted to harassment of a passenger on the disability ground (Chapter 5.4). His employer sought to avail of the defences under sections 11(3) and 42(3) on the basis that comprehensive training had been provided to the driver and Dublin Bus had dealt with the initial complaint against him. The equality officer did

---

[731] DEC-S2006-068. On effective implementation of harassment policies in the employment context see *Dublin Airport Authority v Khatimy*, ADE/05/23; EDA/067, 22 May 2006.

[732] See, for example, *A Bus Customer v A Bus Company*, DEC-S2011-006 (the respondent's employees were interviewed but denied that incident had taken place; vicarious liability imposed nonetheless). The findings of an investigation into an allegation of harassment by an employee were also considered inadequate in *Odion v Techniform (Waterford) Ltd*, DEC-E2007-018.

[733] DEC-S2008-019.

[734] DEC-S2009-029.

not accept those arguments:

> Having fully considered all of the evidence in this matter I am satis-
> fied (i) that the training provided to all drivers in the first instance is
> of a general nature and, while it is customer service oriented, does not
> deal in any depth with the specific requirements of equality legisla-
> tion and (ii) following the formal complaint from the complainant to
> the respondent company about the first incident arising, no specific
> measures were taken to clearly indicate to the driver that his actions
> were regarded as unilateral and not work related. The driver was not
> informed of the specific complaint against him.
>
> I note that the company gave a full apology to the complainant for
> the driver's behaviour following the first incident. However, the
> formal investigation of the first incident by the respondent was never
> completed. I fail to see how the respondent can then state that the
> driver's actions were not in the course of his duty, as this was never
> properly determined (para 9).

Hennessy involved allegations of harassment by staff on an ongoing basis
while the complainant was using the respondent's public transport service.
There was no evidence that employees had received training on the ESA. A
booklet had been circulated on how assistance could be provided to disabled
passengers but it did not address the issue of discrimination. Some complaints
lodged by Mr Hennessy were not investigated, nor were any instructions
issued to staff. The equality officer found that Iarnród Éireann could not avail
of the section 11(3) defence and that it was vicariously liable for the conduct
of staff in the dining car.

In the 2009 EEA case of *Mr A v A Hotel*[735] the employer successfully
invoked the parallel defence provided for under that legislation. The equality officer was satisfied that the respondent had disciplined the employee in
an effort to ensure that the behaviour would not happen again, and accordingly had acted in 'a preventative and remedial way'. A policy statement and
procedure governing equal opportunities and harassment was in place and the
complainant had availed of that process.

7.2.2.4 Identification of the Correct Respondent

On occasion the Equality Tribunal has applied section 42 in identifying the
correct respondent. The Acts do not explicitly provide that only the employer

---

[735] DEC-E2009-003.

or service provider can be liable for prohibited conduct. The prohibitions on direct and indirect discrimination, as well as those on harassment and sexual harassment, direct 'persons' not to engage in prohibited conduct. 'Persons' can refer to natural persons, as well as organisations, public bodies or other entities.[736] Exceptionally, the reasonable accommodation duty is aimed specifically at the 'provider of a service'. However, when these prohibitions are read in conjunction with the sections on the contexts covered by the ESA[737] and the provisions on vicarious liability, the Tribunal has found that complaints should be referred against the service provider or employer as opposed to an individual staff member.

For instance, in *Carr v Gaelscoil Mhainistir Na Corann*[738] the equality officer decided that the complaint should proceed against the board of management of the school in question rather than the school principal:

> I am satisfied that Ms. A was acting in her capacity as School Principal and therefore has no case to answer in her personal capacity. I am satisfied that the correct respondent in these proceedings is the Board of Management of the school, which is the service provider with responsibility for the school and its policies (para 5.3).

In other cases, individual employees have been removed as respondents because they were acting within the course of their employment and so the employer would ultimately be accountable should the case succeed.[739]

7.2.3 Liability for Agents

A principal–agent relationship exists where one party (the agent) acts on behalf of another (the principal). This arrangement is usually set down in a formal written agreement called a contract.[740] For the purposes of the ESA, in theory *both* the principal and the agent can be held liable for discrimination or harassment. To impose liability on the principal, the agent must have been acting with the authority of the principal. That authority may be express or implied. This means that a principal will not be liable for unlawful

---

[736] Section 2.

[737] Sections 5 and 6 use the term 'persons', while section 7 refers directly to educational establishments.

[738] DEC-S2009-023. See also *Burke v Kerry County Council*, DEC-S2011-032, para 4.2.

[739] *Mongans v Clare County Council*, DEC-S2006-084, para 2.3. See also *Mongans v Clare County Council*, DEC-S2008-039.

[740] The Tribunal examines the nature of the principal–agent relationship in *Mongans v Clare County Council*, DEC-S2008-039, para 2.13.

discrimination carried out by its agent where the agent acted in contravention of the principal's express instructions not to discriminate.

Section 42(2) states:

> Anything done by a person as agent for another person, with the authority (whether express or implied and whether precedent or subsequent) of that other person shall, in any proceedings brought under this Act, be treated for the purposes of this Act as done also by that other person.

A principal–agent relationship may exist between a service provider and a range of people or other bodies. For example, a retailer might have contracted with a firm to provide security staff for its premises. In such a case the security staff would be agents of the retailer. A director of a company that provides services acts as the agent of that company.[741]

As underlined in the case of *Axinte v Q-Bar Dublin*,[742] a written policy and related training should be provided to all people acting as agents of a service provider. In that case the Director of the Equality Tribunal found the proprietor of a pub liable for the discriminatory conduct of a doorman employed by security contractors:

> [W]hile the respondent had in place a comprehensive equality policy, the respondent relied on the security sub-contractors to provide training and there was no evidence of procedures being in place to ensure that door persons were trained in equality issues. I refer to section 42(2) of the Equal Status Act which provides that anything done by a person as agent for another person, with the latter's authority, shall be treated for the purposes of the Act as done also by that other person. I conclude therefore that the respondent is vicariously liable for the refusal of service (para 5.7).

She directed the respondent to take steps to ensure that the security personnel were appropriately trained instead of relying on third-party assurances (para 6.3).

A complaint about medical treatment in *Hallinan v O'Donnell*[743] fell within the exemption for matters concerning clinical judgment. When issuing her

---

[741] *Merriman v O'Flaherty's Ltd t/a Reads Print Design and Photocopying Bureau*, DEC-S2011-049, para 5.3.

[742] DEC-S2004-188. See also *Crawford v The Bootlegger Bar*, DEC-S2003-146/147 and *O'Brien and Others v Barry's Hotel*, DEC-S2005-094/097.

[743] DEC-S2006-069.

decision the equality officer observed that the Health Service Executive would be vicariously liable for discriminatory conduct of doctors that was not related to clinical issues. She underlined that the HSE could be found liable in relation to correspondence or other administrative matters. The decision in *A Separated Complainant v A Hospital*[744] reinforces that approach. The Tribunal made it clear that the respondent hospital could be legally responsible for the actions of a consultant surgeon in dealing with the parents of a child who underwent surgery.

As for the liability of agents, insurance brokers and travel agents have been found liable for implementing discriminatory policies set by underwriters and tour operators (i.e. the principals). In *Jordan v Marsh Ireland Ltd*,[745] a case involving a discriminatory condition in an insurance policy, Marsh Ireland Ltd was acting as an agent of the actual insurer (Cigna International) and so was the correct respondent. The equality officer noted that Cigna could have been named as a co-respondent in the complainant's original notification under the ESA.[746] Similar reasoning was applied in *Callan v United Travel*[747] to hold a travel agent liable with respect to a holiday package offered by a tour operator. According to the equality officer the respondent 'carried out the administration as an agent on behalf of the Tour Operator, including the interaction with the customer such as dealing with the booking, invoicing and collection of payments' (para 5.4). The Tribunal's decision was upheld on appeal to the Circuit Court.

In a number of cases the Equality Tribunal applied section 42(2) to attach liability to the Health Service Executive (HSE) when implementing circulars issued by the Department of Health.[748] However, in an appeal from one of those decisions the Circuit Court found that the correct respondent was the Department of Health and that the HSE was not acting as an agent within the terms of section 42(2).[749] The judgment does not elaborate as to why liability could not be attached to the HSE, presumably because both parties accepted that the complaint should have been referred instead against the Department.

---

[744] DEC-S2010-046.

[745] DEC-S2008-054. Applied in *Bisayeva v Westend Management Ltd*, DEC-S2011-030, to render a shopping centre management company (the agent) liable for the conduct of its security personnel who were acting on the instruction of a retailer (the principal) in removing a woman from a shop.

[746] See also *Burke v Lynskey Ryan Insurance Limited, Galway*, DEC-S2006-071, and *O'Donoghue v An Post Ltd t/a One Direct*, DEC-S2005-053.

[747] DEC-S2009-027; see also *Comerford v Trailfinders Ireland Ltd*, DEC-S2011-013.

[748] For example, *A Complainant v Health Service Executive (South)*, DEC-S2009-011, para 5.3 and *Quigley v Health Service Executive*, DEC-S2009-012.

[749] *Health Service Executive v Quigley* (Circuit Court Dublin, Linnane J, unreported, 26 April 2010).

It seems that much rested on the fact that the HSE had implemented the exact terms of the circular and had no discretion to deviate from its terms. This finding suggests that complaints should be pursued against the principal, that is, the service provider who is ultimately responsible for an impugned policy, where the agent exercises no element of discretion in its application. A distinction may therefore emerge in future ESA cases as to how section 42(2) operates to attach liability to the agent as opposed to the principal.

7.3 Liability for Third Parties in Harassment Cases

Service providers are legally responsible for the discriminatory actions of their employees and agents under the vicarious liability principle set out under section 42. Harassment and sexual harassment are included under that general provision, but section 11 goes further in obliging service providers to also protect people from harassment or sexual harassment committed by a third party, subject to a defence.

Section 11 provides:

(1) A person shall not sexually harass or harass (within the meaning of *subsection (4)* or *(5)*) another person ('the victim') where the victim—

(*a*) avails or seeks to avail himself or herself of any service provided by the person or purchases or seeks to purchase any goods being disposed of by the person,

(*b*) is the proposed or actual recipient from the person of any premises or of any accommodation or services or amenities related to accommodation, or

(*c*) is a student at, has applied for admission to or avails or seeks to avail himself or herself of any service offered by, any educational establishment (within the meaning of *section 7*) at which the person is in a position of authority.

(2) A person ('the responsible person') who is responsible for the operation of any place that is an educational establishment or at which goods, services or accommodation facilities are offered to the public shall not permit another person who has a right to be present in or to avail himself or herself of any facilities, goods or services provided at that place, to suffer sexual harassment or harassment at that place.

(3) It shall be a defence for the responsible person to prove that he or she took such steps as are reasonably practicable to prevent the sexual harassment or harassment, as the case may be, of the other person referred to in *subsection (2)* or of a category of persons of which that other person is a member.

Section 11(2) clearly envisages the possibility that service providers can be liable not just for the acts of their employees or agents but also for those of third parties, including other service recipients. It is a defence for the 'responsible person' (i.e. the service or goods provider) to prove that they took reasonably practicable steps to prevent the harassment or sexual harassment of the victim or of any category of persons which includes the victim. Use of the term 'place' suggests that liability is confined to unwanted conduct that occurs at physical locations operated by the service provider. 'Place' includes cyberspace in the form of a website discussion forum according to the Tribunal.[750]

There are very few decisions on harassment by third parties. In an early ESA case, *Sweeney v John Biggins, The Corner Bar*,[751] a pub owner heard a conversation involving derogatory comments about the complainant's Traveller identity made by another customer. According to Mr Sweeney no action was taken when he complained to the owner. The owner did not remember any grievance, and said that he had not intervened because he considered that the complainant was 'giving as good as he got' in the argument. The equality officer could not make a determination about the incident because it had occurred before the Equal Status Act entered into force. Nonetheless, he referred to the harassment provisions and stated: 'Publicans should note … that since the Equal Status Act came into force, the type of situation outlined above could result in a publican being held liable for harassment under the Act' (para 7.8).[752]

The matter was considered directly in *Ms A v A Library*.[753] The equality officer accepted that the complainant has been harassed on the age ground by fellow library users. The harassment consisted of derogatory remarks made by younger people. However, the respondent was entitled to avail of the defence provided for under section 11(3). A policy was in place that requested library users not to disturb others. That policy was communicated via a large sign posted at the entrance and was monitored regularly by staff who watched out

---

[750] *Dalton v Aspire*, DEC-S2009-062, para 5.7.

[751] DEC-S2002-128.

[752] See also the comments of the equality officer in *Campbell v Bus Éireann*, DEC-S2005-197, at para 14.

[753] DEC-S2009-060. The Tribunal has also referred to appropriate signage as a means of preventing harassment of employees by customers: *A Worker v A Hotel*, DEC-E2009-062.

for inappropriate behaviour. Following a complaint by Ms A the senior librarian had asked staff to be especially vigilant in monitoring unruly behaviour and to take appropriate steps should any such activity occur. The equality officer was therefore satisfied that the respondent took adequate steps to investigate the allegations of harassment and to prevent it happening again. Notably, here a general policy that did not refer to discrimination law coupled with a response to a complaint was adequate to meet the obligation to take reasonably practicable steps to 'prevent' harassment by third parties.

Arguably different considerations should apply in assessing liability for harassment in the context of an ongoing service provision relationship, classically the accommodation and education spheres, as opposed to one-off or episodic contacts. In other words, varying thresholds of responsibility should be built into the notion of 'reasonably practicable' steps. At this stage there is insufficient case law to assess the Tribunal's approach but it has indicated that the capacity and resources of the service provider is a relevant factor. The equality officer in *Brooks v BRC Shooting Club*[754] suggested that voluntary bodies with few resources could not be expected to meet the standards imposed on employers in the workplace:

> While I appreciate and acknowledge that it would be unfeasible and unfair to impose the same degree of obligations to such voluntary bodies, the legal obligation to protect service users from harassment and discrimination is unconditional. This means that a service provider must take complaints of harassment and discrimination seriously and investigate them in a manner that is consistent with the principles of natural justice (para 5.10).

The implication here is that while small-scale or voluntary service providers might not be expected to have a comprehensive harassment policy in place, failing to deal adequately with a complaint will make it liable for third-party harassment. In that case the response to a harassment complaint about a fellow club member's behaviour at a meeting was heavily criticised by the equality officer. The board of the respondent club asked ten other members who had attended the meeting in question whether they thought the conduct in question was inappropriate. On foot of their replies the board informed the complainant that the harasser had no case to answer. The equality officer said it was not appropriate 'to presume that a woman is "oversensitive" and ask male members to confirm what she ought to be feeling' (para 5.8). The board appeared to be reluctant to deal with the matter because they were friends with the member who was the subject of the complaint and they formed the view

---

[754] DEC-S2010-042.

that his conduct should be tolerated because it was unintentional. According to the equality officer, '[i]t is not relevant whether the offending person intended or did not intend to cause such offence. What is relevant is what followed subsequent to a complaint' (para 5.8). The respondent had failed to carry out any meaningful investigation and as a result it was liable for the acts of harassment on the gender ground.

A post to an online discussion forum by another service user amounted to harassment on the disability ground in *Dalton v Aspire*.[755] The respondent voluntary organisation was, however, entitled to avail of the section 11(3) defence because it had responded effectively to the complaint. As soon as the issue arose, a message was sent to the forum users requesting that a respectful tone be maintained and warning them that failure to do so would result in posts being deleted. The post in question was removed. The respondent also sent a letter to the complainant seeking clarification about the alleged harassment, in which it reiterated that such behaviour would not be tolerated. The equality officer was 'satisfied that the respondent did all that it could concerning the messages in the discussion forum' (para 5.7).

The reference to a person 'in a position of authority' in the education context (section 11(1)(*c*)) could mean that those responsible for running educational establishments would not be liable for harassment as between students. Liability for such harassment has however been addressed, though not established in a few cases.[756] It would seem, therefore, that the duty placed on 'responsible persons' under subsection (2) is of a general nature and not strictly confined to the situations outlined in subsection (1).

It was not clear from the facts as reported in *Two Complainants (a mother and her son) v A Primary School*,[757] whether the school in question had adopted a harassment policy. While the school had a code of behaviour in place, no harassment policy as such was mentioned and so it seems that the equality officer was satisfied that a reactive response to complaints of bullying and harassment was adequate to avail of the defence.[758] A child who had been

---

[755] DEC-S2009-062. Liability will not accrue if a harassment victim requests the service provider not to take action: *A Minor v Dublin City Council*, DEC-S2011-039.

[756] *Two Complainants (a mother and her son) v A Primary School*, DEC-S2006-028; *A Student v An Educational Establishment*, DEC-S2009-084; *Mrs Z (and on behalf of her three children) v A National School*, DEC-S2010-055.

[757] DEC-S2006-028.

[758] Boards of management are charged, under section 23 of the Education (Welfare) Act 2000, with ensuring that a code of behaviour is drawn up, applied in the school and kept under review. The code must adhere to the guidelines produced by the National Education Welfare Board (2008). The guidelines specify that codes should promote equality for all members of the school community, prevent discrimination and allow for appropriate accommodation of difference, in line with the ESA. Sanctions must not be used in a manner

accused of calling the complainant derogatory names was sanctioned and the complainant was invited to report further incidents. The child who had lodged the harassment complaint was also permitted to go home at lunchtime 'so that he was "out of [harm's] way" in the school yard' (para 6.5). I would argue that this latter step should not be considered an appropriate response to cases of harassment, even though there was evidence that the complainant had been involved in fights with other pupils. The school environment is one in which service providers exercise a considerable degree of control over pupils and so it would seem that an effective harassment policy should be a pre-requisite to satisfy the requirements of the ESA.[759]

A community-based college had such a policy in place. All students had attended a presentation on the policy and had signed an undertaking that they understood its terms and agreed to abide by it.[760] Harassment complaints made by a student on the sexual orientation ground were investigated, and on one occasion another student was sanctioned. Following the incidents a class meeting was held at which the college manager tried to reinforce the importance of maintaining an atmosphere of respect and tolerance. The equality officer was satisfied that the respondent could avail of the section 11(3) defence because it had taken reasonably practicable steps to deal with the complaint and to prevent harassment at the college.

7.4 Instructions to Discriminate and Procurement of Prohibited Conduct

EU law does not specifically provide for vicarious liability but it does stipulate that an 'instruction to discriminate' should be prohibited.[761] However, the concept is ambiguous because the Directives do not define it (De Schutter, 2008; Ahtela, 2005, pp 67–68). It appears to cover the actions of persons who do not themselves engage in prohibited conduct but cause others to do so. According to De Schutter (2008, p 35), the words used in the Directives

---

that discriminates against students and schools should be aware that some sanctions might impact disproportionately on particular groups (National Education Welfare Board, 2008, p 53). Account should be taken of a child's cultural background and special educational needs. The guidelines also point out that: 'Bullying and harassment may lead to inappropriate behaviour by the victim. Schools should respond when such provocation leads to inappropriate behaviour and should not focus solely on the poor behaviour of the student who has been bullied or harassed' (National Education Welfare Board, 2008, p 52).

[759] In *Doherty v Letterkenny Institute of Technology*, DEC-S2010-039, the equality officer criticised the educational establishment's failure to include a harassment policy in its student handbook.

[760] *A Student v An Educational Establishment*, DEC-S2009-084.

[761] See article 2(4) of the Race Directive and article 4(4) of the Gender Goods and Services Directive.

suggest that an instruction to discriminate 'requires that steps be taken by one person "instructing" another, ordering or at least (in the absence of a hierarchical relationship between the two parties) encouraging another person to commit discrimination'. It seems that the instruction need not have been carried out in order to impose liability.

The ESA does not explicitly prohibit the issuing of instructions to discriminate, although it might be argued that the prohibition on procurement or attempted procurement of 'prohibited conduct' includes the issuing of instructions. Section 13 states:

> (1) A person shall not procure or attempt to procure another person to engage in prohibited conduct.

> (2) A person who contravenes *subsection (1)* shall be guilty of an offence.

'Prohibited conduct' means discrimination against, or sexual harassment or harassment of, or permitting the sexual harassment or harassment of a person (section 2). The section is not confined to employees of the procurer, and so it covers third parties including agents.

There has been no case law to date on this aspect of the legislation, perhaps because it is relatively difficult to invoke. As with the other offences provided for under the ESA, either the Minister or the Equality Authority may institute summary proceedings within twelve months of the occurrence of the alleged offence.[762] Crowley (2006, pp 101–103) catalogues a campaign of opposition to the ESA during 2002, which was supported by the Vintners' Federation of Ireland and included a threatened national ban on Travellers' access to pubs. The situation was ultimately resolved through dialogue between various stakeholders, with the Equality Authority briefing the Minister of State with responsibility for equality issues on the procurement offence under the ESA, and advising him 'that this section of the Act could be applied to those involved in seeking to have a blanket ban on serving Travellers imposed by publicans' (Crowley, 2006, p 103). If a resolution had not been reached the Authority might have considered invoking its power to initiate criminal proceedings.

In addition to the procurement offence, the provision on vicarious liability for agents makes it clear that persons cannot discriminate through an intermediary. Where a principal directs or instructs an agent to engage in prohibited

---

[762] Section 44. The penalties for offences under the ESA are set out in section 43. The Supreme Court concluded that the parallel provision in the Employment Equality Bill 1996 was not repugnant to the Constitution. The Court noted that it would have to be proved in the ordinary way that the person in question had an intention to commit the offence: *Article 26 of the Constitution and the Employment Equality Bill 1996, Re* [1997] 2 IR 321 at 369.

conduct both parties can be found liable (Chapter 7.2.3), although in such cases the instruction must have been carried out.

The facts of several complaints disclose evidence of procurement of prohibited conduct. For instance, in *De Burca and Fernandez v Homelocators*[763] a letting agency discriminated on the family status ground, where it apparently complied with a client's request not to rent its property to families with children. Arguably here the client procured prohibited conduct. In *Forde v The Body Clinic*[764] the respondent would not allow the complainant to access its beauty treatment services because she had disclosed that she was epileptic. The equality officer held that it had engaged in less favourable treatment on the disability ground:

> It is clear to me from the evidence provided at the Hearing of this complaint that the respondent's actions in refusing the service to the complainant were primarily on foot of the insurance provider's insistence that service was not to be provided to persons with, inter alia, epilepsy. It should be noted that under Section 13 of the Equal Status Acts it is an offence to procure or attempt to procure another person to engage in prohibited conduct. This does not in any way excuse the respondent's actions in imposing the insurer's conditions in this matter (para 6.2).

The EEA also specifies that a person who procures or attempts to procure another person to discriminate is guilty of an offence.[765] It goes further than the ESA in explicitly defining 'discrimination' as including an instruction to discriminate.[766] This means that employers who instruct an employee or an agent to discriminate against another employee or prospective employee breach the EEA. Inclusion of an instruction to discriminate against service recipients contrary to the ESA would afford employees greater protection.[767] It would cover situations such as that addressed in *Weathersfield Ltd v Sargent*.[768] In that case the UK Court of Appeal found that an employee was discriminated against on racial grounds when she resigned from her job because she

---

[763] DEC-S2004-030/031.

[764] DEC-S2007-085.

[765] Section 14 EEA.

[766] Section 2(1) EEA states that '"discrimination" includes the issue of an instruction to discriminate and, in Part V and VI, includes prohibited conduct within the meaning of the Equal Status Act 2000, and cognate words shall be construed accordingly.' Parts V and VI of the EEA set out the functions and powers of the Equality Authority.

[767] The Equality Authority can take action in such situations but individual complainants may not.

[768] [1999] IRLR 94.

refused to follow her employer's instruction not to hire vehicles to black or Asian customers.[769]

Other provisions of the EEA may also cover instructions to discriminate against service recipients. In particular, the victimisation prohibition should operate to protect employees or agents from less favourable treatment that results from a refusal to carry out an instruction to discriminate.[770] For example, a school principal who is directed by the patron or board of management to expel a pregnant student and is disciplined for failing to do so could claim that he/she was opposing conduct that is unlawful under the ESA.[771]

The Equality Authority (2007a, p 59) has recommended amendments to the ESA aimed at clarifying who can refer a complaint about an instruction to discriminate under the EEA. It suggests that the legislation should specifically provide that the complainant could be the person who receives the instruction to discriminate and not just the person in respect of whom the instruction relates. The Authority has also suggested that the definition of discrimination in the ESA should specifically include an instruction to discriminate.

7.5 Conclusion

Service providers need to be proactive in order to avoid liability under the ESA. The first step is to draw up a written equal status policy, seeking guidance perhaps from the good practice publications of the Equality Authority (Chapter 11.3.2). The policy should then be circulated to all employees and agents (such as security staff or consultant doctors).[772] Holding training sessions on the policy is also advisable in order to ensure, for instance, that employees and agents know how to deal with incidents that may involve harassment or discrimination and are aware of the consequences of breaching the policy. Responsibility for implementation of the policy should be assigned to a senior member of staff. Any incidents that appear to involve discriminatory treatment should be recorded in a logbook. Good practice would also suggest that notices should be displayed on premises advising service users that an equal status policy is in place and that discriminatory conduct is not acceptable.

While all service providers have legal duties under the ESA, the case law accepts that the way these duties are put into practice may differ. Small-scale service providers may have limited resources, and so it may be acceptable

---

[769] See also *Showboat Entertainment Centre Ltd v Owens* [1984] 1 WLR 384.

[770] Section 74(2) EEA.

[771] Section 74(2)(*f*) EEA. An employer who *dismisses* an employee in circumstances amounting to victimisation may be guilty of an offence under section 98 EEA.

[772] Large-scale service providers or those with ongoing relationships with service users (e.g. educational establishments and housing bodies) may choose to consult customers and organisations representing the discriminatory grounds about their experiences.

to have fewer written policies. But in every case service providers should have a complaints procedure and should respond effectively to an allegation of discrimination or harassment, making sure that any person connected with a complaint is not victimised.

8

Positive Action

8.1 Overview

Positive action is a relatively novel means of attempting to secure equality of opportunity. It is generally traced to US government initiatives dating from the 1960s (McCrudden, 2007). As the term 'positive' suggests, these measures go beyond the usual duties of restraint associated with discrimination law. Generally speaking, positive or affirmative action involves policies or actions designed to secure greater participation of under-represented groups in beneficial activities like education and paid work. In the employment arena, positive action measures are used in many countries and usually seek to augment the number of women or minority groups in occupational fields traditionally dominated by others (Baker et al., 2009, pp 131–132).

Such measures are frequently regarded as deviating from the fundamental principle of equal treatment however (Jolls, 2001). Where courts adopt a narrow understanding of equality as requiring everyone to be treated the same, positive action programmes are particularly vulnerable to constitutional challenge (Barmes, 2009; Fredman, 2011, Chapter 5; Nice, 2000; Rutherglen, 2009).[773] This prospect gave rise to carefully drafted substantive equality guarantees under both the South African Constitution and the Canadian Charter of Rights and Freedoms (Bosch, 2007; Hurley, 2007; Naff and Dupper, 2009).[774] An expert group that undertook a review of the Irish Constitution considered the possibility of including explicit protection for positive action (Constitution Review Group, 1996). The group was, however, divided on the issue. Some members believed the matter should be left to the Oireachtas partly

---

[773] But see the UK High Court decision in *Kaur and Shah v London Borough of Ealing* [2008] EWHC 2062 (Admin).

[774] For a recent application of the Canadian Charter in the area of positive action see the Supreme Court of Canada's decision in *R v Kapp* [2008] 2 SCR 483. See Chapter 1.2 for a general discussion of the relationship between discrimination and different conceptions of equality.

because of difficulties in defining the concept with adequate precision. Others felt that a provision would advance equality for marginalised social groups and would give the Government and the Oireachtas constitutional protection for any affirmative action policies they might wish to introduce (subject to the limits imposed by EU law).

The Racial Equality Directive allows member states to introduce legislation providing for positive action in respect of disadvantages suffered by a racial or ethnic group. Article 5 is enabling rather than mandatory: 'With a view to ensuring full equality in practice, the principle of equal treatment shall not prevent any Member State from maintaining or adopting specific measures to prevent or compensate for disadvantages linked to racial or ethnic origin.' Article 6 of the Gender Goods and Services Directive permits similar measures in relation to disadvantages linked to sex.

To date, case law at EU level relates to the realm of employment and the gender ground. We can garner from the principles established in that field that the CJEU will maintain a distinction between 'positive discrimination' and positive action. Basically 'positive discrimination' involves automatic preferences for members of disadvantaged groups (e.g. a recruitment quota) without taking account of the circumstances and 'merits' of each individual affected. Although the case law is not entirely consistent (De Schutter, 2007, pp 801–820), the CJEU regards such 'positive discrimination' as unlawful.[775] Measures then cannot automatically and unconditionally give priority to a member of a disadvantaged group, and in all cases they must be proportionate and be designed to compensate for disadvantages (European Commission, 2009a, pp 22–25).

Burrows and Robison (2006) believe that changes at treaty level[776] and in CJEU case law relating to positive action indicate a shift in the underlying

---

[775] See, for example, *Marschall v Land Nordrhein-Westfalen*, Case C-409/95, ECR 1-6363; *Badeck v Landesan beim Staatsgerichtshof des Landes Hessen*, Case C-158/97, [2000] ECHR 1-1875; *Abrahamsson v Fogelqvist*, Case C-407/98, [2000] ECR 1-5539; *Lommers v Minister Van Landbouw, Natuurbeheer en Visserij*, Case C-476/99, [2002] ECR 1-2891; and *Briheche v Ministre de L'Interieur*, Case C-319/03, [2004] ECR 1-8807. See Waddington and Bell (2011) for a discussion of the reasoning employed in those cases. Future developments in this area may address the relationship between reasonable accommodation, 'positive discrimination' and permissible positive action. Waddington and Bell (2011, p 1518) point out that reasonable accommodations 'possess an individualized character, and are framed in terms of an individual right'. Positive action by contrast is addressed to members of socially or economically disadvantaged groups and no individual entitlement to such measures are provided by law.

[776] Specifically they refer to article 157(4) TFEU (formerly article 141(4) of the EC Treaty), which relates to sex discrimination in the sphere of paid work: 'With a view to ensuring full equality in practice between men and women in working life, the principle of equal treatment shall not prevent any member state from maintaining or adopting measures providing

conception of EU equality law away from a symmetrical and formal model towards one which accommodates measures that are aimed at remedying disadvantage and achieving substantive equality. Significant uncertainties persist and it remains to be seen how the CJEU will deal with positive action outside the field of employment and across different discriminatory grounds (Waddington and Bell, 2011). As De Schutter (2007, p 823) observes, an 'acceptable justification for the allocation of scarce goods will always depend on the sphere in which we are situated'. According to Waddington and Bell (2011), distinct approaches may be required in light of the different forms of inequality experienced by the various social groups covered by EU law.

Within the goods and services context, tensions between positive action measures and the underlying non-discrimination principle are perhaps likely to arise in relation to competitive grants, aids or other benefits.[777] Positive or affirmative action programmes in admissions to third level education are controversial and have been tested frequently within the US legal system (Marin and Horn, 2008).

8.2 Positive Action under the ESA

Section 14(1)(*b*) allows positive action intended to promote equality of opportunity for persons who are disadvantaged or who have been unable to avail of opportunities open to others. It also states that the 'special needs' of individuals or groups can be catered for.[778] The provision is enabling only and so there is no duty on service providers, including public bodies, to take any measures or cater for 'special needs'.[779] Consequently, a failure or refusal to undertake

---

for specific advantages in order to make it easier for the underrepresented sex to pursue a vocational activity or to prevent or compensate for disadvantages in professional careers.'

[777] *MacMahon v Department of Physical Education and Sport, University College Cork,* DEC-S2009-014, involved an application for a sports scholarship. Mr MacMahon argued that the respondent had a policy of positively discriminating in favour of females. However, the Tribunal found no evidence that women were treated more favourably. Consequently, the complainant failed to establish a *prima facie* case of discrimination.

[778] The section provides that the Act shall not prohibit: '(*b*) preferential treatment or the taking of positive measures which are *bona fide* intended to— (i) promote equality of opportunity for persons who are, in relation to other persons, disadvantaged or who have been or are likely to be unable to avail themselves of the same opportunities as those other persons, or (ii) cater for the special needs of persons, or category of persons, who, because of their circumstances, may require facilities, arrangements, services or assistance not required by persons who do not have those special needs.'

[779] See, for example, *Stevens v The Helix Theatre,* DEC-S2008-033: service providers are not obliged to provide positive action for breastfeeding mothers. See also the comments of the Director of the Equality Tribunal concerning Traveller access to education initiatives in *Stokes v Christian Brothers' High School, Clonmel and Department of Education and*

positive action cannot be used as the basis for a discrimination complaint. Rather, as the case law discussed below illustrates, it features as a defence for service providers.[780]

Positive action measures might include providing additional or customised services, separate facilities that take into account special needs, or accelerated access to services. Resources or training opportunities may also be targeted at a particular disadvantaged group. In the education field, for example, the provision could be used to provide English language classes for refugees or subsidies for students from a given background who wish to avail of third level education (Equality Commission, 2009a, pp 57–59). It might also be deployed to establish programmes aimed at enhancing the participation of women and girls in certain sporting activities, or to implement schemes aimed at enhancing the accessibility of premises or services in general (benefiting some individuals across the age, disability, family status and gender grounds). Age criteria are currently used positively to target some goods and services, such as concessions on transport for older and younger people, in an attempt to reduce the disadvantages associated with that group (i.e. lower incomes).[781] Common family status related measures include the provision of distinct car parking spaces to expectant mothers and people accompanied by children in hotels, shopping centres and other venues.

Provided such action is within the parameters laid down in the Acts (and EU law where applicable), it will not amount to discrimination against a group or individual who does not qualify.

A scheme introduced to mitigate the effects of the liberalisation of the taxi industry was the subject of a disability discrimination claim in *McCall v Area Development Management Ltd*.[782] Under its terms certain disabled holders of taxi licences were entitled to compensation. Mr McCall, as a non-disabled person, claimed that he was treated less favourably as he was not eligible for the payment. The scheme was based on the findings of a report produced by the Taxi Hardship Panel. In relation to disabled drivers, the panel noted that taxi licensees who were disabled and incapable of driving could derive their primary income from renting their licence prior to liberalisation in November 2000. The Panel concluded that such persons were now experiencing extreme financial hardship and recommended that, subject to certain conditions, they be paid €13,000. The equality officer found that there was a bona fide intention

---

Skills, DEC-S2010-056. On the non-mandatory nature of positive action in the employment field see *Gillen v Department of Health*, DEC-E2003-035.

[780] *Selenke v Social Welfare Local Office*, DEC-S2011-048, para 5.3.

[781] See also the exemption for preferential rates, fees or charges aimed at certain categories of people under section 16(1), discussed further below.

[782] DEC-S2007-058.

to assist disabled persons whose incomes were reduced and that the Equal Status Act permits such action under section 14(1)(*b*).

Hoey v Area Development Management Ltd[783] involved a challenge to the same scheme, this time under the age ground. Mr Hoey referred a case of direct discrimination as payments were confined to those aged 50 and over and he did not qualify as a result. The equality officer noted that section 14 could be distinguished from exceptions provided for under section 5,[784] in that there is no reference to reasonableness:

> [Section 14(*b*)(ii)] covers treatment which is bona fide intended for a particular purpose and, once it is so intended, it is not for the equality officer to assess whether or not the treatment is reasonable. Even if it is not reasonable, the exemption still applies. It seems to me that the following elements are necessary for the exemption to be invoked: (i) there must be a special need; (ii) the preferential treatment must be bona fide intended to cater for this need; and (iii) the persons benefiting must be persons who, because of their circumstances deriving from the special need, may require assistance (i.e. the preferential treatment) not required by persons without that need (para 17).

According to the respondent the scheme advanced two special needs of people aged over 50: the increased costs of pension provision and the fact that taxi driving work becomes more difficult as one ages due to increased risks of sickness and disability. Applying the provision to the facts before him, the equality officer in effect concluded that the age limit was arbitrary. The needs referred to could not just be attributed to people over 50. The Tribunal decision was overturned on appeal to the Circuit Court. However, the Circuit Court judgment addressed the application of the ESA to the Taxi Hardship Payments Scheme rather than the meaning of section 14(*b*) (Chapter 2.4.3). As a consequence the original decision still provides useful guidance on the operation of the positive action provision.

In *O'Connor v The Icon Night Club*[785] the respondent sought to defend a claim of gender discrimination by invoking section 14(*b*). At issue was a policy of allowing female customers free entry to a club on Thursday evenings. The male complainant was asked to pay an entrance fee and successfully argued that the practice was discriminatory. The equality officer did not accept that the policy was a positive action measure aimed at women within the terms of

---

[783] DEC-S2008-010.
[784] Specifically in sections 5(2)(*d*), (*h*) and (*l*). See Chapters 2.6.4.3 and 2.6.4.4.
[785] DEC-S2004-001.

the legislation. She noted that the respondent had not supplied any evidence establishing that women as a group were disadvantaged in their ability to get into nightclubs. Following established practice the Tribunal could rely on its own specialist knowledge to support such a finding but the equality officer concluded that it was untenable:

> It may be that some groups of women find it more difficult to go out to nightclubs in the evening due to economic disadvantage or lack of childcare support, but the entrance fee involved is a relatively small one, which would not appear to pose difficulties for women gener-ally, and the waiver of the entrance fee is not targeted to any groups of women suffering particular disadvantage. I am satisfied therefore that the [practice] is not a positive action measure taken in good faith in order to reduce barriers confronting women as a disadvantaged group. I believe the measure was taken for commercial reasons aimed at attracting more customers into the nightclub (para 4.6).

The exception provided for under section 16(1) could also be regarded as a form of positive action for certain groups.[786] It provides:

> Imposing or maintaining a reasonable preferential fee, charge or rate in respect of anything offered or provided to or in respect of persons together with their children, married couples, persons in a specific age group or persons with a disability does not constitute—
>
> (*a*) discrimination for the purposes of *section 5* or *6*, or
>
> (*b*) a discriminatory rule, policy or practice for the purposes of *section 8(2)(a)*.

The provision is not, however, linked to ameliorating disadvantage or cater-ing for 'special needs' as section 14(*b*) is. Instead it must be shown that the 'preferential fee, charge or rate' is 'reasonable' and aimed at one of the groups mentioned. It should operate to sanction a range of 'deals' such as family membership rates and admission charges, as well as financial prod-ucts that offer favourable rates for older people. Concessions available only to married couples would discriminate on the sexual orientation ground since gay and lesbian couples are currently barred from marrying as a matter of Irish law.[787] But this exception would appear to permit such differentiation.

---

786 See discussion of *Dalton v Limerick City Council*, DEC-S2004-042, in Chapter 3.3.1.
787 *Zappone & Anor. v Revenue Commissioners & Ors* [2008] 1 IR 417. The High Court judgment is under appeal to the Supreme Court as of 13 July 2012 (*Irish Times*, 2011a).

The amendments effected by the Civil Partnership Act 2010 do not appear to include civil partners within the term 'married couple'.[788]

As discussed above, various exceptions allow for differences in treatment that have a 'benign' purpose. For instance, section 7(3)(e) facilitates the admission of mature students to third level educational institutions (Chapter 2.6.2.2). In relation to registered clubs specifically, section 9(1)(d) permits concessionary rates for club members previously disadvantaged by discriminatory rules and under section 9(2) clubs may take steps to promote equal participation in their governance.

Sections 5(2)(h) and 5(2)(l) also allow for special treatment of certain categories of people. Broadly speaking, differences in treatment are permissible where it is reasonably necessary to do so in order to promote the special interests or meet the distinct needs of certain persons. Case law on those provisions is considered in Chapter 2.6.4.3.

8.3 Conclusion

Positive action is a valuable means of securing equality of opportunity for groups that experience systemic disadvantage. However, the ESA simply permits such measures. Bodies like the Equality Authority, in promoting good practice and working with stakeholders on the implementation of equality policies, seek to incentivise private and public sector organisations to consider positive action as a valuable option (Chapter 11.3.2).

---

[788] Section 103 of the Civil Partnership Act 2010 amended the definition of 'near relative' in section 2(1) of the ESA but left intact the definition of 'married couple'.

9

Registered Clubs

9.1 Overview

Sections 8 to 10 of the ESA apply exclusively to registered clubs, which are bodies that have applied for or hold a certificate of registration under the Registration of Clubs Acts 1904–1999. Registration enables clubs to sell alcohol to members and certain visitors. Clubs that do not hold a liquor licence are governed instead by the general prohibition on discrimination set out under section 5.[789]

The provisions only relate to matters concerning membership of clubs and cases must be taken before the District Court. Currently, the Equality Tribunal hears allegations of discrimination by registered clubs that concern the provision of goods or services that are available to the public, as with other goods and services providers.[790] Indeed, where a club member alleges discrimination in relation to a service that is available to the public (or to a section of the public), he or she may lodge a complaint with the Tribunal in the usual manner. For example, the Tribunal investigated a complaint taken by a member against a registered club because it involved parking facilities that were not confined to members.[791]

Discrimination relating to a club's internal rules and affairs is dealt with distinctly under sections 8–10, e.g. as to who can become a member, conditions of membership and the provision of reasonable accommodation to disabled members. Significantly, the ESA does not ban membership-related

---

[789] See, for example, *Brooks v BRC Shooting Club*, DEC-S2010-042.

[790] See the definition of 'service' in section 2, which includes 'a service or facility provided by a club' to the public.

[791] *Ennis v Navan O'Mahony's Football and Hurling Club*, DEC-S2010-031. The distinction between services offered to the public and the internal private activities of a club offered to, and participated in, strictly by its own members may not be straightforward, as illustrated by the spilt decision of the Canadian Supreme Court in *Gould v Yukon Order of Pioneers* [1996] 1 SCR 571.

discrimination outright. Rather, clubs may discriminate but risk losing their certificate of registration.

In effect the legislation attempts to strike a balance between the right not to be discriminated against and potentially competing rights, such as those relating to privacy, freedom of association and freedom of expression (White, 1997). Decisions in other countries have generated considerable political controversy, particularly where the associations in question are in receipt of public funding (Hunter, 2001).[792] A case concerning Portmarnock Golf Club, in north County Dublin, also attracted a degree of media attention. It is discussed below.

As for the EU position, the Racial Equality Directive does not contain any specific exceptions for clubs or private associations. Its application to those types of bodies will depend on whether they provide goods and services. The preamble to the Directive recognises that non-discrimination must be read in light of other human rights. Recital 4 states, 'It is important to respect fundamental rights and freedoms, including the right to freedom of association. It is also important, in the context of access to and provision of goods and services, to respect the protection of private and family life and transactions carried out in this context.' But recital 17, which concerns positive action measures, envisages the establishment of 'organisations of persons of a particular racial or ethnic origin where their main object is the promotion of the special needs of those persons.'

The Gender Goods and Services Directive is more limited in scope than the Racial Equality Directive. It is explicitly confined to goods and services 'which are offered outside the area of private and family life and the transactions carried out in this context' (article 3(1)). It remains to be seen whether, and to what extent, the reference to 'private and family life' will remove clubs or private associations from the reach of the Directive. Across all areas, the Gender Goods and Services Directive allows different treatment of women and men in two respects. Firstly, 'if the provision of the goods and services exclusively or primarily to members of one sex is justified by a legitimate aim and the means of achieving that aim are appropriate and necessary' (article 4(5)), and secondly, where the different treatment has the aim of preventing or compensating for disadvantages linked to sex (article 6 on positive action). Recital 16 provides examples of differences in treatment that could be justified. Those examples include single-sex voluntary bodies aimed at promoting gender equality or the interests of women and men, and membership of single-sex private clubs, which in turn is linked to the legitimate aim of freedom of

---

[792] See, for example, the US Supreme Court decisions in *Boy Scouts of America et al. v Dale*, 530 US 640 (2000) and *Hurley v Irish-American Gay, Lesbian and Bisexual Group of Boston*, 515 US 557 (1995).

association. The Gender Goods and Services Directive is considered further in Chapter 9.3.

9.2 Discriminating and Non-Discriminating Clubs

According to section 8(2)(*a*), 'discriminating clubs' are ones that have 'any rule, policy or practice which discriminates against a member or an applicant for membership' or clubs where 'a person involved in its management discriminates against a member or an applicant for membership in relation to the affairs of the club.' The prohibition of discriminatory 'practices' should capture forms of grounds-based exclusion that are not documented, but occur nonetheless, such as the informal screening of membership applications.

Section 8(2)(*b*) provides examples of potentially discriminatory acts:

- Refusing to admit a person to membership

- Providing different terms and conditions of membership for members or applicants

- Terminating membership or subjecting a member to a sanction

- Refusing or failing to do all that is reasonable to accommodate the needs of a member or applicant with a disability as required by section 4(1)

Protection from harassment is not afforded to members of registered clubs. The Oireachtas debates suggest that the extension of an express prohibition on harassment to registered clubs was ruled out because of concerns that it would be too draconian, particularly were it to cover harassment as between members, and could give rise to constitutional difficulties.[793] However, actions that might usually constitute harassment may also be considered a form of less favourable treatment and so fall foul of the prohibition on direct discrimination (see Chapter 5.4.4). Seeking protection under the direct discrimination prohibition is more limited because liability can only be attached to a club for the acts of its employees and agents (i.e. harassment by third parties is not covered) (Chapter 7).

Enforcement proceedings and sanctions are detailed in the remainder of section 8. The sole sanction that can be imposed on a discriminating club is the suspension and ultimately the loss of its certificate of registration (and so

---

[793] 162 *Seanad Debates* 25, Cols 1724–1727 (Equal Status Bill 1999: Committee Stage (Resumed)); 514 *Dáil Debates* 4, Cols 818–820 (Equal Status Bill 1999: Report Stage (Resumed)); Select Committee on Justice, Equality, Defence and Women's Rights, 4 November 1999 (Equal Status Bill 1999: Committee Stage (Resumed)).

its licence to sell alcohol).[794] These sanctions are triggered by court proceedings. Along with any other person or legal entity the Equality Authority can apply to the District Court for a determination that a club is a 'discriminating club'.[795]

Section 9 is headed 'non-discriminating clubs' and clarifies what is permissible under the ESA. The first major exception allows clubs to confine membership to a particular group, if the 'principal purpose' of the club is 'to cater only for the needs of' persons within that group:

> 9(1) For the purposes of *section 8*, a club shall not be considered to be a discriminating club by reason only that—
>
> (*a*) if its principal purpose is to cater only for the needs of—
>
> > (i) persons of a particular gender, civil status, family status, sexual orientation, religious belief, age, disability, nationality or ethnic or national origin,
> >
> > (ii) persons who are members of the Traveller community,
> >
> > or
> >
> > (iii) persons who have no religious belief,
>
> it refuses membership to other persons

This provision involves denying membership outright to certain categories of people. It was at the centre of the *Portmarnock* case, which is discussed in the next section.

Other exceptions allow for differences in treatment of members that concern separate but equivalent facilities and benefits, like separate changing rooms for men and women.[796] Clubs may offer different grades of membership such as full and associate, but must open those grades to all groups protected by the ESA.[797] Under section 9(1)(*e*) a club is allowed to provide different treatment

---

[794] During the Oireachtas debates on the Equal Status Bill 1999 opposition TDs unsuccessfully sought an amendment that would have precluded the state from funding clubs that discriminate. Government deputies rejected the proposal because of legal advice to the effect that the proposed measure could be unconstitutional apparently on the grounds of proportionality (see Select Committee on Justice, Equality, Defence and Women's Rights, 4 November 1999). The Minister of State suggested that a department administering a particular scheme should instead make eligibility conditional on the applicant meeting certain standards in the discrimination field (162 *Seanad Debates* Cols 1729–1732).

[795] Section 8(3).

[796] Section 9(1)(*b*).

[797] Section 9(1)(*c*).

to members 'in the category of a particular gender, age, disability, nationality or national origin in relation to sporting facilities or events', where the different treatment is relevant to the purpose of the facilities or events and is reasonably necessary. This would allow, for example, competitions confined to people in certain age groups since a person's age would be relevant to their level of skill in a particular sport and it would be reasonable to hold different events for various age groups. These exceptions mirror those found elsewhere in the ESA and should not prove controversial, except perhaps in relation to the treatment of transgender people (Chapter 3.3.4).

Nothing in section 9 relieves a club of its duty to reasonably accommodate members with disabilities. Also, the 'race' and 'colour' aspects of the race ground are not exempt, either with respect to acquiring membership or treatment of existing members. Clubs whose principal purpose is to cater only for the needs of Travellers are not discriminating clubs, but there is no exemption for the settled community.

Finally, clubs are entitled to enact positive action measures in the form of concessionary rates for members affected by previous rules restricting membership on the basis of gender.[798] Clubs may also reserve places on boards or committees of management and take other measures to promote equal participation in governance.[799]

9.3 Case Law

As recorded in its annual reports, the Equality Authority was often involved in the resolution of allegations that clubs had discriminated on the gender ground in particular (2002, p 43; 2003, p 4; 2004, pp 32, 38–39; 2005b, p 37; 2006b, p 54; 2011a, p 42). However, in 2003 the Authority pursued a case under section 8 for the first time in relation to Portmarnock Golf Club (Fenelon, 2009). It argued that the club was a discriminating club because it refused membership to women. On 20 February 2004 the District Court found that Portmarnock was a discriminating club and subsequently ordered that its licence be suspended for seven days. The club appealed the District Court finding and also challenged the decision in the High Court on the basis that certain provisions of the ESA were unconstitutional. The High Court heard the case in March 2005; the judgment was delivered in June of that year and, while the constitutional challenge failed, the regular appeal was successful.[800]

---

[798] Section 9(1)(*d*).
[799] Section 9(2).
[800] *The Equality Authority v Portmarnock Golf Club* [2005] IEHC 235.

As noted above, the legislation sanctions a single gender club provided that its principal purpose is to cater only for the needs of persons of that gender (section 9(1)(*a*)). Essentially, Portmarnock Golf Club argued that the word 'needs' included social, cultural and recreational needs, and that the principal purpose of the club was to cater for the golfing needs of men. The Equality Authority maintained there must be a logical connection between the objectives of the club and gender. The principal purpose of a golf club, it argued, is not to cater for the needs of persons of a single gender but rather to play golf. O'Higgins J agreed with the club and found that its principal purpose was to cater for the needs of male golfers, and so it came within the exception provided for under section 9.

He went on to consider whether the legislation was unconstitutional. The club's arguments pivoted on the right to freedom of association protected by Article 40.6.1 of the Constitution, which provides:

> The State guarantees liberty for the exercise of the following rights, subject to public order and morality …
>
> iii. – the right of the citizens to form associations and unions. Laws, however, may be enacted for the regulation and control in the public interest of the exercise of the foregoing right.

After considering the wording of the provision and case law concerning restrictions on the right, O'Higgins J did not accept that it could only be interfered with on the grounds of morality and public order. Furthermore, the restrictions imposed by the Equal Status Act did not prevent persons from associating with one another but just allowed for the deprivation of a club licence. The right to hold a social club licence is not a constitutionally protected right and is dependent on the existing statutory regime. O'Higgins J concluded that the restrictions envisaged by the ESA would not strike at the core of freedom of association but would constitute a permissible control and regulation in the public interest of an ancillary activity of the club. The judgment also addressed the applicability of the equality guarantee set out in Article 40.1 of the Constitution. O'Higgins J found that while the guarantee does not directly impose obligations on citizens in their private relations, the Oireachtas is entitled to legislate positively to vindicate and promote the value of equality and such legislation can legitimately have an effect on private individuals.

The Equality Authority appealed the finding that Portmarnock was not a discriminating club to the Supreme Court. The Supreme Court was exclusively concerned with the correct interpretation of section 9, having found that the constitutional question should not have been dealt with by the High

Court. It dismissed the appeal by a majority of three to two.[801] Hardiman J and Geoghegan J, with Macken J concurring, held that the ordinary, natural and literal meaning of the word 'needs' was sufficiently wide to include cultural, social and sporting needs as well as more basic needs such as air or water. Portmarnock Golf Club's principal purpose was to cater for the needs of *men* to play golf. It was therefore entitled to avail of the exception set out under section 9(1)(*a*).

Applying the same rules of interpretation the two dissenting judges arrived at a different conclusion. Denham J and Fennelly J found that the 'principal purpose' of the club was to play golf, not to cater for the needs of men. The club allowed women to play golf (although not as full members), and so it catered for the needs of both men and women and should not be entitled to claim the exemption. According to Fennelly J, it was 'unreal and implausible to suggest that the principal purpose of a Golf Club is not the playing of golf'.[802] He pointed out that the club's own rules state that golf is the purpose to which the club was 'primarily devoted'. Furthermore, the club enjoys tax exemptions as a body that has 'the sole purpose of promoting athletic or amateur games or sports'. On this basis Fennelly J stated, 'golf becomes not only its "principal" but its "sole" purpose.'[803]

It remains to be seen whether the approach adopted by the majority of the Supreme Court will comply with the Gender Goods and Services Directive. As noted above, the Directive's application to private clubs or associations is ambiguous (Chapter 9.1). The Directive allows different treatment on the gender ground in two circumstances. Firstly, 'if the provision of the goods and services exclusively or primarily to members of one sex is justified by a legitimate aim and the means of achieving that aim are appropriate and necessary' (article 4(5)). And secondly, where the different treatment has the aim of preventing or compensating for disadvantages linked to sex (article 6 on positive action). The relevant provisions of that Directive were not in force at the time of the Portmarnock litigation.[804] Nonetheless Hardiman J appeared to accept the club's contention that the Directive permitted single-sex private clubs whatever their composition.[805]

---

[801] *Equality Authority v Portmarnock Golf Club & Ors* [2010] 1 ILRM 237.

[802] *Equality Authority v Portmarnock Golf Club & Ors* [2010] 1 ILRM 237, at p 311.

[803] *Equality Authority v Portmarnock Golf Club & Ors* [2010] 1 ILRM 237, at p 312.

[804] Member states were required to transpose the Gender Goods and Services Directive into national legislation by December 2007. Since the events in question in the Portmarnock case occurred prior to that implementation date the Directive was inapplicable: *Albatross Meats Ltd v Minister for Agriculture & Food, Ireland and the Attorney General* [2007] 1 IR 221, at para 117.

[805] *Equality Authority v Portmarnock Golf Club & Ors* [2010] 1 ILRM 237, at pp 272–273.

Commenting on the High Court judgment in *Portmarnock* in light of EU law Burri and McColgan (2008, p 14) observe:

> It should be recalled here that the Directive applies only in relation to those 'goods and services (...) which are available to the public' and that it does not, therefore, 'bite' on small clubs which could reasonably be regarded as 'private'. But, insofar as the Directive does have application, the exclusion of women from (for example) a prestigious golf club at which, more than likely, numerous 'networking' opportunities are available to men involved in business, the professions and similar, might reasonably be regarded as disproportionate to any legitimate aim, given its potentially damaging impact on women, and therefore as not saved by Article 4(5). Indeed the question might arise whether the aim of such clubs can be regarded as legitimate at all. In the Irish golf club case discussed above, the High Court accepted that 'there is nothing inherently undesirable with persons seeking – in a social context – the society of persons of the same gender'. This may be so, but this is not the same thing as saying that the facilitation of such wishes in the public sphere is a legitimate aim, in particular given the deleterious impact it has on women's ability to network for professional and other reasons. By contrast, a networking organisation of women designed to ameliorate some of the disadvantages suffered by women in business (disadvantages associated with, for example, minority status, sexism, and/or restrictions on networking opportunities associated with childcare responsibilities) might well be regarded as a proportionate means of achieving a legitimate end (furthering equality) under Article 4(5), as well as being justified under Article 6 of the Directive.

In any event, the outcome in *Portmarnock* arguably does not reflect the intention of the Oireachtas when enacting the 2000 Act. Eliminating male-only membership policies in golf clubs appeared to enjoy cross-party support.[806]

9.4 Conclusion

The Supreme Court's findings in the *Portmarnock* case effectively allow registered clubs to decline membership to most of the groups covered by the ESA (Fenelon, 2009). Legislative reform should perhaps be considered in order to better align the ESA with the EU directives. It would afford an

---

[806] See Select Committee on Justice, Equality, Defence and Women's Rights, 4 November 1999 (Equal Status Bill 1999: Committee Stage (Resumed)).

opportunity to re-think the difficult balance to be struck between freedom of association and privacy on the one hand and substantive equality of opportunity on the other. The approach adopted in the UK may be a good starting point. In the process of reforming discrimination law for the purposes of aligning it with EU directives the UK Government approached the question of private clubs in a different manner to the Oireachtas. A consultation paper on the Equality Bill made an express link between a protected characteristic and the purpose of a private association: 'we consider that private clubs ... whose main purpose does not depend on their members having a characteristic protected by discrimination law should not be able to discriminate against their members, associates, applicants for membership or their guests' (Department for Communities and Local Government, 2007, p 156). Under the Equality Act 2010, 'associations' include bodies that have membership criteria such as private clubs and political parties, but only associations with at least 25 members have obligations. The legislation, therefore, protects freedom of association but recognises that larger groupings may provide significant networking opportunities and so forth that should not be denied to members of minority or disadvantaged groups.

II

ENFORCEMENT

10

Activating Discrimination Law

10.1 Introduction

This part examines how the ESA is activated. The provisions can be triggered by individuals who believe they have been subjected to discrimination, or by a specialist equality agency. Ireland's equality infrastructure will undergo considerable change over the coming years. The system for processing discrimination complaints is subject to an ongoing reform process, and the body tasked with overseeing implementation of discrimination law, the Equality Authority, is to be replaced by a new entity.

The primary means of enforcing discrimination law, the individual complaint, is dealt with in Chapter 12. A specialised body dedicated to hearing complaints, the Equality Tribunal, was established in 1999. Processes are designed so that hearings take place more quickly, are less expensive and are less formal than those before ordinary courts (Chapter 11.2). In July 2011 the Government announced the proposed merger of five bodies with responsibility for enforcing employment rights, including the Equality Tribunal.[807] A new body called the Workplace Relations Commission (WRC) will be formally established in 2012 and will ultimately take over the Tribunal's role in determining EEA cases (Department of Jobs, Enterprise and Innovation, 2012). Unfortunately, the fate of complaints under the ESA was not specifically addressed in the discussion papers issued by the Department of Jobs, Enterprise and Innovation (2011a, 2012). A number of submissions to the initial consultation, including that by the Equality Tribunal, recommended that the WRC also hear ESA cases (Department of Jobs, Enterprise and Innovation, 2011b, p 19; Equality Tribunal, 2011b; Irish Council for Civil Liberties, 2011). These matters are revisited in Chapters 11 and 12.

Implementation of the law is currently overseen by a specialist equality agency, namely the Equality Authority. The promotional and development

---

[807] See generally <http://www.djei.ie/employment/rights/erirproject.htm>.

work carried out by the Authority has been crucial in driving voluntary take-up of equality measures. Its role in this regard is considered in Chapter 11.3, as are its enforcement and other powers. In 2012 the Equality Authority will merge with the Human Rights Commission to form the Irish Human Rights and Equality Commission (IHREC). A working group on the IHREC, established by the Minister for Justice, reported in April 2012 (Working Group on the Human Rights and Equality Commission, 2012). It recommended that the current powers and functions exercised by both bodies should be retained, subject to some modifications and enhancements. It remains to be seen, of course, whether and to what extent those recommendations will be reflected in the draft legislation to be published in autumn 2012. The Working Group was guided by the Paris Principles,[808] which emanate from the United Nations and are a set of detailed standards for the establishment and operation of national human rights institutions. An enhanced European dimension to the question of remedies, enforcement and associated specialised agencies has evolved as EU competence in the field of equal opportunity has widened (Ammer et al., 2010; Cormack, 2004; Holtmaat, 2007; Moon, 2007; Obura and Palmer, 2006; Rorive, 2009a; Yesilkagit and Snijders, 2008). Because of the primacy of EU law those standards must be adhered to in the establishment of the new equality infrastructure.

Chapters 11 and 12 deal with how the law operates in practice, examining respectively the role of equality bodies and how individual complaints are heard. The remainder of this chapter sets out some general observations on invoking discrimination law.

10.2 Limits and Benefits of Individual Enforcement

Enforcement of Irish discrimination law relies heavily upon actions taken by individuals. Apart from resolving the actual case, litigation has an important role to play in clarifying legal principles and establishing precedents, as well as raising awareness and having a wider symbolic impact (Barry, 2004, p 7; McCrudden, 1999a, p 300).

However, there are several difficulties with a complaints-led or individual model of enforcement and a substantial body of research has sought to explain low levels of discrimination law claims (e.g. Blom et al., 1995; Engel and Munger, 2003; Handley, 2001; Lerpiniere and Stalker, 2010; McCrudden, Smith and Brown, 1991; Walsh, Conlon, Fitzpatrick and Hansson, 2007). A

---

[808] The 'Paris Principles' were endorsed by the UN Commission on Human Rights in March 1992 (Resolution 1992/54) and by the UN General Assembly in its Resolution A/RES/48/143 of 20 December 1993. On the application of the Paris Principles to equality bodies see further Yesilkagit and Snijders (2008).

major perceived problem with the individual model is that it operates in a *reactive* manner, that is, an objectionable practice must have already occurred for the law to be triggered (Lacey, 1998, pp 20–24; Fredman, 2009). Discrimination will simply go unchallenged unless an individual takes action. A complex set of economic, social and cultural factors affect people's willingness and ability to do so.

Data collected in a 2004 household survey suggests that significant numbers of people are affected by discrimination in Ireland, yet most do nothing about it (Central Statistics Office, 2005; Russell, Quinn, King O'Riain and McGinnity, 2008). While approximately 382,000 or 12.5 per cent of people aged 18 or over felt they had experienced discrimination in the two-year period prior to the survey, almost 60 per cent of them took no action.[809] Only 6 per cent made an official complaint or took legal action, suggesting 'that the cases that make it to the Equality Tribunal represent a very small fraction of all cases of discrimination' (Russell et al., 2008, p 62).

Many studies conclude that discrimination law tends to be accessed by well-resourced and supported individuals.[810] People may not know that a particular practice amounts to unlawful discrimination, or be unaware of various avenues of redress or what making a complaint will entail in terms of costs and so on (Walsh et al., 2007). According to the CSO survey mentioned above, one-fifth of people who reported experiencing discrimination felt they had no understanding of their rights. Over half stated that they understood a little, while only 27.6 per cent felt that they understood a lot (Central Statistics Office, 2005).

Potential sources of discrimination law advice and advocacy within Ireland include the services operated under the auspices of the Citizens Information Board (CIB). The CIB is required to assist and support people in identifying their needs and options and in accessing their entitlements to social services (Citizens Information Board, 2011). The public can access information directly through the Citizens Information website.[811] Significantly, the Citizens Information Services (CISs) have 42 offices located around the country to which people may call for face-to-face advice. Information and advice can also be accessed through the Citizens Information phone service. CISs provide assistance and advocacy support, which may extend to enabling people to make discrimination complaints or even representing them before

---

[809] The survey centred on the nine grounds protected under the ESA and EEA, but respondents could indicate a category 'other' for all responses; some 150,000 of the 381,600 persons that had experienced discrimination availed of that option.

[810] On this debate see Baker et al. (2009, Chapter 7), Barry (2003), Blom et al. (1995), Fredman (2002, Chapter 6) and Lacey (1998, Chapter 1).

[811] <http://www.citizensinformation.ie/>.

bodies like the Equality Tribunal.[812] Some CISs host clinics by the Equality Authority (Citizens Information Board, 2011, p 14). Since 2011 the National Advocacy Service for People with Disabilities has been operating through the CISs.[813] The advocates working for this service assist people with disabilities in enforcing their legal rights and in accessing essential services.

A number of independent law centres currently operate in Ireland. These include the Ballymun Community Law Centre, the Free Legal Advice Centres (FLAC), the Immigrant Council of Ireland, the Irish Traveller Movement Law Centre, Mercy Law Resource Centre and the Northside Community Law Centre.[814] FLAC operates on a nationwide basis and supplies basic information on legal rights to members of the public.[815] The other centres provide legal services to different constituencies, set either by geographic location (Ballymun and Northside) or with reference to a particular area of interest. Mercy Law Resource Centre deals with the legal needs of homeless people, the Irish Traveller Movement Law Centre focuses on the rights of the Traveller community, and the Immigrant Council of Ireland's legal services are availed of by Ireland's migrant population.

Along with inadequate information, fear of retaliation is a major deterrent to litigation (Blom et al., 1995; Rodrigues, 1997). People may be anxious about the reaction of the service provider, employers (current or prospective), colleagues, family members and so on. Concerns about retaliation and privacy more generally may be heightened for members of particular social groups. In relation to lesbian, gay and bisexual individuals, for example, the prospect of being 'outed' is a major barrier (European Group of Experts on Combating Sexual Orientation Discrimination, 2004, Appendix 1; Walsh et al., 2007; European Union Agency for Fundamental Rights, 2009).

In sum, the individual enforcement model serves valuable ends but cannot be expected to deliver full and effective compliance with anti-discrimination law.

10.3 Positive Equality Duties

Other vehicles for implementing discrimination law complement the individual enforcement model (Fredman, 2009). Extension of the ability to litigate (or 'standing') to specialised equality agencies and other bodies is one such mechanism and is considered in Chapter 10.4. But positive equality duties

---

[812] See further <http://www.citizensinformationboard.ie/services/advocacy_services/>.

[813] The Citizens Information Act 2007 gives legislative responsibility to the Citizens Information Board to develop advocacy services for people with disabilities, particularly a personal advocacy service to deal with the most complex cases (Flynn, 2007).

[814] See further <http://www.pila.ie/about-pila/law-centres/>. Please see the Appendix for contact information for these bodies.

[815] See further <http://www.flac.ie/gethelp/>.

are perhaps the most salient development in the field. Such duties take many forms and operate in several jurisdictions (Crowley, 2006, pp 108–112; Fredman, 2009, 2010; Halford, 2009; Hepple, 2010; McLaughlin, 2007; O'Cinneide, 2003; Szabo, 2008). Generally speaking, positive equality duties require duty-bearers to proactively identify and address unlawful discrimination. Organisations may also be required to institute policies or practices that promote equality of opportunity. These measures potentially address the limitations inherent in the individual enforcement model as they do not rely on a victim of discrimination coming forward and are designed to prevent discrimination arising in the first place.

The duties applicable to public sector bodies in the UK are outlined here. Distinct legislation governs the position in Northern Ireland, while the obligations of public bodies in England, Scotland and Wales were dealt with under a series of laws until the advent of the Equality Act 2010.

In Great Britain, the first public sector equality duty dealt with the race ground. The Race Relations (Amendment) Act 2000 directed specified public authorities in carrying out their functions to have due regard to the need to eliminate unlawful racial discrimination, promote equality of opportunity and promote good relations between people of different racial groups. Allied specific duties were imposed on certain public bodies to publish equality schemes demonstrating how the duties are to be fulfilled, involve affected people in the development of the scheme, carry out impact assessments, make arrangements for gathering relevant information, develop action plans, take the steps set out in its action plan and publish a report on compliance. These specific duties are meant to enable better performance of the general duty. Similar obligations were subsequently extended to the disability and gender grounds.[816] Under the terms of the Equality Act 2010 a new public sector equality duty replaced the existing framework. It came into force on 5 April 2011 and covers the grounds of age, disability, gender, gender identity, race, religion and belief, and sexual orientation (Ashtiany, 2010; Hepple, 2011, Chapter 6; Lester and Uccellari, 2008; Vickers, 2011). However, the government that came into power shortly after the 2010 Act came into force watered down the specific duties considerably (Fredman, 2011, pp 311–312).

A statutory body, the Equality and Human Rights Commission, oversees implementation.[817] It may issue a non-compliance notice where it believes that a public authority has failed to abide by the duty. The duties have also given rise to some court challenges, which underline the potential for enhanced accountability on the part of public sector decision makers (Bell, 2010b;

---

[816] Under the Disability Discrimination Act 2005 and the Equality Act 2006.
[817] See further: <http://www.equalityhumanrights.com/>.

Halford, 2009). *Secretary of State for Defence v Elias*[818] was the first case to consider positive duties. It concerned a scheme to compensate ex-prisoners of war that was limited to persons who could establish that they, a parent or grandparent was born in Britain. The criterion was indirectly discriminatory on the race ground. According to the Court of Appeal the scheme was also unlawful because no 'due regard' was had to the question of whether the law promoted equality and good relations between people from different racial groups. Arden LJ explained:

> [I]t is the clear purpose of Section 71 to require public bodies to whom that provision applies to give advance consideration to issues of race discrimination before making any policy decision that may be affected by them. This is a salutary requirement, and this provision must be seen as an integral and important part of the mechanisms for ensuring the fulfilment of the aims of anti-discrimination legislation (para 274).

The UK High Court ruling in *Kaur and Shah v London Borough of Ealing*[819] is another interesting example of the race equality duty's effects. In 2007 Ealing Council decided that in the interests of 'community cohesion' it should only fund organisations that provided services to the whole borough and not just to specific ethnic groups. These revised criteria would deprive South-hall Black Sisters of the opportunity to apply for funding since it provided services to women affected by domestic violence within Afro-Caribbean and Asian communities. The council's decision was challenged on the basis that it did not conduct an impact assessment. The local authority produced one just prior to the hearing and the Court found this to be inadequate. Indeed it went further and said that in looking at whether a measure promotes equality a public body must have regard to substantive equality considerations. According to the Court, 'There is no dichotomy between the promotion of equality and cohesion and the provision of specialist services to an ethnic minority' (para 55). Moses LJ also quoted from the UK Government's 2007 Equalities Review, which emphasises that 'an equal society recognises people's different needs, situations and goals and removes the barriers that limit what people can do and can be' (para 58).[820]

---

[818] [2006] 1 WLR 3213.

[819] [2008] EWHC 2062 (Admin).

[820] On Race Equality Impact Assessments see further *R(C) v Secretary of State for Justice* [2008] EWCA Civ 882. *Eisai v National Institute of Clinical Excellence* [2007] EWHC 1941 (Admin) and *Chavda v London Borough of Harrow* [2008] BLGR 657 both address the disability equality duty.

Section 75 of the Northern Ireland Act 1998 requires designated public authorities to publish 'equality schemes' in which they demonstrate to the satisfaction of the Equality Commission for Northern Ireland (ECNI)[821] how they will have due regard to the need to promote equality of opportunity between certain different individuals and groups (for instance, between men and women, between those with a disability and those without, and between those with dependants and those without) (McCrudden, 1999b; McLaughlin, 2007). Among other things, these schemes must state the authority's arrangements for assessing and consulting on the likely impact of all policies adopted or proposed on the promotion of equality of opportunity. The authority can be required to amend its scheme once the Equality Commission has examined it. If the ECNI receives a complaint about failure to comply it is obliged to investigate or to give the complainant reasons for not investigating. It can also independently conduct an investigation. Ultimately, the ECNI issues a report and if action is recommended and the public body fails to conform within a reasonable time the matter is referred to the Secretary of State for Northern Ireland, who may in turn give directions to the defaulting body.

Writing in the context of racial discrimination, Hepple (2004) argues that such 'fourth generation equality laws' are required to tackle institutional forms of discrimination. Evaluations confirm the duties' potential to enhance accountability and transparency but point to an overly bureaucratic approach to implementation (Fredman, 2010). However, as Vickers (2011, pp 137–138) observes, 'the shortcomings of public duties identified thus far largely relate to the fact that implementation is not as effective as it might be, rather than taking the form of objections to the idea of mainstreaming equality ....'

The Equality Authority and the Irish Human Rights Commission (2004a) called for the enactment of a public sector equality duty in the Republic of Ireland, citing as support the equivalence provisions contained in the Belfast ('Good Friday') Agreement (O'Cinneide, 2005). Similar proposals have been put forward by the coalition of civil society groups and activists that operate as the Equality and Rights Alliance (2011a, 2011b). The Working Group on the Human Rights and Equality Commission (2012) has recommended the introduction of a modest statutory duty on public bodies to have due regard to equality and human rights. 'The purpose of the public sector equality and human rights duty is to ensure that public bodies reflect on and take action on these core values as part of their mainstream service' (Working Group on the Human Rights and Equality Commission, 2012, Chapter 3.34). It does not envisage an external monitoring or enforcement role. Driven by pragmatic concerns about the 'undue burden' and economic costs a more extensive duty would entail, it recommends that each public body should address relevant

---

[821] <http://www.equalityni.org/>.

human rights and equality issues in its strategic plan and report on compliance in its annual reports (Working Group on the Human Rights and Equality Commission, 2012, Chapter 3.42). Failure to comply could not be challenged in judicial review or other court proceedings (Working Group on the Human Rights and Equality Commission, 2012, Chapter 3.41). The IHREC's role 'should be that of facilitation and provision of supports, including guidelines for assessment of the human rights and equality issues that face public sector organisations and training for staff' (Working Group on the Human Rights and Equality Commission, 2012, Chapter 3.43). In this regard it could encourage the development of equality policies by public authorities and prepare tailored codes of practice (Working Group on the Human Rights and Equality Commission, 2012, Chapter 3.45). Operation of the duty should be reviewed after a period of three to five years. The review should assess the effectiveness of the duty and amongst other things consider whether there is a need to implement a formal review and monitoring mechanism (Working Group on the Human Rights and Equality Commission, 2012, Chapter 3.45). It remains to be seen whether the Working Group's suggestions are taken on board by the Oireachtas.

10.4 Third-Party Involvement in Litigation

The EU equality directives specify that organisations with a legitimate interest in ensuring compliance with equality law must be permitted to participate in complaints. For instance, article 7(2) of the Racial Equality Directive provides:

> Member States shall ensure that associations, organisations or other legal entities, which have, in accordance with the criteria laid down by their national law, a legitimate interest in ensuring that the provisions of this Directive are complied with, may engage, either on behalf or in support of the complainant, with his or her approval, in any judicial and/or administrative procedure provided for the enforcement of obligations under this Directive.[822]

---

[822] Recital 19 of the Race Directive states: 'Persons who have been subject to discrimination based on racial and ethnic origin should have adequate means of legal protection. To provide a more effective level of protection, associations or legal entities should also be empowered to engage, as the Member States so determine, either on behalf or in support of any victim, in proceedings, without prejudice to national rules of procedure concerning representation and defence before the courts.' See the virtually identically worded provisions in article 9(2) and recital 29 of the Framework Directive, as well as article 8(3) and recital 21 of the Gender Goods and Services Directive.

There is no definitive case law yet on the type of measures required and a variety of approaches have been adopted throughout the Union (Chopin, Cormack and Niessen, 2004; European Network of Legal Experts in the Non-Discrimination Field, 2005, pp 68–70; Fredman, 2009, pp 15–18). In a 2008 judgment the CJEU found that article 7 allowed, but did not require, national provisions enabling associations 'to bring legal or administrative proceedings … without acting in the name of a specific complainant or in the absence of an identifiable complainant.'[823] It went on to state that it is for the national court to assess whether domestic legislation allows such a possibility.

A complainant or respondent in an ESA case can authorise any individual or body to act as their representative.[824] However, NGOs or other entities like trade unions do not have the legal right to *initiate* an action. The Equality Authority was authorised to provide legal representation to persons taking cases and did so quite frequently, partly on a strategic impact basis (see Chapter 11.3.3). It was also empowered to refer general instances of discrimination. In the light of the CJEU finding just discussed, an equality body should be able to use such a power even where there is no actual victim of discrimination.

Across Europe specialised equality bodies and NGOs are involved in various strategic enforcement initiatives (Ammer et al., 2010; Cormack, 2004; European Roma Rights Centre, INTERIGHTS and the Migration Policy Group, 2004; Obura and Palmer, 2006). These approaches seek to maximise the impact of complaints pursued through the standard system of redress. Collaboration between equality bodies and civil society organisations is crucial (Ammer et al., 2010, pp 174–175; European Commission, 2006, 2009b; European Roma Rights Centre et al., 2004). In particular, NGOs can provide support for victims of discrimination (European Commission, 2006, pp 32–35). The Equality Authority consistently underlined the importance of community sector advocacy (2008b) and promoted its development through, for instance, setting up an accredited Advocacy Studies course in partnership with the Citizens Information Board and Sligo Institute of Technology.[825]

Given their role in securing workers' rights trade unions are frequent participants in cases taken under the EEA and other employment-related laws (O'Sullivan and MacMahon, 2010). In the case of the ESA there is no obvious equivalent to unions. NGOs have not tended to use the legislation in a concerted

---

[823] *Centrum voor Gelijkheid van Kansen en voor Racismebestrijding v Firma Feryn NV*, Case C-54/07, [2008] ECR 1-1587, at para 27.

[824] Section 25A. The Equality Tribunal has no power to veto the complainant's choice of representative: *Clare County Council v Director of Equality Investigations & Anor* [2011] IEHC 303, at para 6.6.

[825] See further <http://www.citizensinformationboard.ie/services/advocacy_services/accredited_advocacy_training_course.html>.

manner but often represent complainants in ESA proceedings.[826] The independent law centres, however, have begun to explore strategic casework as part of their broader public interest law mandate, with the Public Interest Law Alliance coordinating the development of educational and awareness-raising activities between civil society groups, universities and the legal profession. The Irish Traveller Movement's Law Centre engages in a range of initiatives designed to advance the human rights of the Traveller community and it has supported a number of critical ESA cases.[827] Such groups are likely to play an increasingly important role in the development of discrimination law.

In the course of an investigation if the Director of the Equality Tribunal considers it appropriate she or he may 'hear persons appearing to the Director to be interested'.[828] Consequently, NGOs and other interested third parties may be authorised to participate in proceedings by making submissions on relevant matters. To date this has occurred at the instigation of complainants. Such submissions differ from the usual type of evidence introduced by the parties, which will concern the facts of the case. Instead third parties tend to introduce material about the general social context. Representatives of the Irish Traveller Movement, for example, have been called as expert witnesses in cases to give information on the difficulties experienced by Travellers in gaining access to services and on other matters.[829] In a reasonable accommodation case the Tribunal heard expert testimony on the structure of Irish Sign Language and the need for suitably qualified interpreters.[830] Dr Pádraic Kenna, an expert on housing law, gave evidence before the Tribunal as to standard practice in landlord–tenant relations and the impact of evictions in a 2011 case.[831] Given the importance of sociological and statistical evidence to

---

[826] For instance, Disability Legal Resource represented the complainants in *Cementwala v Colbert, Winters Property Management & Crescent Green Ltd*, DEC-S2005-184/186 and *Wellard v Killester College*, DEC-S2008-024. The Free Legal Advice Centres have also supported a number of complainants: see, for example, *Reilly v Abbey Lodge, Celbridge*, DEC-S2002-122/123, *Two Complainants v Department of Education and Science*, DEC-S2003-042/043 and *Tsourova v Trinity College Dublin*, DEC-S2004-162. The Citizens Information Centre Sligo provided representation in *Sweeney v The Ship Inn, Sligo*, DEC-S2002-032. Traveller support groups frequently represent complainants, examples include *Collins v Kyle*, DEC-S2001-019, *O'Reilly v Dragon Inn*, DEC-S2002-017, and *Maughan v Options Store*, DEC-S2002-077.

[827] See <http://www.itmtrav.ie/keyissues/legalunit/>.

[828] Section 25(1).

[829] See, for example, *Reilly v The Licensee, the Foxhunter Pub, Lucan, Dublin*, DEC-S2003-026, and *Sweeney v Saehan Media Ireland Ltd*, DEC-E2003-017.

[830] *Regan v Old Bawn Community School*, DEC-S2010-043. See also *Surridge v Coláiste Bhríde School*, DEC-S2008-050.

[831] *McGreal v Clúid Housing*, DEC-S2011-004.

indirect discrimination cases, academics and NGOs could play an important role in the development of the law in that area (Chapter 4).

10.5 Other Avenues for Challenging Discrimination or Unfair Treatment

As noted above, public bodies are subject to an additional body of discrimination law that may cover incidents falling outside the material or personal scope of the ESA. The ECHR Act 2003 may be especially useful in this regard (Chapter 2.2; Chapter 2.7). Many of those laws are enforced through litigation before the courts, an option that is beyond the resources and capacity of most individuals. However, a wide range of alternative, inexpensive redress mechanisms are available to people who believe they have encountered unfair treatment in the course of dealing with public bodies. The Citizens Information Board (2009a) has published a useful guide to such enforcement and redress bodies, which can be accessed on its website, along with publications on the rights of specific groups.[832] This section outlines briefly the redress mechanisms operated by the Ombudsman and the Ombudsman for Children.

Discrimination encountered in the course of accessing many public services can be raised in a complaint to the Ombudsman (Feldman, 2006; Hogan and Morgan, 2010, Chapter 9).[833] The Ombudsman is not empowered to consider compliance with the ESA as such; rather she can seek to counter flawed decision making by public bodies and in so doing may apply discrimination law and human rights law more generally. The Ombudsman does not have jurisdiction over the substance of a given entitlement or benefit, her role is confined to ensuring that proper procedures are followed (O'Reilly, 2007, p 4).

The main bodies within the remit of the Ombudsman are government departments and offices, local authorities, the Health Service Executive (HSE), voluntary hospitals and voluntary agencies that provide services on behalf of the HSE, and An Post. Activities of third level colleges and universities are not covered. The Ombudsman can examine a complaint about an action taken by one of those bodies if someone has been adversely affected and the action was:

- Taken without proper authority

- Taken on irrelevant grounds

- The result of negligence or carelessness

- Based on incorrect or incomplete information

---

[832] See <http://www.citizensinformationboard.ie/publications/list/>.
[833] See <http://ombudsman.gov.ie/en/>.

- Improperly discriminatory

- Based on an undesirable administrative practice or

- Otherwise contrary to fair or sound administration[834]

Since the complaints process is conciliatory in nature, and no fees are payable, the system enjoys many advantages over litigation before the regular courts (Hogan and Morgan, 2010, pp 434–436). Following an investigation the Ombudsman may make a general recommendation to the body concerned. Recommendations issued are not legally binding, however. Where it appears to the Ombudsman that the response to a recommendation is not satisfactory she may make a special report on the matter to the Oireachtas.[835]

There is a degree of overlap between the public services covered by the ESA and matters that the Ombudsman may investigate, including, for example, public health services, social welfare payments,[836] local authority housing grants and the operation of housing lists. For instance, in 2007 the Equality Authority was involved in the resolution of a complaint about discrimination against single people in access to public housing. The Ombudsman investigated the same policy (Equality Authority, 2008a, pp 33–34). In a 2010 investigation into payment of the Mobility Allowance the Ombudsman drew on ESA principles (Chapter 3.3.2). An investigation into the operation of a waiver scheme for refuse collection charges concluded that the local authority scheme in question discriminated against a couple because they had a child (Office of the Ombudsman, 2011b, pp 68–69). Several of the Ombudsman's investigations concern access to services for disabled people, which is also a common feature of disability ground ESA complaints.[837]

As noted in Chapter 3, several ESA cases fail because there is no evidence of less favourable treatment on a ground. People who experience undue delays in accessing public services or who feel that they have not been dealt with fairly by a public body may have a better prospect of success before the Ombudsman where there is no evidence of discrimination as such. Indeed in a 2012 complaint about delays in processing applications for social welfare payments, the equality officer suggested that since systems failures as opposed to discrimination caused the delay, the matter should have been referred instead to the Ombudsman.[838]

---

[834] Section 4(2), Ombudsman Act 1980.

[835] Section 6(7), Ombudsman Act 1980.

[836] The Ombudsman may investigate issues that have been through the social welfare appeals system, on which see further <http://www.socialwelfareappeals.ie/>.

[837] See further <http://www.ombudsman.gov.ie/en/SampleCases/>.

[838] *Walczak v Minister for Social Protection*, DEC-S2012-011, para 4.10.

In relation to children, the free complaints service offered by the Ombudsman for Children (OCO) may offer an alternative route for resolving disputes with public bodies and schools.[839] The OCO is charged with safeguarding and promoting the rights and welfare of people under the age of eighteen.[840] As part of that role the OCO can investigate complaints about services provided to children by public bodies (including public hospitals).[841] Complaints may also be referred about schools in relation to the performance of their functions under section 9 of the Education Act 1998.[842] Section 9 covers matters like identifying and providing for the educational needs of all students, including those with a disability or other special educational needs, enabling access to student records, establishing and maintaining an admissions policy which provides for maximum accessibility to the school, and promoting equality of opportunity for male and female students. Exclusions to the OCO's mandate are set out in section 11 of the Ombudsman for Children Act 2002. For instance, the OCO cannot investigate complaints about any action taken in the administration of the law relating to asylum, immigration, naturalisation or citizenship. The operation of prisons or other places of detention (e.g. police stations)[843] are also excluded, with the exception of children's detention schools.

The OCO may commence an investigation on similar grounds to the Ombudsman: where a child has or may have been negatively affected by the action or inaction of a relevant body and there has been some form of maladministration, including an action that was 'improperly discriminatory'.[844] Education and health are consistently the largest complaint categories (Ombudsman for Children, 2011, p 37). The case studies of investigations published on the OCO's website cover matters like educational grants, school processes for handling complaints and bullying, access to education for non-Irish national children, supports for children in state care and local authority housing.[845] As with the general Ombudsman, the OCO aims to support the parties to arrive at a mutual understanding of the issues and to resolve the complaint informally. In her 2010 annual report the OCO noted that 'the Office has seen a positive response from public bodies at an early stage in the complaints process with a considerable number of complaints being resolved

---

[839] See generally <http://www.oco.ie/>.

[840] Section 7, Ombudsman for Children Act 2002.

[841] Guides to the complaints process are available here <http://www.oco.ie/publications/complaints-and-investigations.html>.

[842] Section 9, Ombudsman for Children Act 2002.

[843] The Garda Síochána Ombudsman Commission investigates complaints made by the public concerning the conduct of Gardaí, as well as cases referred to it by the Garda Commissioner. See further: <http://www.gardaombudsman.ie/>.

[844] See sections 8–10, Ombudsman for Children Act 2002.

[845] <http://www.oco.ie/complaints/case-studies.html>.

at that stage. This reflects a focus on the part of the Office to encourage the achievement of local redress between parties where it considers a good basis exists for this to occur' (Ombudsman for Children, 2011, p 36).

Finally, a number of other procedures may be used to challenge actions taken by schools (O'Mahony, 2009). Decisions to refuse enrolment, to expel a student or to suspend student for twenty or more days in any school year can be appealed to the Secretary General of the Department of Education and Skills.[846] Appeals are heard by an Appeals Committee established by the Minister, which is made up of three independent people with appropriate expertise and experience. Where attempts to resolve the matter through facilitation are not successful the Appeals Committee will re-hear the matter in full and may substitute its own judgment for that of a school's board of management.[847] A decision to suspend or exclude a student may implicate the various discrimination prohibitions set out in the ESA. In evaluating the school's decision an Appeals Committee may take into account 'the duties on schools or their boards imposed by or under any enactment', which would include its obligations under the ESA.[848] Schools have additional duties towards disabled children under the Education for Persons with Special Educational Needs Act 2004 (O'Mahony, 2006, 2009), but many relevant sections have yet to be commenced. It sets out a range of services that must be provided to children with special educational needs, reinforcing the reasonable accommodation duty under the ESA (Chapter 6.7). The services include assessments, education plans and support services. Implementation of those services is allocated to numerous bodies including two statutory bodies: the National Council for Special Education and the Special Education Appeals Board. The Appeals Board has yet to be established.[849]

10.6 Conclusion

At the beginning of the previous decade Irish anti-discrimination law was quite advanced in European terms. However, significant funding cuts and a failure to upgrade the compliance mechanisms means that it now compares poorly

---

[846] Section 29, Education Act 1998, as amended by section 4 of the Education (Miscellaneous Provisions) Act 2007. A guidance note and an appeals form are available on the Department's website: <http://www.education.ie/home/home.jsp?maincat=&pcategory=17216&ecategory=42741&sectionpage=12251&language=EN&link=link001&page=1&doc=38947>.

[847] *Board of Management of St. Molaga's National School v Secretary General of the Department of Education and Others* [2010] IESC 57.

[848] Section 29(4)(*g*), Education Act 1998.

[849] See further: <http://www.citizensinformation.ie/en/education/the_irish_education_system/special_education.html>.

to the Northern Irish system in particular. The establishment of the IHREC provides an opportunity to bolster the individual enforcement model with further proactive measures for tackling discrimination and advancing equality of opportunity. Legislating for fourth generation equality laws would be an important move in not only enhancing the effectiveness of the law but also in sending out a wider symbolic message about the causes of discrimination.

11

Equality Bodies

11.1 Introduction

From 1999 to 2012 the Equality Authority and the Equality Tribunal operated as two entirely distinct specialised equality bodies. These bodies formed a core strand of Ireland's equality and human rights infrastructure and their composition, structure and powers were shaped by international legal standards as well as indigenous practice. As noted in the previous chapter, the Tribunal, which hears and resolves discrimination law cases, is to be wound down. Its functions will be taken over by a new body called the Workplace Relations Commission (Department of Jobs, Enterprise and Innovation, 2012). The Equality Authority played a promotional, advisory and advocacy role in the field of equality of opportunity, in addition to enjoying some enforcement powers. From late 2012 the IHREC will carry out those functions in a revised form (Chapter 10.1; Chapter 11.3).

EU law has a relatively limited influence on the mandate and structure of equality bodies across the 27 member states.[850] While Union law on the substance of discrimination law is quite prescriptive, states are left far more discretion when it comes to enforcement mechanisms. Both the Racial Equality Directive[851] and the Gender Goods and Services Directive[852] do oblige member states to establish a specialised body to promote equal treatment on

---

[850] Two EU-level bodies were established in recent years: the European Institute for Gender Equality and the European Union Agency for Fundamental Rights. Effectively these bodies engage in research, compile reports on the status of human rights and gender equality within the Union, raise awareness (in collaboration with NGOs) and provide advice to EU institutions and the member states. Neither body has the power to legislate or hear complaints. See further: <http://www.eige.europa.eu/> and <http://www.fra.europa.eu/fraWebsite/home/home_en.htm>.

[851] Article 13 of Directive 2000/43/EC.

[852] Article 12 of Directive 2004/113/EC; see also article 20 of the Recast Directive (2006/54/EC).

the grounds covered by those instruments. However the standards required are vague and imprecise according to some commentators (Cormack, 2004; Moon, 2007, pp 887–891; Rorive, 2009a). At a minimum, the bodies should be in a position to furnish independent advice and assistance, conduct independent surveys and studies, and publish independent reports and recommendations (Moon, 2007, p 888).

Furthermore, the European Union has ratified and Ireland has signed the UN Convention on the Rights of Persons with Disabilities. Article 33 obliges the Government, upon ratification, to designate a framework with one or more independent mechanisms to 'promote, protect and monitor' compliance with the Convention. Either the IHREC or the National Disability Authority could operate as the 'independent' mechanism (Working Group on the Human Rights and Equality Commission, 2012, Chapter 3.32).

11.2 The Equality Tribunal

The Equality Tribunal is an independent, quasi-judicial forum for the resolution of complaints under the ESA and the EEA, as well as discrimination claims under the Pensions Acts 1990–2008. In operation since 1999, it comprises the Director of the Equality Tribunal, equality officers and equality mediation officers.[853] Cases are resolved either through mediation or through a process known as an investigation. Decisions issued are legally binding. As discussed further in Chapter 12, all hearings are conducted in private, no fees are payable and the procedures adopted are designed to facilitate self-representation.

Currently the Tribunal operates from sites in central Dublin and Portlaoise (Equality Tribunal, 2009a, p 7, 2010a, p 5). Hearings are held in Dublin and at various locations around the country (Equality Tribunal, 2010a, p 15).

The Tribunal and its proposed successor, the Workplace Relations Commission, are organs of the state for the purposes of the ECHR Act 2003 and so are obliged to carry out their functions in a manner that complies with the Convention.[854] In practice, this duty is most likely to impact on the time frame within which cases are processed, and other matters covered by the right to fair procedures under article 6 (Equality Tribunal 2007b, p 16). For many years the Equality Authority's annual reports referred to delays in the appointment of equality officers, the scheduling of hearings and the delivery of recommendations before the Equality Tribunal (e.g. Equality Authority, 2006b, p 15, 2007a, pp 18–20, 2008a, pp 25–26). In her contribution to the Tribunal's

---

[853] The Equality Tribunal was initially called the Office of the Director of Equality Investigations (ODEI). It took over the resolution of equality cases from the Labour Relations Commission.

[854] See sections 1 and 3 of the ECHR Act 2003.

Statement of Strategy 2008–2010 the former Director of the Tribunal noted that additional posts had been secured to enable the elimination of delays and that procedures would be revised accordingly (Equality Tribunal, 2007b). However, a significant increase in employment equality cases undermined the progress made. In 2011 three years was the expected time frame from embarking on an EEA case to completion (*Irish Times*, 2011b). The number of ESA cases declined in recent years and in 2010 were being heard within about one year (Woulfe, 2010, p 65).[855] Very ambitious time frames for processing and resolving cases are set out in the documentation concerning the proposed Workplace Relations Commission (Department of Jobs, Enterprise and Innovation, 2012).

Delay in processing an ESA claim before the Equality Tribunal was considered in *Kelly v The Equality Tribunal*.[856] Mr Kelly contended that the Tribunal had violated its statutory duty to act compatibly with article 6 of the European Convention on Human Rights. That duty is set out under section 3 of the ECHR Act 2003. Applying the test developed by the European Court of Human Rights, the High Court found that a delay of four years and six months was not unreasonable. Under the Convention the reasonableness of the length of proceedings is assessed with reference to the complexity of the case, the conduct of the applicant and of the relevant authorities, and the importance of what is at stake for the applicant in the litigation. Gilligan J took the view that 'on any interpretation of the factual events nothing of any significant importance could have been or be deemed to have been, at stake for the plaintiff'.[857] The complaint in question concerned access to a place on a third level course and the plaintiff pursued equivalent studies elsewhere. Other referrals under the ESA concern matters that have a profound impact on an individual's life and so the case may be distinguished on the facts. For example, in *Faulkner v St Ita's & St Joseph's School, Tralee*,[858] which addressed access to 'special needs' education, the equality officer commented, 'I believe that Mrs Faulkner and her son have suffered a serious injustice at the hands of St Ita's & St Joseph's School, Tralee and that a major opportunity to cater for her son's special educational needs has been lost.' In *Oršuš v Croatia*[859] the European Court of Human Rights found that article 6 was breached where a

---

[855] There was a 19 per cent drop in ESA complaints in 2009: <http://www.equalitytribunal. ie/Press-Releases-1/Press-Releases/2009-Annual-Statistics.17828.shortcut.html>.   There was a further 15 per cent reduction in 2010 (Equality Tribunal, 2011a, p 6).
[856] [2008] IEHC 112.
[857] *Kelly v The Equality Tribunal*, [2008] IEHC 112, para 58.
[858] DEC-S2006-037.
[859] *Oršuš v Croatia* (2009) 49 EHRR 26; this finding was subsequently upheld by the Grand Chamber of the Court: *Oršuš v Croatia* (2011) 52 EHRR 7. See also *Somjee v United Kingdom* (2003) 36 EHRR 16, in which a delay of approximately eight years in

case concerning segregation of Roma children in primary schools lasted for just under five years. In reaching that conclusion the Court placed particular emphasis on what was at stake for the applicants, namely their right to education (at para 48).

It appears that the Director endeavoured to expedite proceedings where there was an urgent dimension to the case. For instance, a complaint about admission to a secondary school was heard within four months of referral.[860]

All bodies that hear discrimination cases are also bound by the ESA, at least with respect to the exercise of those functions that are services within the meaning of section 2. The adjudication function of public bodies is not a service and so not open to challenge under the terms of the ESA.[861] However, the customer service aspects of their operations are covered (Chapter 2.4.4). In this context the reasonable accommodation duty is perhaps the most significant (see generally Chapter 6). Tribunal literature underlines its commitment to ensuring that services are accessible and take account of the different needs of participants in proceedings:

> The Tribunal provides modern and accessible offices and meeting rooms that fully meet with occupational, health and safety standards. The Tribunal has a range of technology, which improves accessibility and assists in delivering quality service and facilities to our staff and customers, including documents in Braille and audio format, full wheelchair access and sign language and other language interpretation when sought, and hearing rooms which are air-conditioned

---

hearing the applicant's claims of racial discrimination under UK employment law breached article 6(1).

[860] *Stokes v Christian Brothers' High School, Clonmel and Department of Education and Skills*, DEC-S2010-056. See also *Murray v Irish Life and Permanent TSB*, DEC-S2010-004.

[861] Discriminatory decision making or adjudication could, however, be challenged under the terms of the ECHR Act 2003 using article 14 in conjunction with article 6. An Australian equality body was found to have engaged in discrimination in *Oberoi v Human Rights and Equal Opportunity Commission* [2001] FMCA 34. Mr Oberoi referred a race discrimination complaint about the conduct of a conciliation officer who was dealing with a case before the Human Rights and Equal Opportunity Commission (HREOC). Another commission officer investigated the complaint and he reported that the complainant's perception of events was affected by his depression and therefore lacked credibility. When the case was dismissed Mr Oberoi lodged a further complaint alleging that the HREOC had discriminated against him. The magistrate held that Mr Oberoi had received less favourable treatment because of his disability. The assigned investigator had assumed that the complainant's credibility was compromised by a disability without any evidence that it had such an affect. A similar complaint would probably fall outside the scope of the ESA because assessing a person's credibility in the context of legal proceedings is an adjudicatory function. An ECHR challenge would be possible, however.

and equipped with 'deaftech' for hearing-impaired clients (Equality Tribunal, 2011a, p 13).

The Workplace Relations Commission will also be bound to ensure that its systems and procedures are accessible. As a public body it must comply with the accessibility obligations set out under the Disability Act 2005 (Citizens Information Board, 2009b; see further Chapter 6.8). Further guidance as to what is required may be available once the Circuit Court judgment in the appeal from *Fogarty v Employment Appeals Tribunal*[862] is delivered (Chapter 2.4.4).

11.3 The Equality Authority

11.3.1 Overview

The Equality Authority was set up under the Employment Equality Act 1998, and was formally established on 18 October 1999. It replaced the Employment Equality Agency and enjoyed a more extensive set of powers than its predecessor. It was charged with working towards the elimination of discrimination and promoting equality of opportunity in the spheres of employment and the provision of goods and services.[863] The Authority's major roles are outlined below.

In 2012 the Authority will merge with the Human Rights Commission to form a new Irish Human Rights and Equality Commission (IHREC). The recent history of funding for both bodies suggests that allocation of adequate resources will be contentious in the formation of the IHREC. The Authority's budget was drastically cut in Budget 2009 from approximately €5.9 million to €3.3 million, which represented a 43 per cent reduction (Equality and Rights Alliance, 2010, p 8). According to the Equality and Rights Alliance (2009), the Equality Authority's capacity to carry out the full range of its functions was severely compromised as a result. These concerns prompted Niall Crowley to resign his position as Chief Executive in December 2008 (*Irish Times*, 2008c). The severity of the cuts was criticised in a report on equality bodies commissioned by the European Commission (Ammer et al., 2010, p 142). Significantly, the UN Committee on the Elimination of Racial Discrimination expressed 'grave concern' over the 'disproportionate budget cuts' imposed on the Authority as well as on the Irish Human Rights Commission (United Nations Committee on the Elimination of Racial Discrimination, 2011, para 11). In response to a complaint lodged by the Equality and Rights Alliance the European Commission found that a budgetary cut alone was not sufficient to

---

[862] DEC-S2009-087.
[863] Section 39 EEA; section 39 ESA.

render Ireland liable to an action for breach of the Directives. However, it also noted that specialised bodies should be in a position to fulfil their mandate.[864]

In light of these considerations the Working Group on the Human Rights and Equality Commission (2012, Chapter 4.14) recommended that the legislation setting up the IHREC include a provision which states, 'The Commission shall be provided with sufficient resources to ensure that it can carry out each of its functions effectively.'

11.3.2 Promotion, Development and Research

As detailed in the Authority's annual reports, its development section engaged in a range of activities aimed at promoting equality of opportunity. For instance, it conducted equality reviews, which comprise equal opportunity audits and examinations of organisations' policies, practices and procedures.[865] The Authority had the power to either invite a particular business or group of businesses to conduct a review or instigate one itself (firms with fewer than 50 employees are exempt). A 'business' for these purposes includes all providers of goods and services regulated by the ESA, including educational establishments, accommodation providers and public sector bodies.[866] Depending on the outcome of the review an equality action plan might issue, suggesting or requiring the employer(s) or service provider(s) concerned to effect changes. An 'action plan is a programme of actions to be undertaken ... to further the promotion of equality of opportunity'.[867] Failure to comply could be referred to the ordinary courts.

A template was developed during 2000 and 2001 in consultation with representative community organisations, the Irish Business and Employers' Confederation (IBEC) and the Irish Congress of Trade Unions (ICTU) (Equality Authority, 2001, p 56). Several reviews were undertaken every year on a cooperative basis with large-scale employers in the private and public sectors. In conjunction with teachers, the Authority developed a template for conducting equal status reviews in primary schools (Equality Authority, 2008b, p 94, 2009b, p 13). Guidelines on embedding equality in second level school development planning were published in 2010 (Equality Authority and School Development Planning Initiative, 2010). These initiatives should dovetail well with other work conducted on the duties of schools, which include a tailored publication on the ESA (Equality Authority, 2005c) that has been circulated

---

[864] See further: <http://eracampaign.org/get-informed>.
[865] See Part VI EEA.
[866] Matters concerning members and access to membership of registered clubs are exempt from equality reviews: section 69(7) EEA.
[867] Section 69(2) EEA.

to all primary and second level educational institutions (Crowley, 2006, pp 45–46). A further significant measure is the initiative against homophobic bullying, which was originally developed in partnership with the youth NGO BeLonGTo (Equality Authority, 2010b, p 58). Guidelines for conducting equality impact assessments in the vocational education sector were produced in 2007 and were then implemented on a pilot basis by County Donegal VEC (Equality Authority, 2009b, pp 12–13).

A Public Sector Equality Learning Network, which supports state and semi-state bodies to share expertise and develop good practice, was established in 2007. In 2009 it developed an equal status training module and an equality screening toolkit, which were piloted the following year (Equality Authority, 2010b, pp 57–58). These and other templates for embedding equality in public service provision are collated in two recent publications, which draw on implementation lessons and should be a significant resource for public sector organisations (Equality Authority, 2011b, 2011c). As noted in Chapter 7, equal status policies, and in particular complaints systems, are crucially important for private sector bodies in meeting their ESA obligations. A template for devising and implementing such policies is available in a publication entitled *Guidelines for Equal Status Policies in Enterprises* (Equality Authority, 2005d).

Reasonable accommodation for disabled people is the subject of several good practice publications and associated projects (e.g. An Chomhairle Leabharlanna and Equality Authority, 2003; RGDATA and Equality Authority, 2004).[868] For example, in 2008 the Irish Pharmacy Union and the Irish League of Credit Unions were involved in such projects (Equality Authority, 2009b, p 45). A wide range of stakeholders have contributed to good practice guidelines on the age ground, spanning sectors such as hospitality, transport and leisure (e.g. Equality Authority, 2010c; Equality Authority and National Youth Council of Ireland, 2008; McGivern, 2007). Other awareness raising and educational measures include initiatives which have run over consecutive years such as Traveller Focus Week, Anti-Racism Workplace Week and Say No to Ageism Week.

The Equality Authority was charged with keeping the ESA and several employment laws including the EEA under review and where appropriate making proposals for its amendment. It also had the power to establish advisory committees and to prepare draft codes of practice.[869] The only code drawn up was the Sexual Harassment and Harassment at Work Code of Practice (Chapter 7.2.2.3). The research section undertook and commissioned

---

[868] RGDATA is a body that represents the independent retail grocery sector in Ireland. See further: <http://www.rgdata.ie/>.
[869] Section 56 EEA.

research, which has contributed significantly to understanding the causes and effects of inequality within Ireland.[870] It produced a substantial body of publications that are available on the Authority's website. Many of the published studies address matters of concern across all the discriminatory grounds while others highlight issues of especial concern to some disadvantaged groups. For example, a particularly innovative methodology involving situation testing was used in a recent study to explore the extent of discrimination based on ethnic or national origins in recruitment processes (McGinnity, Nelson, Lunn and Quinn, 2009, 2010). Five hundred equivalent CVs were sent by the researchers in response to advertised vacancies for jobs in administration, finance and retail sales. Candidates with Irish names are over twice as likely to be asked to attend an interview as are candidates with an African, Asian or German name.[871]

11.3.3 Information, Legal Advice and Representation

The Equality Authority was tasked with providing information to the public on the ESA and several employment laws including the EEA.[872] It raised awareness of equality legislation and disseminated information on the rights and responsibilities it entails through various routes, including its website and responses to calls to the Public Information Centre (Equality Authority, 2008b, pp 73–79, 2009a, pp 12–13, 2010b, pp 12–21). Under the Government decentralisation programme the Public Information Centre was relocated to Roscrea in 2007. The Working Group on the Human Rights and Equality Commission (2012, Chapter 4.28–4.29) has recommended that the offices in Roscrea be closed and staff relocated to the single Dublin-based office that should house the IHREC.

The Public Information Centre operated in tandem with the Equality Authority's legal division. People taking proceedings under the EEA, the ESA or the Intoxicating Liquor Act 2003 could apply to the Equality Authority for assistance.[873] Individuals who contacted the Authority and requested assistance were informed of the applicable criteria and were informed at the outset whether their complaint qualified. If it did, 'preliminary assistance'

---

[870] Section 57 EEA.

[871] Rorive (2006, p 33) explains that situation testing entails 'setting up a situation, a sort of role play, where a person is placed in a position to commit discrimination without suspecting that he or she is being observed. This person is presented with fictional "candidates", some of whom possess a characteristic that may incite discriminatory behaviour. Observers aim to compare his or her attitude towards people bearing this characteristic compared to others without it.' See further Rorive (2009b) and Moon (2007, pp 909–914).

[872] Section 39 EEA.

[873] Section 67 EEA.

was authorised. The person's file was usually then assigned to a solicitor who entered into correspondence with the respondent and then proceeded to process an application for 'substantial assistance' (Equality Authority, 2011a, p 54).

The Equality Authority's in-house legal section worked on a substantial number of case files in any given year (e.g. Equality Authority, 2010b, pp 22–41, 2011a, pp 26–55). In 2010, for instance, 116 new case files were opened (Equality Authority, 2011a, p 4). The range and depth of assistance provided in any given case depended on several factors. Many complaints were resolved through an agreed settlement between the parties with the assistance of the Authority's solicitors. Complainants often decided to withdraw their complaint upon receipt of advice that the case was unlikely to succeed, because of the length of time it would take to reach a resolution or because of the possibility of incurring costs (Equality Authority, 2011a, pp 26–27). Not all people, therefore, who received preliminary assistance wanted or needed to apply for substantial assistance.

Given the limits on available resources it was not possible to provide substantial assistance to everyone who qualified for preliminary assistance (Equality Authority, 2011a, p 54). It provided such assistance according to criteria that were set down by the Board of the Equality Authority.[874] In line with the relevant legislative provision, a complaint was supported partly on the basis of its perceived strategic significance.[875] These factors were balanced with assistance criteria that took account of the particular circumstances of the complainant, including the complexity of the case, access to alternative supports (such as a trade union) and the relationship between the applicant and respondent. Even a cursory examination of the Tribunal's published decisions reveals that the Equality Authority has represented complainants in many of the ground-breaking cases under the ESA and the EEA. In 2011, for example, they represented Mr McGreal in establishing a case of age discrimination by a provider of housing to older people[876] and assisted the complainant in the first proven case of discrimination against a transsexual person.[877] Clearly the substantial expertise built up by the Authority's legal section has shaped the contours of Irish discrimination law and has enabled particularly vulnerable individuals to vindicate their rights.

According to the Working Group on the Human Rights and Equality Commission (2012, Chapter 3.13) the Equality Authority's legal assistance function will transfer fully to the IHREC. It notes that the Public Information Centre 'does more than provide information on entitlements' and that it

---

[874] <http://www.equality.ie/en/Information/Criteria-for-Representation/>.
[875] Section 67 EEA.
[876] *McGreal v Clúid Housing*, DEC-S2011-004.
[877] *Hannon v First Direct Logistics Limited*, DEC-E2011-066.

'reports into the Legal section with details of cases that may be suitable for assistance/representation' (Working Group on the Human Rights and Equality Commission, 2012, Chapter 4.35). For that reason it suggests that the Centre should report to the head of a legal claims division in the IHREC. However, the report also implies that the assistance criteria ought to be revised to emphasis more strongly the strategic value of cases (Chapter 3.10–3.11). Any revision of the criteria will be a matter for the incoming Commissioners.

11.3.4 Enforcement

Irish discrimination law granted the Equality Authority quite a significant role in enforcement but, as discussed further below, some of its powers were never invoked.

This section outlines the Authority's powers to take legal action, to conduct equality reviews and to undertake inquiries.

As noted above, the Authority played a crucial role in supporting complaints taken by individuals (Chapter 11.3.3). It was also able to commence litigation on its own initiative, a power enjoyed by counterparts in some other jurisdictions (Ammer et al., 2010; McColgan, 2005, p 357; Obura and Palmer, 2006). In defined circumstances the Equality Authority could refer discriminatory practices or instances of discrimination against an individual to the Director of the Equality Tribunal.[878] Referrals of individual cases could take place where it was not reasonable to expect the potential complainant to make such a reference. One such reference was made under the ESA in 2004 (Equality Authority, 2005b, p 58) but it is not clear whether the Tribunal ultimately heard the case. A complaint referred against Aer Lingus and AIG Insurance was settled prior to hearing in 2007 (Equality Authority 2008a, pp 45–46).

The Equality Authority enjoyed exclusive legal standing in relation to discriminatory advertising. Under section 12 of the ESA a person shall not publish or display, or cause to be published or displayed, an advertisement that indicates an intention to engage in prohibited conduct or might reasonably be understood as indicating such an intention. 'Advertisement' is widely defined to include 'every form of advertisement, whether to the public or not and whether in a newspaper or other publication, on television or radio or by display of a notice or by any other means …'.[879] Bolger and Kimber (2000,

---

[878] Section 23. Section 38A(3) applies the same principles on the burden of proof to complaints that are referred by the Equality Authority: 'Where, in any proceedings arising from a reference of a matter by the Authority to the Director under section 23(1), facts are established by or on behalf of the Authority from which it may be presumed that prohibited conduct or a contravention mentioned in that provision has occurred, it is for the respondent to prove the contrary.'

[879] Section 12(3).

p 454) describe the ban on discriminatory advertising as 'puzzling' because it is aimed at material which indicates an *intention* to discriminate or harass.

The Authority referred a complaint against Ryanair in 2000 (Crowley, 2006, pp 78–79).[880] That case concerned discriminatory advertising in employment and so was dealt with under the equivalent provision to section 12 under the EEA.[881] The Tribunal found that the use of the word 'young' as a job require-ment in an employment advertisement amounted to discrimination on the age ground. The Equality Authority's annual reports detail interventions it has taken with respect to discriminatory advertising (e.g. Equality Author-ity, 2008b, pp 48–50, 2009b, pp 36–37, 2010b, p 26, 2011a, pp 38–39). The age, gender, marital status and race grounds tend to predominate. Examples of advertisements that could violate section 12 would include a letting agent describing premises as unsuitable for students (indirect discrimination on the age ground) or families with young children (family status ground). Members of the public may lodge complaints about discriminatory advertising with the Advertising Standards Authority for Ireland.[882]

In common with other equality bodies across Europe, the Equality Author-ity had statutory powers that facilitated enforcement of discrimination law beyond the context of an individual case (Ammer et al., 2010, pp 97–98; Barry, 2003; McColgan, 2005, pp 357–407; White, 2006). Significantly, such powers mean that the burden of enforcement is not placed exclusively on people who have experienced discriminatory treatment. Furthermore, since an organisa-tion or an entire service provision sector may be tackled, there is potential for effecting change on a large scale.

As discussed above, the Authority could conduct an equality review of an organisation with more than 50 employees, without being invited to do so (Chapter 11.3.2).[883] The review could result in an action plan designed to elim-inate discriminatory practices and align the organisation fully with its legal obligations. The Equality Authority was also empowered to conduct inquiries for any purpose connected with its functions, either on its own initiative or at the request of the Minister for Justice.[884] Recommendations could ensue and if necessary a non-discrimination notice obliging the person(s) in default to remedy the identified breaches of anti-discrimination law. The statutory provi-sions appeared to empower the Authority to carry out both 'named person' inquiries (i.e. ones directed at a specified employer or service provider) and

---

[880] *The Equality Authority v Ryanair*, DEC-E2000-014; in *Burke v FÁS* [2004] ELR 332 the Labour Court confirmed that only the Equality Authority could make complaints about advertisements.

[881] Section 10 EEA.

[882] See further: <http://www.asai.ie/>.

[883] See Part VI EEA.

[884] Sections 58–66 EEA.

general inquiries (White, 2006). General inquiries could address a particular sector or issue. Neither form was undertaken but implementation issues were explored during 2007 (Equality Authority, 2008b, p 101). Barry (2003, p 426) observes that the 'carrying out of an inquiry would require substantial resources. It is a particularly useful power in situations where claimants may be very vulnerable or where there is a dearth of information.' Experience from other jurisdictions suggests that apart from resource constraints, 'named person' inquiries have often been subject to successful and lengthy court challenges (Hepple, 2011, pp 149–154; McColgan, 2005, pp 357–407). The past decade witnessed renewed use of general investigations and inquiries by the UK equality bodies (O'Brien, 2005; White, 2006) and the Equality and Human Rights Commission, which commenced work in 2007 (Spencer, 2008). For example, in 2009 the EHRC conducted inquiries into race discrimination in the construction industry and the gender pay gap within the finance sector (Equality and Human Rights Commission, 2009a, 2009b).

One of the stated goals of the Equality Authority (2006c, p 25) under its third strategic plan was to 'test the full range of functions and powers' it enjoys 'in order to assess and identify the most effective mix of these for the implementation of its mandate'. It alluded to conducting a small number of inquiries and equality reviews (Equality Authority, 2006c). The subsequent plan, which ran from 2009 to 2011, did not refer to inquiries or reviews (Equality Authority, 2009c), which is perhaps to be expected given the significant cuts to its funding over that period. The plan did, however, list taking 'cases under the equality legislation in the name of the Equality Authority as appropriate', as one of its strategic objectives (Equality Authority, 2009c, p 14).

11.4 Conclusion

We will see the establishment of a new equality body in 2012. According to the Working Group on the Human Rights and Equality Commission (2012), the new IHREC should be equipped with an extensive range of powers that will enable it to foster respect for equality and human rights. The Working Group recommended that the current powers and functions exercised by both the Equality Authority and the Human Rights Commission should be retained in a modified form and strengthened in some respects. The envisaged compliance and enforcement powers ought to include the ability to produce good practice guidelines and research, to issue codes of practice, to carry out equality reviews, to take various forms of legal action and to conduct inquiries. It remains to be seen whether this advice is followed and in particular whether the IHREC will be furnished with sufficient resources to carry out its mandate.

12

The Individual Complaint

12.1 Introduction

This chapter examines the processes involved in making an individual complaint under the ESA. It first explains which cases are currently heard by the Equality Tribunal and briefly examines the role of the courts. The various steps involved in referring a complaint are then examined. The remainder of the chapter deals with what happens during and after a hearing.

12.2 Forum of Redress

12.2.1 Introduction

The Equality Tribunal is the primary forum for hearing and determining discrimination complaints under the ESA.[885]

As Figure 1 illustrates, the ordinary courts also play a significant role in enforcement, by hearing some cases at first instance and also dealing with appeals.

The Tribunal will continue to function until the new employment rights infrastructure is put in place. Legislation providing for the amalgamation of five employment rights bodies will apparently be published in autumn 2012 (Department of Jobs, Enterprise and Innovation, 2012). Yet, the process of

---

[885] At present, it is not clear whether the ESA can be pleaded at first instance outside the Tribunal system. According to the High Court in *Doherty v South Dublin County Council* [2007] 2 IR 696 and in *Prendergast v The Higher Education Authority* [2009] 1 ILRM 4, a case under the ESA cannot be made at first instance before the ordinary courts; instead such claims must be lodged with the Equality Tribunal (apart from in the limited situations outlined in Chapter 12.2). However, in other cases courts have examined whether the Acts were breached: *Clare (A Minor) v Minister for Education and Science and Others* [2004] IEHC 350 and *O'Donnell (a minor) & Ors v South Dublin County Council* [2007] IEHC 204.

Figure 1: Forum of Redress

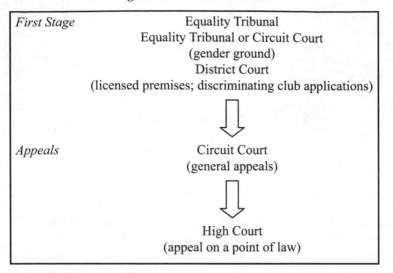

First Stage	Equality Tribunal
	Equality Tribunal or Circuit Court
	(gender ground)
	District Court
	(licensed premises; discriminating club applications)
	⇩
Appeals	Circuit Court
	(general appeals)
	⇩
	High Court
	(appeal on a point of law)

winding down the Tribunal could take a considerable period of time given the need to process the complaints that are currently in the system.

A new body, the Workplace Relations Commission (WRC), will assume responsibility for dealing with EEA cases at first instance. A revised Labour Court will hear appeals from the WRC. The current reform blueprint does not address what will happen to ESA complaints (Department of Jobs, Enterprise and Innovation, 2012). Two options appear feasible. The first and most preferable option is for the WRC and Labour Court to also deal with ESA cases. It is also possible that the District Court could be designated as the primary forum. For reasons elaborated upon in the following section, it is submitted that the District Court is not a suitable venue for discrimination cases. Staff of the Equality Tribunal (2011b, p 2) have put forward cogent arguments as to why the WRC should continue its work on equal status matters:

1. Certain areas, such as vocational education, are covered by both Employment Equality and Equal Status legislation.

2. Both [A]cts are governed by a single EU directive, the [R]acial [E]quality [D]irective[,] and other EU directives.

3. Both Acts are intertwined. It would be a complex process to disentangle them. To leave them within the same jurisdiction would minimise the extent of legislative change required.

4. Disputes about access to goods and services, which is what the Equal Status Act is about, would be within the ambit of the Department of Jobs, Enterprise and Innovation.

5. The Equality Tribunal has 11 years' experience of interpreting the Equal Status Acts.

6. There is no obvious alternative informal forum.

7. Equal Status cases are a small proportion of the total case load of the Equality Tribunal.

Civil society groups have also argued that the WRC would be preferable to the District Court, pointing especially to the specialised knowledge required to apply discrimination law, and the benefits of an informal redress system for unrepresented complainants (Equality and Rights Alliance, 2011c; Irish Council for Civil Liberties, 2011).

12.2.2 The District Court

Registered clubs are subject to specific rules under the ESA as regards applications for membership and the treatment of club members (Chapter 9). The Equality Tribunal does not deal with alleged discrimination in relation to those matters. Instead the appropriate course of action is to apply to the District Court for a determination that the club is a 'discriminating club' (Chapter 9).[886]

From 2004 discrimination claims concerning incidents that took place on or at the point of entry to licensed premises *must* also be brought before the District Court.[887] This has resulted in a decline in the number of cases taken against such service providers (Equality Authority, 2008b, pp 55–56).[888]

---

[886] Section 8(3) ESA.

[887] Section 19, Intoxicating Liquor Act 2003.

[888] The Council of Europe advised the Irish Government to 'monitor the impact of the recent changes to the complaint mechanisms for non-discrimination cases so as to ensure that they do not harm the accessibility or effectiveness of the remedies available and ensure that the structures concerned are adequately resourced' (Committee of Ministers, 2007, p 2). In a subsequent report the Government maintained that the Intoxicating Liquor Act was operating as an effective redress mechanism (Council of Europe, Secretariat of the Framework Convention for the Protection of National Minorities, 2011). However, as the Irish Council for Civil Liberties (2011) points out, much of the evidence relied upon in support of that claim is not robust. Only a few cases now proceed annually to a full hearing before the District Court and no qualitative data about people's experience of using the Court was provided.

Licensed premises include most obviously pubs, but also registered clubs,[889] hotels and many restaurants. Not all incidents concerning such premises are dealt with by the District Court. First, the alleged discrimination must have occurred on or at the point of entry to the premises. As a result cases that involve dealings with a hotel, pub or a restaurant that occur over the phone, for instance, would not be covered.[890] Nor would incidents that take place in a part of a hotel or club that is not covered by the licence.[891] Second, where the alleged discrimination concerned the provision of accommodation (including ceasing to provide accommodation) or any related services or amenities, the Tribunal retains jurisdiction.[892] So, for example, a person who alleges that they were harassed when checking into a hotel for an overnight stay should refer a complaint to the Equality Tribunal.

The transfer of jurisdiction to the District Court for some cases of discrimination has introduced considerable complexity for lay litigants. Obviously, initiating a court case poses much greater difficulties than completing the user-friendly forms developed by the Equality Tribunal. The Tribunal forms contain fields under which complainants (and respondents) enter information relevant to the complaint. Forms are processed centrally by the Tribunal and the equality officer assigned to the case corresponds directly with the parties. It seems that similar processes and forms will be used by the Workplace Relations Commission, which should assume responsibility for ESA cases when the relevant laws come into force (Department of Jobs, Enterprise and Innovation, 2012).[893] By contrast, proceedings before the District Court have to be initiated using a document called a 'civil summons', for which a €22 fee must be paid.[894] The appropriate District Court is the one in which the licensed premises is situated.[895] A person who believes that they have experienced discrimination while travelling or on holiday, therefore, faces a significant hurdle in lodging

---

[889] Section 23 of the Intoxicating Liquor Act 2003 applies the provision on the jurisdiction of the District Court (i.e. section 19) to registered clubs. Registered clubs do not usually fall within the definition of licensed premises.

[890] See *Ward v Menlo Park Hotel*, DEC-S2011-042.

[891] See *McGuffin and Harte v Eyre Square Hotel*, DEC-S2008-051, para 5.10.

[892] Section 19(1) of the Intoxicating Liquor Act 2003.

[893] A form for making an employment complaint is already in use and can be downloaded from the website of the Workplace Relations Commission: <http://www.workplacerelations.ie/en/services/howtomakeacomplaint/>.

[894] The procedures and relevant forms are set out in the District Court Rules: District Court (Equal Status Act 2000) Rules 2006 (SI 161/2006). See also: <http://www.courts.ie/rules.nsf/lookuppagelink/District%20Court%20Rules%20Index>. Further information on the processes involved is available from the website of the Citizens Information Board: <http://www.citizensinformation.ie/en/justice/civil_law/>. The current fees for District Court proceedings are set out in the District Court (Fees) Order 2012 (SI 108/ 2012).

[895] Section 24, Intoxicating Liquor Act 2003.

a complaint with the appropriate court office. Persons who wish to lodge a complaint on behalf of a child have to fill out an authorisation form and lodge it with the clerk of the District Court along with the civil summons.[896]

Furthermore, with some narrow exceptions, court hearings are not heard in private (Chapter 12.5.2). This may act as a considerable deterrent to people who are concerned about the publicity a case may generate. The option of resolving a case through mediation is not available (Chapter 12.4) and costs may be awarded against the losing party (Chapter 12.5.3). Both complainants and respondents are therefore compelled to engage in an adversarial and potentially expensive process. For people who do pursue a case before the District Court the Citizens Information Board (2009a, p 15) advises, 'People quite often appear in the District Court without a solicitor or barrister. If you want to start an action in the District Court you can go along to the Clerk of the Court and you will be told how to go about it.'

A 2011 case illustrates further technical difficulties faced by complainants.[897] Two men argued that their gym membership was terminated when it was discovered that they were members of the Travelling community. During the Tribunal's investigation of the complaint, however, it emerged that the respondent publican's licence covered an extensive area including the gym. As a result the gym was a licensed premise and so the case could not proceed before the Tribunal.

A successful discrimination case against a licensed premise can lead to an award of compensation up to a maximum amount of €6,348.69. The District Court judge may also order the licensee to take 'a course of action' or make an order for temporary closure of the premises.[898] Where an order has been made under subsection (3) any person may make an objection, related to the prohibited conduct concerned, to the renewal of the licence.[899]

12.2.3 The Circuit Court and High Court

Claims on the gender ground are treated exceptionally: since 2008 they may be brought before either the Tribunal or the Circuit Court.[900] The distinct treatment of that ground is due to CJEU judgments concerning levels of awards and the right to an effective judicial process under article 6 of the Equal Treatment Directive (see further Chapter 12.6).

---

[896] The relevant District Court rules can be viewed here: <http://www.courts.ie/rules.nsf/pagescurrent/90C150A9B632EB4480256D2B0046A08B?opendocument&l=en>.

[897] *Dunne v Planet Health Club*, DEC-S2011-018.

[898] Section 19(3) of the Intoxicating Liquor Act 2003.

[899] Section 19(10) of the Intoxicating Liquor Act 2003.

[900] Section 21 ESA.

The regular court system also hears appeals from first instance decisions. A general right of appeal against decisions of the Equality Tribunal or the District Court lies to the Circuit Court and a further appeal on a point of law can be brought before the High Court.[901] Regular appeals involve a full re-hearing of law and fact before the Circuit Court.[902] Appeals on a point of law are more limited in scope and will generally rely on the facts as established by the original body. The appeal will instead rest on arguments about how a particular legal provision has been applied or interpreted.[903] Parties to a case also have the option of applying for judicial review. According to the Supreme Court the appropriate procedure and remedy is judicial review, as opposed to a statutory appeal on a point of law, 'where the method or manner by which the decision is reached is attacked rather than the actual decision itself'.[904]

12.3 Referring a Complaint

12.3.1 Introduction

A person who believes they have been discriminated against when accessing goods or services is obliged to notify the service provider in writing of their intention to seek redress under the ESA. This notification must be sent to the service provider within two months of the incident in question. Chapter 12.3.4 discusses the notification process in detail. Following that process the individual may decide to refer a complaint to the Equality Tribunal by filling out the relevant form.[905] The form is available on request from the Tribunal and can also be downloaded from its website. A complaint that is referred in another written format will still be valid since the forms are administrative rather than statutory in nature.[906]

---

[901] Section 28. Appeals against District Court orders concerning registered clubs are dealt with in section 8(8) of the ESA. In relation to licensed premises see section 19(8) of the Intoxicating Liquor Act 2003.

[902] The required procedures and forms are set out in the Circuit Court Rules (Equal Status Acts 2000 to 2004) 2006 (SI 349/2006).

[903] The scope of an appeal on a point of law under parallel employment equality provisions has been considered in a number of cases. In *National University of Ireland, Cork v Ahern* [2005] 2 IR 577 the Supreme Court held that, although findings of fact must be accepted by the High Court on appeal, that court could still examine the basis upon which those facts were found: the relevance or admissibility of the matters relied on in determining the facts were questions of law. See also *Calor Teoranta v McCarthy* [2009] ELR 281.

[904] *Faulkner v Minister for Industry and Commerce* [1997] ELR 106, per O'Flaherty J at p 111.

[905] See generally the 'Guide to Procedures in Equal Status Cases' page on the Equality Tribunal's website: <http://www.equalitytribunal.ie/Equal_Status_/Guide-to-Procedures/>.

[906] See, for example, *A Female Employee v A Building Products Company*, DEC-E2007-036

12.3.2 Locus Standi

Under section 21 a person who claims that prohibited conduct has been directed against him or her may seek redress by referring a case to the Tribunal.[907] Someone who is not directly affected by alleged discriminatory treatment has no legal standing (or *locus standi*) and so cannot take a case in place of persons who may be so affected. But there are some limited exceptions. In relation to children the general rules on legal capacity apply. An adult such as a parent can lodge a complaint on behalf of a child. A person who does so is known as a 'next friend'. Additionally, section 20 allows a parent, guardian or other person acting in place of a parent to refer a claim on behalf of a person who is unable do so effectively, by reason of an intellectual or psychological disability.[908] Finally, where it is not reasonable to expect a potential complainant to take a case before the Tribunal, the Equality Authority can do so (Chapter 11.3.4).

A man who complained of discriminatory treatment could not establish that he had legal standing under the ESA in the 2009 case of *A Complainant v A Local Authority*.[909] The complaint concerned a clause in a tenancy agreement signed by a member of the man's extended family, which stipulated that no member of the Traveller community could visit or live in the house. However, because the complainant was not a service recipient but just a visitor to the house there was no legal relationship between him and the local authority. He could, therefore, not seek redress under the Acts.

In *Gloria (Ireland's Lesbian and Gay Choir) v Cork International Choral Festival Ltd*[910] the Equality Tribunal found that Gloria, as an unincorporated association of persons, did not have *locus standi*. A claim of direct

---

and *Kingspan Building Products v A Worker* (REE/02/01; EET/024, 11 April 2002).

[907] A cause of action under the ESA survives a person's death and so may be pursued by the deceased's estate: *Hegarty v Area Development Management Ltd*, DEC-S2009-004, paras 4.1–4.3. The equality officer accorded persuasive weight to the UK case of *Harris v Lewisham & Guy's Mental Hospital Health NHS Trust* [2000] 3 ALL ER 769. He found that a discrimination complaint was a 'cause of action' within the meaning of section 7(1) of the Civil Liability Act 1961 which provides, 'On the death of a person on or after the date of the passing of this Act all causes of action (other than excepted causes of action) vested in him shall survive for the benefit of his estate.' See also *Hendrick v National Learning Network t/a Roslyn Park College*, DEC-S2009-013, and the employment case of *Ibidunni v Boston Scientific (Ireland) Limited* [2011] ELR 158.

[908] See, for example, *Ms A (on behalf of her sister Ms B) v Aer Lingus*, DEC-S2009-038, and *Mrs X (on behalf of her daughter, Ms Y) v The Minister for Social & Family Affairs*, DEC-S2009-039. This change was effected under the Equality Act 2004. See the discussion of the pre-2004 Act position in *A Complainant v FÁS*, DEC-E2003-029.

[909] DEC-S2009-059.

[910] DEC-S2008-078.

discrimination on the sexual orientation ground was referred when the respondent had removed the description of Gloria as Ireland's gay and lesbian choir from promotional material for the festival in question. Having considered several provisions in detail and various principles of interpretation, the equality officer concluded:

> Whilst the term 'person' is usually interpreted broadly to include corporate and unincorporated bodies, I am satisfied that a contrary intention is evident from the Equal Status Acts given the manner in which the discriminatory grounds are set out and the particular definition of 'person' as contained in the Acts. I am therefore of the view that the legislative intent in this regard was to protect individuals and not bodies from discrimination (para 5.5).[911]

The net effect of the decision is that only individual persons can act as complainants under the ESA, while potential respondents may include unincorporated associations, public bodies, individuals and legal persons such as corporations.[912]

There is no provision in Irish anti-discrimination law for class actions but complainants can refer a single grouped case encompassing individual claims.[913] In a grouped case a complaint must be referred by each person involved and a decision is issued in respect of every complaint (e.g. where all the complainants are denied access to the same service on the same occasion). Class actions allow a representative number of individuals to take a case on behalf of a wider group of people against a single defendant where their cases are related or similar (Fredman, 2011, p 285).

---

[911] The finding in *Gloria* appears to be in line with the intention of the Oireachtas, see 162 *Seanad Debates* Cols 1647–1654. See the decision of the Federal Court of Australia in *Access For All Alliance (Hervey Bay) Inc. v Hervey Bay City Council* [2007] FCA 615.

[912] Section 2(1) ESA provides as follows: '"person", as that term is used in or in relation to any provision of this Act that prohibits that person from discriminating or from committing any other act or that requires a person to comply with a provision of this Act or regulations made under it, includes an organisation, public body or other entity …'. See *McCall v Area Development Management Ltd*, DEC-S2007-058.

[913] See, for example, *McCann, Collins and 31 Others v Eircom Ltd*, DEC-S2003-076/108; *Mongans v Clare County Council*, DEC-S2008-039, para 7.17; and *McCarthy v Grooveyard Ltd*, DEC-S2009-069. The High Court ruled out use of class actions in the employment case of *Verbatim Ltd v Duffy and Others* [1994] ELR 159. See also the decisions of the Tribunal in *Johnson and Sixty-Five Others v Tesco Ireland Limited*, DEC-E2001-024, and *Mongans v Clare County Council*, DEC-S2006-087.

12.3.3 Time Limits

A complaint must be referred to the Tribunal within six months of the last alleged incident or the most recent occurrence in a chain of incidents.[914] Before that referral, the complainant must also notify the service provider of their intention to take an ESA case. Notification must be sent within two months of the alleged discriminatory treatment. Before looking at notification in more detail (Chapter 12.3.4), this section examines when the time limits run from.

Not all discrimination involves one-off events like denial of access to a shop. Many complainants will experience discriminatory treatment in the course of an ongoing relationship, such as renting accommodation, or in the context of an arrangement with a service provider like a contract. In such cases, the time runs from the 'most recent' or 'last' occurrence of prohibited conduct.[915] Section 21(11) elaborates on the date on which discrimination occurs where an act is carried out over a period of time:

> For the purposes of this section prohibited conduct occurs—
>
> (*a*) if the act constituting it extends over a period, at the end of the period,
>
> (*b*) if it arises by virtue of a provision which operates over a period, throughout the period.

In *Dublin City Council v Deans*[916] Hunt J referred to the housing and medical situation of the complainant as 'open and evolving' over the course of her dealings with the city council. The Court found that Ms Deans was entitled to wait until the respondent's most senior medical officer had reviewed her file before referring a complaint; in other words, his decision marked the 'most recent occurrence' of alleged prohibited conduct under the ESA.[917]

It is important to appreciate that the time limits run in relation to discriminatory acts carried out by the respondent and so where an alleged discriminatory decision is appealed to an independent body complainants should not wait

---

[914] Section 21(6). See generally *Persaud v The Shelbourne Hotel*, DEC-E2004-075, and *Lindberg v Press Photographers Association of Ireland*, DEC-S2011-041, para 4.2.

[915] Section 21(6)(*a*) and section 21(2)(*a*).

[916] Circuit Court Dublin, Hunt J, unreported, 15 April 2008, at p 33.

[917] See also *Morrell v Hogan's Bar, Ballina*, DEC-S2003-001; *Mrs A (on behalf of her son B) v A Boys National School*, DEC-S2009-031, at para 4.4; *James v Cork Institute of Technology*, DEC-E2010-076; *Walczak v Minister for Social Protection*, DEC-S2012-011. For a discussion of the difference between a once-off decision with continuing consequences for the complainant and an act extending over a period of time see *McGrath v University of Dublin, Trinity College*, DEC-S2010-006.

until the outcome of that appeal to notify.[918] They should, in other words, notify the respondent of their intention to refer a complaint as soon as the respondent has issued a final decision on their application.

A term in an insurance contract will operate throughout the duration of that contract, and so a complaint can be referred within six months of its termination even though the provision may have been in place for a number of years.[919]

Where several instances of alleged discrimination are raised and some fall outside the time limit the Tribunal will investigate each one provided that they are similar and related (Equality Tribunal, 2004, pp 84–86). However, that 'is not to say, that complaints going back over a very lengthy period would have to be considered, as an issue of prejudice might arise. But this is something that would fall to be dealt with in the course of the hearing in any particular case.'[920]

The Director may extend the period for lodging a complaint up to a maximum of twelve months if she is satisfied that 'reasonable cause' prevented timely referral.[921] It is up to the complainant to apply for an extension of time. Principles developed in the employment arena oblige the complainant to supply reasons that both explain and justify the delay.[922] According to the Labour Court and the High Court, relevant factors may include whether the complainant was represented or not[923] and the complainant's migrant status and consequent limited knowledge of the law,[924] as well as engagement between the parties with a view to resolving the matter.[925]

As discussed in the next section the Director may also extend the period for notifying a respondent and in exceptional circumstances may dispense with the notification requirement.

---

[918] *Lennon v Health Service Executive*, DEC-S2009-063.

[919] *King v The Voluntary Health Insurance Board*, DEC-S2008-116.

[920] McGovern J in *County Louth VEC v The Equality Tribunal* [2009] IEHC 370, at para 6.2.

[921] Section 21(6)(*b*).

[922] *Minister for Finance v Civil and Public Service Union* [2007] ELR 36. In that case Laffoy J found that 'reasonable cause' does not include a situation where a person only decided to take a case having realised that it could succeed because of media coverage of a relevant court judgment. This reasoning was applied in *Lennon v Health Service Executive*, DEC-S2009-063.

[923] *Cementation Skanska v Neary* (WTC/03/34; DWT/03/49, 7 November 2003).

[924] *Singh & Singh Ltd t/a Gaylord Tandoori Restaurant v Guatam & Ors* (WT/05/62; DWT0544, 5 December 2005).

[925] *Murphy v Minister for Social Welfare* [1987] IR 295; *O'Donnell v Dun Laoghaire Corporation* [1991] ILRM 301.

12.3.4 The Notification Requirement

Prior to lodging a complaint with the Tribunal written notification must be forwarded to the goods or services provider.[926] An official form can be used but is not mandatory.[927] In other words, an ordinary letter is acceptable provided that it satisfies the requirements discussed below. Given that those requirements are quite technical it is advisable to use the notification form (Form ES.1) provided by the Tribunal on its website.[928]

The notification must be sent within two months of the alleged discriminatory event[929] and must state the nature of the allegation and the complainant's intention to seek redress under the Acts if not satisfied by any reply received. Both of these criteria are essential. For example, in *Ennis v Navan O'Mahony's Football and Hurling Club*[930] a letter in which the complainant stated, 'will ye do something about this, or will I?' but did not mention the ESA or the Tribunal was not accepted as valid notification. The notification requirement was not complied with in *O'Brien and McCarthy v Ruarí's Bar, Tralee*[931] because the notification form contained inaccurate information about the alleged act of discrimination. It referred to refusal of admission by a doorman, whereas subsequently the complainants maintained that they had been refused service inside the pub in question. The equality officer explained that notification serves two purposes: it alerts the respondent at an early stage about 'the nature of the allegation and the fact that a complaint is being considered against them and, secondly, it affords the respondent the opportunity of communicating directly with the complainant with a view to resolving the issue between themselves without recourse to the Equality Tribunal'. It is also vital to identify the

---

[926] Section 21(2) ESA. The provisions on notification also apply to gender ground complaints lodged at first instance with the Circuit Court. There is no obligation to send notification where a case is pursued against a licensed premise under section 19 of the Intoxicating Liquor Act 2003.

[927] *Mongans v Clare County Council*, DEC-S2008-039.

[928] The form can be downloaded here: <http://www.equalitytribunal.ie/Forms/Equal-Status-Act-Forms/>.

[929] Under section 21(2A), 'the date of notification is the date on which the notification is sent, unless it is shown that the notification was not received by the respondent.' This provision was interpreted purposively in *Fitzgerald v McCaul*, DEC-S2011-026. In that case the complainant sent a notification form by registered post and when it was returned marked 'not called for', he re-sent the form again by registered post. The second letter was also returned marked 'not called for'. Even though the respondent had not received the notification the equality officer found that the notification was valid. To find otherwise would undermine the purpose of the ESA by allowing a respondent to avoid discrimination proceedings by simply failing to collect the notification.

[930] DEC-S2010-031. See also *Litzouw v Matthews Property Management*, DEC-S2010-026.

[931] DEC-S2007-039.

complainant in any notification. For that reason correspondence between a solicitor and a respondent did not meet the requirements of section 21.[932]

A 2009 case failed because the complainant could not establish that the respondent had received the notification, which she had delivered in person.[933] The decision underlines the need to obtain a receipt upon delivery and/or to retain proof of postage.

Relevant information may also be sought in the notification 'with a view to assisting the complainant in deciding whether to refer the case to the Director'.[934] This provision is aimed at helping a person to decide whether or not a complaint is viable. A respondent is not obliged to answer any questions but where they fail to do so, answer in a way that is false or misleading, or answer in a way that is non-responsive the Director may draw adverse inferences if the case comes before the Tribunal.[935] The following kinds of information may be sought in the notification:

- Information as to the respondent's reasons for doing or omitting to do a relevant act and as to the practices or procedures material to a relevant act

- Information about the treatment of other persons in a similar situation to the complainant (excluding confidential information)

- Such other information as in the circumstances it is reasonable for the complainant to require (excluding confidential information)[936]

Confidential information is broadly defined as information relating to a particular individual where that individual does not consent to its disclosure. There is no requirement that the information be personal or private in nature.[937]

The time limit for notification can be extended to a maximum of four months for 'reasonable cause' and in exceptional circumstances the

---

[932] *Neary v Dublin Airport Authority*, DEC-S2010-036.

[933] *Jackson v Ann's Hot Bread Shop*, DEC-S2009-018. See also *Maughan v Brady's Public House*, DEC-S2006-046.

[934] Section 21(2)(*b*).

[935] Section 26. On the Tribunal's power to draw inferences from a failure to provide information see *Iarnród Éireann v Mannion* [2010] IEHC 326.

[936] Section 21(8).

[937] Section 21(9). In *Kelly v National University of Ireland*, Case C-104/10, (2010/C 134/29) the CJEU stated that neither the Burden of Proof Directive (97/80/EC) nor the Equal Treatment Directive (2002/73/EC) generally entitle an applicant for vocational training to access information about the qualifications of the other applicants based on a suspicion of discrimination. However, it is for the national court to decide whether the aim of Directive 97/80/EC requires a disclosure of such facts in individual cases.

Director may waive the notification requirement.[938] The complainant must seek the extension of time and provide reasons that both explain and justify the delay.

The power to waive the notification requirement may only be exercised where it is fair and reasonable in all the circumstances of the case. In particular, the Director must have regard to the extent to which the respondent is, or is likely to be, aware of the circumstances raised in the complaint and the risk of any prejudice to the respondent's ability to deal with the complaint.[939] In *Ennis v Navan O'Mahony's Football and Hurling Club*[940] the notification sent by the complainant did not meet the technical requirements of the ESA but the respondents had been put on notice that Mr Ennis regarded the incident in question as a serious matter that he intended to take further. A complaint was referred to the Tribunal well within the six-month time limit. The equality officer was satisfied that in these exceptional circumstances there was no prejudice to the respondent and so he dispensed with the notification requirement.

Cases are frequently dismissed for failure to notify the respondent within the two-month period. For example, in *Adeduntan v Vodafone Ireland*[941] the equality officer found that the case could not be heard as the notification was sent ten months after the incident complained of (the disconnection of a phone). A complaint about an airline's policy on carrying pregnant women was dismissed where notification was sent some two weeks outside the time limit. Reasonable cause for the delay was not presented and the Tribunal was 'mindful' of the fact that the complainant had the benefit of legal advice.[942] Likewise, an application for extension of time failed in *Yambasu and Brave v Abby Taxis*.[943] The equality officer was satisfied that the complainant had put no exceptional circumstances forward:

> I noted on the day of the hearing that Mr Brave had a very good command of the English language. He informed me that he had been in Ireland since the year 2000 and had been a taxi driver for some eight years. I also note that the complainant is legally represented in this case (para 4.5).

---

[938] Section 21(3). The power to dispense with notifications was introduced in the Equality Act 2004.

[939] Section 21(3)(*a*)(ii) and section 21(3)(*b*).

[940] DEC-S2010-031.

[941] DEC-S2008-110.

[942] *Wood v Aer Lingus*, DEC-S2009-061. See also *Reen v City of Cork VEC*, DEC-S2005-024.

[943] DEC-S2011-007.

If either party disagrees with the Tribunal's decision on an extension of time (in relation to notification of the service provider or referral to the Tribunal) it may be appealed to the Circuit Court within 42 days.[944]

An investigation cannot begin until the Director is satisfied that either the respondent has replied to the notification or at least one month has passed since it was sent.[945]

The obligation to notify the respondent in writing leaves little time for reflection. It assumes literacy and knowledge of the English language (Barry, 2003). Also, as the Equality Authority (2008b, p 27) points out:

> Claimants who have ongoing relationships with potential respond-
> ents (for example school pupils) or claimants who are dependent on
> the respondent for the provision of services (for example residents in
> long-term residential settings) would perceive the issuing of written
> notification as being potentially very damaging to relationships and/
> or services they may depend on.

12.4 Mediation of Complaints

Mediation is available as an alternative to investigation of complaints.[946] A case that is considered suitable is dealt with by the Tribunal's mediation service provided neither party objects (Equality Tribunal, 2011c, p 7). Over one-quarter (27 per cent) of complaints received by the Tribunal in 2010 were referred to mediation (Equality Tribunal, 2011a, p 4). The complainant or respondent can withdraw from the mediation process at any stage and request that an investigation be conducted instead. The process aims to enable the parties to reach a confidential and legally enforceable resolution, known as a mediation agreement. If an agreement is not reached the mediator issues a non-resolution notice, at which point the complainant may apply (within 28 days) to have the case returned for investigation.[947] Although the terms of settlements are not published, the Tribunal's annual *Mediation Review* publication provides general information about the mediation service along with data on resolutions. The mediation route takes less time than an investigation. An average period of eight months is recorded in the Tribunal's most recent *Mediation Review* (Equality Tribunal, 2011c, p 6).

Assuming that ESA cases are transferred to the Workplace Relations Commission, complainants and respondents will be offered an 'early

---

[944] Section 21(7A).
[945] Section 21(4) ESA.
[946] See generally section 24 ESA.
[947] Section 24(6) ESA.

resolution service' in place of a hearing (Department of Jobs, Enterprise and Innovation, 2012).

12.5 Investigation of Complaints

12.5.1 Introduction

Section 25 governs the investigation process. It provides that where a complaint has been referred to the Director and is not resolved by mediation 'the Director shall investigate the case and may, as part of that investigation and if the Director considers it appropriate, hear persons appearing to the Director to be interested.'[948] As discussed further in the next section, investigations are heard in private. The Minister for Justice has the power to issue regulations specifying the procedures and time limits to be followed by the Director in carrying out an investigation, having consulted with the Director and the Equality Authority.[949] No such regulations were produced. Guidance on the procedures followed in ESA cases are, however, available on the Tribunal's website.[950] According to that guide:

> If the complaint does not go to mediation or mediation is unsuccessful then, the complainant is asked for a submission/statement. The complainant's submission/statement will form an important part of the equality officer's investigation and should contain a clear and comprehensive written account of the complaint. It should set out details of the link between the ground and the alleged discrimination, the facts of the complaint such as the dates of the alleged discrimination, details of the specific allegations, the parties involved and any other information that is needed to set out the full facts of the complaint. It should include all relevant support documentation such as copies of letters, etc. The submission/statement should also include any legal arguments the complainant wants to make.[951]

When the submission or statement is received it is sent to the respondent, who is invited to send the Tribunal a 'replying submission'. This should be equally comprehensive and will be forwarded to the complainant.

---

[948] Section 25(1). This section was amended by section 28 of the Civil Law (Miscellaneous) Provisions Act 2011.

[949] Section 25(3).

[950] According to Hedigan J, the 'guidelines are not a legal interpretation of the Act. They are for general guidance only. A failure to comply with them is not, therefore, a good ground for a judicial review': *Clare County Council v Director of Equality Investigations & Anor* [2011] IEHC 303, at para 6.4.

[951] <http://www.equalitytribunal.ie/Equal_Status_/Guide-to-Procedures/>.

The ESA was amended in 2011 to enable the Tribunal to deal with cases on the basis of written submissions only.[952] If the Director decides to adopt that course of action, he or she must notify the parties to the case in writing. Either party can object to having the case dealt with on the basis of written submissions and, provided they do so within 28 days, the complaint will be dealt with through an oral hearing.

Once an equality officer has been assigned to the case and a hearing is scheduled the complainant and respondent will be asked to provide a list of the witnesses they intend to call.[953] Reasonable notice will be given of the hearing, which may take place in Dublin or at another location that is more convenient to the parties. In 2009 and 2010, because of budgetary constraints, the Tribunal held external hearings at fewer venues (Equality Tribunal, 2010a, p 15, 2011a, p 13).

12.5.2 Privacy

Equality Tribunal hearings are held in private.[954] Additionally, in some instances the parties' identities are concealed in published decisions. This is established practice in the case of sexual harassment complaints and many of those concerning the disability and sexual orientation grounds (Equality Tribunal, 2009b, p 5). Where the complainant is a child, the names of the parties to the case are also frequently recorded by the use of random initials. Anonymity has been applied in other sensitive cases, such as those involving criminal matters.[955] Outside of those situations, however, the Tribunal might not grant a request that the identities of the parties be concealed.[956] Complainants who are offered anonymity can waive it if they wish.[957]

A case may end up in the regular court system on appeal, and in that event a private hearing and anonymity cannot be secured. Under the Constitution all court proceedings are conducted in public unless a specific statutory exemption applies (Hogan and Whyte, 2003, pp 731–751; Equality Authority, 2008b, p 37). The Civil Law (Miscellaneous Provisions) Act 2008 provides for a limited exemption, which may apply to some appeals from the Equality Tribunal or to discrimination cases heard by the District Court. Under section 27 of

---

[952] Section 25(2A) as inserted by section 19 of the Civil Law (Miscellaneous Provisions) Act 2011.

[953] <http://www.equalitytribunal.ie/Equal_Status_/Guide-to-Procedures/>.

[954] Under sections 24(3) (mediation) and 25(2) (investigation).

[955] See, for example, *A Nigerian National v A Financial Institution*, DEC-S2005-114.

[956] *Lavery v Health Service Executive (Mid-Western Region)*, DEC-E2008-046, para 5.8.

[957] The complainant in *O'Regan v The Bridge Hotel, Waterford* (DEC-S2004-037) waived anonymity because he wanted the discriminatory actions of the hotel in question to be publicised.

that Act a court in civil proceedings may grant anonymity to a party or witness where the person is suffering from a medical condition and being identified as having that condition would cause undue stress to the person.[958] The term 'medical condition' is not defined but it will overlap to some extent with the disability ground, affording some complainants the possibility of having their privacy protected. A transsexual person might also seek to invoke the provision. Court cases taken on behalf of children may be heard in private under section 45(1)(c) of the Courts (Supplemental Provisions) Act 1961.

It should also be noted that both the Racial Equality Directive (article 7(1)) and the Gender Goods and Services Directive (article 8) oblige member states to ensure that judicial and administrative procedures for the enforcement of its provisions are 'available' to aggrieved individuals. These requirements open up the possibility that in given cases effective enforcement will entail non-disclosure of a person's identity, as occurred in an employment case involving a transsexual woman before the Northern Ireland Court of Appeal.[959] She had unsuccessfully applied for various orders to secure anonymity due to fear of intimidation and physical attacks. Referring to article 6(1) of the Amended Equal Treatment Directive the Court stated (at para 22):

> Member States are required by the Directive to ensure that procedures for the enforcement of obligations under the Directive are available to all persons who consider themselves wronged by failure to apply the principles of equal treatment to them. If it is established by the evidence that the appellant will be unable to enforce an obligation because of the risk to her physical safety, unless the procedure can afford her sufficient protection as to allow her to do so, the obligation under the Directive will not be met.

It is evident from the approach adopted here that the obligation to make procedures 'available' entails more than technical availability.

12.5.3 Representation and Costs

Although Tribunal processes are relatively informal, the inaccessible language used in the legislation and the complexity of some legal concepts means that

---

[958] According to Hogan J, because it is a 'remedial provision designed to complement the traditional concepts of medical confidentiality in a legal setting' section 27 'can be interpreted "as widely and liberally as can fairly be done"': *Temple Street v D. and Anor* [2011] IEHC 1, at para 23, citing *Bank of Ireland v Purcell* [1989] IR 327.

[959] *JR5 v Department of Agriculture and Rural Development* [2007] NICA 19. See also *X v Stevens (Commissioner Metropolitan Police Service)* [2003] IRLR 411.

complainants might need professional legal assistance. A complainant may be faced with a 'repeat player' (Galanter, 1974; Hirsh, 2008), such as a government department, leading to a serious imbalance of resources and knowledge. O'Sullivan and MacMahon's (2010) survey of EEA cases heard by the Tribunal from 2001 to 2007 revealed that complainants who were represented by the Equality Authority or a trade union enjoyed higher success rates than those who represented themselves. However, lay litigants had a marginally higher success rate than people who employed private lawyers (barristers and solicitors). Research conducted on parallel UK legislation suggests that those who have the benefit of legal representation enjoy higher success rates, but that an inquisitorial tribunal system can mitigate the disadvantages experienced by lay litigants (Gaze and Hunter, 2009).[960] Equality officers are trained to take account of the imbalance of power that may arise where one party is unrepresented (O'Sullivan and MacMahon, 2010, p 343).

As discussed in Chapter 11.3.3, the Equality Authority represented and therefore met the costs incurred by a limited number of complainants. Tribunal proceedings are not covered by the civil legal aid scheme, and so anyone who hires a lawyer will have to pay for his/her services out of their own funds (Free Legal Advice Centres, 2005, pp 26–28). In contrast with proceedings before the ordinary courts where costs generally follow the event (i.e. are paid by the losing side), each party before Equality Tribunal must bear their own costs.[961] Where a case reaches the Circuit Court or ultimately the High Court on appeal costs may be awarded against the unsuccessful party, which raises

---

[960] The Tribunal released statistics on the level of representation in 2003. In equal status cases 42 per cent of complainants, and 28 per cent of respondents, did not use legal representation. Approximately 25 per cent of all parties were unrepresented (Equality Tribunal, 2004, p 4).

[961] The Equality Act 2004 effected an amendment to the Equal Status Act 2000, which empowers the Director to award expenses where an investigation is obstructed or impeded. Legal costs are excluded from the definition of 'expenses' for these purposes: section 37A. In *Mongans v Clare County Council*, DEC-S2007-012, the complainants were directed to pay the respondents €400 in expenses for failure to attend hearings and leaving Tribunal proceedings without a valid excuse. Expenses were also awarded where the complainant obstructed and impeded an investigation by failing to attend a hearing in *Byrne v Ms A and the National University of Ireland, Galway*, DEC-S2009-077, and in *Oladimeji v Fingal County Council*, DEC-S2010-008. The penalty was applied to the representative of the complainants (Ms Rosen) in *Sweeney v Clare County Council*, DEC-S2008-072. Apparently Ms Rosen had instructed her clients not to attend an earlier hearing convened by the equality officer and this was found to warrant the payment of €200 to the county council for 'obstructing and impeding the investigation.' Similar findings were issued in a series of cases, for example *O'Donoghue v Clare County Council*, DEC-S2008-070; *Sweeney v Clare County Council*, DEC-S2008-071; and the related case of *Mongans v Clare County Council*, DEC-S2008-039.

the stakes considerably for individuals and other parties with limited means.[962] For instance, the High Court awarded costs against a young complainant in a reasonable accommodation case, which had initially been successful before the Tribunal (*Irish Times*, 2010).

12.5.4 Investigative Powers and Procedures before the Tribunal

Equality officers enjoy significant powers in carrying out their functions.[963] These include the power to enter premises, obtain information and inspect work, and the ability to seek court orders directing that persons cooperate with investigations. As these powers suggest, the Equality Tribunal is intended to be an investigative forum. Barry (2004, p 16) explains that the 'inquisitorial model means that the pursuit and defence of a claim is not wholly dependent on the ability and capacity of the individual litigant to marshal relevant evidence and present complex legal arguments.' Accordingly, equality officers need not rely exclusively upon material introduced by the parties in arriving at a decision. In several investigations equality officers have sought additional factual information from the parties, in particular it seems when seeking to establish whether a pattern of differential treatment can be established or discounted.[964] If adequately resourced the investigative capacity of the Tribunal could perhaps have been enhanced. While entering premises for the purposes of inspecting work occurs regularly in EEA equal pay cases, it appears that the power to enter premises in order to obtain material information has never been used in an ESA investigation. However, given the significant constraints on the Tribunal's resources even journeys outside Dublin for the purposes of holding hearings have been curtailed (Equality Tribunal, 2010a).

According to the Tribunal's guide to procedures the format of a hearing is as follows:

> The Equality Officer will direct the hearing and may look for formal identification of either party or any witnesses. It is the responsibility of the parties and their representatives to ensure that all information is before the Equality Officer on the day of the hearing including any documents or witnesses relevant to the case. The Equality Officer will ask questions of each party and of any witnesses attending. S/he will also give each party the opportunity to give evidence, make legal points, cross-examine and the opportunity to respond to the other

---

[962] *Joyce v Madden* [2004] 1 ILRM 277.
[963] See sections 33–37 ESA.
[964] See, for example, *MacMahon v Department of Physical Education and Sport, University College Cork*, DEC-S2009-014, at para 4.14.

side. The witnesses may be allowed to remain or may be asked to come in only for their own evidence. The Equality Officer will decide what is appropriate, taking into account fair procedures, arrangements which will best support the effective and accurate giving of evidence, and the need to protect privacy during sensitive evidence.

Given the Tribunal's objective to provide an accessible forum, the Equality Officer will ensure that unrepresented complainants or respondents are not placed at a disadvantage in so far as he or she can.[965]

The processes and rules of evidence are less formal than those encountered in regular litigation. According to the Supreme Court, 'Tribunals exercising quasi judicial functions are frequently allowed to act informally – to receive unsworn evidence, to act on hearsay, to depart from the rules of evidence, to ignore courtroom procedures, and the like – but they may not act in such a way as to imperil a fair hearing or a fair result.'[966]

In a 2009 judgment the High Court endorsed the Equality Tribunal's ability to decide how a hearing should be conducted subject to the principles of natural and constitutional justice: *County Louth VEC v The Equality Tribunal*.[967] For that reason the equality officer was entitled to exclude witnesses for the respondent VEC while the complainant was giving evidence. The VEC's representative was present during the testimony and was in a position to question the complainant. Witnesses were able to give their own account of events and where necessary counter the complainant's version of what had happened. An appropriate balance was therefore struck between ensuring the complainant was not intimidated and affording the respondent an opportunity to test the case against it.

On occasion equality officers adopt a flexible approach to some of the more technical aspects of pursuing a complaint. Several cases went ahead where the complainant had not identified the 'correct' respondent when lodging the complaint. In those situations the equality officer was satisfied that despite technical errors the correct respondent had been put on notice of the complaint.[968] Complaints will not succeed where the party identified as the respondent is not responsible for the act or omission on which the case

---

[965] <http://www.equalitytribunal.ie/Equal_Status_/Guide-to-Procedures/>.

[966] *Kiely v The Minister for Social Welfare (No. 2)* [1977] IR 276, per Henchy J at p 281. See also *Goodman v Hamilton* [1992] 2 IR 542 and *Calor Teoranta v McCarthy* [2009] ELR 281.

[967] [2009] IEHC 370. As of July 2012 the case is under appeal to the Supreme Court. See also *Clare County Council v Director of Equality Investigations & Anor* [2011] IEHC 303.

[968] See, for example, *Corcoran and Others v The One Foot Inn, Burnfoot, Co. Donegal,*

is based. For example, a case referred against the Department of Education failed, as the board of management of a school was responsible for the decision in question.[969]

The Tribunal frequently allows claims to proceed where the precise ground or type of discrimination was not specified in the original referral of the complaint. For example, an equality officer investigated an allegation of victimisation in *A Post-Leaving Certificate Student v An Educational Institution*[970] even though the issue was not specifically raised in the complaint form:

> In all the circumstances of the present complaint, I am satisfied that it is lawful under the Acts for me to address any issue, including that of victimisation, which appears to me on the facts to fall within the scope of the Acts. The Equal Status Acts are Acts '… to prohibit types of discrimination … and … to provide for investigating and remedying certain discrimination and other unlawful activities' and Section 25 of the Acts requires me to investigate the complaint. In so doing, my jurisdiction is not limited by the same rules and procedures as the District, Circuit or Superior Courts. It is wider than that, particularly where a party is unrepresented, and cannot be restricted by the complainant's failure to tick a box on a non-statutory form (para 5.14, footnote omitted).

The equality officer considered that the respondent had adequate notice of the allegation through subsequent correspondence, was afforded the opportunity to make oral submissions on the matter and to make further written submissions following the hearing (paras 5.14–5.16). According to the Supreme Court, where a quasi-judicial body introduces any element into a case that has not been previously considered the parties must be afforded an adequate

---

DEC-S2007-004; *Comerford v Trailfinders Ireland Ltd*, DEC-S2011-013; and *Egan v Young Fine Gael*, DEC-S2011-001.

[969] *Lyamina v The Department of Education and Science*, DEC-S2009-016. See also *McClean v The Revenue Commissioners*, DEC-S2004-016.

[970] DEC-S2009-043; applied in *Ms A v A Library*, DEC-S2009-060, and in *McGrath v University of Dublin, Trinity College*, DEC-S2010-006. See also *Stokes and Others v Hoban's Pub, Dysart*, DEC-S2006-066, and *A Separated Complainant v A Hospital*, DEC-S2010-046, paras 5.6–5.8. In *Byrne v Association of Irish Racecourses*, DEC-E2008-008, the equality officer relied on the High Court judgment in *Long v The Labour Court and Others* (High Court, Johnson J, unreported, 25 May 1990) to establish 'the right of an Equality Officer to consider cases before him or her under provisions of the relevant legislation that the complainant or the complainant's representative have not sought to invoke, if it appears from the evidence that those provisions should be applied to the case at hand' (at para 5.18).

opportunity to address the new issues.[971] The Equality Tribunal's approach was addressed specifically in *County Louth VEC v The Equality Tribunal*.[972] McGovern J found that the Tribunal was entitled to hear matters that went beyond those set out in the complaint form provided the general nature of the complaint remained the same and the respondent was afforded a reasonable opportunity to deal with it in compliance with the principles of natural and constitutional justice.

In other cases the Tribunal has accepted testimony about matters that fall outside the time period covered by the Acts. For example, in *O'Shea v Hennessy Salon Supplies Ltd, Cork*[973] the Tribunal heard evidence of interactions between the complainant and respondent that took place prior to the alleged discriminatory incident because it could assist in clarifying the nature of their relationship. That information was especially relevant in victimisation cases, according to the equality officer.[974]

12.5.5 Dismissal of Complaints

Section 22(1) provides that a complaint may be dismissed at any stage if the Director is of the opinion that it has been made in bad faith or is frivolous, vexatious, misconceived or relates to a trivial matter. A decision to dismiss may be appealed to the Circuit Court within 42 days.[975]

A complaint on the religion ground was dismissed on the basis that it was trivial in *An Individual v A Garda Station*.[976] The complainant had objected to the fact that a number of bibles were freely available for the use of the public in a Garda station. The Director noted the importance of the state's constitutional obligations to guarantee freedom of conscience. However, she found that the complainant had failed to show any discrimination or any personal detriment as such in the practice complained of.

The criterion of 'bad faith' implies that a complainant is acting fraudulently, deceitfully or dishonestly according to the equality officer in *Mongans v Clare County Council*.[977] She derived the meaning of 'frivolous and vexatious' from a number of Superior Court judgments, which essentially refer to cases that

---

[971] *State (Irish Pharmaceutical Union) v Employment Appeals Tribunal* [1987] ILRM 36. See also *County Louth VEC v The Equality Tribunal* [2009] IEHC 370 and *Galway–Mayo Institute of Technology v Employment Appeals Tribunal* [2007] IEHC 210.

[972] [2009] IEHC 370. Applied in *Clare County Council v Director of Equality Investigations & Anor* [2011] IEHC 303, at para 6.5 and *Hennessy v Thurles Town Council*, DEC-S2010-012.

[973] DEC-S2004-092.

[974] See also *Brooks v BRC Shooting Club*, DEC-S2010-042.

[975] Section 22(2).

[976] DEC-S2001-025.

[977] DEC-S2008-039.

have no reasonable prospect of succeeding (at paras 5.4–5.6).[978] Finally, the equality officer found that '[a] complaint is misconceived if it is incorrectly based in law, for example, if the complaint did not relate in any way to the nine discriminatory grounds under the Equal Status Acts it would be misconceived' (para 5.8).[979] A complaint against the Garda Síochána Ombudsman Commission was dismissed on the ground that it was misconceived in a 2010 decision.[980] The Commission's decision-making function was not a 'service' and so the matter did not fall within the ambit of the ESA. Similarly, an age discrimination complaint referred by a volunteer worker was misconceived, as the respondent was not providing that worker with a service.[981]

A second category in which a case may be dismissed is when a complainant is found to have ceased to pursue his/her case under section 38:

(1) Where a case is referred to the Director and, at any time after the expiry of one year from the date of the reference, it appears to the Director that the complainant has not pursued, or has ceased to pursue the reference, the Director may dismiss the reference.

(2) As soon as practicable after dismissing a reference, the Director shall give notice in writing of that fact to the complainant and the respondent.

(3) Where a reference is dismissed under this section, no further proceedings may be taken in relation to that reference, but nothing in this section prevents a person from making a further reference in relation to the same matter (subject to any applicable time limit).

A decision to dismiss under this section cannot be appealed[982] but a complainant could lodge a new complaint (provided it is within the usual time limits, e.g. where the discriminatory act is ongoing).

The power to dismiss for failure to pursue was considered by the High Court in *Eagle Star Life Assurance Company of Ireland Ltd v Director of the Equality Tribunal & Anor*.[983] Ms Treanor, an equality officer, had referred a complaint to the Equality Tribunal against Eagle Star in 2002 on the basis

---

[978] See also *Egan v Young Fine Gael*, DEC-S2011-001, at para 4.4.

[979] See *Fitzgerald v Minister for Community, Equality and Gaeltacht Affairs* [2011] IEHC 180: the Director was entitled to dismiss a complaint as misconceived since it did not fall within any of the discriminatory grounds provided for under the ESA. Specifically, the race ground did not cover the complainant's status as a farmer (Chapter 2.3.7).

[980] *O'Neill v Garda Síochána Ombudsman Commission*, DEC-S2010-037.

[981] *Neary v Louth County Council*, DEC-S2011-020.

[982] See *Clare County Council v Judge Kenny* [2008] IEHC 177, at para 43.

[983] [2009] ELR 295.

that the imposition of an increased premium on her income protection policy discriminated against her on the disability ground. Due to the potential conflict of interest the Tribunal appointed a temporary external equality officer to hear the case in 2006. Eagle Star argued that the complaint should be dismissed because Ms Treanor had not pursued it. It also disputed the jurisdiction of the Tribunal to hear the complaint in light of the definition of 'disability' under the ESA, contending that obesity did not amount to a disability. The Equality Tribunal proceeded to find in favour of Ms Treanor and Eagle Star sought to quash its findings by way of judicial review.

According to the High Court, section 38 does not impose a requirement on individuals 'to continuously inquire as to the status of their complaint and thereby impose pressure on the Tribunal to accelerate the adjudicative process'.[984] Rather the purpose of the section was to allow the Tribunal to clear cases from its files that had 'become moribund'. The delay in hearing the case was due to the backlog of cases at the Tribunal and the time it took to secure a temporary equality officer. Hedigan J found that the Tribunal had acted in accordance with the terms of section 38 in declining to dismiss the complaint: the complainant had complied with the relevant time limits and had furnished the information sought by the Tribunal in a prompt and efficient manner. The High Court also declined to override the interpretation of the disability ground adopted by the Tribunal on the basis that upon judicial review the courts should not 'prematurely trespass into the special jurisdiction assigned to the Tribunal by the 2000 Act'.[985]

Finally, it should be noted that there is no power to dismiss a complaint in the event that a complainant does not attend the Equality Tribunal hearing. Where an equality officer is satisfied that adequate notice of the hearing was received by the parties and that there are no factors that would merit deferring it, he/she will generally go on to find that the complainant has failed to establish a *prima facie* case. The investigation will then be concluded and a decision issued in favour of the respondent.

12.6 Redress

Following the investigation equality officers issue a written decision as soon as practicable. All decisions are published on the Tribunal's website. Where

---

[984] *Eagle Star Life Assurance Company of Ireland Ltd v Director of the Equality Tribunal & Anor* [2009] ELR 295, at para 29.

[985] *Eagle Star Life Assurance Company of Ireland Ltd v Director of the Equality Tribunal & Anor* [2009] ELR 295, at para 38. On deference to administrative bodies and tribunals when exercising specialist expertise see also *Henry Denny & Sons (Ireland) Ltd v Minister for Social Welfare* [1998] 1 1R 3 and *Meadows v Minister for Justice, Equality and Law Reform* [2010] IESC 3.

the complainant succeeds the decision will include an order for redress, which can take the form of monetary compensation and/or other specified courses of action directed at the respondent.

Compensation of up to €6,348.69 in total can be ordered under the ESA.[986] The average award in 2007 was €2,751, but it fell to €1,664 in 2008 (Equality Tribunal, 2008, p 18, 2009a, p 17). In 2009 the figure was €2,198 and it remained at a similar level of €2,128 the following year (Equality Tribunal, 2010a, p 12, 2011a, p 10).

Under EU law sanctions for findings of discrimination must be effective, proportionate and dissuasive.[987] In the context of employment cases on the gender ground the CJEU has established that compensation ceilings are not compatible with those requirements (Bolger and Kimber, 2000, pp 424–427; Higgins, 2003). As noted above, claims under the gender ground are treated exceptionally; they can be taken directly to the Circuit Court and as a result can attract higher compensation awards.[988] However, the limit on compensation remains under section 19 of the Intoxicating Liquor Act 2003 for gender discrimination in relation to licensed premises. This anomaly ought to be dealt with by appropriate legislation.

A report by the European Network of Legal Experts in the Non-Discrimination Field (Tobler, 2005b, p 39) points to the disparity between Irish provisions on remedies for gender discrimination and other claims, stating, 'there can be no doubt that upper limits on compensation for discrimination are not acceptable either in the case of either the Race or Employment Framework Directives.'[989] Since EU law, in the form of the Racial Equality Directive, applies to similar terrain as that governed by the ESA, the threshold of €6,348.69 ought to be removed (at least in respect of the race and Traveller community grounds). The CJEU has found that national rules on sanctions implementing the Racial Equality Directive must be effective, proportionate and dissuasive even where there is no identifiable victim.[990]

---

[986] Section 27.

[987] See article 15 of the Racial Equality Directive and article 8(2) of the Gender Goods and Services Directive.

[988] Indeed there is no limit on the amount of compensation payable. Section 76(c) of the Civil Law (Miscellaneous Provisions) Act 2008 amended sections 21 and 27 of the ESA to allow for the distinct treatment of claims on the gender ground. These provisions came into force on 20 July 2008 under the terms of SI 274/2008.

[989] In *Fagan v The Office of the Revenue Commissioners* (DEC-E2008-004) the equality officer applied EU principles concerning redress to an age discrimination claim in employment. The complainant was awarded €60,000 in compensation.

[990] *Centrum voor Gelijkheid van Kansen en voor Racismebestrijding v Firma Feryn NV*, Case C-54/07, [2008] ECR 1-1587.

The ESA provides that compensation may be awarded for 'the effects of the prohibited conduct concerned'.[991] According to the Tribunal effects may include:

- *Social/personal impact*: humiliation, upset, anger, stress and, where discrimination is severe or repeated, a contribution to an overall lessening of self-esteem/empowerment, increased exclusion from the mainstream social and economic currents, and a loss of confidence in the fairness and legitimacy of the society in which a person lives or works. This is the human rights aspect of discrimination: that it is an affront to the dignity of the human person.

- *Practical impact (e.g. loss of amenity)*: this would vary depending on the nature of the goods or services which have been refused to the individual. For instance, the non-provision of a drink would be considered less serious than not being able to get accommodation, being sacked from a job or being physically harassed.

- *Financial impact*: this would include loss of earnings, the cost of travelling further to obtain accommodation or to get served in a pub, not being admitted to an event for which tickets had been purchased, or having to pay higher rent for alternative accommodation because the accommodation sought was refused for discriminatory reasons.[992]

In deciding on the level of compensation other factors weighed up include evidence of a general discriminatory policy, whether discrimination was acknowledged and an apology offered, and whether the respondent had taken genuine measures to comply with the ESA subsequent to the act of discrimination.[993] The behaviour of the complainant may also be taken into account. For example, in *Wall v Wicklow Cabs*[994] the award was €50 in light of an admission by the complainant that he had acted aggressively immediately following the act of discrimination.

Equality officers can also order persons to take specified courses of action.[995] Goods and services providers are frequently tasked with ensuring that admissions policies[996] and other procedures[997] are compliant with the legislation.

---

[991] Section 27(1)(*a*).

[992] *Delaney and Others v The Kilford Arms, Kilkenny*, DEC-S2002-033/036, para 9.2.

[993] *Delaney and Others v The Kilford Arms, Kilkenny*, DEC-S2002-033/036, para 9.2.

[994] DEC-S2002-001. See also *Cementwala v Colbert, Winters Property Management & Crescent Green Ltd*, DEC-S2005-184/186.

[995] Section 27(1)(*b*) ESA.

[996] See, for example, *O'Brien (on behalf of Quilligan) v Daly's Supermarket, Killarney*, DEC-S2005-098.

[997] See, for example, *A Nigerian National v A Financial Institution*, DEC-S2005-114.

Such measures, particularly where the respondent is a large organisation, can have significant effects beyond the immediate case. For example, in *Hennessy v Network Catering/Iarnród Éireann*,[998] having established that the complainant was subjected to harassment on the disability ground, the equality officer ordered the respondent to 'display a clearly visible notice, in the dining car or in any other place on the train where there is a designated wheelchair space, stating that customers with disabilities are protected by the Equal Status Acts. The notice should also state that passengers with disabilities are welcome to travel and enjoy the amenity of the train without interference. This notice should be displayed within four weeks of this Decision' (para 5.3). In addition, she directed that all staff be trained on the requirements of anti-discrimination law. As we saw above, the finding in *Reilly v Health Service Executive*[999] effectively led to the closure of the Castle Street Social Welfare office (Chapter 3.3.9). In the reasonable accommodation case of *Two Complainants (a mother and her son) v A Primary School*[1000] the equality officer ordered the respondent school to put in place a system facilitating early identification of students who have disabilities or learning difficulties with the aim of directing these students to the appropriate educational services quickly. According to Woulfe (2010, p 66), imposing 'a time limit is very important in terms of implementation as open-ended orders in terms of carrying out reviews and changing policy and procedure can lead to long delays and at times failure by respondents to implement such orders.'

On appeal the Circuit Court has occasionally set aside an order issued by the Tribunal. For example, in *Dublin City Council v Deans*[1001] the equality officer had directed that the council revise its scheme of priority for processing housing applications in relation to disabled persons to take further account of medical reports and applicants' particular disabilities. Hunt J found, however, that the order interfered unduly with the city council's discretion in maintaining and operating its housing plan. The order for compensation was upheld.

The adequacy of the remedies provided for under the ESA is likely to feature in future case law. In 2008 the European Commission (2008, para 2.1) announced that it is examining the effectiveness of national penalties and time limits to bring actions before national courts, stating, 'these are two fundamental issues for discouraging discriminatory behaviour and giving victims effective legal remedies.'

---

[998] DEC-S2009-029.

[999] DEC-S2007-059.

[1000] DEC-S2006-028.

[1001] Circuit Court Dublin, Hunt J, unreported, 15 April 2008.

12.7 Appeals and Enforcement of Tribunal Decisions

Either party may appeal the equality officer's decision in writing to the Circuit Court within 42 days of the date of issue marked on the decision.[1002] A copy of the notice of appeal must be sent to the Tribunal. If no appeal is lodged during that time, the decision becomes legally binding. In the event that the respondent doesn't comply with a Tribunal order enforcement is largely a matter for the successful complainant, who must make an application to the Circuit Court.[1003] However, a complainant can seek assistance from the Equality Authority in bringing enforcement proceedings.[1004] The Equality Authority can also bring enforcement proceedings itself with the consent of the complainant where it considers that the decision or settlement is unlikely to be implemented without its intervention.[1005]

12.8 Conclusion

Ireland's equality infrastructure will change substantially over the coming years. The system for processing discrimination complaints is subject to an ongoing reform process. The future path for pursuing ESA complaints will be determined when relevant legislation is published in 2012. Given the significant benefits of the processes adopted by specialised tribunals over formal court proceedings, it would be preferable for the Workplace Relations Commission to assume responsibility for resolving equal status cases once the Equality Tribunal is wound down.

[1002] Section 28. See generally Circuit Court Rules (Equal Status Acts 2000 to 2004) 2006 (SI 349/2006).
[1003] Section 31.
[1004] Section 67 EEA.
[1005] Section 31(4)(*b*).

References

Ahtela, Karoliina (2005) 'The Revised Provisions on Sex Discrimination in European Law: A Critical Assessment', *European Law Journal* 11(1), 57–78.

Ammer, Margit, Niall Crowley, Barbara Liegl, Elisabeth Holzleithner, Katrin Wladasch and Kutsal Yesilkagit (2010) *Study on Equality Bodies Set up under Directives 2000/43/EC, 2004/113/EC and 2006/54/EC* (Utrecht: Human European Consultancy and Ludwig Boltzmann Institute of Human Rights).

Aphramor, Lucy (2009) 'Disability and the Anti-Obesity Offensive', *Disability & Society* 24(7), 897–909.

Ashtiany, Sue (2010) 'The Equality Act 2010: Main Concepts', *Equal Rights Review* 2010(5), 25–30, <http://www.equalrightstrust.org/ertdocumentbank/Sue%20Ashtiany.pdf>.

Association for Higher Education Access and Disability (nd) *Disclosure* (Dublin: AHEAD).

Bacik, Ivana (2003) 'Harassment', in C. Costello and E. Barry (eds.), *Equality in Diversity: The New Equality Directives* (Dublin: Irish Centre for European Law), 151–176.

Baker, John, Kathleen Lynch, Sara Cantillon and Judy Walsh (2009) *Equality: From Theory to Action* (2nd edition, Basingstoke: Palgrave Macmillan).

Bamforth, Nicolas, Maleiha Malik and Colm O'Cinneide (2008) *Discrimination Law: Theory and Context, Text and Materials* (London: Sweet & Maxwell).

Banda, Sibo (2009) 'Taking Indirect Horizontality Seriously in Ireland: A Time to Magnify the Nuance', *Dublin University Law Journal* 31, 263–297.

Barmes, Lizzie (2007) 'Constitutional and Conceptual Complexities in UK Implementation of the EU Harassment Provisions', *Industrial Law Journal* 36(4), 446–467.

Barmes, Lizzie (2009) 'Equality Law and Experimentation: The Positive Action Challenge', *Cambridge Law Journal* 68(3), 623–654.

Barnard, Catherine and Bob Hepple (2000) 'Substantive Equality', *Cambridge Law Journal* 59, 562–585.

Barnes, Colin (1991) *Disabled People in Britain and Discrimination: A Case for Anti-Discrimination Legislation* (London: Hurst).

Barnes, Colin and Geoffrey Mercer (2005) *The Social Model of Disability: Europe and the Majority World* (Leeds: Disability Press).

References

Barnett, Laura (2008) *Freedom of Religion and Religious Symbols in the Public Sphere* (Ottawa, ON: Law and Government Division, Parliamentary Research Branch, Canadian Parliament), <http://www.parl.gc.ca/content/LOP/ResearchPublications/2011-60-e.htm>.

Barry, Eilís (2003) 'Different Hierarchies – Enforcing Equality Law', in C. Costello and E. Barry (eds.), *Equality in Diversity: The New Equality Directives* (Dublin: Irish Centre for European Law), 411–434.

Barry, Eilís (2004) 'Strategic Enforcement: From Concept to Practice', in J. Cormack (ed.), *Strategic Enforcement and the EC Equal Treatment Directives* (Brussels: Equinet), 4–17.

Barry, Eilís (2006) 'Interventions and *Amicus Curiae* Applications: Making Individual Enforcement More Effective', in S. Obura and F. Palmer (eds.), *Strategic Enforcement: Powers and Competences of Equality Bodies* (Brussels: Equinet), 31–42.

Bell, Mark (2007) 'Direct Discrimination', in D. Schiek, L. Waddington and M. Bell (eds.), *Cases, Materials and Text on National, Supranational and International Non-Discrimination Law* (Oxford: Hart Publishing), 185–321.

Bell, Mark (2009) 'Advancing EU Anti-Discrimination Law: The European Commission's 2008 Proposal for a New Directive', *Equal Rights Review* 2009(3), 7–18, <http://www.equalrightstrust.org/ertdocumentbank/mark%20bell.pdf>.

Bell, Mark (2010a) 'Combating Discrimination in Areas Outside Employment: The Anticipated Impact of the Proposed New Directive', in Equality Authority (ed.), *Expanding Equality Protections in Goods and Services: Irish and EU Perspectives* (Dublin: Equality Authority), 11–25.

Bell, Mark (2010b) 'Judicial Enforcement of the Duties on Public Authorities to Promote Equality', *Public Law* 2010, 672–687.

Binchy, William (2008) 'New Family Structures: The School's Relations with Unmarried, Separated or Divorced Parents of Pupils', in School of Law, Trinity College Dublin (ed.), *Legal Issues Facing School Principals and Teachers in 2008: Some Practical Solutions* (Dublin: School of Law, Trinity College Dublin).

Blom, Judith, Barry Fitzpatrick, Jeanne Gregory, Robert Knegt and Ursula O'Hare (1995) *The Utilisation of Sex Equality Litigation Procedures in the Member States of the European Community: A Comparative Study* (Luxembourg: Office for Official Publications of the European Communities).

Bolger, Marguerite (2004) 'Discrimination on Grounds of Religion: Theory and Practice', *Irish Employment Law Journal* 1(2), 48–56.

Bolger, Marguerite and Cliona Kimber (2000) *Sex Discrimination Law* (Dublin: Round Hall, Sweet & Maxwell).

Bolger, Marguerite and Cliona Kimber (2009) 'Employment Equality', in M. Regan (ed.), *Employment Law* (Dublin: Tottel Publishing), 413–524.

Bond, Laurence, Frances McGinnity and Helen Russell (2010) *Making Equality Count: Irish and International Research Measuring Equality and Discrimination* (Dublin: Liffey Press).

References

Bosch, Grete (2007) 'Restitution or Discrimination? Lessons on Affirmative Action from South African Employment Law', *Web Journal of Current Legal Issues* 2007(4), <http://webjcli.ncl.ac.uk/2007/issue4/bosch4.html>.

Brown, Chris (2001) 'The Race Directive: Towards Equality for All the Peoples of Europe?', *Yearbook of European Law* 21, 195–227.

Burri, Susanne and Aileen McColgan (2008) *Sex-Segregated Services* (Luxembourg: Office for Official Publications of the European Communities).

Burrows, Noreen and Muriel Robison (2006) 'Reforming Positive Action', *Journal of Law and Society* 33, 24–41.

Campbell, Liz, Shane Kilcommins and Catherine O'Sullivan (2010) *Criminal Law in Ireland: Cases and Commentary* (Dublin: Clarus Press).

Central Statistics Office (2005) *Quarterly National Household Survey: Module on Equality, Fourth Quarter 2004* (Dublin: Stationery Office).

Central Statistics Office (2007a) *Equality in Ireland* (Dublin: Stationery Office).

Central Statistics Office (2007b) *Census 2006 – Volume 13* (Dublin: Stationery Office).

Central Statistics Office (2010) *National Disability Survey 2006 Volume 2* (Dublin: Stationery Office).

An Chomhairle Leabharlanna and the Equality Authority (2003) *Library Access* (Dublin: Equality Authority).

Chopin, Isabelle, Janet Cormack and Jan Niessen (eds.) (2004) *The Implementation of European Anti-Discrimination Legislation: Work in Progress* (Brussels: Migration Policy Group).

Citizens Information Board (2009a) *Where to Complain: A Guide to Enforcement and Redress Bodies* (Dublin: Citizens Information Board), <http://www.citizensinformationboard.ie/publications/providers/downloads/where_to_complain_2009.pdf>.

Citizens Information Board (2009b) *Accessible Information for All* (Dublin: Citizens Information Board), <http://www.citizensinformationboard.ie/publications/social/downloads/Accessible_Information_For_All.pdf>.

Citizens Information Board (2011) *Annual Report 2010* (Dublin: Citizens Information Board), <http://www.citizensinformationboard.ie/about/downloads/annual_report2010.pdf>.

Clifford, Jarlath (2011) 'The UN Disability Convention and Its Impact on European Equality Law', *Equal Rights Review* 2011(6), 11–25, <http://www.equalrightstrust.org/ertdocumentbank/ERR06_jarlath_article.pdf>.

Coates, Dermot, Fiona Kane and Kasey Treadwell Shine (2008) *Traveller Accommodation in Ireland: Review of Policy and Practice* (Dublin: Centre for Housing Research), <http://www.housing.ie/Our-Publications/Archive/Traveller-Specific-Accommodation.aspx>.

Collins, Anthony and James O'Reilly (2004) *Civil Proceedings and the State* (2nd edition, Dublin: Round Hall).

Commission on Assisted Human Reproduction (2005) *Report of the Commission on Assisted Human Reproduction* (Dublin: Stationery Office).

References

Committee of Ministers (2007) *Resolution CM/ResCMN (2007) 10 on the Implementation of the Framework Convention for the Protection of National Minorities by Ireland* (Strasbourg: Council of Europe), <https://wcd.coe.int/ViewDoc.jsp?id=1156203&Site=CM&BackColorInternet=C3C3C3&BackColorIntranet=EDB021&BackColorLogged=F5D383?>.

Compton, Alicia and Maryrose Dillon (2010) 'Practice and Procedure', *Irish Employment Law Journal* 7(4), 114.

Conaghan, Joanne (1986) 'The Invisibility of Women in Labour Law: Gender Neutrality in Model Building', *International Journal of Sociology of Law* 14, 377–392.

Conaghan, Joanne (1999) 'Enhancing Civil Remedies for (Sexual) Harassment: S.3 of the Protection from Harassment Act 1997', *Feminist Legal Studies* 7, 203–214.

Connolly, Michael (2009a) 'Rethinking Victimisation', *Industrial Law Journal* 38(2), 149.

Connolly, Michael (2009b) 'Homophobic Harassment Where No One Is Gay', *Cambridge Law Journal* 68(2), 265–268.

Constitution Review Group (1996) *Report of the Constitution Review Group* (Dublin: Stationery Office).

Coolahan, John, Caroline Hussey and Fionnuala Kilfeather (2012) *The Forum on Patronage and Pluralism in the Primary Sector: Report of the Forum's Advisory Group* (Dublin: Department of Education and Skills), <http://www.education.ie/servlet/blobservlet/fpp_report_advisory_group.pdf?language=EN&igstat=true>.

Cormack, Janet (ed.) (2004) *Strategic Enforcement and the EC Equal Treatment Directives* (Brussels: Equinet).

Council of Europe Commissioner for Human Rights (2009) *Human Rights and Gender Identity* (Strasbourg: Office of the Commissioner for Human Rights Council of Europe), <https://wcd.coe.int/ViewDoc.jsp?id=1476365>.

Council of Europe, Secretariat of the Framework Convention for the Protection of National Minorities (2011) *Third Report Submitted by Ireland Pursuant to Article 25, Paragraph 2 of the Framework Convention for the Protection of National Minorities*, 18 July 2011, ACFC/SR/III (2011) 004, <http://www.coe.int/t/dghl/monitoring/minorities/3_FCNMdocs/Table_en.asp#Ireland>.

Craig, Paul and Gráinne de Búrca (2007) *EU Law: Text, Cases and Materials* (4th edition, Oxford: Oxford University Press).

Crowley, Niall (2006) *An Ambition for Equality* (Dublin: Irish Academic Press).

Curran, John (2008) 'Victimisation: A New Remedy for Employees', *Irish Employment Law Journal* 5(1), 4–13.

Curtin, Deirdre (1989) *Irish Employment Equality Law* (Dublin: Round Hall).

Daly, Eoin (2008) 'Religious Freedom and the Denominational Education Model in the Republic of Ireland: The Shortcomings of "Accommodationist" Reform', *Education Law Journal* 9(4), 242–258.

Daly, Eoin (2009) 'Restrictions on Religious Dress in French Republican Thought: Returning the Secularist Justification to a Rights-Based Rationale', *Dublin University Law Journal* 31, 154–182.

Day, Shelagh and Gwen Brodsky (1996) 'The Duty to Accommodate: Who Will Benefit?', *Canadian Bar Review* 75, 433–473.

De Londras, Fiona and Cliona Kelly (2010) *European Convention on Human Rights Act: Operation, Impact and Analysis* (Dublin: Round Hall).

De Schutter, Olivier (2005a) *The Prohibition of Discrimination under European Human Rights Law: Relevance for EU Racial and Employment Equality Directives* (Luxembourg: Office for Official Publications of the European Communities), <http://www.non-discrimination.net/publications>.

De Schutter, Olivier (2005b) 'Reasonable Accommodations and Positive Obligations in the European Convention on Human Rights', in A. Lawson and C. Gooding (eds.), *Disability Rights in Europe* (Oxford: Hart Publishing), 35–63.

De Schutter, Olivier (2007) 'Positive Action', in D. Schiek, L. Waddington and M. Bell (eds.), *Cases, Materials and Text on National, Supranational and International Non-Discrimination Law* (Oxford: Hart Publishing), 757–869.

De Schutter, Olivier (2008) 'The Liability of Legal Persons in Anti-Discrimination Law', *European Anti-Discrimination Law Review* 6/7 (Luxembourg: Office for Official Publications of the European Communities), 33–41.

De Wispelaere, Jurgen and Judy Walsh (2007) 'Disability Rights in Ireland: Chronicle of a Missed Opportunity', *Irish Political Studies* 22(4), 517–543.

Degener, Theresia (2004) *Definition of Disability* (Brussels: EU Network of Independent Experts on Disability Discrimination), <http://www.pedz.uni-mannheim.de/daten/edz-ath/gdem/04/disabdef.pdf>.

Department for Communities and Local Government (2007) *Discrimination Law Review – A Framework for Fairness: Proposals for a Single Equality Bill for Great Britain* (London: Department for Communities and Local Government).

Department of Education and Science (2007) *Audit of School Enrolment Policies* (Dublin: Department of Education and Science).

Department of Education and Science (2008) *Report on the Need for a Guidance Note to Schools when Reviewing their Policies on School Uniforms* (Dublin: Department of Education and Science).

Department of Education and Skills (2011) *Discussion Paper on a Regulatory Framework for School Enrolment* (Westmeath: School Governance Section, Department of Education and Skills).

Department of Health and Children (2005) *Adoption Legislation: 2003 Consultation and Proposals for Change* (Dublin: Stationery Office).

Department of Jobs, Enterprise and Innovation (2011a) *Consultation on the Reform of the State's Employment Rights and Industrial Relations Structures and Procedures*, <http://www.djei.ie/employment/rights/erirproject.htm>.

Department of Jobs, Enterprise and Innovation (2011b) *Summary and Analysis of Responses to the Consultation on the Reform of the State's Employment*

Rights and Industrial Relations Structures and Procedures, <http://www.djei. ie/employment/rights/erirproject.htm>.

Department of Jobs, Enterprise and Innovation (2012) *Blueprint to Deliver a World-Class Workplace Relations Service*, <http://www.workplacerelations. ie/en/media/Blueprint%20for%20a%20World%20Class%20Workplace%20 Relations%20Service%20April%202012.pdf>.

Department of Transport (2006) *Sectoral Plan for Accessible Transport under the Disability Act 2005* (Dublin: Department of Transport).

Dine, Janet and Bob Watt (1995) 'Sexual Harassment: Moving Away From Discrimination', *Modern Law Review* 58, 343–363.

Disability Rights Commission (2006) *DDA 1995 Code of Practice: Rights of Access – Services to the Public, Public Authority Functions, Private Clubs and Premises* (London: Her Majesty's Stationery Office).

Donlan, Séan Patrick and Rónán Kennedy (2006) 'A Flood of Light? Comments on the Interpretation Act 2005', *Judicial Studies Institute Journal* 6(1), 92–139.

Doyle, Oran (2008) *Constitutional Law: Text, Cases and Materials* (Dublin: Clarus Press).

Eardly, John (2005) 'Religious Discrimination', in A. Mooney-Cotter and J. Moffatt (eds.), *Discrimination Law* (London: Cavendish), 149–165.

Eichhorn, Lisa (2002) 'Hostile Environment Actions, Title VII, and the ADA: The Limits of the Copy-and-Paste Function', *Washington Law Review* 77, 575–638.

Ellis, Evelyn (2003) 'Social Advantages: A New Lease of Life', *Common Market Law Review* 40, 639–659.

Emens, Elizabeth (2008) 'Integrating Accommodation', *University of Pennsylvania Law Review* 156(4), 839–922.

Engel, David M. and Frank W. Munger (2003) *Rights of Inclusion: Law and Identity in the Life Stories of Americans with Disabilities* (Chicago, IL: University of Chicago Press).

Epp, Charles (2010) *Making Rights Real: Activists, Bureaucrats, and the Creation of the Legalistic State* (Chicago, IL: University of Chicago Press).

Equality and Human Rights Commission (2009a) *Race Discrimination in the Construction Industry Inquiry Report* (Manchester: Equality and Human Rights Commission), <http://www.equalityhumanrights.com/legal-and-policy/ inquiries-and-assessments/inquiry-into-race-in-the-construction-industry/ inquiry-report/>.

Equality and Human Rights Commission (2009b) *Financial Services Inquiry: Sex Discrimination and Gender Pay Gap Report of the Equality and Human Rights Commission* (Manchester: Equality and Human Rights Commission), <http:// www.equalityhumanrights.com/legal-and-policy/inquiries-and-assessments/ inquiry-into-sex-discrimination-in-the-finance-sector/index.html>.

Equality and Rights Alliance (2009) *Downgrading Equality and Human Rights: Assessing the Impact* (Dublin: ERA), <http://www.eracampaign.org/uploads/ Downgrading%20Equality%20&%20Human%20Right%20Assessing%20 the%20Impact.pdf>.

References

Equality and Rights Alliance (2010) *Shadow Report to UNCERD in Response to the Irish Government's Combined Second and Third Progress Report under ICERD* (Dublin: ERA), <http://www2.ohchr.org/english/bodies/cerd/docs/ngos/ERA_Ireland78.pdf>.

Equality and Rights Alliance (2011a) *A Roadmap to a Strengthened Equality and Human Rights Infrastructure in Ireland* (Dublin: ERA), <http://www.eracampaign.org/uploads/ERA%20Roadmap%202011.pdf>.

Equality and Rights Alliance (2011b) *Response on Proposed Merger of the Equality Authority and the Irish Human Rights Commission* (Dublin: ERA), <http://www.eracampaign.org/uploads/Equality_&_Rights_Alliance-_Submission_to_merger_working_group.pdf>.

Equality and Rights Alliance (2011c) *Submission on Reform of the State's Employment Rights and Industrial Relations Structures and Procedures* (Dublin: ERA), <http://www.eracampaign.org/uploads/ERA%20submission%20on%20Reform%20of%20Employment%20Rights%20Structures.pdf >.

Equality Authority (2001) *Annual Report 2000* (Dublin: Equality Authority).

Equality Authority (2002) *Annual Report 2001* (Dublin: Equality Authority).

Equality Authority (2003) *Annual Report 2002* (Dublin: Equality Authority).

Equality Authority (2004) *Annual Report 2003* (Dublin: Equality Authority).

Equality Authority (2005a) *Equal Status Acts 2000–2004 and the Provision of Health Services* (Dublin: Equality Authority).

Equality Authority (2005b) *Annual Report 2004* (Dublin: Equality Authority).

Equality Authority (2005c) *Schools and the Equal Status Act* (2nd edition, Dublin: Equality Authority).

Equality Authority (2005d) *Guidelines for Equal Status Policies in Enterprises* (Dublin: Equality Authority).

Equality Authority (2006a) *Traveller Ethnicity* (Dublin: Equality Authority).

Equality Authority (2006b) *Annual Report 2005* (Dublin: Equality Authority).

Equality Authority (2006c) *Strategic Plan 2006–2008: Embedding Equality* (Dublin: Equality Authority).

Equality Authority (2007a) *Annual Report 2006* (Dublin: Equality Authority).

Equality Authority (2007b) *Equality News* Spring–Summer 2007 (Dublin: Equality Authority).

Equality Authority (2008a) *Annual Report 2007* (Dublin: Equality Authority).

Equality Authority (2008b) *The Role and Aspirations of the Non-Governmental Sector in Articulating and Representing the Interests of Groups Experiencing Inequality* (Dublin: Equality Authority).

Equality Authority (2009a) *Casework Activity 2008* (Dublin: Equality Authority).

Equality Authority (2009b) *Annual Report 2008* (Dublin: Equality Authority).

Equality Authority (2009c) *Strategic Plan 2009–2011: Equality for All in a Time of Change* (Dublin: Equality Authority).

Equality Authority (2010a) *Guide to the Equal Status Acts 2000–2008* (Dublin: Equality Authority).

Equality Authority (2010b) *Annual Report 2009* (Dublin: Equality Authority).

Equality Authority (2010c) *Towards Age-Friendly Provision of Goods and Services* (2nd edition, Dublin: Equality Authority).

Equality Authority (2011a) *Annual Report 2010* (Dublin: Equality Authority).

Equality Authority (2011b) *Embedding Equality in Public Services: What Works in Practice* (Dublin: Equality Authority).

Equality Authority (2011c) *Equality Benefits Tool* (Dublin: Equality Authority).

Equality Authority and National Youth Council of Ireland (2008) *Stereotyping of Young People: Resource Pack* (Dublin: Equality Authority).

Equality Authority and School Development Planning Initiative (2010) *Guidelines for Second Level Schools on Embedding Equality in School Development Planning* (Dublin: Equality Authority).

Equality Tribunal (2004) *Legal Review 2003* (Dublin: Equality Tribunal).

Equality Tribunal (2006) *Annual Report 2005* (Dublin: Equality Tribunal).

Equality Tribunal (2007a) *Annual Report 2006* (Dublin: Equality Tribunal).

Equality Tribunal (2007b) *Statement of Strategy 2008–2010* (Dublin: Equality Tribunal).

Equality Tribunal (2008) *Annual Report 2007* (Dublin: Equality Tribunal).

Equality Tribunal (2009a) *Annual Report 2008* (Dublin: Equality Tribunal).

Equality Tribunal (2009b) *Legal Review 2008* (Dublin: Equality Tribunal).

Equality Tribunal (2010a) *Annual Report 2009* (Dublin: Equality Tribunal).

Equality Tribunal (2010b) *Mediation Review 2009* (Dublin: Equality Tribunal).

Equality Tribunal (2011a) *Annual Report 2010* (Dublin: Equality Tribunal).

Equality Tribunal (2011b) *Response of the Equality Tribunal to the Consultation on the Reform of the State's Employment Rights and Industrial Relations Structures and Procedures* (Dublin: Equality Tribunal).

Equality Tribunal (2011c) *Mediation Review 2010* (Dublin: Equality Tribunal).

European Commission (2006) *Combating Discrimination: A Training Manual* (Luxembourg: Office for Official Publications of the European Communities).

European Commission (2008) *Communication from the Commission to the European Parliament, the Council, the European Economic and Social Committee and the Committee of the Regions of 2 July 2008 – Non-Discrimination and Equal Opportunities: A Renewed Commitment*, COM (2008) 420.

European Commission (2009a) *International Perspectives on Positive Action Measures: A Comparative Analysis in the European Union, Canada, the United States and South Africa* (Luxembourg: Office for Official Publications of the European Communities).

European Commission (2009b) *The Role of NGOs and Trade Unions in Combating Discrimination* (Luxembourg: Publications Office of the European Union).

European Commission against Racism and Intolerance (2007) *Third Report on Ireland: CRI (2007) 44* (Strasbourg: ECRI).

European Group of Experts on Combating Sexual Orientation Discrimination (2004) *Combating Sexual Orientation Discrimination in Employment: Legislation in Fifteen EU Member States* (Brussels: European Commission).

References

European Network of Legal Experts in the Non-Discrimination Field (2005) *Developing Anti-Discrimination Law in Europe: The 25 EU Member States Compared* (Luxembourg: Office for Official Publications of the European Communities).

European Network of Legal Experts in the Non-Discrimination Field (2007) *European Anti-Discrimination Law Review* 5 (Luxembourg: Office for Official Publications of the European Communities).

European Roma Rights Centre, INTERIGHTS and the Migration Policy Group (2004) *Strategic Litigation of Race Discrimination in Europe: From Principles to Practice*, <http://www.migpolgroup.com/publications_detail.php?id=198>.

European Union Agency for Fundamental Rights (2009) *Homophobia and Discrimination on Grounds of Sexual Orientation and Gender Identity in the EU Member States: Part II – The Social Situation* (Vienna: EUAFR), <http://www.fra.europa.eu/fraWebsite/attachments/FRA_hdgso_report-part2_en.pdf>.

Fahey, Elaine (2009) 'A Constitutional Crisis in a Teacup: The Supremacy of EC Law in Ireland', *European Public Law* 15(4), 515–522.

Farkas, Lilla (2006) 'A Good Way to Equality: Roma Seeking Judicial Protection against Discrimination in Europe', in European Network of Legal Experts in the Non-Discrimination Field, *European Anti-Discrimination Law Review* 3 (Luxembourg: Office for Official Publications of the European Communities), <http://www.migpolgroup.com/public/docs/27.European%20Anti-discriminationLawReview-Issue3_EN_04.06.pdf>.

Farkas, Lilla and European Network of Legal Experts in the Non-Discrimination Field (2007) *Segregation of Roma Children in Education* (Luxembourg: Office for Official Publications of the European Communities), <http://ec.europa.eu/social/BlobServlet?docId=2019&langId=en>.

Farrell, Michael (2008) 'The Use of the ECHR Act in the Courts to Assist the Vulnerable and Disadvantaged', paper presented at the Irish Human Rights Commission and Law Society of Ireland Annual Conference, *The European Convention on Human Rights Act, 2003 Five Years On*, 8 November, Law Society of Ireland, Blackhall Place, Dublin, <http://www.ihrc.ie/download/doc/paper20081108_annconf_farrell.doc>.

Fay, Ronnie (2008) 'Castle Street to finally End', *Equality News* Winter 2007/2008 (Dublin: Equality Authority).

Feldman, Estelle (2006) 'The Ombudsman: Redressing the Balance for Older People', in E. O'Dell (ed.), *Older People in Modern Ireland: Essays on Law and Policy* (Dublin: First Law), 353–370.

Fenelon, Larry (2009) 'Discriminating Tastes', *Law Society Gazette* 103(10), 16–19.

Filinson, Rachel (2008) 'Age Discrimination Legislation in the UK: A Comparative and Gerontological Analysis', *Journal of Cross-Cultural Gerontology* 23(3), 225–237.

Finlay, Mary (2003) 'Indirect Discrimination and the Article 13 Directives', in C. Costello and E. Barry (eds.), *Equality in Diversity: The New Equality Directives* (Dublin: Irish Centre for European Law), 135–150.

Flynn, Eilionóir (2007) 'Access to Services for People with Disabilities', *Cork Online Law Review* 2007(2), 14–23, <http://corkonlinelawreview.com/editions/2007/COLR%202007%20Full.pdf>.

Flynn, Eilionóir (2009) 'Ireland's Compliance with the Convention on the Rights of Persons with Disabilities – Towards a Rights-Based Approach for Legal Reform?', *Dublin University Law Journal* 31, 357–385.

Flynn, Leo (1995) 'Gender Equality Laws and Employers' Dress Codes', *Industrial Law Journal* 24, 255–272.

Fredman, Sandra (2002) *Discrimination Law* (Oxford: Oxford University Press).

Fredman, Sandra (2009) *Making Equality Effective: The Role of Proactive Measures* (European Commission Directorate-General for Employment, Social Affairs and Equal Opportunities), <http://ec.europa.eu/social/BlobServl et?docId=4551&langId=en>.

Fredman, Sandra (2010) 'Positive Duties and Socio-Economic Disadvantage: Bringing Disadvantage onto the Equality Agenda', *European Human Rights Law Review* 2010(3), 290–304.

Fredman, Sandra (2011) *Discrimination Law*, (2nd edition, Oxford: Oxford University Press).

Fredman, Sandra and Sarah Spencer (2006) 'Beyond Discrimination: It's Time for Enforceable Duties on Public Bodies to Promote Equality Outcomes', *European Human Rights Law Review* 6, 598–606.

Free Legal Advice Centres (2004) *Equality Bill 2004 Part III: Proposed Amendments to the Equal Status Act 2000* (Dublin: FLAC).

Free Legal Advice Centres (2005) *Access to Justice: A Right or a Privilege?* (Dublin: FLAC).

Free Legal Advice Centres (2009) *One Size Doesn't Fit All: A Legal Analysis of the Direct Provision and Dispersal System in Ireland, 10 Years On* (Dublin: FLAC).

Galanter, Marc (1974) 'Why the "Haves" Come Out Ahead: Speculations on the Limits of Legal Change', *Law and Society Review* 9, 95–160.

Gannon, Brenda and Brian Nolan (2005) *Disability and Social Inclusion in Ireland* (Dublin: Equality Authority; National Disability Authority).

Gaze, Beth and Rosemary Hunter (2009) 'Access to Justice for Discrimination Complainants: Courts and Legal Representation', *UNSW Law Journal* 32(3), 699–724.

Gender Recognition Advisory Group (2011) *Report of the Gender Recognition Advisory Group*, <http://www.welfare.ie/EN/Policy/Legislation/Pages/gragreportjune11.aspx>.

Glendenning, Dympna (2008a) 'Section 29 Appeals: Will the Education (Miscellaneous Provisions) Act 2007 Make a Difference?', in School of Law, Trinity College Dublin (ed.), *Legal Issues Facing School Principals and*

Teachers in 2008: Some Practical Solutions (Dublin: School of Law, Trinity College Dublin).

Glendenning, Dympna (2008b) *Religion, Education and the Law* (Dublin: Tottel Publishing).

Gold, Richard (2009) 'Faith and Race Discrimination in Education: Implications of Recent Judgments for Schools', *Education Law Journal* [2009], 23–32.

Gooding, Caroline and Catherine Casserley (2005) 'Open for All? Disability Discrimination Laws in Europe Relating to Goods and Services', in A. Lawson and C. Gooding (eds.), *Disability Rights in Europe: From Theory to Practice* (Oxford: Hart Publishing), 135–162.

Government of Ireland (2007) *National Action Plan for Social Inclusion 2007–2016* (Dublin: Stationery Office).

Griffiths, John (1999) 'The Social Working of Anti-Discrimination Law', in T. Loenen and P.R. Rodrigues (eds.), *Non-Discrimination Law: Comparative Perspectives* (The Hague: Kluwer Law International), 313–330.

Halford, John (2009) 'Paying Attention to Inequality: The Development of the Positive Equality Duties', *Judicial Review* [2009], 21–32.

Halley, Janet (2002) 'Sexuality Harassment', in W. Brown and J. Halley (eds.), *Left Legalism: Left Critique* (Durham; London: Duke University Press), 80–104.

Handley, Peter (2001) '"Caught Between a Rock and a Hard Place": Anti-Discrimination Legislation in the Liberal State and the Fate of the Australian Disability Discrimination Act', *Australian Journal of Political Science* 36, 515–528.

Hannett, Sarah (2003) 'Equality at the Intersections: The Legislative and Judicial Failure to Tackle Multiple Discrimination', *Oxford Journal of Legal Studies* 23(1), 65–86.

Hatzis, Nicholas (2011) 'Personal Religious Beliefs in the Workplace: How Not to Define Indirect Discrimination', *Modern Law Review* 74(2), 287–305.

Health Service Executive (2009a) *Staff Guidelines for Obtaining Consent for Non Emergency Treatment/Services from Parents of Children and Young People Under the Age of 18 Years*, <http://www.hse.ie/eng/services/Publications/services/Children/medconsentpub.html>.

Health Service Executive (2009b) *'Your Service, Your Say': The Policy and Procedures for the Management of Consumer Feedback to Include Comments, Compliments and Complaints in the Health Service Executive (HSE)*, <http://www.hse.ie/eng/services/Publications/Your_Service,_Your_Say_Consumer_Affairs/Policies/Feedback.html>.

Healthcare Commission (2009) *Equality in Later Life: A National Study of Older People's Mental Health Services* (London: Healthcare Commission), <http://www.cqc.org.uk/sites/default/files/media/documents/equality_in_later_life.pdf>.

Hepple, Bob (2004) 'Race and Law in Fortress Europe', *Modern Law Review* 67, 1–15.

References

Hepple, Bob (2010) 'The New Single Equality Act in Britain', *Equal Rights Review* 2010(5), 11–24, <http://www.equalrightstrust.org/ertdocumentbank/bob%20hepple.pdf>.

Hepple, Bob (2011) *Equality: The New Legal Framework* (Oxford: Hart Publishing).

Hickey, Tom (2009) 'Domination and the Hijab in Irish Schools', *Dublin University Law Journal* 16(1), 127–153.

Higgins, Imelda (2003) 'Enforcement and the New Equality Directives', in C. Costello and E. Barry (eds.), *Equality in Diversity: The New Equality Directives* (Dublin: Irish Centre for European Law), 391–409.

Hirsh, Elizabeth (2008) 'Settling for Less? Organizational Determinants of Discrimination-Charge Outcomes', *Law and Society Review* 42, 239–272.

HM Treasury and BIS (2011) *The Plan for Growth* (London: Her Majesty's Stationery Office), <http://www.hm-treasury.gov.uk/ukecon_growth_index.htm>.

Hogan, Gerard and David Gwynn Morgan (2010) *Administrative Law in Ireland* (4th edition, Dublin: Thomson Round Hall).

Hogan, Gerard and Gerry Whyte (2003) *Kelly: The Irish Constitution* (4th edition, Dublin: Lexis Nexis).

Holtmaat, Rikki (2007) *Catalysts for Change? Equality Bodies According to Directive 2000/43 – Existence, Independence and Effectiveness* (Luxembourg: Office for Official Publications of the European Communities), <http://ec.europa.eu/social/BlobServlet?docId=2015&langId=en>.

Honeyball, Simon (2007) 'Discrimination by Association', *Web Journal of Current Legal Issues* 4, <http://webjcli.ncl.ac.uk/2007/issue4/honeyball4.html>.

Howard, Erica (2008) 'Race and Racism: Why Does European Law Have Difficulty with Definitions?', *International Journal of Comparative Labour Law and Industrial Relations* 21(4), 5–29.

Hunter, Nan D. (2001) 'Accommodating the Public Sphere: Beyond the Market Model', *Minnesota Law Review* 85, 1591–1637.

Hurley, Mary C. (2007) *Charter Equality Rights: Interpretation of Section 15 in Supreme Court of Canada Decisions* (Ottawa, ON: Law and Government Division, Parliamentary Research Branch, Canadian Parliament), <http://www.parl.gc.ca/content/LOP/ResearchPublications/bp402-e.htm>.

Hynes, Geraldine (2010) 'Discrimination in Financial Services', in Equality Authority (ed.), *Expanding Equality Protections in Goods and Services: Irish and EU Perspectives* (Dublin: Equality Authority), 41–50.

Irish Council for Civil Liberties (2008) *Submission to the Joint Committee on Justice, Equality, Defence and Women's Rights on the Immigration, Residence and Protection Bill 2008 (as initiated)* (Dublin: ICCL).

Irish Council for Civil Liberties (2011) *Preliminary Submission on the Consultation of the Reform of the State's Employment Rights and Industrial Relations Structures and Procedures* (Dublin: ICCL).

Irish Human Rights Commission (2004a) *Travellers as an Ethnic Minority under the Convention on the Elimination of Racial Discrimination: A Discussion Paper* (Dublin: IHRC).

Irish Human Rights Commission (2004b) *Observations on the Equality Bill* (Dublin: IHRC).

Irish Human Rights Commission (2004c) *Observations on the Disability Bill 2004* (Dublin: IHRC).

Irish Human Rights Commission (2006) *ESCR Discussion Document* (Dublin: IHRC).

Irish Human Rights Commission (2007) *Amicus Submission:* Lawrence v Ballina Town Council (Dublin: IHRC).

Irish Human Rights Commission (2009) *Annual Report 2008* (Dublin: IHRC).

Irish Human Rights Commission (2010) *Discussion Paper on Religion and Education* (Dublin: IHRC).

Irish Times (2007a) 'Catholic Schools Say Enrolment Policy Not Illegal', 28 September 2007.

Irish Times (2007b) 'Catholic Schools' Policy Defended', 15 September 2007.

Irish Times (2007c) 'Authority's Stance May Change All Schools' Policies', 13 September 2007.

Irish Times (2008a) 'Traveller Family Fails in Damages Claim Concerning Housing Delays', 1 August 2008.

Irish Times (2008b) 'Judge Criticises Lack of Laws on Fertility Treatment', 4 February 2008.

Irish Times (2008c) 'Equality Chief Resigns over Budget Cuts', 12 December 2008.

Irish Times (2010) 'Costs Awarded to State in Dyslexia Action', 19 June 2010.

Irish Times (2011a) 'Lesbian Couple Weigh Up Whether to Continue Appeal', 22 October 2011.

Irish Times (2011b) 'Backlog of 1,700 Equality Cases', 7 April 2011.

Jolls, Christine (2001) 'Antidiscrimination and Accommodation', *Harvard Law Review* 115, 642–699.

Joyce, David (2003) 'The Historical Criminalisation of Travellers in Irish Law', *Irish Criminal Law Journal* 13(4), 14–17.

Kelly, Eileen (2008) 'Accommodating Religious Expression in the Workplace', *Employee Responsibilities and Rights Journal* 20, 45–56.

Kilcommins, Shane, Emma McClean, Maeve McDonagh, Siobhán Mullally and Darius Whelan (2004) *Extending the Scope of Employment Equality Legislation: Comparative Perspectives on the Prohibited Grounds of Discrimination* (Dublin: Stationery Office).

Kilkelly, Ursula (ed.) (2009) *ECHR and Irish Law* (2nd edition, Bristol: Jordans).

Kirkland, Anna (2006) 'What's at Stake in Transgender Discrimination as Sex Discrimination?', *Signs: Journal of Women in Culture and Society* 32(1), 83–109.

References

Lacey, Nicola (1998) *Unspeakable Subjects: Feminist Essays in Legal and Social Theory* (Oxford: Hart Publishing).

Law Reform Commission of Ireland (2000) *Report on Statutory Drafting and Interpretation: Plain Language and the Law*, LRC 61 – 2000 (Dublin: LRC).

Law Reform Commission of Ireland (2005) *Consultation Paper on Vulnerable Adults and the Law: Capacity*, LRC CP 37 – 2005 (Dublin: LRC).

Lawson, Anna (2008) *Disability and Equality Law in Britain: The Role of Reasonable Adjustment* (Oxford: Hart Publishing).

Lerpiniere, Jennifer and Kirsten Stalker (2010) 'Taking Service Providers to Court: People with Learning Disabilities and Part III of the Disability Discrimination Act 1995', *British Journal of Learning Disabilities* 38, 245–251.

Lester, Anthony and Paola Uccellari (2008) 'Extending the Equality Duty to Religion, Conscience and Belief: Proceed with Caution', *European Human Rights Law Review* 2008(5), 567–573.

Liukko, Jyri (2010) 'Genetic Discrimination, Insurance, and Solidarity: An Analysis of the Argumentation for Fair Risk Classification', *New Genetics and Society* 29(4), 457–475.

Lockwood, Graeme (2011) 'The Widening of Vicarious Liability: Implications for Employers', *International Journal of Law and Management* 53(2), 149–164.

MacKay, Wayne and Kim Piper (2009) *Adding Social Condition to the Canadian Human Rights Act* (Ottawa, ON: Canadian Human Rights Commission), <http://www.chrc-ccdp.ca/pdf/sc_eng.pdf>.

MacKinnon, Catherine A. (1979) *Sexual Harassment of Working Women: A Case of Sex Discrimination* (London; New Haven, CT: Yale University Press).

Makkonen, Timo (2002) *Multiple, Compound and Intersectional Discrimination: Bringing the Experiences of the Most Marginalized to the Fore* (Turku: Institute for Human Rights, Åbo Akademi University), <http://www.abo.fi/instut/imr/norfa/timo.pdf>.

Malik, Maleiha (2008) *'From Conflict to Cohesion': Competing Interests in Equality Law and Policy* (London: Equality and Diversity Forum), <http://www.edf.org.uk/blog/wp-content/uploads/2009/02/competing-rigts-report_web.pdf>.

Marin, Patricia and Catherine Horn (2008) *Realizing Bakke's Legacy: Affirmative Action, Equal Opportunity, and Access to Higher Education* (Sterling, VA: Stylus Publishing).

Mason, Gail (2002) 'Harm, Harassment and Sexuality', *Melbourne University Law Review* 26, 596–622.

Mawhinney, Alison (2010) 'International Human Rights Law and the Place of Religion in Schools', paper presented at the Irish Human Rights Commission/TCD Conference, *Religion and Education: A Human Rights Perspective*, 27 November, Trinity College Dublin, <http://www.ihrc.ie/publications/list/ihrc-discussion-paper-religion-education/>.

McColgan, Aileen (2005) *Discrimination Law: Text, Cases and Materials* (2nd edition, Oxford: Hart Publishing).

McColgan, Aileen (2007a) 'Reconfiguring Discrimination Law', *Public Law* 2007, 74–94.

McColgan, Aileen (2007b) 'Harassment', in D. Schiek, L. Waddington and M. Bell (eds.), *Cases, Materials and Text on National, Supranational and International Non-Discrimination Law* (Oxford: Hart Publishing), 477–560.

McColgan, Aileen (2009) 'Class Wars? Religion and (In)equality in the Workplace', *Industrial Law Journal* 38(1), 1–29.

McCrudden, Christopher (1982) 'Institutional Discrimination', *Oxford Journal of Legal Studies* 2, 303–367.

McCrudden, Christopher (1999a) 'Regulating Discrimination: Advice to a Legislator on Problems Regarding the Enforcement of Anti-Discrimination Law and Strategies to Overcome Them', in T. Loenen and P.R. Rodrigues (eds.), *Non-Discrimination Law: Comparative Perspectives* (The Hague: Kluwer Law International), 295–312.

McCrudden, Christopher (1999b) 'Mainstreaming Equality in the Governance of Northern Ireland', *Fordham International Law Journal* 22, 1696–1775.

McCrudden, Christopher (2004) (ed.) *Anti-Discrimination Law* (2nd edition, Aldershot: Ashgate).

McCrudden, Christopher (2007) *Buying Social Justice: Equality, Government Procurement and Legal Change* (Oxford: Oxford University Press).

McCrudden, Christopher, David J. Smith and Colin Brown (1991) *Racial Justice at Work* (London: Policy Studies Institute).

McGinnity, Frances, Jacqueline Nelson, Peter Lunn and Emma Quinn (2009) *Discrimination in Recruitment: Evidence from a Field Experiment* (Dublin: Equality Authority and Economic and Social Research Institute).

McGinnity, Frances, Jacqueline Nelson, Peter Lunn and Emma Quinn (2010) 'Are Eamon and Eithne More Employable than Hardeep and Heike? Evidence from a Field Experiment in Ireland', in L. Bond, F. McGinnity and H. Russell (eds.), *Making Equality Count: Irish and International Research Measuring Equality and Discrimination* (Dublin: Liffey Press).

McGivern, Yvonne (2007) *Implementing an Action Plan to Promote More Age Friendly Transport Services* (Dublin: Equality Authority).

McGlennan, Tony (2010) 'Faith in Equality: The Making of the Equality Act (Sexual Orientation) Regulations (Northern Ireland) 2006' in Equality Authority (ed.), *Expanding Equality Protections in Goods and Services: Irish and EU Perspectives* (Dublin: Equality Authority), 87–94.

McIlroy, Cat (2009) *Transphobia in Ireland* (Dublin: Transgender Equality Network Ireland).

McLaughlin, Eithne (2007) 'From Negative to Positive Equality Duties: The Development and Constitutionalisation of Equality Provisions in the UK', *Social Policy & Society* 6(1), 111–121.

McVeigh, Robbie (2007) 'Ethnicity Denial and Racism: The Case of the Government of Ireland against Irish Travellers', *Translocations* 2(1), 90–133.

Mental Health Foundation (2009) *All Things Being Equal: Age Equality in Mental Health Care for Older People in England* (London: MHF), <http://www.mentalhealth.org.uk/content/assets/PDF/publications/all_things_being_equal.pdf>.

Monaghan, Karon (2007) *Equality Law* (Oxford: Oxford University Press).

Moon, Gay (2007) 'Enforcement Bodies', in D. Schiek, L. Waddington and M. Bell (eds.), *Cases, Materials and Text on National, Supranational and International Non-Discrimination Law* (Oxford: Hart Publishing), 871–954.

Morgan, Sinéad (2009) 'Disability Discrimination – How Far Does It Extend?', *Irish Employment Law Journal* 6(3), 70–73.

Mullally, Siobhán and Darren O'Donovan (2011) 'Religion in Ireland's "Public Squares": Education, the Family and Expanding Equality Claims', *Public Law* 2011, 284–307.

Naff, Katherine and Ockert Dupper (2009) 'Footprints through the Courts: Comparing Judicial Responses to Affirmative Action Litigation in South Africa and in the United States', *International Journal of Comparative Labour Law and Industrial Relations* 25(2), 157–189.

National Consultative Committee on Racism and Interculturalism (2006) *Potentially Discriminatory HIV Testing by Financial Institutions* (Dublin: NCCRI).

National Council on Ageing and Older People (2005) *Perceptions of Ageism in Health and Social Services in Ireland* (Dublin: NCAOP).

National Council for Curriculum and Assessment (2006) *Intercultural Education in the Post-Primary School* (Dublin: Stationery Office).

National Council for Special Education (2006) *Guidelines on the Individual Education Plan Process* (Dublin: Stationery Office).

National Disability Authority (2005a) *How Far towards Equality: Measuring How Equally People with Disabilities Are Included in Irish Society* (Dublin: NDA).

National Disability Authority (2005b) *Review of the Effectiveness of Part M of the Building Regulations* (Dublin: NDA).

National Disability Authority (2005c) *Recommended Accessibility Guidelines for Public Transport Operators in Ireland* (Dublin: NDA).

National Disability Authority (2006) *Code of Practice on Accessibility of Public Services and Information Provided by Public Bodies* (Dublin: NDA).

National Economic and Social Forum (1996) *Equality Proofing Issues*, Report 10 (Dublin: Stationery Office).

National Economic and Social Forum (2008) *Fifth Periodic Report on the Work of the NESF*, Report 37 (Dublin: Stationery Office).

National Educational Welfare Board (2008) *Developing a Code of Behaviour: Guidelines for Schools* (Dublin: NEWB), <http://www.newb.ie/downloads/pdf/guidelines_school_codes_eng.pdf>.

Nice, Julie A. (2000) 'Equal Protection's Antinomies and the Promise of a Co-Constitutive Approach', *Cornell Law Review* 85, 1392–1425.

References

O'Brien, Nick (2005) 'The GB Disability Rights Commission and Strategic Law Enforcement: Transcending the Common Law Mind', in C. Gooding and A. Lawson (eds.), *Disability Rights in Europe: From Theory to Practice* (Oxford: Hart Publishing), 249–263.

Obura, Soraya and Fiona Palmer (eds.) (2006) *Strategic Enforcement: Powers and Competences of Equality Bodies* (Brussels: Equinet).

O'Cinneide, Colm (2003) *Taking Equal Opportunities Seriously: The Extension of Positive Duties to Promote Equality* (London: Equality and Diversity Forum/ Equal Opportunities Commission).

O'Cinneide, Colm (2005) *Equivalence in Promoting Equality: The Implications of the Multi-Party Agreement for the Further Development of Equality Measures for Northern Ireland and Ireland* (Dublin: Equality Authority and Equality Commission for Northern Ireland).

O'Cinneide, Colm (2010) 'Multiple Discrimination and the Distinctions between Discrimination Grounds in EU Law', in Equality Authority (ed.), *Expanding Equality Protections in Goods and Services: Irish and EU Perspectives* (Dublin: Equality Authority), 26–40.

O'Connell, Donncha, Siobhán Cummiskey, Emer Meeneghan and Paul O'Connell (2006) *ECHR Act 2003: A Preliminary Assessment of Impact* (Dublin: Dublin Solicitors Bar Association and the Law Society of Ireland).

O'Connell, Rory (2008) 'From Equality Before the Law to the Equal Benefit of the Law: Social and Economic Rights in the Irish Constitution', in E. Carolan and O. Doyle (eds.), *The Irish Constitution: Governance and Values* (Dublin: Thomson Round Hall), 327–346.

Office of the Ombudsman (2011a) *Too Old to Be Equal? An Ombudsman Investigation into the Illegal Refusal of Mobility Allowance to People over 66 Years of Age* (Dublin: Office of the Ombudsman), <http://www.ombudsman. gov.ie/en/Reports/InvestigationReports/April2011-TooOldtobeEqual/>.

Office of the Ombudsman (2011b) *Annual Report 2010* (Dublin: Office of the Ombudsman), <http://www.ombudsman.gov.ie/en/Reports/AnnualReports/ AnnualReportoftheOmbudsman2010/>.

O'Mahony, Conor (2006) *Educational Rights in Irish Law* (Dublin: Thomson Round Hall).

O'Mahony, Conor (2009) 'National Mechanisms for Protecting the Right to Education', paper presented at the Irish Human Rights Commission Annual Conference, 21 November, Law Society of Ireland, Blackhall Place, Dublin, <http://www.ihrc.ie/download/pdf/paper20091121_annconf_omahony.pdf>.

Ombudsman for Children (2011) *Annual Report 2010* (Dublin: OCO), <http:// www.oco.ie/assets/files/annual-report/Annual-Report2010.pdf>.

O'Neill, Garrett (2010) 'A Synopsis of Discrimination in Respect of Public Housing Accommodation Services', in Equality Authority (ed.), *Expanding Equality Protections in Goods and Services: Irish and EU Perspectives* (Dublin: Equality Authority), 51–61.

Ontario Human Rights Commission (2005) *Policy and Guidelines on Racism and Racial Discrimination* (Toronto, ON: OHRC), <http://www.ohrc.on.ca/sites/default/files/attachments/Policy_and_guidelines_on_racism_and_racial_discrimination.pdf>.

Ontario Human Rights Commission (2007) *Policy and Guidelines on Discrimination because of Family Status* (Toronto, ON: Ontario Human Rights Commission), <http://www.ohrc.on.ca/en/policy-and-guidelines-discrimination-because-family-status>.

O'Reilly, Emily (2007) 'Human Rights and the Ombudsman', presentation by the Ombudsman of Ireland at the Biennial Conference of the British and Irish Ombudsman Association, 27 April, University of Warwick.

O'Sullivan, Michelle and Juliet MacMahon (2010) 'Employment Equality Legislation in Ireland: Claimants, Representation and Outcomes', *Industrial Law Journal* 39(4), 329–354.

Oxera (2009) *The Use of Age-Based Practices in Financial Services* (London: Oxera Consulting).

Patmore, Glenn (1999) 'Moving towards a Substantive Conception of the Anti-Discrimination Principle: *Waters v Public Transport Corporation of Victoria* Reconsidered', *Melbourne University Law Review* 23, 121–143.

Pilgerstorfer, Marcus and Simon Forshaw (2008) 'Transferred Discrimination in European Law: Case C-303/06, *Coleman v Attridge Law* [2008] ICR 1128, [2008] IRLR 722 (ECJ)', *Industrial Law Journal* 37, 384–393.

Power, Conor (2003) 'Marital Status and Family Status', in C. Costello and E. Barry (eds.), *Equality in Diversity: The New Equality Directives* (Dublin: Irish Centre for European Law), 313–328.

Quill, Eoin (2005) 'Employers' Liability for Bullying and Harassment', *International Journal of Comparative Labour Law and Industrial Relations* 21(4), 645–666.

Redmond, Mary (2002) 'A Level Playing Field', *Law Society Gazette* 96(7), 18–21.

Rees, Neil, Katherine Lindsay and Simon Rice (2008) *Australian Anti-Discrimination Law: Text, Cases and Materials* (Sydney, NSW: The Federation Press).

Rehnstrom, Jeanette (2005) 'Preconceptions', *Gay Community News* 191, 12–15.

Reynolds, Barry (2008) 'When Equal Treatment Is Not Enough: A Review of Recent Decisions in the Management of International Workers', *Irish Employment Law Journal* 5(3), 94.

RGDATA and the Equality Authority (2004) *Serving the Community* (Dublin: Equality Authority).

Ringelheim, Julie (2010) 'The Prohibition of Racial and Ethnic Discrimination in Access to Services under EU Law', in European Network of Legal Experts in the Non-Discrimination Field (ed.), *European Anti-Discrimination Law Review* 10 (European Commission Directorate-General for Employment,

Social Affairs and Inclusion), <http://www.migpolgroup.com/publications_detail.php?id=279>.

Rodrigues, Peter R. (1997) 'The Dutch Experience of Enforcement Agencies: Current Issues in Dutch Anti-Discrimination Law', in M. MacEwen (ed.), *Anti-Discrimination Law Enforcement: A Comparative Perspective* (Aldershot: Ashgate), 50–64.

Rorive, Isabelle (2006) 'Situation Tests in Europe: Myths and Realities', in European Network of Legal Experts in the Non-Discrimination Field (ed.), *European Anti-Discrimination Law Review* 3 (Luxembourg: Office for Official Publications of the European Communities), 31–37, <http://www.migpolgroup.com/publications_detail.php?id=172>.

Rorive, Isabelle (2009a) 'A Comparative and European Examination of National Institutions in the Field of Racism and Discrimination', in K. Boyle (ed.), *New Institutions for Human Rights Protection* (Oxford: Oxford University Press), 137–173.

Rorive, Isabelle (2009b) *Proving Discrimination: The Role of Situation Testing* (Brussels: Centre for Equal Rights and Migration Policy Group), <http://www.migpolgroup.com/publications_detail.php?id=230>.

Russell, Helen, Emma Quinn, Rebecca King O'Riain and Frances McGinnity (2008) *The Experience of Discrimination in Ireland: Analysis of the QNHS Equality Module* (Dublin: Equality Authority).

Rutherglen, George (2009) '*Ricci v. DeStefano*: Affirmative Action and the Lessons of Adversity', *Supreme Court Review* 2009, 83–114.

Ryan, Desmond (2008) 'Making Connections: New Approaches to Vicarious Liability in Comparative Perspective', *Dublin University Law Journal* 30, 41–70.

Ryan, Desmond and Raymond Ryan (2007) 'Vicarious Liability of Employers: Emerging Themes and Trends and their Potential Implications for Irish Employment Law', *Irish Employment Law Journal* 4, 3–8.

Ryan, Sandra (2008) 'Fertility Clinics still Operating in Limbo', *Irish Medical Times*, 28 June, <http://www.imt.ie/news/features/2008/06/fertility-clinics-still-operating-in-limbo.html>.

Samuels, Harriet (2004) 'A Defining Moment: A Feminist Perspective on the Law of Sexual Harassment in the Workplace in the Light of the Equal Treatment Amendment Directive', *Feminist Legal Studies* 12, 181–211.

Sandland, Ralph (2008) 'Developing a Jurisprudence of Difference: The Protection of the Human Rights of Travelling Peoples by the European Court of Human Rights', *Human Rights Law Review* 8(3), 475–516.

Schiek, Dagmar (2007) 'Indirect Discrimination', in D. Schiek, L. Waddington and M. Bell (eds.), *Cases, Materials and Text on National, Supranational and International Non-Discrimination Law* (Oxford: Hart Publishing), 323–475.

Schiek, Dagmar (2009) 'From European Union Non-Discrimination Law towards Multidimensional Equality Law for Europe', in D. Schiek and V. Chege (eds.), *European Union Non-Discrimination Law: Comparative Perspectives on Multidimensional Equality Law* (London; New York, NY: Routledge-Cavendish), 3–28.

Schiek, Dagmar, Lisa Waddington and Mark Bell (eds.) (2007) *Cases, Materials and Text on National, Supranational and International Non-Discrimination Law* (Oxford: Hart Publishing).

Sheppard, Colleen (2001) 'Of Forest Fires and Systemic Discrimination: A Review of *British Columbia (Public Service Employee Relations Commission) v. B.C.G.S.E.U.*', *McGill Law Journal* 46, 533–559.

Smith, Tyson and Michael Kimmel (2005) 'The Hidden Discourse of Masculinity in Gender Discrimination Law', *Signs: Journal of Women in Culture and Society* 30(3), 1827–1849.

Smyth, Emer, Merike Darmody, Frances McGinnity and Delma Byrne (2009) *Adapting to Diversity in Irish Schools: Irish Schools and Newcomer Students* (Dublin: Economic and Social Research Institute).

Solanke, Iyiola (2009) 'Putting Race and Gender Together: A New Approach to Intersectionality', *Modern Law Review* 72(5), 723–749.

Spencer, Sarah (2008) 'Equality and Human Rights Commission: A Decade in the Making', *The Political Quarterly* 79(1), 6–16.

Szabo, Gabrielle (2008) *Mainstreaming Equality in the ACT: An Equality Duty for the ACT Discrimination Act* (Canberra ACT: Australian Capital Territory Human Rights Commission), <http://www.hrc.act.gov.au/res/mainstreaming%20equality.pdf>.

Temperman, Jeroen (2010) 'State Neutrality in Public School Education: An Analysis of the Interplay Between the Neutrality Principle, the Right to Adequate Education, Children's Right to Freedom of Religion or Belief, Parental Liberties, and the Position of Teachers', *Human Rights Quarterly* 32(4), 865–897.

Thornton, Margaret (2002) 'Sexual Harassment: Losing Sight of Sex Discrimination', *Melbourne University Law Review* 26, 422–444.

Tobler, Christa (2005a) *Indirect Discrimination: A Case Study into the Development of the Legal Concept of Indirect Discrimination under EC Law* (Antwerpen; Oxford: Intersentia).

Tobler, Christa (2005b) *Remedies and Sanctions in EC Non-Discrimination Law* (Luxembourg: Office for Official Publications of the European Communities).

Tobler, Christa and European Network of Legal Experts in the Non-Discrimination Field (2008) *Limits and Potential of the Concept of Indirect Discrimination* (Luxembourg: Office for Official Publications of the European Communities).

Tobler, Christa and Kees Waaldijk (2009) 'Case C-267/06, *Tadao Maruko v Versorgungsanstalt der Deutschen Buhnen*, Judgment of the Grand Chamber of the Court of Justice of 1 April 2008', *Common Market Law Review* 46(2), 723–746.

References

Transgender Equality Network Ireland (2010) *Submission to the Gender Recognition Advisory Group* (Dublin: TENI), <http://www.teni.ie/attachments/714a4ffb-3240-496b-8905-06002a24d6c7.PDF>.

Trinity College Dublin, School of Law (2002) *The Criminal Trespass Legislation* (Dublin: School of Law, Trinity College Dublin).

Turner, Jenny (2003) 'Minority Rights Protection in the United Kingdom', in European Centre for Minority Issues (ed.), *European Yearbook of Minority Issues: Volume 1* (The Hague; London; New York, NY: Kluwer Law International), 395–424.

Uccellari, Paola (2008) 'Banning Religious Harassment: Promoting Mutual Tolerance or Encouraging Mutual Ignorance?', *Equal Rights Review* 2008(2), 7–28, <www.equalrightstrust.org/ertdocumentbank/Paola%20article.pdf>.

United Nations Committee on the Elimination of Racial Discrimination (2005) *Conclusions and Recommendations of the Committee on the Elimination of Racial Discrimination, Ireland* (UN Doc. CERD/C/IRL/CO/2).

United Nations Committee on the Elimination of Racial Discrimination (2011) *Concluding Observations of the Committee on the Elimination of Racial Discrimination* (UN Doc. CERD/C/IRL/CO/3-4).

United Nations Human Rights Committee (2008) *Concluding Observations of the Human Rights Committee, Ireland* (UN Doc. CCPR/C/IRL/CO/3).

Vandenhole, Wouter (2005) *Non-Discrimination and Equality in the View of the UN Human Rights Treaties Bodies* (Antwerpen; Oxford: Intersentia).

Vickers, Lucy (2006) 'Is all Harassment Equal? The Case of Religious Harassment', *Cambridge Law Journal* 65(3), 579–605.

Vickers, Lucy (2011) 'Promoting Equality or Fostering Resentment? The Public Sector Equality Duty and Religion and Belief', *Legal Studies* 31(1), 135–158.

Vizkelety, Béatrice (2008) 'Discrimination Law – The Canadian Perspective', in European Network of Legal Experts in the Non-Discrimination Field (ed.), *European Anti-Discrimination Law Review* No. 6/7 – 2008 (Luxembourg: Office for Official Publications of the European Communities), 23–32, <http://www.migpolgroup.com/publications_detail.php?id=175>.

Waddington, Lisa (2007) 'Case C-13/05, *Chacón Navas v. Eurest Colectividades SA*', *Common Market Law Review* 44, 487–499.

Waddington, Lisa (2009) 'Case C-303/06, *S. Coleman v. Attridge Law and Steve Law*', *Common Market Law Review* 46, 665–681.

Waddington, Lisa and Mark Bell (2011) 'Exploring the Boundaries of Positive Action under EU Law: A Search for Conceptual Clarity', *Common Market Law Review* 48, 1503–1526.

Walsh, Judy and Fergus Ryan (2006) *The Rights of De Facto Couples* (Dublin: Irish Human Rights Commission).

Walsh, Judy, Catherine Conlon, Barry Fitzpatrick and Ulf Hansson (2007) *Enabling Gay, Lesbian and Bisexual Individuals to Access their Rights under*

Equality Law (Belfast; Dublin: Equality Commission for Northern Ireland and Equality Authority).

Ward, Paul (2010) *Tort Law in Ireland* (The Hague: Kluwer Law International).

Whelan, Darius (2009) *Mental Health Law and Practice: Civil and Criminal Aspects* (Dublin: Round Hall).

White, Myra (2006) 'Formal Investigations and Inquiries', in S. Obura and F. Palmer (eds.), *Strategic Enforcement: Powers and Competences of Equality Bodies* (Brussels: Equinet), 25–30.

White, Stuart (1997) 'Freedom of Association and the Right to Exclude', *Journal of Political Philosophy* 5(4), 373–391.

Whittle, Richard (2002) 'The Framework Directive for Equal Treatment in Employment and Occupation: An Analysis from a Disability Rights Perspective', *European Law Review* 27, 303–326.

Whyte, Gerry (2002) *Social Inclusion and the Legal System: Public Interest Law in Ireland* (Dublin: Institute of Public Administration).

Whyte, Gerry (2010) 'Religion and Education: The Irish Constitution', paper presented at the Irish Human Rights Commission/TCD Conference, *Religion and Education: A Human Rights Perspective*, 27 November, Trinity College Dublin, <http://www.ihrc.ie/publications/list/professor-gerry-whyte-paper-on-religion-and-educat/>.

Wintemute, Robert (1997) 'Recognising New Kinds of Direct Sex Discrimination: Transsexualism, Sexual Orientation and Dress Codes', *Modern Law Review* 60(3), 334–359.

Women's Health Council (2009) *Infertility and Its Treatments: A Review of Psycho-Social Issues* (Dublin: WHC).

Working Group on the Irish Human Rights and Equality Commission (2012) *Report to the Minister for Justice and Equality and Defence*, <http://www.inis.gov.ie/en/JELR/20120419-WorkingGroupRpt-HumanRightsEqualityCommission.pdf/Files/20120419-WorkingGroupRpt-HumanRightsEqualityCommission.pdf>.

Woulfe, Carol Ann (2010) 'Disability Discrimination in Education: An Irish Perspective' in Equality Authority (ed.), *Expanding Equality Protections in Goods and Services: Irish and EU Perspectives* (Dublin: Equality Authority), 62–74.

Yesilkagit, Kutsal and Berend Snijders (2008) *Between Impartiality and Responsiveness: Equality Bodies and Independence* (Brussels: Equinet).

Appendix: Further Resources

Accessing Case Law

Ireland: Equality Tribunal decisions under the Equal Status Acts
All decisions issued by the Equality Tribunal under the Equal Status Acts 2000–2011 are published on its website:
http://www.equalitytribunal.ie/

Ireland: Ordinary Courts
Hardcopies
The main sources of written court judgments are the *Irish Reports* (IR) and *Irish Law Reports Monthly* (IRLM) – these hardcopy judgments are published annually in bound volumes and can be consulted in the law section of university libraries.

Electronic format
There are three freely accessible online Irish case law databases:

British and Irish Legal Information Institution:
http://www.bailii.org
Judgments of the Superior Courts back to mid-1990s

The Irish Legal Information Initiative:
http://www.ucc.ie/law/irlii/
Contains many judgments of High Court and Supreme Court (goes back to 1997 but 'leading cases' section contains some earlier judgments). Can search within databases chronologically (date of judgment) and alphabetically (name of case). Also has index of leading cases by subject matter and index of recent cases.

The Courts Service:
http://www.courts.ie/
Extensive database of High Court and Supreme Court judgments. Supreme Court judgments from 2001 to present, High Court judgments from 2003. Can search by year or by court. Internal search function as well.

Court of Justice of the European Union
http://curia.europa.eu/

European Court of Human Rights
http://www.echr.coe.int/

International human rights law and cases from other countries

World Legal Information Initiative:
http://www.worldlii.org/

PILnet Database on Anti-Discrimination and Equality Law:
http://www.pilnet.org/

European Union Agency for Fundamental Rights, Case Law Database:
http://www.fra.europa.eu/fraWebsite/research/case-law/case-law_en.htm

Contact List

Statutory Bodies

Equality Authority
Dublin Office
Equality Authority
Clonmel Street
Dublin 2
Tel: +353 1 4173336
Lo-Call: 1890 245 545
Email: info@equality.ie
Website: http://www.equality.ie

Roscrea Office
The Equality Authority
Birchgrove House
Roscrea
Co. Tipperary
Information – Lo-Call: 1890 245 545
Tel: +353 505 24126
Fax: +353 505 22388
Email: info@equality.ie
Website: http://www.equality.ie

Equality Tribunal
3 Clonmel Street
Dublin 2
Lo-Call: 1890 34 44 24
Tel: + 353 1 4774100

Fax: + 353 1 4774141
Email: info@equalitytribunal.ie
Website: http://www.equalitytribunal.ie

Workplace Relations Customer Service
Department of Jobs, Enterprise and Innovation
O'Brien Road
Carlow
Lo-Call: 1890 80 80 90
Tel: +353 59 9178990
Online Enquiry Form: http://www.workplacerelations.ie/en/services/contactus/
Website: http://www.workplacerelations.ie/en/

National Disability Authority
25 Clyde Road
Dublin 4
Tel: +353 1 6080400
Fax: +353 1 6609935
Email: nda@nda.ie
Website: http://www.nda.ie/

Office of the Ombudsman
18 Lower Leeson Street
Dublin 2
Lo-Call: 1890 223 030
Tel: +353 1 6395600
Email: ombudsman@ombudsman.gov.ie
Website: http://www.ombudsman.gov.ie

Office of the Ombudsman for Children
Millennium House
52–56 Great Strand Street
Dublin 1
Freephone: 1800 202 040
Tel: +353 1 8656800
Email: oco@oco.ie
Website: http://www.oco.ie

Citizens Information
Lo-Call: 1890 777 121
Tel: +353 21 4521600
Website: http://www.citizensinformation.ie/en/
Citizens Information Centres: http://centres.citizensinformation.ie/

Non-Governmental Organisations

Ballymun Community Law Centre
Tel: + 353 1 8625805
Website: http://www.bclc.ie/

Equality and Rights Alliance, Ireland
Tel: + 353 1 8148860
Email: rachel@eracampaign.org
Website: http://www.eracampaign.org/

Free Legal Advice Centres (FLAC)
Information and Referral Line: 1890 350 250
Tel: +353 1 8745690
Fax: +353 1 8745320
Website: http://www.flac.ie/contact/

Immigrant Council of Ireland, Legal Service
Tel: +353 1 6740200
Email: info@immigrantcouncil.ie
Website: http://www.immigrantcouncil.ie/services/legal-service

Irish Council for Civil Liberties (ICCL)
9–13 Blackhall Place
Dublin 7
Tel: +353 1 7994504
Fax: +353 1 7994512
Website: www.iccl.ie

Irish Traveller Movement Law Centre
Tel: +353 1 6796577
Fax: +353 1 6796578
Email: itmtrav@indigo.ie
Website: http://www.itmtrav.ie/keyissues/legalunit

Mercy Law Resource Centre
Tel: +353 1 4537459
Fax: +353 1 4537455
Email: info@mercylaw.ie
Website: http://www.mercylaw.ie/

Northside Community Law Centre
Tel: +353 1 8477804
Fax: + 353 1 8477563
Email: info@nclc.ie
Website: http://www.nclc.ie/

Index